Institutional Economics
Volume I

Schools of Thought in Economics

Series Editor: Mark Blaug

Emeritus Professor of the Economics of Education, University of London and Consultant Professor of Economics, University of Buckingham

For greater convenience, a cumulative index to all titles in this series will be published in a separate volume number 12.

Institutional Economics
Volume I

Edited by

Warren J. Samuels

Professor of Economics
Michigan State University

EDWARD ELGAR

Published by
Edward Elgar Publishing Limited
Gower House
Croft Road
Aldershot
Hants GU11 3HR
England

Gower Publishing Company
Old Post Road
Brookfield
Vermont 05036
USA

British Library Cataloguing in Publication Data

Institutional economics. — (Schools of thought in
  economics; 5).
  1. Institutional economics I. Samuels, Warren J. (Warren Joseph),
  1933– II. Series
  330.15'5

Library of Congress Cataloging-in-Publication Data

Institutional economics/edited by Warren J. Samuels.
  p. cm. — (Schools of thought in economics; 5)
  Includes indexes.
  1. Institutional economics. I. Samuels, Warren J.,
  1933–. II. Series.
  HB99.5.I56. 1988   88–16347
  330–dc19   CIP

ISBN 1 85278 057 6 (vol. I)
     1 85278 116 5 (3 volume set)

Printed and bound in Great Britain at
The Camelot Press Ltd, Southampton

Contents

Acknowledgements

The editor and publishers wish to thank the following who have kindly given permission for the use of copyright material.

American Economic Association for articles: Clarence E. Ayres (1951), 'The Co-ordinates of Institutionalism', *American Economic Review*, 41, May pp. 47–55; John R. Commons (1931), 'Institutional Economics', *American Economic Review*, 21, December, pp. 648–57; Allan G. Gruchy *et al*, (1957), 'A New Look at Institutionalism: Discussion', *American Economic Review Supplement*, 47, May, pp. 13–27; Wesley C. Mitchell (1935), 'Commons on Institutional Economics', *American Economic Review*, 25 (4), December, pp. 635–52.

Association For Evolutionary Economics for articles: Allan G. Gruchy (1969), 'Neo-institutionalism and the Economics of Dissent', *Journal of Economic Issues*, 3, March, pp. 3–17; Marc R. Tool (1981), 'The Compulsive Shift to Institutional Analysis', *Journal of Economic Issues*, 15 (3), September, pp. 569–92; J. Ron Stanfield (1980), 'The Institutional Economics of Karl Polanyi', *Journal of Economic Issues*, 14 (3), September, pp. 593–614; Malcolm Rutherford (1983), 'J.R. Commons's Institutional Economics', *Journal of Economic Issues*, 17 (3), September, pp. 721–44.

Kyklos-Verlag for articles: K.W. Kapp (1976), 'The Nature and the Significance of Institutional Economics', *Kyklos*, 29, pp. 209–32; Ervin K. Zingler (1974); 'Veblen vs Commons: A Comparative Evaluation', *Kyklos*, 27(2), pp. 322–44.

The Scandinavian Journal of Economics for article: K.W. Kapp (1968), 'In Defense of Institutional Economics', *Swedish Journal of Economics*, 70, March, pp. 1–18.

Southern Economic Journal for article: Edwin E. Witte (1954), 'Institutional Economics as Seen by an Institutional Economist', *Southern Economic Journal*, 21, October, pp. 131–40.

University of Texas Press and the author for article: William Breit (1973), 'The Development of Clarence Ayres's Theoretical Institutionalism, *Social Science Quarterly*, Vol. 54, No. 2, September, pp. 244–57. Copyright 1973.

Western Economic Association International and the author for articles: Donald A. Walker (1977), 'Thorstein Veblen's Economic System', *Economic Inquiry*, 15 (2),

April, pp. 213–37; Donald A. Walker (1979), 'The Institutionalist Economic Theories of Clarence Ayres', *Economic Inquiry*, 17 (4), October, pp. 519–38.

Every effort has been made to trace all the copyright holders but if any have been inadvertently overlooked the publishers will be pleased to make the necessary arrangement at the first opportunity.

In addition the publishers wish to thank the Library of the London School of Economics and Political Science and the British Library Document Supply Centre for their assistance in obtaining these articles.

Publisher's note
Every effort has been made to reproduce exact copies of the articles and papers reprinted in this volume. Unfortunately, it proved impossible to find copies of Chapters 7 and 13 in a sufficiently good condition for facsimile reproduction. These articles have been re-typeset in a style similar to the first printing. For ease of reference, the pagination in the original article has been printed in brackets [ ] in the text.

Introduction

Economics, for at least a century, has been diverse and heterogeneous. It has increasingly consisted of a dominant mainstream neoclassical orthodoxy and a diverse heterodoxy. Moreover, both the neoclassical mainstream and all heterodox schools themselves have been heterogeneous, each with several diverse formulations or understandings of its basic doctrines. Heterodox economics has been dominated by various versions of Marxism but there has been more to heterodox economics than Marxism. The principal alternative to Marxism within heterodox economics has been American institutionalism. Institutional economics has provided critiques of both neoclassical and Marxian economics and, especially, an alternative conception of the economy and of doing economics.

There have been three historic meanings to institutionalism. First, it has been a protest movement against both (1) the market economy as it has actually been institutionalized in twentieth century America (and, by extension, the entire West) and (2) the dominant school of market (neoclassical) economics which it perceives as basically a body of self-perception and self-justification by those who identify with the market economy, that is, as an emanation of the system itself. As such, there has been great uniformity to the diagnoses or interpretations of the American economy by institutionalists. They see it as essentially a corporate system, one dominated by business, especially the giant corporations. Institutionalists differ, however, with regard to prescription. Some perceive a technological imperative at work which mandates large-scale enterprise and the present system of private–public planning, and prescribe what they consider to be a democratization of the system through conscious democratic government planning. Others are wary of the concentration of power which they perceive resident in the existing corporate system and which they also anticipate in any system of government planning – which they think will likely be dominated by the corporations and only effectively consummate and legitimize the existing system of private–public planning. These institutionalists prescribe, alternatively, a political economy which in their view is both truly structurally competitive and not dominated by business.

The second historic meaning of institutionalism has been problem-solving. Institutionalists have typically and self-consciously followed the path of American pragmatism, in which the meaning of anything resides in its instrumental role and consequences. They also have been problem oriented and have, accordingly, sought to help work out solutions to the problems of a large, increasingly prosperous, urban industrial economy. Most of their research interests and proposed policy solutions have dealt with aspects of what has come to be called the welfare state: public utility regulation, protective labour legislation, labour relations legislation (the legalization and institutionalization of labour unions), worker compensation for industrial injury and unemployment, and social security, as well as narrower and more locally specialized problems. Many, if not all, of these solutions have been controversial because they have involved working out accommodations between parties with conflicting interests. To the institutionalist, problem solving is typically conflict resolution; it is also the reworking of the legal foundations of the economic system through cooperative, collective institutions, which themselves may be the object of reformation.

Thirdly, institutional economics, no less than other schools of economic thought, has attempted to create a body of knowledge. I shall examine the distinguishing characteristics of this facet in greater detail below.

Mainstream neoclassical economics itself can be similarly identified. It, however, affirms the market economy, generally, but by no means universally, as it has actually come to be institutionalized, and it certainly affirms its theory of how the market economy works. It also represents an approach to problem-solving, this notwithstanding the fact that it can readily be taken to signify that market solutions are ipso facto optimal and that there is no substantive need for problem-solving policy. And it certainly constitutes a body of knowledge.

Institutional economics differs from neoclassical economics in certain important technical respects. First, institutionalists are generally infinitely less interested in working out determinate solutions to technical intellectual problems or puzzles. Second, they are not at all interested in working out narrow, static equilibrium solutions, or the technical conditions of the existence and/or stability of an equilibrium. They find the empty formalism of such deterministic and equilibrium analyses either quite irrelevant to, or, because of the necessary limiting assumptions, quite presumptuous when applied to, real world problems. Third, they specifically reject the common presumptive optimality reasoning typically found in the application of neoclassical models to questions of policy. Institutionalists insist that there are as many optimal results as there are presumed initial distributions of entitlements; that is, that there is no unique optimal solution, only solutions respectively giving effect to the structure of power which gives rise to them.

Considered, then, as a body of knowledge, the relation of institutional to neoclassical market economics is rather complex but straightforward. The relationship includes the different scope of variables which they bring to bear in analysis and their different conceptions of the central problem(s) of economics. Looking at the latter first, whereas neoclassical economics is principally concerned with the basic economic problems of the allocation of resources, the determination of the level of aggregate income, output, employment and prices, and the distribution of income, institutional economics is principally concerned with a different, additional basic economic problem: the organization and control of the economic system, especially its structure of power. Thus, when it comes to the scope of variables, institutionalists generally pursue a broader range of variables and a longer explanatory chain. For example, whereas neoclassical economists explain the allocation of resources in terms of, first, the operation of the market and, second, the operation of demand and supply in the market, institutional economists go deeper to, third, the structure of institutions which form the market and the structure of rights which govern whose interests count in effectuating demand and supply; fourth, the operation of government (and other social control processes) in (re)forming the structure of market institutions and rights; and, fifth, the processes in which interested groups compete for the use of government in order to influence allocation and especially distribution through controlling the structure of rights and institutions pertinent to the market. Institutionalists thus see at least two processes simultaneously operative in the economy: the working out of the power structure which ultimately governs allocation, and the working out of optimal, gains-from-trade maximizing results within the existing power structure. A third process is that of the spread of the logic of industrialization understood as a cultural process.

The central problem of institutional economics is thus the organization and control of the economy, especially its structure of power. It is the organization and control problem which institutionalists tend to read into any practical or analytical question. In the institutionalist view, the market is an institutional complex; it is formed by institutions; and it interacts with other institutional complexes in society. The fundamental institutionalist position, then, is that it is not the market which allocates resources but that the market gives effect to the institutions (or power structure) which form and operate through it. This is in direct contrast with the market-oriented neoclassical view. It is also in conflict with the Marxian view with its typical emphasis on the mode of production as the driving force behind institutional, superstructural change. The institutionalists insist on both the enormous impact of technology and the role of human choice – exercised through the mediating, or weighting, influence of power structure.

The institutionalists also insist that the problem of organization and control of the economic system is fundamentally one of the distribution of power in society and economy. They stress the importance of both the structure of power and the often-obfuscated struggles to alter the structure of power.

Institutionalism thus differs from mainstream economics in its emphases (1) that the economy is more than the market; (2) that the economy has to be studied dynamically or evolutionally, as well as holistically; (3) that while it is important to study the behaviour of individuals (methodological individualism), it is also, and perhaps more, important to study group problems, forces and processes (methodological collectivism); and, *inter alia*, (4) that is is important to study empirical phenomena empirically and not solely through artificial or contrived a priori deductive exercises.

Actually, power is but one of three coordinate facets of institutional economics, the others being knowledge and psychology. With regard to knowledge, institutionalists assume neither perfect knowledge nor fully its perceived close cousin, bounded rationality, but stress uncertainty, the role of institutions in countering, channelling or otherwise compensating for uncertainty, the importance of belief rather than knowledge per se, the learning process governing the acquisition of facts and preferences, and the importance of tooled or instrumental knowledge, such as that embodied in technology. With regard to psychology, institutionalists reject both explicit and implicit hedonism, preferring to concentrate on the fact of diverse and kaleidoscopic psychic states, on the role of custom and habit, especially status emulation, and the role of work as a mode of realizing and enjoying one's social identity (rather than as disutility in comparison with the utility derived from consuming goods).

But institutionalists have focused on power. They have been interested in the (re)formation of rights through custom and through law, in the (re)formation and functioning of the working rules of law and custom, in the interrelation of nominally legal and market processes, and in the values resident in the rights structures and working rules which govern whose/which interests are to count.

Institutionalists have thus argued that institutions are important for economic performance and should be studied as such, an implicit criticism of analyses which abstract from, or take implicit normative positions on, institutions. However, institutionalists themselves take two very different positions on institutions. One tradition of institutionalism, following the work of John R. Commons, considers institutions as one set of the critical explanatory variables governing economic organization, control and performance. Another tradition, taking its lead from Thorstein Veblen and Clarence Ayres, distinguishes between institutions and technology. It generally treats technology – by which is meant tool-using, broadly comprehended – as the progressive, as well as the explanatory force, in the economy; and institutions as ceremonial and inhibitive, serving principally to reinforce established positions of power and status, thereby to prevent the introduction of technology. The latter position is much more complex, inasmuch as it also recognizes, along with the much criticized hierarchy-reinforcement function, both the necessary affirmation of continuity and the necessary making of decisions through structured decision-making processes and institutions.

It is not saying too much that one significant difference among institutionalists is that some, generally in the Veblen–Ayres tradition, consider their work to be mutually exclusive from neoclassical economics, whereas others, generally in the Commons tradition, consider that institutional and neoclassical economics are much more complementary than contradictory. In either case, however, institutionalism and neoclassicism are competitive with regard to both their respective claims for attention and their differing understandings of what the economy is all about.

This is the first of a three-volume collection of representative articles on and in the institutionalist tradition. The first group of articles in this volume serves to introduce institutionalism as a distinctive and coherent school of economic thought. Many of these articles present identifications and defences of institutionalism by institutionalists themselves, especially the articles by Clarence Ayres, John Commons, Edwin Witte, Allan Gruchy, Marc Tool, and K. W. Kapp. Ayres, Gruchy and Tool, are in the Veblenian tradition of institutionalism. Witte joins Commons in the alternative tradition to which the latter's name is typically given. Kapp is less neatly classified but represents the general thrust of the school. One set of materials (Gruchy *et al.*) derives from a session of the American Economic Association and contains statements from institutionalists and non-institutionalists; particular attention is called to the statements by Ayres and Parsons. The article by Witte is a splendid example of institutionalism as a problem-solving approach (but also much more); and that by Gruchy, of institutionalism as critique, or dissent. Tool argues that the content of institutional economics is so important that non-institutionalists have been compelled to adopt institutional analysis even when not recognizing or acknowledging it as such.

The second group of articles in this volume introduces the work of specific leading institutionalists. The article by Donald Walker treats Veblen; those by Wesley Mitchell and Malcolm Rutherford, Commons; those by Walker and William Breit, Ayres; that by Ron Stanfield, Karl Polanyi; and those by David Hamilton and E. Zingler, the contrast between Commons and Veblen, the two acknowledged leaders of the school. Limitations of space prevent inclusion of materials on other writers, for example, Wesley Mitchell himself, Gunnar Myrdal, and John Kenneth Galbraith, among others.

Together these two groups of articles constitute a comprehensive introduction to institutionalism as a whole and to the particular ideas of specific leading institutionalists, and thereby to a quite different kind of economics than is found in either the neoclassical or Marxian schools.

Warren J. Samuels

Part I
Institutional Economics:
Overview

[1]

INSTITUTIONAL ECONOMICS

THE CO-ORDINATES OF INSTITUTIONALISM

By Clarence E. Ayres
University of Texas

I

The word institutionalism has been in general use for something more than thirty years as the standard designation of a certain way of thinking in economics or approach to economic problems. However, the development of that way of thinking covers a much longer time span. If there is any one point of general agreement with regard to institutionalism, it is that of the pre-eminent influence of Thorstein Veblen; and this circumstance alone extends the period of development of this way of thinking in economics at least to the closing years of the last century.

But Veblen did not appear in a cultural vacuum. As time passes, it is becoming increasingly clear that his ideas form a part of a considerable stream.[1] I do not think that I can be accused of having failed to give Veblen his due, even if I declare that an institutionalist has quite as much to learn from John Dewey and the instrumentalists as from Veblen and his interpreters. Moreover, I agree with those writers who see in Veblen's ideas, no less than those of Dewey, a development of the empiricism of C. S. Peirce[2] and a response to Darwinian evolution[3] and to the infant science of cultural anthropology.[4]

Institutionalism itself does not exist in isolation. The same intellectual influences and the same pattern of social events which have given direction to institutionalism have also produced other developments, seemingly unrelated in origin and early development but clearly consonant with institutionalism, and lending greater significance to it as they also derive greater clarity and deeper perspective from institu-

[1] See Allan G. Gruchy, *Modern Economic Thought: The American Contribution* (New York: Prentice Hall, 1947); Joseph Dorfman, *The Economic Mind in American Civilization* (New York: Viking, 1949), Vol. III; Morton G. White, *Social Thought in America* (New York: Viking, 1949).

[2] See Stanley M. Daugert, *The Philosophy of Thorstein Veblen* (New York: King's Crown Press, 1950); also Gruchy, *op. cit.*, pp. 32 ff.

[3] See Richard Hofstadter, *Social Darwinism in American Thought* (Philadelphia: University of Pennsylvania Press, 1944).

[4] For a recent discussion of a related factor, see Louis Schneider, *The Freudian Psychology and Veblen's Social Theory* (New York: King's Crown Press, 1948). See also John S. Gambs, *Beyond Supply and Demand: A Re-appraisal of Institutional Economics* (New York: Columbia University Press, 1946), pp. 47 ff.

tionalism as a basic social philosophy. I refer to such things as the economic-planning movement and the underconsumptionist movement of which Keynesian economics is the most formidable expression. There is a natural affinity, so to speak, between institutionalism and all such developments which seems to me highly significant.[5]

In the present paper I shall have time to note only the principal features of the institutionalist landscape. Indeed, I shall limit myself to three. All three are well known; but they are known somewhat as distant mountains are recognized by travelers. Are they isolated peaks, dating perhaps from different geologic epochs? Or are they related features of a single massif? To many commentators they have seemed to be quite distinct, and they have therefore, naturally, failed to make a pattern; and even those who have postulated a relationship by which the institutionalist position is somehow oriented have nevertheless found it difficult to figure out just what that relationship may be. The difficulty, I think, is only one of perspective. Seen in a perspective that brings all three features into view simultaneously, institutionalism appears clearly as a single intellectual massif, and as such a significant part of the whole intellectual landscape of our time.

II

Institutionalism has been identified with behaviorism as long and as consistently as it has been identified at all; and over the entire span this association has been a source of general puzzlement. It has been recognized as a fact that institutionalists demur at the psychological assumptions of classical price theory, and that they propose to make somewhat different assumptions. But exactly what is the difference has remained obscure.

That obscurity has been due to various circumstances. As is usual in such cases, the criticism of the classical conception of human nature has developed bit by bit and has seemed to apply to the details of price behavior: the excessive rationality which classical price theory has seemed to postulate, the hedonistic flavor of the traditional conception of wants, the teleological implications of the "invisible hand," and all that sort of thing. Even when criticism has been wholesale, it has too often been couched in terms of "the eighteenth-century climate of opinion," a characterization which is bound to seem opaque to all denizens of the twentieth century.

Meantime, the word behaviorism has also proved confusing. As

[5] See C. E. Ayres, "The New Economics," *Southwest Review,* Summer, 1948, pp. 223 ff.

things have turned out, that word has come to be applied to the particular crotchets of John Broadus Watson and his closest associates rather than to the trend of the whole science of psychology away from psycho-physical parallelism and the stuff of which the "mind" is made and toward a functional conception of human behavior. Needless to say, institutionalism is properly identified with behaviorism in the latter sense. Moreover, what is significant is not so much the rejection of mind-stuff as the cultural corollary of the functional conception of behavior.

The greater is the significance of learning in human behavior, the greater is the significance of what is learned; that is to say, culture. What is wrong with classical price theory is its mental atomism. Economics is the study of the economy; and classical economics (in its entirety) is an attempt to explain economic patterns as the consequence of the concatenation of the individual acts of a vast concourse of individual human beings who are what they are "by nature." But human beings are not what they are in any intelligible sense of the phrase "by nature." Human beings are social phenomena. Social patterns are not the logical consequents of individual acts; individuals, and all their actions, are the logical consequents of social patterns.

All that institutionalism proposes to do is to accept the full significance of the conception of human nature which is now axiomatic, not only to all present-day psychologists but to all social scientists. Strangely enough, economists themselves do not commonly deny that human nature (or individuality, or selfhood) is a social phenomenon. Except for very occasional reversions to neo-Cartesianism,[6] even the most orthodox economists do not explicitly reject the premises of twentieth century psychology and the other social sciences, notwithstanding the fact that contrary assumptions are implicit in their own work. The explanation of this anomaly is to be found, I believe, in what might be called professional inertia. The business of devising graphs to represent various price patterns has become an enterprise of such magnitude that one can easily devote his life to it without ever pausing to reflect that the whole significance of the enterprise derives from assumptions which all other scholars now judge to be highly questionable.

For price patterns can be conceived to reveal the character of the economy only if some of those patterns be regarded as the consequence of a human nature that is antecedent to all social patterns while others are regarded as evidence of "unnatural interference." Recognizing that human nature is itself a social phenomenon obviously does not mean

[6] See, for example, F. A. Hayek, "The Facts of the Social Sciences," *Ethics*, October, 1943, pp. 1 ff.

abjuring the use of price data, any more than it means abjuring the use of census data. But it does mean abandoning price theory; that is, the attempt to read the character of the economy in the horoscope of price. We do not consider census data useless because nobody thinks of it as containing a theory of the economy; and there is nothing in the social conception of human nature that would invalidate the statistical treatment of price data. It does invalidate price theory; and on this account alone the so-called "behavioristic" assumptions of institutionalism are indeed highly significant.

III

The consequences of those assumptions are by no means altogether negative. Another linkage by which institutionalism has always been identified has been with anthropology, and this also has been a perennial source of confusion and misunderstanding. Does it mean only that economists must accept human evolution as a fact? But no economist denies that fact. Or does it mean only that economics must take account of the process of social change? But economics has always done so. Economics does not assume the economy to be static, and never has. Economic theory has always been—since long before the time of Adam Smith—a theory of economic development.

The truth is that the significance of the anthropological aspect of institutionalism can be grasped only in conjunction with its behavioristic aspect. What is at issue is not the fact of change, but rather how it comes about. If human nature is not antecedent to social structure, then it is quite useless to try to find an explanation of the development of that structure by procedures which begin with a contrary assumption, and an alternative explanation must be sought. Moreover, if human nature itself is a social phenomenon, that alternative explanation must necessarily be couched in terms of social forces.

This is the reason for the insistent concern of institutionalists with social institutions and with "workmanship," or technology. That concern has its origin not in a sort of literary interest in describing the social scenery in which economic activity occurs but rather in the conviction that social change (including economic development) can be explained only in terms of social forces and not in terms of "human" wants or "natural" scarcity—both of which are of course defined by prevailing institutions and the state of the industrial arts.

Thus the substance of institutionalism is its attempted identification and differentiation of what Veblen called "the larger forces moving obscurely in the background" of the surface phenomena of the market place. That effort was Veblen's lifelong preoccupation. It has also been the constant underlying concern of John Dewey for well over half a century.[7] Briefly, the theory is that technology (including science) is the dynamic force by which modern civilization (and even, perhaps, all civilization) has been shaped. This is not to say that technology is an external force, external either to human behavior or to social structure. Most emphatically it is not, though much of the misunderstanding of institutionalism derives from the supposition that it is. Indeed, critics seem to feel no embarrassment over denying that civilization is shaped by technology, which for this purpose they themselves regard as an external force, and then turning about and reproaching institutionalists for talking as though machines invent themselves. Actually, institutionalism does neither. It does not postulate that machines invent themselves nor does it treat "the state of the industrial arts" as something external either to human behavior or to social structure.

In recognizing the dynamic character of technology, institutionalism of course does not minimize the importance of the institutional patterns of our own, or any other, society. How could it? The very tag, "institutionalism," signalizes the insistence of Veblen and the institutionalists generally upon the importance of prevailing institutions in the determination of the wants and scarcities that prevail in any community or in any given part of it. Those institutions of course derive from pre-existing institutions and the immemorial past, of which they retain as much as circumstances permit and from which they derive their sanction. But the circumstances which shape and modify and attenuate the institutional heritage are those of technology.

In all this, institutionalism seems to be in line with modern thinking generally. Who would now deny that modern Western civilization has been largely shaped, and is still being shaped, by science and the machine process? Who would now deny that present-day institutions are the "residues" of ancient institutions? To recognize that present-day society is divided into upper, middle, and lower strata is of course to recognize that feudalism is still with us. And to recognize the significance of "mobility" in modern society and of the "fluidity" of modern institutions—to recognize that feudalism persists only as a "residue"—is to recognize what Veblen ironically called the "contamination" of ancient beliefs, sentiments, and habits by the discipline of science and the machine.

---

[7] A brief but explicit statement to this effect by Mr. Dewey himself appears in Joseph Dorfman, *Thorstein Veblen and His America* (New York: Viking, 1934), p. 450. Anyone to whom this suggestion comes as a surprise should reread the opening pages of John Dewey, *The Quest for Certainty* (New York: Minton, Balch, 1929). See also Idus L. Murphree, *Technology and Institutions* (Library of the University of Texas, 1946: unpublished thesis). The writer states in his preface: "This thesis will point out, by constant reference to Dewey's writing, what a large part that distinction plays in his thinking, a fact which is generally ignored."

In these circumstances I find the common judgment of institutionalism—that it is all very interesting, but that it has no theory and no principles—somewhat embarrassing. That is, I feel embarrassed for people who entertain such thoughts. Institutionalism is an attempt to find an answer to the sixty-four dollar question that confronts all economics: what does the economy mean? Institutionalism proposes to find that meaning in the interplay of institutions and technology, which in turn are its basic analytical principles, just as classical theory has sought the meaning of the economy in the interplay of wants and scarcity, which (transliterated into demand and supply) constitute its basic principles. To insist, as some economists now seem to do, that only curve-plotting is economic theory is to forget the theoretical presumptions from which alone the significance of curve-plotting derives.

IV

Economic theory is rightly identified as value theory. From the beginning, one of its central problems has been the relation of value-in-exchange to value-in-use. It was at this point that pecuniary analysis seemed to penetrate most deeply into the meaning of the economy; for it seemed to discover in the operation of the market the closest possible approximation to the value judgments of the community. It is likewise at this point that institutionalism has seemed to display its most strategic weakness.

I am afraid that institutionalist writers must bear a large measure of responsibility for this misunderstanding. Their zeal for objectivity has led many institutionalists to devote themselves almost exclusively to empirical studies to the neglect of the interpretation of the facts their studies have disclosed. Veblen went even farther afield. By his ironical disclaimer of any moral judgment he misled a whole generation of students into supposing that he really did regard waste and usefulness as morally neutral categories, and that his whole analysis was therefore rudderless. In doing so I am afraid that he contributed substantially to the cultural relativism that was just coming into vogue during his most active years.

But it is our responsibility not to be misled. Irony notwithstanding, a theory of value is implicit in all of Veblen's work. Surely no one could read *The Theory of the Leisure Class* and still declare that Veblen really thought just as well of waste as he did of workmanship! Surely there can be no doubt about his evaluation of pecuniary employments and industrial employments! Further, such judgments were by no means the naïve expression of the prejudices of a simple country boy who understood about hoes and combines but never quite comprehended the subtleties of money and credit, as some writers have supposed. Veblen saw that tool-using (or instrument-using, as Dewey has preferred to say) is physically productive, a creative process that underlies all the achievements of mankind; and that the exploits by which some men are always seeking to get the better of others are an impediment to workmanship and creative achievement. This basic ethical principle—the instrumental theory of value, as it is now generally known—runs through all of Veblen's work, and is one of the foundation principles of institutionalism.

Critics often say that whatever institutionalism may be, one thing is certain: it is not a theory of value. Such a statement could mean various things. It could mean that it is not a theory of price; and that is, of course, true. To anyone who is so completely obsessed with the notion that price is the sole valid and objective measure of value that he has come to use the terms "value" and "price" interchangeably, any proposal to seek an objective criterion of value in some other aspect of human endeavor than buying and selling will no doubt seem to be an abandonment of value theory. The issue of ultimate ends is perhaps more serious. To anyone who thinks of value as necessarily derivative from goals which an Almighty Creator (or His modern successor, the Almighty Community) has arbitrarily imposed upon mankind, the proposal to find the criterion of value in the instrumental (tool-using) process, and disvalue in its retardation or arrest, will appear to be a confusion of "ends" with "mere means."

But why "must" values derive from a priori "ends"? Why "must" we attach greater significance to the irrational beliefs and sentiments of the community than we do to the actual, objective, and unquestionably cumulative achievements of hand and brain? After all, scientific know-how and industrial technology are social creations, no less, certainly, than tribal beliefs and community sentiments. Whatever direction science and technology have given and may continue to give to social development is no less the dictate of the community than any other part of our social heritage. One may fail to find "normative" significance in what Edwin Cannan once called "the heritage of improvement." But to assume that none is to be found is to ignore not only Veblen and Cannan and institutionalism generally, and not only the very extensive and formidable work of John Dewey and the instrumentalists, but also the work of many other reputable and accomplished scholars who do not bear these tags—such, for example, as Professor C. I. Lewis.[8]

It is of course apparent that if the technological or instrumental or

---

[8] See C. I. Lewis, *An Analysis of Knowledge and Valuation* (Chicago: Open Court, 1946).

54   AMERICAN ECONOMIC ASSOCIATION

scientific process does contain a valid criterion of value, and therefore of human welfare, then society is not utterly dependent upon the assessments of the market as the sole alternative to the (no more arbitrary but far less palatable) pronouncements of a dictator. In its philosophy of workmanship, institutionalism provides a theoretical foundation for general social and economic planning, one which completely nullifies the a priori supposition of its critics that planning can never be anything but arbitrary.[9] One may doubt the validity of such a theory. But are those who wish to avoid the asperities of dictatorship then well advised to ignore such an alternative to the arbitrary dictates both of tyrants and of markets?

V

At the conclusion of discussions such as this, I have sometimes been asked, "Who, besides yourself, holds these views?" One obvious answer is, "Nobody; and even I have never made this particular statement before, and never will again!" But neither the question nor its answer is very significant. No two of us think exactly alike over the whole of any area as large as the one we have been traversing. The important thing is not agreement or disagreement among persons, but rather logical relationships among ideas. What I have tried to do is to point to a series of relationships by virtue of which a certain set of ideas seem to form a pattern. Granted the possibility of error and the certainty of incompleteness, still any such set of logical affinities, if it exists at all, must touch the work of a very considerable number of people—some closely and many more at least to some degree. I believe that it could be shown quite easily that the work of all those who have been widely recognized as institutionalists bears a close and significant relationship to some such pattern as the one I have tried to draw; and I believe further that a very great deal of work which is not explicitly identified as institutionalist in character is nevertheless complementary to institutionalist theory and itself derives added significance from that fact.

This is true most particularly of empirical studies, or descriptive economics. As I have tried to indicate elsewhere,[10] the very substantial increase of interest in what is actually going on at various points and in various regions of the economy, though it contributes little or nothing to institutionalist theory, is institutionalist in motive and institutionalist in result. One of the most important consequences of classical price theory is that it makes detailed knowledge of what is going on

[9] This point is discussed in my article cited above, pp. 227 ff.
[10] "Piecemeal Revolution," *Southwestern Social Science Quarterly*, June, 1949, pp. 12 ff.

in the economy unnecessary. Since, in the absence of unnatural re-
straints, the economy will take care of itself, no one need bother
about details. The very great number of students who have nevertheless done so, especially during the past half-century, seems to indicate
that we do not trust the invisible hand quite as unreservedly as strict
orthodoxy stipulates. Conversely, the more we know of what is
actually going on, the better prepared we are to deal with our problems realistically and the more likely we are to try to do so.

Simply to identify institutionalism with empiricism is a mistake.
Descriptive studies are the spadework of institutionalist thinking; but
they do not produce a body of theory by spontaneous generation.
Nevertheless, they do quite visibly give evidence of "the cultural incidence of the machine process." One of my most empirical colleagues
remarked one day after perusing one of my effusions, "Why do you
go to so much trouble to establish 'keeping the machines running' as
a principle of social action? I would accept it without argument!"
Now the shift of focus from keeping prices in equilibrium to keeping
machines running seems to me to have a vast significance of which—at
that moment, at least—my colleague was unaware; and precisely on
that account his unconsidered willingness to adopt a technological criterion of welfare struck me as highly suggestive.

Without being fully aware of its implications (since, after all, most
people are not social philosophers), the whole world has come to accept
physical production as the criterion of a sound economy. Institutionalism is nothing more, and nothing less, than the intellectual implications
of that axiom.

[2]

INSTITUTIONAL ECONOMICS

An institution is defined as collective action in control, liberation and expansion of individual action. Its forms are unorganized custom and organized going concerns. The individual action is participation in bargaining, managing and rationing transactions, which are the ultimate units of economic activity. The control by custom or concerns consists in working rules which govern more or less what the individual can, must, or may do or not do. These are choices, resolved into performance, forbearance or avoidance while participating in transactions. The working rule of the Supreme Court is due process of law. The universal principles, that is, similarities of cause, effect, or purpose, discoverable in all transactions, are scarcity, efficiency, futurity, working rules and limiting factors under volitional control. These reveal themselves in a negotiational, or behavioristic, psychology of persuasion and coercion in bargaining transactions, command and obedience in managerial transactions, argument and pleading in rationing transactions.

Transactions determine legal control, while the classical and hedonic economics was concerned with physical control. Legal control is future physical control. The three social relations implicit in transactions are conflict, dependence and order. Social philosophies differ economically according to the kind of transactions which they place uppermost.

The difficulty in defining a field for the so-called institutional economics is the uncertainty of meaning of an institution. Sometimes an institution seems to mean a framework of laws or natural rights within which individuals act like inmates. Sometimes it seems to mean the behavior of the inmates themselves. Sometimes anything additional to or critical of the classical or hedonic economics is deemed to be institutional. Sometimes anything that is "economic behavior" is institutional. Sometimes anything that is "dynamic" instead of "static," or a "process" instead of commodities, or activity instead of feelings, or mass action instead of individual action, or management instead of equilibrium, or control instead of laissez faire, seems to be institutional economics.[1]

All of these notions are doubtless involved in institutional economics, but they may be said to be metaphors or descriptions, whereas a *science* of economic behavior requires analysis into similarities of cause, effect or purpose, and a synthesis in a unified system of principles. And institutional economics, furthermore, cannot separate itself from the marvelous discoveries and insight of the classical and psychological economists. It should incorporate, however, in addition, the equally important insight of the communistic, anarchistic, syndicalistic, fascistic, coöperative and unionistic economists. Doubtless it is the effort to cover by enumeration all of these uncoördinated activities of the various schools which gives to the name institutional economics that reputation of a miscellaneous, nondescript yet merely descriptive, character of so-called "economic behavior," which has long since relegated the crude Historical School.

[1] Cp. *Proceedings*, Amer. Econ. Assn. Suppl., Mar., 1931, p. 134 ff; *Amer. Econ. Rev.*, Mar., 1931, p. 67 ff; Atkins and others, *Economic Behavior* (1930).

If we endeavor to find a universal circumstance, common to all behavior known as institutional, we may define an institution as collective action in control, liberation and expansion of individual action.

Collective action ranges all the way from unorganized custom to the many organized going concerns, such as the family, the corporation, the trade association, the trade union, the reserve system, the state. The principle common to all of them is greater or less control, liberation and expansion of individual action by collective action.

This control of the acts of one individual always results in, and is intended to result in, a gain or loss to another or other individuals. If it be the enforcement of a contract, then the debt is exactly equal to the credit created for the benefit of the other person. A debt is a duty enforced collectively, while the credit is a corresponding right created by creating the duty. The resulting social relation is an economic status, consisting of the expectations towards which each party is directing his economic behavior. On the debt and duty side it is the status of conformity to collective action. On the credit and right side it is a status of security created by the expectation of the said conformity. This is known as "incorporeal" property.

Or, the collective control takes the form of a *tabu* or prohibition of certain acts, such as acts of interference, infringement, trespass; and this prohibition creates an economic status of liberty for the person thus made immune. But the liberty of one person may be accompanied by prospective gain or loss to a correlative person, and the economic status thus created is exposure to the liberty of the other. An employer is exposed to the liberty of the employee to work or not to work, and the employee is exposed to the liberty of the employer to hire or fire. The typical case of liberty and exposure is the goodwill of a business. This is coming to be distinguished as "intangible" property.

Either the state, or a corporation, or a cartel, or a holding company, or a coöperative association, or a trade union, or an employers' association, or a trade association, or a joint trade agreement of two associations, or a stock exchange, or a board of trade, may lay down and enforce the rules which determine for individuals this bundle of correlative and reciprocal economic relationships. Indeed, these collective acts of economic organizations are at times more powerful than the collective action of the political concern, the state.

Stated in the language of ethics and law, to be developed below, all collective acts establish relations of rights, duties, no rights and no duties. Stated in the language of individual behavior, what they require is performance, avoidance, forbearance by individuals. Stated in the language of the resulting economic status of individuals, what they provide is security, conformity, liberty and exposure. Stated in language of cause, effect or purpose, the common principles running through all of them are the principles of scarcity, efficiency, futurity, the working rules of collective action and the limiting and complementary factors of economic theory. Stated in language of the operation of working rules on individual action, they are expressed by the auxiliary verbs of what the individual can, cannot, must, must not, may or may not *do*. He "can" or "cannot," because collective action will or will not come to his aid. He "must" or "must not," because collective action will compel him. He "may," because collective action will permit him and protect him. He "may not," because collective action will prevent him.

It is because of these volitional auxiliary verbs that the familiar term "working rules" is appropriate to indicate the universal principle of cause, effect or purpose, common to all collective action. Working rules are continually changing in the history of an institution, and they differ for different institutions; but, whatever their differences, they have this similarity that they indicate what individuals can, must, or may, do or not do, enforced by collective sanctions.

Analysis of these collective sanctions furnishes that correlation of economics, jurisprudence and ethics which is prerequisite to a theory of institutional economics. David Hume found the unity of these three social sciences in the principle of scarcity and the resulting conflict of interests, contrary to Adam Smith who isolated economics from the others on assumptions of divine providence, earthly abundance and the resulting harmony of interests. Institutional economics goes back to Hume. Taking our cue from Hume and the modern use of such a term as "business ethics," ethics deals with the rules of conduct arising from conflict of interests, arising, in turn, from scarcity and enforced by the *moral* sanctions of collective *opinion;* but economics deals with the same rules of conduct enforced by the collective economic sanctions of *profit* or *loss* in case of obedience or disobedience, while jurisprudence deals with the same rules enforced by the organized sanctions of *violence*. Institutional economics is continually dealing with the relative merits and efficiency of these three types of sanctions.

From this universal principle of collective action in control, liberation and expansion of individual action arise not only the ethical concepts of rights and duties and the economic concepts of security, conformity, liberty and exposure, but also of assets and liabilities. In fact, it is from the field of corporation finance, with its changeable assets and liabilities, rather than from the field of wants and labor, or pains and pleasures, or wealth and happiness, or utility and disutility, that institutional economics derives a large part of its data and methodology. Institutional economics is the assets and liabilities of concerns, contrasted with Adam Smith's Wealth of Nations.

But collective action is even more universal in the unorganized form of custom than it is in the organized form of concerns. Custom has not given way to free contract and competition, as was asserted by Sir Henry Maine. Customs have merely changed with changes in economic conditions, and they may to-day be even more mandatory than the decrees of a dictator, who perforce is compelled to conform to them. The business man who refuses or is unable to make use of the modern customs of the credit system, by refusing to accept or issue checks on solvent banks, although they are merely private arrangements and not legal tender, simply cannot continue in business by carrying on transactions. These instruments are customary tender, instead of legal tender, backed by the powerful sanctions of profit, loss and competition, which compel conformity. Other mandatory customs might be mentioned, such as coming to work at seven o'clock and quitting at six.

If disputes arise, then the officers of an organized concern—a credit association, the manager of a corporation, a stock exchange, a board of trade, a commercial or labor arbitrator, or finally the courts of law up to the Supreme Court of the United States—reduce the custom to precision by adding an organized sanction.

This is the common-law method of making law by the decision of disputes. The decisions, by becoming precedents, become the working rules, for the time being, of the particular organized concern. The historic "common law" of Anglo-American jurisprudence is only a special case of the universal principle common to all concerns that survive, of making new law by deciding conflicts of interest, and thus giving greater precision and organized compulsion to the unorganized working rules of custom. The common-law *method* is universal in all collective action, but the technical "common law" of the lawyers is a body of decisions. In short, the common-law method is itself a custom, with variabilities, like other customs. It is the way collective action acts on individual action in time of conflict.

Thus collective action is more than *control* of individual action—it is, by the very act of control, as indicated by the aforesaid auxiliary verbs, a *liberation* of individual action from coercion, duress, discrimination, or unfair competition by other individuals.

And collective action is more than control and liberation of individual action—it is *expansion* of the will of the individual far beyond what he can do by his own puny acts. The head of a great corporation gives orders whose obedience, enforced by collective action, executes his will at the ends of the earth.

Thus an institution is collective action in control, liberation and expansion of individual action.

These individual actions are really *trans*-actions instead of either

individual behavior or the "exchange" of commodities. It is this shift
from commodities and individuals to transactions and working rules of
collective action that marks the transition from the classical and hedonic
schools to the institutional schools of economic thinking. The shift is
a change in the ultimate unit of economic investigation. The classic and
hedonic economists, with their communistic and anarchistic offshoots,
founded their theories on the relation of man to nature, but institutionalism is a relation of man to man. The smallest unit of the classic
economists was a commodity produced by labor. The smallest unit of
the hedonic economists was the same or similar commodity enjoyed by
ultimate consumers. One was the objective side, the other the subjective
side, of the same relation between the individual and the forces of nature.
The outcome, in either case, was the materialistic metaphor of an automatic equilibrium, analogous to the waves of the ocean, but personified
as "seeking their level."

But the smallest unit of the institutional economists is a *unit of activity*—a transaction, with its participants. Transactions intervene between the labor of the classic economists and the pleasures of the hedonic
economists, simply because it is society that controls access to the forces
of nature, and transactions are, not the "exchange of commodities,"
but the alienation and acquisition, between individuals, of the *rights* of
property and liberty created by society, which must therefore be nego-
tiated between the parties concerned before labor can produce, or consumers can consume, or commodities be physically exchanged.

Transactions, as derived from a study of economic theories and of
the decisions of courts, may be reduced to three economic activities, distinguishable as bargaining transactions, managerial transactions and
rationing transactions. The participants in each of them are controlled
and liberated by the working rules of the particular type of moral,
economic or political concern in question.[2]

The bargaining transaction derives from the familiar formula of a
market, which, at the time of negotiation, before goods are exchanged,
consists of the best two buyers and the best two sellers on that market.
The others are potential. Out of this formula arise four relations of
possible conflict of interest, on which the decisions of courts have built
four classes of working rules.

(1) The two buyers are competitors and the two sellers are competitors, from whose competition the courts, guided by custom, have
constructed the long line of rules on fair and unfair competition.

(2) One of the buyers will buy from one of the sellers, and one of
the sellers will sell to one of the buyers, and, out of this economic choice
of opportunities, both custom and the courts have constructed the rules

[2] Cp. Commons, *Legal Foundations of Capitalism*, pp. 47 ff. (1924).

of equal or unequal opportunity, which, when reduced to decisions of disputes, become the collective rules of reasonable and unreasonable discrimination.

(3) At the close of the negotiations, one of the sellers, by operation of law, transfers title to one of the buyers, and one of the buyers transfers title to money or a credit instrument to one of the sellers. Out of this double alienation and acquisition of title arises the issue of equality or inequality of bargaining power, whose decisions create the rules of fair and unfair price, or reasonable and unreasonable value.[3]

(4) But even the decisions themselves on these disputes, or the legislative or administrative rules prescribed to guide the decisions, may be called in question, under the American System, by an appeal to the Supreme Court, on the ground that property or liberty has been "taken" by the governing or judicial authority "without due process of law." Due process of law is the working rule of the Supreme Court for the time being, which changes with changes in custom and class dominance, or with changes in judges, or changes in the opinions of judges, or with changes in the customary meanings of property and liberty.

Hence the four economic issues arising out of that unit of activity, the bargaining transaction, are competition, discrimination, economic power and working rules.

The habitual assumption back of the decisions in the foregoing classes of disputes is the assumption of equality of willing buyers and willing sellers in the bargaining transactions by which the ownership of wealth is transferred by operation of law. Here the universal principle is scarcity.

But the assumption back of managerial transactions, by which the wealth itself is produced, is that of superior and inferior. Here the universal principle is efficiency, and the relation is between *two* parties, instead of the *four* parties of the bargaining transaction. The master, or manager, or foreman, or other executive, gives orders—the servant or workman or other subordinate must obey. Yet a change in working rules, in course of time, as modified by the new collective action of court decisions, may distinguish between reasonable and unreasonable commands, willing and unwilling obedience.

Finally the rationing transactions differ from managerial transactions in that the superior is a collective superior while the inferiors are individuals. Familiar instances are the log-rolling activities of a legislature in matters of taxation and tariff; the decrees of communist or

[3] Cp. article "Bargaining Power," John R. Commons, *Encyclopaedia of Social Sciences.*

fascist dictatorships; the budget-making of a corporate board of directors; even the decisions of a court or arbitrator; all of which consist in rationing either wealth or purchasing power to subordinates without bargaining, although the negotiations are sometimes mistaken for bargaining, and without managing, which is left to executives. They involve negotiation, indeed, but in the form of argument, pleading, or eloquence, because they come under the rule of command and obedience instead of the rule of equality and liberty. On the borderline are partnership agreements which ration to the partners the benefits and burdens of a joint enterprise. These rationing transactions, likewise, in the American system, are subject finally to the working rules (due process of law) of the Supreme Court.

In all cases we have variations and hierarchies of the universal principle of collective action controlling, liberating and expanding individual action in all the economic transactions of bargaining, managing and rationing.

Since institutional economics is behavioristic, and the behavior in question is none other than the behavior of individuals while participating in transactions, institutional economics must make an analysis of the economic behavior of individuals. The peculiar quality of the human will in all its activities, distinguishing economics from the physical sciences, is that of choosing between alternatives. The choice may be voluntary, or it may be an involuntary choice imposed by another individual or by collective action. In any case the choice is the whole mind and body in action—that is, the will—whether it be physical action and reaction with nature's forces, or the economic activity of mutually inducing others in the transaction.

Every choice, on analysis, turns out to be a three-dimensional act, which, as may be derived from the issues arising in disputes, is at one and the same time, a performance, an avoidance, and a forbearance. Performance is the exercise of power over nature or others; avoidance is its exercise in one direction rather than the next available direction; while forbearance is the exercise, not of the total power except at a crisis, but the exercise of a limited degree of one's possible moral, physical or economic power. Thus forbearance is the limit placed on performance; performance is the actual performance; and avoidance is the alternative performance rejected or avoided—all at one and the same point of time.

It is from forbearance that the doctrine of reasonableness arises, while performance means either rendering a service, compelling a service, or paying a debt, but avoidance is non-interference with the performance, forbearance or avoidance of others. Each may be a duty or a liberty, with a corresponding right or exposure of others, and each may be enforced, permitted, or limited by collective action according to the then working rules of the particular concern.

If institutional economics is volitional it requires an institutional psychology to accompany it. This is the psychology of transactions, which may properly be named negotiational psychology. Nearly all historic psychologies are individualistic, since they are concerned with the relation of individuals to nature, or to other individuals, treated, however, not as citizens with rights, but as objects of nature without rights or duties. This is true all the way from Locke's copy psychology, Berkeley's idealistic psychology, Hume's skeptical psychology, Bentham's pleasure-pain psychology, the hedonistic marginal utility psychology, James' pragmatism, Watson's behaviorism, and the recent Gestalt psychology. All are individualistic. Only Dewey's is socialistic.

But the psychology of transactions is the psychology of negotiations. Each participant is endeavoring to influence the other towards performance, forbearance or avoidance. Each modifies the behavior of the other in greater or less degree. This is the psychology of business, of custom, of legislatures, of courts, of trade associations, of trade unions. In popular language it resolves into the *persuasions* or *coercions* of bargaining transactions, the *commands* and *obedience* of managerial transactions, or the *arguments* and *pleadings* of rationing transactions. All of these are negotiational psychology. It may be observed that they are a behavioristic psychology.

But these are only names and descriptions. A scientific understanding of negotiational psychology resolves it into the smallest number of general principles, that is, similarities of cause, effect or purpose, to be found in all transactions, but in varying degree. First is the personality of participants, which, instead of the assumed equality of economic theory, is all the differences among individuals in their powers of inducement and their responses to inducements and sanctions.

Then are the similarities and differences of circumstance in which personalities are placed. First is scarcity or abundance of alternatives. This is inseparable from efficiency, or the capacity to bring events to happen. In all cases negotiations are directed towards future time, the universal principle of futurity. Working rules are always taken into account, since they are the expectations of what the participants can, must or may do or not do, as controlled, liberated or expanded by collective action. Then, in each transaction is always a limiting factor whose control by the sagacious negotiator, salesman, manager or politician, will determine the outcome of complementary factors in the immediate or remote future.

Thus negotiational psychology is the transactional psychology which offers inducements and sanctions according to the variable personalities and the present circumstances of scarcity, efficiency, expectation, working rules and limiting factors.

Historically this transactional psychology may be seen to have changed, and is changing continuously, so that the whole philosophies of capitalism, fascism or communism are variabilities of it. In the common-law decisions it is the changing distinctions between persuasion and coercion or duress, persuasion being considered the outcome of a reasonable status of either equality of opportunity, or fair competition, or equality of bargaining power, or due process of law. But economic coercion and physical duress are denials of these economic ideals, and nearly every case of economic conflict becomes an assumption or investigation, under its own circumstances, of the negotiational psychology of persuasion and coercion. Even the managerial and rationing negotiations come under this rule of institutional change, for the psychology of command and obedience is changed with changes in the status of conformity, security, liberty or exposure. The modern "personnel" management is an illustration of this kind of change in negotiational psychology.

All of this rests on what may be distinguished as three social relations implicit in every transaction, the relations of conflict, dependence and order. The parties are involved in a conflict of interests on account of the universal principle of scarcity. Yet they depend on each other for reciprocal alienation and acquisition of what the other wants but does not own. Then the working rule is not a foreordained harmony of interests, as assumed in the hypotheses of natural rights or mechanical equilibrium of the classical and hedonic schools, but it actually creates, out of conflict of interests, a workable mutuality and orderly expectation of property and liberty. Thus conflict, dependence and order become the field of institutional economics, builded upon the principles of scarcity, efficiency, futurity and limiting factors derived from the older schools, but correlated under the modern notions of working rules of collective action controlling, liberating and expanding individual action.

What then becomes of the "exchange" of physical commodities and the production of wealth, as well as the consumption of wealth and satisfaction of wants by consumers, which furnished the starting points of the classical, hedonic, communist and other schools of economists? They are merely *transferred to the future*. They become expectations of the immediate or remote future, secured by the collective action, or "institution," of property and liberty, and available only after the conclusion of a transaction. Transactions are the means, under operation of law and custom, of acquiring and alienating legal control of commodities, or legal control of the labor and management that will produce and

1931]   *Institutional Economics*   **657**

deliver or exchange the commodities and services, forward to the ultimate consumers.[4]

Institutional economics is not divorced from the classical and psychological schools of economists—it transfers their theories to the *future* when goods will be produced or consumed or exchanged as an outcome of present transactions. That future may be the engineering economics of production of the classical economists or the home economics of consumption of the hedonic economists, which depend on *physical* control. But institutional economics is *legal* control of commodities and labor, where the classical and hedonic theories dealt only with physical control. *Legal control is future physical control.* Future physical control is the field of engineering and home economics.

Thus it may be seen how it was that the natural rights ideas of the economists and lawyers created the illusion of a framework, supposed to be constructed in the past, within which present individuals are supposed to act. It was because they did not investigate collective action. They assumed the fixity of existing rights of property and liberty. But if rights, duties, liberties and exposures are simply the changeable working rules of all kinds of collective action, looking towards the future, then the framework analogy disappears in the actual collective action of controlling, liberating and expanding individual action for the immediate or remote future production, exchange, and consumption of wealth.

Consequently the final social philosophy, or "ism"—which is usually a belief regarding human nature and its goal—towards which institutional economics trends is not something foreordained by divine or natural "right," or materialistic equilibrium, or "laws of nature"—it may be communism, fascism, capitalism. If managerial and rationing transactions are the starting point of the philosophy, then the end is the command and obedience of communism or fascism. If bargaining transactions are the units of investigation then the trend is towards the equality of opportunity, the fair competition, the equality of bargaining power, and the due process of law of the philosophy of liberalism and regulated capitalism. But there may be all degrees of combination, for the three kinds of transactions are interdependent and variable in a world of collective action and perpetual change, which is the uncertain future world of institutional economics.

JOHN R. COMMONS

University of Wisconsin

[4] On this subject see Commons, "The Delivered Price Practice in the Steel Market," *Amer. Econ. Rev.*, Sept., 1924. Also F. A. Fetter, *The Masquerade of Monopoly* (1931).

[3]

INSTITUTIONAL ECONOMICS AS SEEN BY AN INSTITUTIONAL ECONOMIST[1]

EDWIN E. WITTE

University of Wisconsin

I can best present my ideas about the nature and values of institutional economics by giving a brief account of how I became an institutional economist. Like most others, I am largely a product of my training and experience. Most of my ideas on economics date from my graduate student days and my earliest experiences in governmental service.

The economist who most influenced my thinking was John R. Commons. I came to economics and to Commons late in the period of my formal education. As an undergraduate and in the first two years of graduate work, I majored in history. I shifted to economics because my major professor, Frederick Jackson Turner, who first stressed the importance of the frontier in American history, left Wisconsin and told me that the best historian among many good historians on our campus was John R. Commons, although he was attached to the economics department. I had discovered Commons earlier through student debating, which was the center of my interests as an undergraduate. With Turner gone, I took his advice and shifted to economics and to Commons.

I have never regretted doing so, although history and biography have ever remained my pastime reading. I had courses with other distinguished economists and learned enough economic theory to pass the Ph.D. examination. But it was principally from Commons that I got the ideas I am expounding in this article. I got these ideas not from what Commons said in class or from his writings, but from working with him on the practical problems in which he was then interested.

Commons at that time was formulating the forward looking protective labor legislation which brought great fame to Wisconsin forty years ago: the industrial commission act, workmens' compensation, and improved child labor law, a women's hours of labor law, a minimum wage act, the first modern apprenticeship law, and the present type of industrial safety legislation. He had all of his graduate students work on some aspect of these problems. Ever modest and always giving credit to his students even for ideas which really came from him, he inspired his students to work on the practical problems assigned to them with a devotion and intensity they did not develop in any other courses. They sought answers and were guided to seek facts having bearing on the subject wherever they might be found, regardless of academic disciplines.

In the last quarter century of his life, Commons tried to pull together into a comprehensive, systematic body of economic thought the theoretical ideas he

---

[1] This article is adapted from an address at the meeting of the Central New York Economics Conference at Wells College, Aurora, N. Y., November 21, 1953.

developed out of the work he did on practical public policy problems.[2] I vaguely recall that even then he was beginning to formulate his theoretical economic ideas. They were lost upon me. I confess that I have had the same difficulty in following Commons' terminology and some of his reasoning which so many students of his later theoretical writings have experienced. But new to economics as I was, I grasped something of Commons' philosophy of economics in action, which seems to me to be central in institutional economics.

After one year of classroom work with Commons, I got my first job in public employment. This came about because Commons was named a member of the first Industrial Commission of Wisconsin. Like several others of his students, I entered the employ of the Industrial Commission, after qualifying through a civil service examination. My first assignment was a field study to find out why many employers were rejecting workmen's compensation. That was the first step in the enactment of the first state law regulating workmen's compensation insurance. Later, when President Wilson appointed Commons a member of the Industrial Relations Commission of 1914–1915, I again went with him, and made a field study of the use of injunctions in labor disputes. I cite these studies, not because my reports were very important or influential, but because they illustrate the sort of economic policy questions with which I have had to deal all my life.

After that, I had one more year of graduate study, during which I was Commons' teaching assistant. In the forty years since then, I have always been a public employee, half the time in the state or national government service in policy-making positions,[3] the other half as a professor and administrator in a state university. Quite often I have carried on both types of governmental service simultaneously—as do many other economists. That has been my life, and in everything that I have done I have found the institutional approach to economics that I got from John R. Commons in my formative years to be invaluable.

WHAT IS INSTITUTIONAL ECONOMICS?

Institutional economics is often regarded as a school or would-be school of economic thought, competitive with such other schools of economic thought as the classical school, the historical school, the Austrian school, the neo-classists, the Keynesians, the Marxists, and still others. Looked upon in this light, I think, there is a good deal of merit in the criticism that there is no such thing as institutional economics. Some of the best known economists classified as institutional

[2] Commons' major books dealing with economic theory, all published in New York by Macmillan, were *The Legal Foundations of Capitalism* (1924), *Institutional Economics* (1935), and *Economics in Action* (1950, posthumous).

[3] Among the governmental positions the author has held were those of Secretary of the Industrial Commission of Wisconsin, 1917–1922; Chief, Wisconsin Legislative Reference Service, 1922–1933; Executive Director, U. S. Commission on Economic Security, 1934–1935 (which sponsored the Social Security Act of the United States); Member, Wisconsin State Planning Board, 1935–1938; Member, Wisconsin Labor Relations Board, 1937–1939; Chairman, Detroit Regional War Labor Board, 1943–1944; Public Member, National War Labor Board, 1944–1945; Member, Atomic Energy Labor Relations Panel, 1948–1953.

economists made major contributions in what all economic theorists regard as the domain of economics. But none of them, nor all of them combined, have developed anything like a complete, self-contained, independent theory of the price mechanism or the functioning of the economic system.

Institutional economics, as I conceive it, is not so much a connected body of economic thought as a method of approaching economic problems. This method is what might be called a practical problems approach. Institutional economists are not so much concerned with the explanation of all economic phenomena as with the solution of particular economic problems of immediate significance. John R. Commons studied labor problems to find out what was the best way for dealing with industrial conflict, with child labor, industrial accidents, sweat shop wages, and many similar questions. Wesley Mitchell studied the business cycle, not only to fit this phenomenon into the general body of economic theory or even merely to understand the cycle, but to learn what might be done to minimize the effects of its fluctuations. It is the practical problems approach which above all others characterizes institutional economics. It is a method of studying economic phenomena rather than a connected body of thought expressing the "timeless and placeless laws" which govern what Frank Knight has referred to as "the economic calculus of individual preference."[4]

In studying economic policy problems, which has always been their great interest, rather than "the equilibrium of individualism" and the "science of the price mechanism"—again using some of Frank Knight's revealing characterizations of orthodox economics—the institutional economists have never confined themselves to economic theory. They have freely disregarded the lines of division between the several academic disciplines. They are concerned with the correct answers to public policy questions and not solely with what economic theory may contribute to these answers. In seeking solutions of practical problems, they try to give consideration to all aspects of these problems: economic (in the orthodox use of that term), social, psychological, historical, legal, political, administrative, and even technical. Although they cannot be expert in all of these, they find it necessary to try to understand all of the aspects which enter into a particular situation or problem with which they are concerned.

The practical problems approach which the institutional economists adopt has led them to regard economics as something broader than Boulding's "a discipline of logic which may be applied to the interpretation of all economic problems, past or present."[5] All economic policy questions are within the scope

---

[4] The clauses credited to Professor Knight are taken from his Presidential Address at the meeting of the American Economic Association in 1950, "The Role of Principles in Economics and Politics," *American Economic Review*, March 1951. While holding the view that economics has a broader scope than Professor Knight believes, the author desires to repeat the tribute he expressed in presiding at a meeting on institutional economics at the 1950 convention of the American Economic Association. While Professor Knight is, perhaps, the most orthodox of orthodox economists, he gave more opportunity in the convention program for which he was responsible to institutional economists to present their views than had been accorded them for many years.

[5] K. E. Boulding, *Economic Analysis*, New York, 1948, p. 8.

of economics, and the institutionalists hold that they must be considered in their totality. ~ holistic

Institutional economists are not concerned solely with what many other economists call "economic motives"—the quest for gain, the profit motive, or the maximizing of something or other. Whatever leads men to act in economic matters as they do is within their scope of interest. To the institutional economists, economic man is pretty much fiction; but the social or whole man is reality and the center of all economic activity and its purpose. Non-economic motives are to them not merely factors interfering with the operation of economic laws, but an essential part of the total situation which must be taken into consideration in arriving at a true explanation of economic life and the laws which govern its functioning.

And the institutionalists do not regard economic laws to be timeless and place-less. As they deal with public policy questions, they seek not universal natural laws but solutions applicable to a particular time, place, and situation. The early American institutionalists were heavily indebted to economists of the German historical school, who were the teachers of many of them. These first American institutionalists—Ely, Patten, Seligman, James and still others of that generation —who incidentally were the founders of the American Economic Association— studied economics in Germany in the late eighteen seventies and early eighteen eighties and had as their teachers some of the most distinguished of German historical economists. Probably through this contact, the early American institutionalists came to appreciate that what is a sound economic policy in one situation will not do in another. That has been a characteristic of the approach of the institutionalists to economic problems ever since. Far more than orthodox economists, the institutionalists have been interested in the development of economic policies and in economic change. As Bushrod Allin expressed this aspect of institutional economics in his thought-provoking article, "Is Group Choice a Part of Economics"[6] (which I commend to all who would like to get a clearer grasp of institutional economics), "economic events of the present have meaning only in the light of the known past and the expected future."

An equally if not even more basic characteristic of the institutionalists' approach to economics is their interest in the institutional background of the time, place, and situation. Institutional economists have not gone along with the view expressed in a leading elementary textbook: "economics assumes technology and institutions and leaves the problem of income distribution to the statesman."[7] To find the solution of economic policy problems, the institutional set-up must be understood. Institutions cannot be taken for granted, as they are man-made and changeable. Changes in the working rules are possible and occur frequently, although normally only slowly. Institutional economists believe that, for the

[6] Bushrod Allin, "Is Group Choice a Part of Economics?" in *Quarterly Journal of Economics*, LXVII, pp. 362–379. Another recent thought-provoking article written from an institutional point of view is Roy Blough, *The Role of the Economist in Federal Policy Making* (Urbana, Ill.: University of Illinois, the Institute of Government and Public Affairs).

[7] P. A. Samuelson, *Economics* (New York, 1951), pp. 14–15.

correct interpretations of different economies and developments, account needs to be taken of the diverse and changing institutions. In seeking solutions of the economic policy questions which interest them, they do not rule out the possibility of changes in institutions. As Bushrod Allin observes in his fine article, it is astonishing that at a time when the natural sciences have gone beyond seeking the automatic laws of nature to the purposeful control of nature (he cites the development of hybrid corn from the original wild plant, Indian maize, as an example), so many theoretical economists, in their quest for the certainty of the natural sciences, see nothing for them to do but to find out what are the automatic laws which govern all economic phenomena. Theoretical economists using the model building approach either consider only a static situation or one in which only a limited number of variations can be introduced. In contrast, the institutional economists in dealing with economic policy problems must take account of all factors in our dynamic society and must not lose sight of the fact that changes are possible in just about every factor.

Institutional economics has often been attacked by advocates of the orthodox approach as being only descriptive, not analytical. It is true that the institutional economists have always been very much concerned with the discovery and presentation of facts. Institutionalists have a great regard for statistics and field studies. To them all economic laws rest upon facts, not assumptions—all the facts, and not merely those which their critics term "strictly economic facts."

In arriving at conclusions, institutional economists have generally relied upon induction rather than deduction. They reason and develop theories—although they do not have a general theory which answers all economic questions. But in theorizing, they concern themselves with facts, not models. They do not construct an economic man, but are concerned with what real men do and think. John R. Commons constantly told his students: "Go out and observe, as well as read and think. Find out what are the facts and all the pertinent facts, and then reach conclusions on the basis of the facts." Institutional economists have relied far more on direct observations than model building and have not been content to make of economics an exercise in logic.

All or most of the institutional economists have been pragmatists, studying facts, not for their own sake, but to solve problems and to make this a better world to live in. I do not want to be understood as claiming that orthodox economic theorists have not had the same objective. Most major advances in economic theory have come as a by-product of intensive study of practical economic problems with a view toward their solution. There have been reformers among orthodox economists, as well as among the institutionalists. But the followers of most orthodox schools of economics should also recognize that the institutionalists have not been satisfied with finding facts and describing situations, although they have placed great store in discovering the facts and in accurate descriptions. They have been most purposeful in all their studies and have ever sought improvement and advancement, no less than economists of other schools and far more than many of their critics.

Concluding my attempt to give you my concept of institutional economics, let me deal briefly with the most distinctive feature of the body of economic thought developed by my mentor, John R. Commons. Other institutional economists, notably Veblen, had something of the same view, as, I believe, have all present day economists who call themselves institutionalists.

This is the emphasis upon the associational aspects of the present day American economy and, to a lesser extent, of all western economies. Commons, like the English founding fathers, regarded his field of study to be "political economy," not an "economics" which has little, if any, relation to government. He, like all institutionalists, was not primarily interested in the economies of the firm and the maximizing of private profits. His interests centered in public policy questions, in which government often has a large role. But he assigned an even more important place to voluntary associations. He recognized that governmental actions are to a very large extent determined by the pressures and interactions of our many voluntary associations. He often called this "collective bargaining," using this term in a far broader meaning than the negotiation, conclusion, and living under labor-management agreements.

Man, while an individual being, is also a gregarious creature. Americans with all their individualism have always demonstrated great capacity for tackling economic problems in association with their fellows. This feature of the American way of life was noted as early as the eighteen thirties by de Toqueville in his *Democracy in America*[8]—the first book on the American way of life written by a European visitor which attracted world wide attention. Most pioneer settlements were associational in character and it was on the frontier that there was developed the concept of a government one of whose primary functions is to help people in their economic activities—"a government of the people, by the people, and for the people," as expressed by the greatest of all Americans, Abraham Lincoln—a product of the frontier. And what was true of the pioneer days is even more true today. This is the age of the ever increasing governmental participation in economic life, of the corporations, the trade unions, the cooperatives, the trade associations, the employers' associations, the associations of commerce, the farmers' organizations, the many professional associations, and numerous other organizations primarily serving economic purposes and profoundly affecting economic life. This is also the age of group patterns of thinking and action. Nowhere else are associations, democratically organized, so important as in individualistic America. In fact, one of the basic differences between totalitarianism and democracy has lain in their attitudes toward private associations. Totalitarianism, whether of the communist or fascist brand, has always suppressed the free trade unions and made all other associations subservient to the state. In contrast, freedom of associations is one of the cornerstones of democracy. Never have associations and group action been so important as they are today in all western nations, particularly the United States.

To institutionalists who look upon Commons as their mentor, group action looms larger than individual action in the present day economy. In contrast,

[8] Alexis de Tocqueville, *De la Democratie en Amerique*. Translated by Henry Reeve (New York, 1898).

many orthodox economists deal primarily with "the calculus of individual preferences" and treat associational action as but an interference with the operation of the natural economic laws. While it is recognized that there are corporations, their great importance in the present day economy is obscured by treating them as firms not essentially different from individual entrepreneurs. And the trade unions are regarded as being at one and the same time powerful, dangerous, and impotent organizations. Such treatment of the associational aspects of our economy seemed unreal to Commons and represents the principal criticism which the present day institutional economists direct against the economics taught in most economic theory courses.

VALUES AND POSSIBILITIES IN INSTITUTIONAL ECONOMICS

Coming now to an appraisal of institutional economics, it is very clear that the institutional economists have not to date developed a complete body of economic theory which incorporates the dominant importance of associations in the economy of the United States or the non-economic facts and motives which influence economic decisions. Such a general theory may or may not be developed in the future.

Institutional economists, however, have only made major contributions towards a better understanding of particular aspects of the present day economy and the American way of life. Who will gainsay the contributions of Wesley Mitchell to the theory of the business cycle, or challenge the importance of the many insights into industrial relations supplied by the pioneer work of John R. Commons, or the acuteness of Thorstein Veblen's analysis of non-economic motives which enter into economic decisions? Coming to a still living institutional economist, the theory of the labor movement advanced by my colleague, Selig Perlman, has such vitality that after twenty-five years it is still the principal subject of discussion among academic students of labor. To institutionalists belongs much of the credit for the development of statistics as a part of the standard equipment of most economists. Institutionalists have made great contributions in such widely ranging fields as economic history, agricultural and land economics, public finance, public utilities, labor economics, industrial evolution and many others —which, if not considered economics by some devotees of abstract economic theory, are certainly taught today as economics in most American universities.

Very certain is it that economics has profited immensely from the emphasis the institutionalists have given to the gathering of facts. There are economists who think we have all the facts we need for a true understanding of the economy and its functioning. But there is scarcely a branch of economics as taught in universities in which major advances have not been made as more facts have become available. To use the fields of labor economics as an illustration, until the vast volume of statistics which has been developed in connection with social security and wage controls became available, it did not seem so unrealistic to assume that substantially all workers are employed full time and work all year long except in periods of depression, and that there is a single wage rate for a given class of labor in an area or community. The wealth of information which has become available has proven both these assumptions to be false. Factual information of this character I believe to be a first step toward the development of sounder economic theories than we now have which, all too often, are based on logical reasoning from false assumptions.

Coming to another aspect of the contributions made to date by institutional economics, I do not claim that it has been the key which has opened an increasing number of positions to economists in government and business and also a few positions in labor. But it is my view that economists, to whatever school they belong, make extensive use of the approaches of institutional economics in such employments, and in most of the work they do make little use of abstract economic theory. This is particularly true in policy-making positions or as advisers to policy-makers, as distinguished from the preparation of research reports which are scarcely read by anyone.

Aside from the use made of the approaches of institutional economics in work done by economists in the employ of government, industry and labor, it is my observation that economists, to whatever school they may belong, practically always go beyond economic theory in nearly all work they do on practical public policy questions. Institutional economics is not, generally, the economics of the classroom, but is the economics of substantially all economists when they tackle practical issues.

There is at present a vogue for interdisciplinary research bringing together social scientists from many academic disciplines to work on practical problems each from the point of view of his specialization. The great foundations increasingly subsidize only such interdisciplinary research. I do not claim that such an interdisciplinary approach to social problems is valueless. Though it is very time-consuming, I do not doubt that there is real value in getting social scientists of different disciplines to understand each other. But to date interdisciplinary research has not produced any very startling or even many productive results.

While not taking the position that the large expenditures now being made for interdisciplinary research represent money not put to the best possible use, it is clear that most study of economic policy questions must still be made in a much less expensive manner. The economist working on economic policy questions often must make use of knowledge in many fields in which he is not a specialist and cannot generally refer a part of his problem to colleagues from other disciplines working with him. It is possible and profitable for the economist to consult specialists from other fields, but the decisions he comes to on policy problems generally must be his own and not those of a group with whom he works. And to be sound they must take into account more than abstract economic theory. The economist who works on practical public policy questions almost necessarily must be something of an institutional economist.

Making such claims for institutional economics, I nevertheless believe that institutional economics to date has not realized its fullest possibilities. It is my hope that the approach of institutional economics—reliance upon facts and induction and the utilization of information which economic theorists generally classify as non-economic—will result in better explanations of the economy and its functioning than we now have.

INSTITUTIONAL ECONOMICS   139

In expressing this hope, I want to leave no doubt that I do not condemn economic theory, economic theorists, or other schools of economic thought. I urge only that institutional economics be not ruled out as not being economics and that something more than abstract economic theory be included in our economics courses in colleges.

As the chairman for many years of the economics department of a large university, which has an institutional economics tradition, I was instrumental in bringing in many orthodox economists, because it is my belief that the economics departments of major universities should have among them representatives of all the principal schools of economic thought. But I have become somewhat concerned about the ever-increasing emphasis on general economic theory and model building in nearly all economics courses. The situation seems to me to have become such that master's degree candidates in applied fields have to devote so much time to general economic theory and its modern methods of expression that many of them have little time to learn much of anything else. Ph.D. candidates devote so much time to getting ready for the theory examinations that most of them do nothing on their theses until they have gone into teaching or other positions, with the result that many either never finish their theses or produce only inferior studies. I most sincerely hope that the report on graduate study in economics made by my good friend Howard Bowen, formerly at Illinois and now at Williams, sponsored by the American Economic Association,[9] will not result in even more concentration on economic theory in the training of graduate students.

Most of all, I am concerned by the trend, manifested at many universities and in textbooks, to make the elementary economics courses for undergraduates almost pure theory courses and to heavily infuse abstract theory and models into the beginning courses in applied fields. Casual inquiries I have made at many institutions lead me to believe that the percentage of university students electing economics courses has decreased in recent years, as emphasis upon abstract theory has increased. I believe also that the low reputation in which economists are held by businessmen[10] and the general public is due to their fondness for abstractions. In the present age of witch-hunting, it may make economists less liable to be falsely branded as communists, to write and speak in a language

[9] Graduate Education in Economics, *American Economic Review*, XLIII, Pt. 2, September 1953.

[10] The opinion which businessmen have of academic economists has been well expressed by Dexter M. Keezer, Vice President of the McGraw-Hill Publishing Company, a former professor of economics and college president, in an unpublished article, "Note on a Dangerous Disrelish," privately circulated in November 1953:

"The businessman, in turn, tends to view the professor of economics as occupied primarily with obstruse irrelevancies or, when he ventures into the world of practical affairs, doing so with an irritating if not positively deleterious ignorance or disregard of crucial business relations."

Keezer adds the further comment:

"A striking aspect of the fogginess of the communication between academic economists and businessmen is found in the fact that most businessmen who took a college course in economics can see virtually no connection between the contents of the course and the range of experience they encounter in the field of business."

which no one understands, but this also operates to minimize their possibilities for influencing thought and action. To me the very scant knowledge or appreciation of economic truth and facts retained in after life by our undergraduate students strongly suggests the need for trying new methods rather than more of the same.

But I freely acknowledge that the weight of opinion among professional economists is against me and that I may be wrong. I do not ask that model building be kept out of economics or that the abstract theorists or the mathematical economists be banned from the profession. Nor have I any thought of seriously challenging their dominance in the professional organizations and periodicals. I grant that they have added to economic knowledge and helped solve many economic problems. I do not take the view that they have nothing further to contribute. I would let them pursue economic truths in their own way, even though I and, I believe, many others interested in economic problems may not understand them.

A few years ago I was approached by members of the American Economic Association who were interested in the formation of an Institutional Economic Association because they felt that they were being treated as outcasts. That was probably because I was the first President of the Industrial Relations Research Association. While I felt and still believe that the latter organization, which seeks to bring together social scientists from all disciplines interested in industrial relations together with its practitioners in industry and labor, serves a most useful purpose, I am opposed to any separate organization of the institutional economists. I want to keep the supporters of the institutional approach to economic problems among the economists, not as a group distinct from them.

What I seek is tolerance of the heterodox practitioners among the economists. I also make a plea for the revival, on an experimental basis, of the sort of training in economics which many of the men of my graduate student days and earlier received, which centered around a thesis devoted to a practical public policy problem. It is my thought that economics is far too vital a field of study to be cast into a single mould. Institutional economics, I submit, is an approach to economics which should not be ruled out because it has not become a general economic theory explaining all economic phenomena.

[4]

DISCUSSION

ALLAN G. GRUCHY: Professor Boulding's new look at institutionalism gives rise to a combined moralistic, verbal, and scientific attack on this type of economics. Since his moralistic and verbal onslaughts on the institutionalists turn out to be moralizing and preachment rather than scientific analysis, I shall dismiss these onslaughts as being quite irrelevant to our main concern, which is a scientific appraisal of institutionalism. Boulding's scientific appraisal of institutional economics is defective on two main counts. First, he incorrectly defines institutionalism as "the description and understanding of institutions." Using this omnibus definition, he can classify any social scientist who studies institutions as an institutionalist. This is why he includes William Petty, Robert Owen, Graham Wallas, Harold Laski, Emile Durkheim, and many other social scientists in his grab-bag of institutionalism. The correct definition of institutionalism is that this type of economics is a study of the disposal of scarce means within the framework of our developing economic system. It rounds out economic science by providing a theory of the going economic system, or, in other words, a theory of capitalism. Institutionalists study institutions only as subsidiary parts of a larger matrix in the form of the economic order. If Boulding wishes to make a significant analysis of institutionalism, he should first elucidate the theoretical position of the institutionalists as it is revealed in their theory of the American capitalistic system. In a very real sense he has not made contact with institutionalism, because he has no interest in what is of prime importance to the institutionalists; namely, a theory of capitalism.

The second criticism of Boulding's look at institutionalism relates to the main thesis of his paper, which is that institutionalism is essentially or primarily a movement of dissent from basic economic theory. According to Boulding, institutionalism is only a particular manifestation of a much broader movement of dissent which goes far beyond institutionalism, so far indeed that it can be said to include even Boulding himself. This view of institutionalism is not supported by an examination of the nature and the history of the movement. Institutionalism is only secondarily a movement of dissent from analytical economics. What Boulding has failed to grasp is that institutionalism is primarily a positive, creative movement which aims at broadening the nature and scope of economic science by pushing beyond basic theory to create a theory of our developing economic system.

As anyone knows who has taken the time to read and digest the very extensive body of institutionalist writings, the great bulk of this material has nothing at all to do with dissent from analytical economics. Veblen's *Theory of Business Enterprise, Absentee Ownership,* and *Vested Interests and the Common Man,* Mitchell's essays on the role of money, the theory of consumption, and his theory of economic guidance, Clark's *Studies in the Economics of Overhead Costs, Social Control of Business,* and *Guideposts in Time of*

13

Change, and Gardiner Means's *The Modern Corporation and Private Property* and *The Modern Economy in Action* have nothing to do with dissent from received economic theory. The economic interpretations in these and other writings of the institutionalists are the pieces with which they have constructed their mosaic of the American capitalistic system. Out of these volumes has emerged the essence of institutionalism; namely, a theory of the American economic system. If criticism of institutionalism is to be significant and relevant, it must inquire into the real core of this type of economic thought and analyze the theory of capitalism which institutionalism has added to the body of pure theory. One may not agree with the institutionalists' theory of the American economic system, but he misses the mark rather completely if he fails to understand that this theory is the very essence and primary concern of institutionalism.

The institutionalists' totalistic concept of the economic system is not the same as Boulding's over-all concept. Whereas he analyzes the economic system in terms of an elaborate, highly abstract mathematical model, the institutionalists study the economic system in terms of a concrete, historical type of economic activity by means of which scarce resources are allocated. While Boulding's view of the economic system is useful as a first approximation to an understanding of economic reality, the institutionalists' view of the economic system is necessary for a full interpretation of the flow of concrete economic events.

The institutionalists do not repudiate or dispense with pure or basic economic theory. What they have done over the years is to take the basic theory of Marshall, Keynes, and others and place it in the larger setting of a theory of the evolving economic system. We see recent statements of this theory of the total economic system in J. M. Clark's *Guideposts in Time of Change.* in the annual reports of the Council of Economic Advisers for the years 1946-53 which develop the concept of an American doctrine of mutual adjustment between the economy's private and public sectors, and also in the publications of the National Planning Association such as *The American Economy in 1960.* The institutionalist theory of capitalism runs in terms of the continued march towards industrialization, the spread of collective action in control of individual action, the growing inability of the free market system to remove automatically discrepancies between the nation's income and product flows, the development of imbalances between prices and costs and between savings and investment, and the expansion of government action to reduce these discrepancies and imbalances.

Theories of the total economic system are very important because men work and live with them. These theories bridge the gulf between basic economic theory and economic policy recommendations. For example, Keynes placed his basic theory of national income determination in the framework of his theory of British capitalism when he came to make his policy recommendations. Likewise, the institutionalists use their theory of capitalism as a springboard for the recommendation of economic policies.

To say that institutionalism is nothing more than a past historical interlude, or at best a negativistic movement of dissent, indicates only wishful

thinking. Recent and current economic trends in this country and elsewhere
are the surest guarantee that institutionalism will continue to be a significant
and, in some quarters, a thriving movement. The Employment Act of 1946
calls for an integrated, holistic attack on the nation's economic problems.
But before such an attack can be made successfully, we must have an adequate over-all interpretation of the functioning of our mixed enterprise system.
Since the institutionalist movement has specialized in providing just such an
interpretation, it bids fair to remain a significant movement in economic
thought. This is so because institutionalism, in terms of economic policy, leads
to national economic programming for full employment and stable growth
without inflation. Recent developments in economic theory and in techniques
of economic analysis have made national economic programming an effective
type of economic program, and so have indirectly lent support to the institutionalist movement. The use of national economic budgets for the projec-
tion of full employment total output goals, of input-output studies to determine the labor, raw material, and capital requirements of these goals, of
flow-of-funds accounting to measure the financial needs of an expanding total
output—all these developments have pointed in the direction of more successful
national economic programming activities, and so of a more effective transla-
tion of institutional economic thought into concrete economic practice.

Institutionalism as a point of view and as a body of economic interpretation
is now thoroughly embedded in the progressive wing of the Democratic Party.
While institutionalism is not at present prominently situated in academic
halls, it does appear to have permanent riparian rights on the banks of the
Potomac River. The strong policy orientation of the institutionalist movement
and its willingness to grapple with pressing economic problems make its continued survival and future progress hardly a matter of doubt.

FOREST G. HILL: Professor Boulding says he originally found the American
institutionalists misguided and unpromising. Today he is interested in dynamics, integration of economics with other social sciences, and the empirical
bearing of economic theory; he even risks calling this work neo-institutionalism. His own career supports his thesis that the direct impact of institutionalism on economic theory has been small but its indirect influence large. However, he may be forced to this conclusion by the way he defines institutionalism and economic theory.

Professor Boulding suggests that a sociology of dissent would help us understand such critics of traditional thought as Veblen, Commons, and Mitchell.
But why has their main influence been indirect, delayed, and received with
hostility? We apparently need a sociology of orthodoxy even more. To understand changes in economic thought calls for a realistic theory of knowledge
and an intimate awareness of intellectual history. This poses a major problem in social science analysis, upon which Mitchell has done extremely challenging work. However, economists have less interest in this problem today
than three or four decades ago.

We need Boulding's distinction between scientific and moral dissent, between criticism of institutions and of analytical content. However, he should

explicitly discuss both elements of dissent, not just the scientific. Since his remarks reflect moral disapproval of Veblen, coolness toward Mitchell, and admiration for Commons, an explicit, reasoned treatment is in order. Not only economic institutions but also the intellectual traditions and procedures of economics pose moral issues; the latter, unfortunately, Boulding does not here acknowledge. Values become intricately involved in economic analysis: problems must be chosen for analysis, assumptions made about man and society, and policy implications drawn from the analysis. These selected problems, assumptions, and policy conclusions inevitably pose normative issues. Elsewhere, Boulding has recognized this ethical aspect of economics; and A. B. Wolfe, J. M. Clark, and Clarence Ayres have emphasized this intriguing subject.

In Joseph Dorfman's view, Veblen and Mitchell tended to prevent a rigid orthodoxy from developing in America. This purpose was shared by Commons and others. They urged the study of major problems of economic change and policy through comprehensive historical, psychological, and empirical methods. Since they sought to enlarge and reorient economic analysis, they were not only dissenters or challengers of orthodoxy, as Boulding uses these terms, but also reformers of intellectual tradition. In assessing the development and significance of institutionalism, we cannot merely view it as purely negative dissent, lumping the major institutionalists in with Boulding's "hundred-and-one dissenters." Valid appraisal requires analysis of their theoretical position and the unique elements in their thinking. It is essential to go beyond the prevailing stereotyped criticisms of their work, as we may note with Veblen and Mitchell.

The fact that Veblen had an unusual personality and career reveals little about his theoretical significance. A careful reading of Veblen will not show that he used an "instinct psychology" or "racist anthropology." He was concerned not with instinctive or racist behavior, but institutionally shaped behavior. His analysis, after all, stressed the evolution and functioning of economic institutions. He used the "instinct of workmanship" and "parental bent" to analyze and evaluate institutions, not ultimate motivation; and the social psychology he used resembled that of John Dewey, once his colleague at the University of Chicago.

Veblen did not think highly of the engineers, whom he viewed as incurably conservative; their neglect of him would have brought no remorse. His influence in the field of law bore particularly on industrial and financial regulation. His stimulus to the study of industrial organization affected economics much more than law. Commons had far greater interest than Veblen in the legal aspects of economic organization. Through his students, Veblen had some effect on labor economics, and especially business cycle analysis through Mitchell. Veblen influenced consumer economics and the theory of the firm enough to bear mention.

I am puzzled that Boulding should interpret Veblen and Mitchell without using the term business cycles or citing their numerous methodological essays. Their work in these two fields is central to the issue of their "scientific" influence on economic theory. To see Mitchell's work in any other light would dispute the recognition accorded him as the first recipient of this Association's Francis A. Walker medal for "a contribution of the highest distinction to economics." He was clearly more than an "economic entomologist," or collector of time series. It is unwarranted to say that he merely "collected figures," gave us only "purely empirical leads and lags," "was not . . . much interested" in the integration of economics with other social sciences, "made only a small impact on academic economics," and was not concerned with "the description and understanding of institutions as such."

Mitchell questioned Veblen's method of reasoning and verifying, not his institutional analysis. Mitchell acknowledged that his conception of the money economy—the foundation of his work on business cycles—was Veblenian. He undertook the analysis of business cycles to demonstrate how economic institutions actually function. He regarded this analysis as a work in general economic theory, designed to show that empirical theorizing can throw light on the operation and control of institutions. That his work had a central theoretical core has been affirmed by Arthur F. Burns, J. M. Clark, Milton Friedman, Rutledge Vining, and even Joseph Schumpeter. Mitchell's development of this theoretical structure was hardly implicit or haphazard. He surveyed the theoretical literature for insights, hypotheses, and questions. He then elaborated his empirical inquiries within the theoretical structure of the money economy. This analytical procedure hardly suggests amateurish theorizing carried on *ab ovo*, without reference to established doctrines. His cyclical analysis should hold great significance for developing dynamic theory. Does Boulding fail to see the theoretical character of Mitchell's work? Does he define "pure theory" in such a way that Mitchell's work falls outside the sacred preserve? Such questions are essential to clarify his attitude toward Mitchell.

In his pragmatic approach, Mitchell formulated his theoretical work to aid policy making. He felt that economic theory could have the objective, empirical, scientific character required in shaping policy. His theoretical approach, designed to cope with problems of economic performance, should lend purpose and usefulness to government planning and welfare economics. His extensive service to government rivaled that of Commons. As government researcher, consultant, and planner, Mitchell, too, deserves notice as an early brain truster and intellectual origin of the New Deal. His students have also been prominent in government work, continuing to the present time—notably, with the President's Council of Economic Advisers.

Despite Boulding's doubt, Mitchell's interest in the integration of economics with other social sciences was second only to business cycles. Like Veblen, he urged economists to study institutions and human nature. Several of his numerous articles on the relation of economics to other disciplines are included in *The Backward Art of Spending Money*, whose title may conceal their theoretical nature. Some of these emphasize psychological problems and the relation between economics and psychology.

Integration of economics with other social sciences strikes Boulding as desirable but hitherto premature. Earlier efforts at integration were perhaps more belated and inadequate than premature. This work had to begin sometime; there is no reason to wait until these disciplines individually reach a more perfect state. It may be neither candid nor charitable to say that economics is more advanced than related fields. We must avoid being smug or provincial about our supposed technical superiority; we should seize every opportunity for Point Four aid to neighboring disciplines; and we may well benefit from a high export multiplier, unless we let the intellectual terms of trade shift against us. Our export surplus, free-trade policy, and academic good will in related fields have not been notable. Potential gains from interdisciplinary exchange have been present all along, are growing rapidly, and must be systematically tapped if the social sciences are to maximize their productive benefit. Some concreteness is thus in order as to what is premature and what is appropriate for integration in the social sciences.

Professor Boulding offers an interesting perspective of the larger movement taking place in economics. This perspective has greater merit than his commentary on the major institutionalists. J. M. Clark suggests that the revolution under way in economic thought is far broader than the designation "Keynesian." Although Professor Boulding puts Keynes at the forefront of this movement, he thinks Commons will be accorded a leading place among institutionalists. While Commons deserves increased attention, Veblen and Mitchell have probably had greater influence on American economic thought. Mitchell may have done more than Keynes to advance economics as an empirical science and an integral part of the social sciences.

FRANK H. KNIGHT: Professor Boulding's excellent paper has covered most of what seems to me worth saying about institutionalism—short of a treatise in problems and methods in the social sciences. In my few minutes I can add little and most of it has been said before, even by me and from the platform of this Association. Rather than pick out points to approve or criticize, I shall survey the topic in a slightly different way. Besides the limit of time—and personal limitations—I face a special embarrassment: presumably put on the program as an adversary—"Satan" is the Biblical word—I am in fact as "institutionalist" as anyone, in a positive sense. I diverge only in not damning "economics" in its essential meaning. That is what the label stands for rather than any positive import. It is a cry of revolt. a call for "anything but" discussion of ends and means and free co-operation. Formally promoting something called by some vague name sounds better than merely using orthodoxy as a cuss word. I also abhor orthodoxy, in its correct historical meaning; but that does not make me denounce the multiplication table, the Pythagorean Theorem, or the laws of motion, though all of these are as unrealistic as the purest pure theory of economics—to use another institutionalist epithet. Nor does hating orthodoxy move me to deny that men economize and organize for efficiency through the purchase and sale of goods and services in markets. Boulding has also made the obvious point that condemning analytical economics is rooted in dislike of the organization it describes—an emotion bound up with refusing to examine it objectively, in critical comparison with possible alternatives.

It is trite to say that economics, like any analytical science, must include more than the most general theoretical principles. There can be no clear line marking where to stop, or especially to start, or what to take as given. If time allowed even a sketch of the scope-and-method problem, a main theme would be the impossibility of a sharp division of labor between disciplines in the study of man and society. Specialization there must be, but it cannot be at all as definite as in the natural sciences; and it is not very definite there, as we move up the scale from mechanics, ether-physics (as it used to be called), and chemistry through the many branches of biology to man. But man belongs to all these realms and a great many more—dealt with by the numerous psychologies and sociologies—and a complete account of man would involve all the sciences, in a highly pluralistic approach.

To limit my field and keep to the center of our topic, I cut off all the lower levels of subject matter to which human phenomena belong and glance at two main and special categories required in their study. One, as would be guessed, will be means-end rationality, or simply economic behavior. For the other, institutionalism is a fitting name, with tradition, convention, and culture as rough equivalents, and especially "historicism." Man, we all know, is a social animal. That is nothing new in the world, but social life on an institutional basis, largely replacing instinct, emerges with *homo.* He has a history, in a sense so distinctive that Dilthey and Ortega could say he has no nature but "only" a history—which might read, "only institutions." The process of his development must have been for ages entirely institutional or cultural, after biological evolution ceased. Institutions are connected with speech; and very late in the story, men began to talk about their history and about matters now treated by the natural sciences. For ages, their talk was fictional, in terms of doings of mythical, supernatural heroes or monsters, whose will also controlled ordinary events; but they were thought to be subject to influence, by magical practices. Natural man hates facts of life in general, biological or other. With us today, this attitude has been partly outgrown, in certain fields, mainly from causes other than understanding and love of truth. Human nature is still, as always, essentially romantic. Very lately, talk about causes has begun to be mixed with a little rational objectivity; but this is largely offset by the fact that, in Hume's famous adage, reason is the slave of the passions. For, about human passions, little can be said in a systematic way, and most of that little comes by way of psychopathology.

We study any subject matter for one or both of two reasons: the special satisfaction we call explanation and knowledge for use in controlling a future course of events. All this, too, has its history, as does everything, including history itself, and historical process is basically institutional. The satisfaction of explanation is itself one of the passions, and as mysterious and varied as any. I have noted that until recently it was animistic: myth and superstition (or religion, depending on whether it is ones own or some other that is referred to). A very short time ago in history, rationality—also a passion—

began to intrude among the older ones. Starting in astronomical prediction (n.b., no thought of "control"!), it soon spread into physics and medicine, founding modern progressive technology. Later still, as the idea of objectivity crept into thinking about society—against the utmost opposition of the custodians of sanctity—it largely ran to the equally absurd notion of solving dynamic value problems of taste and judgment by using the same "scientific method" which had transformed life in the field of men's dealings with passive nature; that is, to solving them by denying that such problems exist.

Modern thought explains things either scientifically or historically, chiefly the former in natural phenomena, the latter in human. Both methods have some application in both fields; but on these complex relations I can note only that while historical knowledge seems to explain, it is of little use for predicting the future and hardly any for control. For example, cosmology and biological evolution are quite satisfying as explanation but are not useful for guiding action.

Human society must always be largely of the original institutional character; custom and habit must rule most of what people feel, think, and do. Institutions, I repeat, are more or less explained historically rather than scientifically and are little subject to control. The ideal type is language, about which we can do so little that we hardly think of trying. For that reason, linguistics is the most scientific of the social disciplines—repeat, "for that reason," and note that it is scientific as the word applies to history, and then incompletely so; otherwise prediction, even in theory, could be only hypothetical. We need history to predict or to tell us what we cannot change; we know little enough about the facts, and virtually nothing about causality, or why history seems to explain while itself crying, mostly in vain, for explanation.

Very lately, as noted, institutional change began to produce individualistic mental life; hence individuals are also institutional, in that sense. As men became aware of social institutions, they took up attitudes towards them— chiefly romantic, love and hate. At long last, they have begun to be a little bit rational, i.e., to distinguish and appraise critically, following upon the growth of the scientific attitude towards nature. Most fundamental for objective thought are organization for war and for the treatment of crime. In this last field, science would be particularly applicable, if it existed. In fact, more knowledge raises more doubts about punishment—its effects, its purpose, even the meaning of crime.

One of the latest products of institutional change is individual rationality, in the twofold sense of trying to use means effectively—economically—to achieve ends and to adapt institutions to allow freedom to do so. But those who go that far commonly go on to demand an impossibly complete freedom, ignoring other values which conflict with freedom, become more important at some point, and have to be balanced against it in some compromise. In this connection have arisen two great and distinctive modern institutional systems, closely interrelated: free enterprise and democratic government; also the sciences which study them: economics and politics. The former—the orthodoxy of institutionalist scorn—yields laws which both explain and enable prediction in the twofold sense needful for intelligent action; i.e., predicting what will happen if no action is taken and predicting the consequences of any action proposed. The other half of the social-action problem is agreement in evaluating cultural ideals; on that, no positive science sheds any light, and history not much; it is a matter for critical judgment. As to the free-market economy, nobody thinks it perfect, but most rate it better, as the main framework, than the alternatives, some form of political compulsion. It has the supreme merit of enabling people to co-operate without specific agreement on values, which they would never reach once the forces of institutional history ceased to effect it, unconsciously or through the opium of superstitious fear. Thus it is the only system of reasonably free co-operation possible on any considerable scale. That men are not completely rational in managing their affairs—a favorite lash on the institutionalist whip—is true, but hardly implies that a government, which must be run by men, will be both wise and benevolent in managing those of everybody. However, the role of economics is to predict, not to judge. Its predictions are much less accurate than those of laboratory physical science; but they are better than those based on physical theory alone and much better than most other social predictions—say those underlying criminal procedure or political lawmaking.

KENNETH H. PARSONS: Professor Boulding has invited us, in this brilliant and scholarly paper, to make amends for the neglect which economists in America have accorded to three former members of this Association—two of them past-presidents. Of the three men on his honor roll of dissenters in American economics, I admit to more interest in Professor Commons than to either of the other two—Veblen or Mitchell. Consequently, I was pleased to learn of his judgment, that although Commons' work may now be the most neglected, his contribution will eventually likely be the most valuable. I think this estimate is well founded. But, especially I am grateful to Professor Boulding for the breadth and tolerance of his views, on the scope of the field of economics.

Even so, I found the basic logic of his paper a bit difficult—once I attempted to move from the literary to the analytical level of criticism. For the moment at least I have concluded that the difficulty in getting at the deeper issues is to be found in the simple fact that Professor Boulding does not state them. I am not sure that they can be stated very clearly for so many points of view in a very short space.

For my brief part in this occasion, I shall elaborate a bit on Professor Boulding's analysis of Commons' work; then make some suggestions on the problem involved in bringing together insights into economic life achieved in differing frames of reference.

Professor Boulding passed rather lightly over Commons' interest in research. Since this is the very key to the understanding of Commons' contribution, I want to add a few comments on this point.

John R. Commons was an investigator, first to last—even when he was in the classroom. His writings are predominantly progress reports on his research and should be read with this qualification in mind.

The research which he did, especially during his middle and later years, was designed to be instrumental for experiments in industrial democracy or the creation of a public service state. He was always working close to problems of policy and administration. The character of his research opportunities and responsibilities influenced both his research and the ideas which were projected therefrom.

Commons began his research career at Wisconsin with the monumental *Documentary History of American Industrial Society* (1910). This work did much to crystallize in his mind his theories of social movements and labor economics and in fact virtually established the study of labor history and trade-unionism as university subjects. In the meantime, he had begun his research in industrial accidents which resulted in the creation of the State Industrial Commission, of which Commons was the principal architect and one of the first administrators. Out of this experience he got a vision of the potentialities for public service of hard-headed progressive businessmen and labor leaders—through appeals to their own self-interest, by administrative arrangements that provided the means for conciliating conflicts and rewarding efficient effort and management. In devising insurance protection against accidents, he insisted that the rates be adjustable to the incidence of accidents in each firm in order to reward progressive industrialists. He concluded that this required an employer's mutual type of insurance company rather than a state fund which would almost surely have uniform rates set by the legislature. He carried this same determination to protect efficient and progressive management over into the individual employer rating provisions of the Wisconsin Unemployment Compensation Act which was designed by him—enacted in 1932, but first introduced in the state legislature in 1921. Meanwhile he had designed and drafted a public utility law in 1907—after some years of research in which he found the fundamental problem to be that of devising regulatory provisions which would meet the due process clauses of the constitutions. In this investigation he discovered the extent and significance of the changing meaning of property in the U.S. during the last quarter of the nineteenth century. This led to seventeen years of study of the development of the Anglo-American political economy which is reported in his *Legal Foundations of Capitalism* (1924). This book is surely one of the few great research contributions in our time to economic literature. In this study, Commons traces out the changing conception of government and property which occurred during the evolution of British economy from feudalism to modern capitalism. One can see there the way in which the private practices of businessmen, guilds, and landlords were generalized and made into the public law of the land. Furthermore, he traces out similar changes in this country in the conception of property, giving us altogether a quite unparalleled analysis of the ways in which the basic economic structure of an economy changes with the economic development of a free society.

In his theoretical synthesis he conceived of himself as working in the main tradition of political economy. The subtitle of his *Institutional Economics* was *Its Place in Political Economy*. It seemed to him that modern economics lacked basic reference points for the analysis of conflicts of interest and collective action in all its forms.

When I turn from such considerations of what Professor Commons actually achieved in a long lifetime of systematic and devoted inquiry to the criteria which Professor Boulding sets up for evaluating the possible contributions of the institutionalist to the improvement of the main body of economic theory, superficially Commons' career would seem to be a treasury of possibilities. In terms of dynamics, he understood at least some of the deeper sources of dynamism in the American economy. Who else has been so ingenious in formulating the conditions of willing participation as he—in his protection of incentives in accident and unemployment compensation programs and in the realization of the creative productivity potential of treating labor with dignity and respect. Perhaps others have understood the mainsprings of willing effort as well but surely not many.

Similarly he was remarkably successful, it seems to me, in his investigation of the interrelations of the different aspects of the structure of human action which are usually analyzed in the separate social science disciplines, yet kept his perspective as an economist and his feet on the ground, so to speak. He investigated court decisions to be able to understand the economic theories of judges who were forced to make decisions, in these rigorous laboratories of the human will, on cases involving millions, or even billions, of dollars in property values. But out of it came not a book on law but on the legal foundations of capitalism.

Commons' work was literally designed to be supplementary to and complementary to traditional economics. He considered the achievements of equilibrium economics to be great and indispensable, but he thought that important facets of economic life were by-passed in this market-resource analysis. Yet despite all this, despite the facts of his contributions to the understanding of the dynamics of economic life, his success in being both truly a social scientist and an economist and his achievements in economic research, is there not a real intellectual gulf between him and those who approach economics in a more conventional manner but also desire to broaden the theoretical base of economics. Why?

The answers to this question appear to me to be very complex. Here we can only suggest some of the issues and the directions which a more adequate comment would require. I suspect, however, that a considerable part of the confusion and disagreement in recent years over matters pertaining to economic theory stem from our lack of agreement on the technical issues underlying the systematic formulations of ideas. In the hope of making my remarks more comprehensible and at the risk of seeming tedious, I am listing the issues which seem to me to be involved in developing a systematic set of ideas in economic theory.

1. The basic ingredient, so to speak, of economic theory is insight into the meaningful and strategic interconnections within the true character of economic affairs. These insights, once formulated, are themselves refined, as the insight about diminishing returns has gradually evolved into the conception of variable proportions.

2. These insights to be productive must be formulated into rigorous "if then" propositions in which the essential and necessary relations are formulated, as the basic insight of the relation of dearness to scarcity is formulated

into what I take to be the basic proposition in the theory of demand: if scarce, then dear.

3. Economic theory, as I understand it, is the name we give to the series of propositions which are deduced, by rigorous attention to possible implications, from the original insights, formulated into propositions. This body of theory does not function as a description of the economic system, for they are not descriptions in the precise meaning of the term. Rather the theory operates as abstract propositions within the processes of inquiry, as a part of the way economists think. The propositions are systematized around assumptions which we might call the "as if" premises of economic thought. We evidently postulate, in these assumptions what we might call our big ideas about the character of the economy, "as if" it were of that character.

4. Economic analysis, including economic theory, must, I am persuaded, honor the basic distinction made by philosophers between fact and value. The problem of ascertaining what is fact is different from that of appraising or even understanding the processes of valuation.

I do not believe that we can integrate the insight achieved by the great minds in economics into a unified theory, or theories, unless and until we find some mutually accepted and fundamental, common grounds upon which to base our arguments.

When we really understand the lack of communication between the views of Professor Commons and his formulations and the main stream of economic thought—to use Professor Boulding's simile—we may likely find differing positions on these basic issues, but particularly on the kinds of facts which the different insights emphasize. Essentially, Professor Commons approached economics from the major premise or postulate of treating the economy as a social organization. The facts in his work are therefore social facts—which accounts for the contributions which Professor Boulding noted to the integration of economics with the other social sciences.

From such social premises Commons analyzed the commonly recognized economic relationships, with the effect noted by Professor Boulding. Exchange, he analyzed as transactions. This formulation opened up the way for distinguishing the bargaining transactions of the market place from the rationing and managerial transactions which operate within the great corporate enterprises. Similarly, the firm of conventional economics he analyzed as a going concern—a social organization held together by judgment and the expectations of the participants. Private property turned out to be sets of social relationships, with the intangible property of the ownership of market opportunities being the hallmark of modern capitalism.

This general frame of reference also enabled him to incorporate into his system of ideas his insights regarding the volitional character of man the citizen, noting the significance and the means of eliciting the willing participation of citizens in the economic enterprise. This insight he generalized into the basic proposition that willing participation is the leading principle of organization in a free economy. Similarly, he saw the significance of security of expectations in the creation of economic order where citizens have significant degrees of freedom. It is approximately correct to say that Commons placed primary emphasis in his formulation on the conditions and the means of general economic order in an age where citizens, corporations, and labor unions have economic power; whereas traditional economics in recent decades has been concerned primarily with formulating the conditions of general equilibrium of optimum resource use.

The economic theory which Professor Boulding refers to variously as academic economics, static economics, or as having the basic abstraction of the commodity, embraces those basic insights into economic life, I infer, which have been systematized around the postulate of treating the economy as if it were a mechanism. This systematizing seems to me to stem from the Ricardian base, built originally upon analogies to the Newtonian conception of natural mechanics. During the intervening decades the great insights of such strategic interrelations as those among the characters of demand, proportionality, interest rates, investment, and levels of employment, etc., have been gradually incorporated within the body of theory of equilibrium economics.

What is often overlooked in comments upon this body of theory, in my judgment, is that it has actually been the postulate of mechanism which has operated to define the relevancy of inclusion or exclusion rather than the character or actual nature of the economic system from which the insights have been drawn. This comment needs immediate qualification, however, by noting that the existence of a large ingredient of mechanism in our modern economy gives genuine relevance to the postulate—under industrialization and the price system—or the concatenation of industry and the pecuniary calculus—to use Veblen's phrase—and, more recently, the somewhat independent career of the stream of purchasing power. However, I do not see that this system of ideas either directs attention to, or gives systematic guidance for, the analysis of distinctions between public and private, for example. This has the effect of actually neglecting public and social considerations; for it is the private, individual, net income position of firms and individuals which is at the very heart of the systems of equilibria. Neither is there any systematic guidance to the analysis of questions relating to the evaluation of alternative economic systems: communism, capitalism, socialism, etc. This system of ideas is evidently useful in policy analysis primarily in estimating the effects of this or that measure upon the commodity-production-price-income complex. Characteristically, such policy measures are implicitly treated as something external to the economic system—as interferences.

The analysis of value or valuation in our economy runs in different terms: the parallels or comparisons between Commons' and the more traditional views involve different issues. The minimum basic categories for the understanding of the problem of evaluation in a free economy seem to be two: the individual or private; or the social or public.

The deeper issue for economic analysis is actually to be found in the interrelations between the two areas of valuation. Briefly—and therefore dogmatically—this is where we seem to come out, starting from the two different basic positions. In equilibrium analysis there appears to be an inherent tendency to elevate private considerations to the status of public values. Correlatively, there is the tendency to elevate efficiency to the status of an absolute value. These follow, I infer, from the general objective of specifying the conditions requisite to general equilibrium, generalized from the requirements for the net income position of individuals or firms.

In Commons' analysis the problems of social valuation or public value turn out to be details in the more inclusive considerations of social organization. He saw, as I interpret him, that whatever scope society accords individual choice and valuations is a consequence of the latitude for discretionary action which is built into the system. Thus, the problem of public value, in his view, was that of determining the reasonableness of the working rules—which rules define the limits to which individual or private action must be performed, if at all. It is through the assured zones of discretion or security of expectations that individual freedom becomes effective and may become power.

Commons was as much devoted to the improvement in the efficiency of resource use as any economist. But he considered this achievement, as I interpret him, to be necessarily indirect in a free society. He viewed public policy as affecting the use of resources through the reproportioning of inducements, opportunities, and disabilities. In short, a free society requires that efficiency be achieved through freedom, security, and the dignity of man, not through their sacrifice.

CLARENCE E. AYRES: In closing this unusually interesting and profitable discussion I am taking the liberty to enter in the record of this meeting the following two points.

First, as I see it, the object of dissent is the conception of the market as the guiding mechanism of the economy or, more broadly, the conception of the economy as organized and guided by the market. It simply is not true that scarce resources are allocated among alternative uses by the market. The real determinant of whatever allocation occurs in any society is the organizational structure of that society—in short, its institutions. At most, the market only gives effect to prevailing institutions. By focusing attention on the market mechanism, economists have ignored the real allocational mechanism. Hence the hiatus between economics and the other social studies, all of which are concerned with various aspects of the institutional structure of society. Economics is more advanced than those others—in the wrong direction.

Second, what determines the relative scarcity or relative plentifulness of all resources is the state of the industrial arts. Ours is an industrial economy. That is the paramount fact of the modern economic system; and the recognition of that fact is the most constructive achievement of institutionalists generally. Formless and inchoate as the writings of institutionalists have been, that emphasis runs through them all, as it runs through all the writings of Thorstein Veblen. Notwithstanding all his obvious faults and frailties, Veblen's recognition of the significance of workmanship, the machine process, and the state of the industrial arts will classify him in centuries to come as a great constructive pioneer.

Professor Boulding has mentioned my impudent suggestion that he himself had showed institutionalist leanings. The reason was that in his book by that title he has attributed "the organizational revolution" to twentieth-century technology, and I think rightly so. We owe the vast industrial system of which we are the lucky beneficiaries not to the acquisitive instinct and not to the calculating spirit of the "counting house" but to the accidents of acculturation through which in earliest modern times Western Europe became the seedbed of scientific and technological revolution, and also to the unique fluidity of the institutional patterns of Western society—itself a consequence of the turmoil of preceding centuries—by grace of which the technological break-through occurred.

We are now witnessing the impact of our own industrial revolution upon all the rest of the world, and as we do so the significance of the technological processes and of institutional resistances is being brought home to us far more vividly than ever before. I agree with Professor Boulding that it is circumstances such as these rather than the persuasions of any dissenters that will give direction to the economic studies of the future. I agree with him, too, in thinking it unlikely, and perhaps even undesirable, that the main stream of future economic thinking will be known as institutionalism. But in the years to come economists will be increasingly concerned with the technological and institutional realities by which gross national product, the level of consumption, and the level of employment are determined.

[5]

NEOINSTITUTIONALISM AND THE ECONOMICS OF DISSENT

Allan G. Gruchy

It is a pleasure to bring the honor of serving as President of the Association for Evolutionary Economics to a close with the opportunity to discuss some of the intellectual currents running through our Association. Since the Association is a very young organization, its future is quite naturally a matter of very great concern to all of us. I am not going to attempt to predict the future of our Association. However, I know that it was in the minds of its founders, when they came together in Washington, D. C., nine years ago, that this Association should have a unique function to perform—one not performed by old line economic associations. However otherwise this unique function may be described, it is clearly that of providing an outlet for economic dissent—dissent from what goes under the heading of conventional or standard economics.

If ever there was a fortunate coincidence, it was that the Association for Evolutionary Economics was organized at a time when dissent in many fields was running high. It is my conviction that this Association has a golden opportunity to provide a forum for economic dissenters at a time when old line economic associations and the economics profession in general are not providing the intellectual leadership called for by the times. Economic dissenters like Clarence E. Ayres, John K. Galbraith, Gunnar Myrdal, Adolph Lowe, Gerhard Colm, and others of a similar intellectual bent assert that conventional economics, as one sees it in standard economics textbooks and advanced economic writings, is hobbled with an excessively narrow view of the science of economics that concentrates on means and not ends; on inputs and not outputs; and on efficiency without asking the question of efficiency for what? The economics profession today directs its main energy to turning out technicians of knowledge who are experts in optimizing the decision-making process, but who do not display much concern for the purposes or goals of this decision-making. Our successful conventional economics textbook writers, following Lionel Robbins with his vintage 1925 definition of economic science, have given wide circulation to the idea that economics is concerned primarily with means and not with ends. It is not surprising then that in the current era of great crisis with respect to goals or values, conventional economics, having little to say about such ends, has become quite

The author is Professor of Economics at the University of Maryland. This paper was the presidential address for the 1968 Association for Evolutionary Economics's convention in Chicago, Illinois, December 27-29. All articles in this issue were papers presented at the same convention.

4   ALLAN G. GRUCHY

irrelevant to much of what concerns the man on the street or the student on the college campus. If ever there was a need to make economics a more relevant science, that need is now pressing for attention. Meeting this need is the aim of the economic dissent coming from Ayres, Galbraith, Myrdal, and other critics of conventional economics.

These dissenting economists, as scientists, do not propose to tell the people what goals they should seek to achieve. However, they do propose to explain to the people how their wants or goals come into being, how these wants are greatly influenced by the large industrial corporations, how collective wants in the public sector are frequently unmet because there are no strong lobbying forces at work in the public sector promoting these collective wants, how obstacles are placed in the path of meeting wants not catered to by the private market place, how the failure of the private sector to take full account of all social costs not only lowers the quality of life but also indirectly lowers the productivity of labor, and how our archaic governmental system is unprepared today to take a comprehensive view of national needs or to take the necessary steps with the cooperation of the public to make sure that these national needs are assigned proper priority.

Economic dissent falls into two categories. There are first those dissenters who criticize the way that the current economic system operates and who disapprove of many of the consequences of these operations. These dissenters usually operate outside the academic world and do not concern themselves with the inadequacies of standard or conventional economics. I am referring to such dissenters as Michael Harrington, Vance Packard, Ralph Nader, William H. Whyte, David Bazelon, and even Rachel Carson, who wondered if the day would come when our chemical companies would have achieved the miracle of a "silent spring." These dissenters have vividly and forcefully called attention to our noisy, dirty, and ugly cities, to the pollution of air and water, to the destruction of our heritage of buildings and urban areas of great historical significance, to the need to preserve the last landscape, and to the spread of what one critic has called the "materialistic Babbitism" of our affluent society.

The second group of economic dissenters is comprised of the academic world whose main concern is the inadequacies of conventional economics. Academic dissenters range from those at one end of the scale who simply want somehow to make standard economics more realistic to those at the other end of the scales who would reconstruct conventional economics into more social and less technical science. Those academic economic dissenters, who would be satisfied if conventional economics were made more realistic, argue that there should be more empirical feedback in the work of the conventional economic theorists so that conventional economic theory and economic practice would be more closely related. Dissent of this negative and unchallenging nature deplores the use of excessive abstraction and would like to see conventional economics shored up with the aid of more empirical studies.

Other economic dissenters in the academic world assert that conventional economics is too limited in scope, and that, since human problems are frequently more than economic in nature, an interdisciplinary approach is necessary if we are to tackle these problems successfully. The weaknesses or deficiencies of conventional economics are to be overcome not by reconstructing this economics, but by combining conventional economics with the other social sciences in the work of dealing with human problems. Those economic dissenters who merely want conventional economics to have more empirical feedback, or who would integrate conventional economics with the other social sciences in an interdisciplinary approach, present no basic challenge to conventional economics. This is so because the basics of conventional economics, as incorporated in its narrow definition of the nature and the scope of economic science, are left intact by the academic dissenters of the types just described.

There is a third and more fundamental type of academic economic dissent that is a distinct challenge to the view of economics held by standard or conventional economists. This type of dissent is positive and constructive in the sense that it challenges the view of economics cultivated by conventional economists and offers a different view of economics to replace that of the conventional economists. The economic dissenters who, I believe, present a constructive challenge to economic orthodoxy of both the Marshallian and Keynesian types include such well-known economists as Clarence E. Ayres, John K. Galbraith, Gunnar Myrdal, Gerhard Colm, and Adolph Lowe. Their economics I describe as neoinstitutional economics.

Perhaps some will think that I should apologize for calling attention to the institutionalist movement in economic thought. I know that in the minds of a majority of academic economists institutional economics is now regarded as something that has had its day and, as Professor Kenneth Boulding said a decade or so ago at one of these conventions, should now be placed among the museum exhibits. This attitude towards institutionalism was brought forcefully to my attention two years ago when I accidentally fell into the company of a young graduate student in economics from one of the most prestigious universities on the West Coast. Upon being introduced to me, this young student said that he was happy to shake my hand as he understood that I was the last of the institutionalists. I am sure that this young graduate was faithfully reproducing the views and opinions of the distinguished economics professors in that far western economics graduate school.

Whether or not this conventional view of institutional economics is wishful thinking—and I think it is—the fact remains that today we have a large body of economic thought that lies outside the boundaries of conventional economics. More than this it presents a significant challenge to conventional economics. My examination of the work of Ayres and others with a similar approach to economics leads me to the views that these critics of conventional economics are working in the institutionalist tradition, and that we can properly regard their work as basically an extension of the work of Veblen, Sombart, Hobson, Commons, Clark, Mitchell, and other heterodox economists of the first three decades of this century. However, the work of Galbraith, Colm, Lowe, and Myrdal is not the work of mere disciples. Thorstein Veblen has not cast his long shadow over these present-day institutionalists. None of these economists except for Ayres was influenced greatly in his formative years by Veblen and his work. For reasons to which I shall soon turn I prefer to call the work of current institutionalists "neoinstitutional economics" to distinguish it from the "old institutionalism" of Veblen.

The intellectual image that Veblen presented is significantly different from the image presented by the neoinstitutionalists. Veblen gave the impression that he would dispense with the inherited analytical or marginalist economics of his time, and that the mechanics or technics of economic decision-making would have no place in his technocratic regime of workmanship of the future. Also, Veblen did not clearly indicate what he thought were his own theoretical contributions with the result that both he and later institutionalists were criticized on the ground that they had not only dispensed with conventional economic theory, but had also put nothing in its place. Furthermore, Veblen's emphasis on the discipline of the machine process opened him to the criticism made by the conventional economists that his work was adversely affected by the acceptance of an untenable technological determinism.

The view that Veblen was an unsophisticated technocrat with little regard for the niceties of standard economic theory persists to this very day. As recently as 1968 Raymond Aron asserted that "Veblen made the mistake of thinking that the industrial order—the order of production—was sufficient unto itself," and was not subject "to the requirements of economic calculation."[1] Whether or not these views concerning the work of Veblen are well-founded—and I believe that they are not—they continue to find widespread acceptance among conventional economists. Such criticisms, however, cannot be made against the neoinstitutionalists, since they have been careful to avoid opening themselves to the criticisms to which Veblen has been subjected. The neoinstitutionalists cannot be described as anti-theoretical technocrats; they do not dispense with the basic building blocks of standard economic theory; and they avoid what is alleged to be Veblen's technological determinism. What the neoinstitutionalists do is to round out the standard or conventional economics of our time by making economics less of a technical and more of a social science. Of special importance in this connection is the neoinstitutionalists's theory of the modern industrial system with its central concept of the logic of the process of industrialization.

The neoinstitutionalists very clearly state that they have taken much

[1]Aron, Raymond, *Progress and Disillusion*, 1968, p. 187.

from the work of standard economists of the past and the present.
Ayres, for example, explains in *The Industrial Society*: "This is not to
say that all the inquiries of all the economists have been a complete waste
of time. . . . The investigations of economists have given us a wealth of
knowledge of price relationships the effect of which is to show how the
various economic activities affect each other. All this is of great value."[2]
Galbraith tells us in *The New Industrial State,* in referring to the work of
standard economists, "I have drawn on their work, quantitative and
qualitative, at every stage; I could not have written without their prior
efforts."[3] Likewise François Perroux in his article on the domination
effect of large industrial corporations informs us that his excursions beyond
conventional economics involve no disavowal of standard economic
theory.[4] Rather than dispense entirely with conventional economics, the
neoinstitutionalists accept it for what it is worth, and then go beyond it
to develop a broader economics which is concerned not only with decision-
making in the market place, but also with the guidance of the larger
evolving economic system. It is precisely at this point that the neoinstitutionalists part company with the conventional economists. The neoinstitutionalists have a larger view of economic reality which leads them to
believe that their version of economics is much more relevant to the
major problems of our time.

The contrast between the conventional economists and neoinstitutional
economists is quite clearly indicated by inquiring into what these two
types of economists think economics is all about. The conventional line,
as presented in some of our most successful economics textbooks, is
that, there is no consumer problem, since, as Professor Paul Samuelson puts it, "What things will be produced is determined by the votes of
consumers . . . every day in their decisions to purchase this item or that."[5]
In other words, student readers of these textbooks are informed that the
market mechanism ordinarily satisfies consumer wants, but does not create
them even though we annually spend 17 billion dollars on advertising.
Furthermore, from the conventional point of view, deviations from a
perfectly competitive economic system can be taken care of adequately by
appropriate antitrust measures and various forms of the public regulation
of industry. Since the allocation of resources in our mixed enterprise system is said to present no real problem, the only big issue is the rate of
economic growth or the annual increase in real gross national product.
According to conventional economists there is nothing like increases in
gross national product to measure an economy's performance. Professor

[2]Ayres, Clarence E., *The Industrial Economy*, 1952, p. 36.

[3]Galbraith, John Kenneth, *The New Industrial State*, 1967, p. 402.

[4]Perroux, Francois, "The Domination Effect and Modern Economic Theory," *Social
Research*, Vol. 17, No. 2, June 1950, p. 188.

[5]Samuelson, Paul A., *Economics, An Introductory Analysis*, Sixth Edition, 1964,
p. 40.

8   ALLAN G. GRUCHY

Campbell McConnell tells us in his widey read textbook that national
income accounting "allows us to keep tab on the economic health of
society. . . . It is generally agreed . . . that the best available indicator of
an economy's health is its annual total output of goods and services."[6]

According to the neoinstitutionalists this view of the measure of an
economy's health does not stand up under close scrutiny. This is so because the national income accounting that is presented in our most
widely used economics textbooks is an incomplete and biased form of
accounting. It takes note of all the "goods" produced, but leaves out what
Joan Robinson has called "negative goods," or what Ezra J. Mishan in his
study of *The Costs of Economic Growth* calls the "bads." We know
why conventional national income accounting accounts only for "goods,"
and ignores "bads" or the social costs of economic growth. The answer is
that "goods" can be quantified and measured in the market place, but
"bads" in the form of social disamenities frequently cannot be quantified,
and so do not appear in the market place. This "goods-bads" problem is
readily handled by conventional economists largely by ignoring it. One
very well-known conventional economist, who felt constrained to make
at least some mention of the vital difference between pecuniary and real
social costs in his textbook, calls the attention of his student readers to
this problem in a footnote in an appendix to a chapter.

It is all so very clear to the conventional economist: every extra billion
dollars's worth of gross national product marks a step forward toward a
healthier economy. As Professor Samuelson explains, "Although [eco-
nomic] growth presents challenges, the subject is really a cheerful one."[7]
Of course this is an unfortunate case of circular reasoning. Economic
health is measured in terms of gross national product, and an increase in
gross national product is regarded as an improvement in economic health.
According to Colm, Galbraith, Myrdal, and other neoinstitutionalists,
conventional national income accounting as it is currently used is a poor
device for measuring economic health. Economic health is not something
that can always be quantified. It is a condition that can be approached
or improved by creating some things and by not creating other things—
by creating "goods" and by not creating "bads," with the people, led by
protest groups and aided by technical experts, deciding what is a "good"
and what is a "bad." The neoinstitutionalists would say that an affluent
society is healthy when its resources are allocated in such a way as to
create not only an abundance of goods and services, but also cities free
from excessive noise, pollution, and ugliness where citizens have adequate leisure, when they are fully informed about the social costs of
economic growth, when nature's balance is preserved, and when industrial technology is adjusted to mankind and not mankind to technology.

[6]McConnell, Campbell R., *Economics: Principles, Problems, and Policies,* Second
Edition, 1963, p. 166.
[7]Samuelson, Paul A., p. 792.

Gunnar Myrdal speaks for the neoinstitutionalists when he states that the ultimate purpose of economics is to "find out where we are heading."[8] Or, in other words, whose goals does the economic system serve, and whose goals does it fail to serve? In Myrdal's opinion, and also that of other neoinstitutionalists, the ultimate purpose of economics is to provide an interpretation of the way in which the industrial system operates with respect to the satisfaction of personal and collective wants or goals. To put the matter simply, the contrast between conventional and neoinstitutional economics is a contrast between "market economics" and "systems economics."

The main issue today in the field of economics, in the opinion of the neoinstitutionalists, is not "efficiency," but rather it is wants, goals, or values. In the past few decades standard economists have made great strides in developing the theory of optimizing or economizing. The theory of economic decision-making has been improved by important advances in both mathematical economics and econometrics. While economizing the use of scarce resources or inputs will always be a matter of great importance to all economists and to the general public, economizing or optimizing the use of scarce resources is not what is of major importance today to a large part of the population in an affluent society. The main concern today of an important section of the general population in Western Europe and the United States is not how to use scarce inputs more efficiently, but how to get the economic system to serve the people by producing what they want, or would want if they were free agents, free from dominating influence of the large industrial corporations which control much of the press, radio, and television, and so are able to impose their scheme of values on the general public. There is a growing concern today with the following three value problems which are of great interest to the neoinstitutionalist critics of conventional economics: (1) to what extent are wants or goals in the private sector of the nation's economic system created by producers and not by consumers, with the result that consumers are induced to purchase a never-ending flow of consumer gadgets and other goods of doubtful private and social utility; (2) what obstacles are placed in the path of collective want determination in the public sector by forces working from out of the private sector, and by the archaic and ineffective institutional arrangements found in our public sector; and (3) to what extent does conventional economics ignore the social costs of economic growth in the form of external diseconomies such as air and water pollution, the spoilation of the natural environment, and the destruction of the nation's historical heritage by the bulldozer and the speculating land developer—all of which lower the quality of life.

The neoinstitutionalists observe that the economic system is a goal- or want-directed system. Individuals, groups, and classes participate in the activities of the economic system with the aim of securing their wants or

[8]Myrdal, Gunnar, *An International Economy, Problems and Prospects*, 1956, p. 314.

goals. The economic system is not a monolithic system or metaphysical entity which gives expression to some vague national interest that is supposed to be common to all individuals and groups. The American economic system is not a monolithic capitalist system. On the contrary, there is in the American economy the state capitalism of the public sector, the large-scale capitalism of the big business sector, and the small-scale, laissez-faire capitalism of small business and the farmers. The economy moves to a great extent in the direction of the goals of those individuals and groups who have enough power to influence the economy and guide it towards the satisfaction of their wants.

The neoinstitutionalists define economics to be the study of the evolving pattern of human relationships which is concerned with the disposal of scarce resources for the satisfaction of personal and collective wants. What the neoinstitutionalists do is to place economizing or economic decision-making within the framework of the evolving economic system. Since the economic sytem's ulitmate concern is with human wants or goals and how they are achieved, economizing is tied up with wants or goals; and the main question confronting economists should be optimizing or economizing for what purposes or goals.

The conventional economist precludes any analysis of the existing and emerging goals of individuals and groups and the question as to whether or not these wants are being achieved, by defining economics so as to exclude the wants or goals problem. Professor Samuelson, in defining economics, states, "As a science, economics can concern itself only with the best means of attaining given ends."[9] Professor McConnell has expressed the same view much more succinctly with the observation that economics is "the science of efficiency."[10] Duplicating Samuelson and McConnell, conventional economists reduce economics to the technical subject of economic decision-making or decision theory in which, as one specialist in decision theory recently explained, "Rationality, as decision theorists think of it, has nothing to do with what you want, but only with how you go about implementing your wants."[11] The conventional economist asserts that economists have no business inquiring into the nature or origins of human wants or goals, because people are said to know what they want and to cast dollar votes for what they want. In effect, what the conventional economist says is that the market mechanism is a want-serving or want-satisfying mechanism. The neoinstitutionalists disagree with the conventional view of the nature of the market mechanism and assert that in the modern industrial society the market mechanism is in many cases a want-creating mechanism. Consumers do not always freely

[9]Samuelson, Paul A., *Economics, An Introductory Analysis*, First Edition, 1948, p. 314.

[10]McConnell, Campbell R., p. 25.

[11]Ward, Edwards, "Decision Making," *International Encyclopedia of the Social Sciences*, Vol. 4, 1968, p. 35.

express what they want through dollar votes. Instead, they buy what the large corporations induce them to buy with the aid of advertising and high-pressure or subtle salesmanship.

According to Galbraith, Myrdal, Ayres and other critics of conventional economics, the social system, including the economic system, is an institutional arrangement by means of which people seek to achieve their wants. To the social scientist people are goal-creating, goal-possessing, and goal-achieving individuals, and the social sciences, including economics, are properly concerned with the goals or wants of people. Economic goals are data which can be documented, analyzed with regard to their origins and what influences have shaped them, the conflicts among these goals, their impact on the nation's production and distribution systems, and what aids or militates against their being achieved. These goals can be treated objectively, and the scientific method can be applied to them in the sense that generalizations can be made about them. There is nothing normative about any such want or goal analysis. What is being done is to widen the scope of economic analysis to include studies of existing means and existing economic goals and their interrelationships. It is for this reason that Ayres states, "Economics is nothing if it is not a science of value."[12]

When the neoinstitutionalists, along with Ayres, state that economics is a science not of efficiency but of values, they are not raising any normative issues in the form of what "ought" to be. What they do say is that economics, viewed not as a technical but as a social science, deals with the material aspects of values or wants. The economist as a social scientist is concerned not with efficiency alone, but with efficiency in relation to the wants of the individuals and groups operating within the evolving economic system. These individuals and groups are interested in such wants as economic abundance, economic freedom, economic security, economic justice, and economic quality. The economist as a social scientist is interested in explaining how the evolving industrial system supplies these wants or does not provide them, how these wants may be achieved with the use of scarce resources, how individuals and groups are in conflict with regard to whose wants should be assigned a high priority, and how conflicts with regard to the satisfaction of wants may be reduced or eliminated.

In an affluent society consideration of people's wants or goals may take precedence over considerations of economic efficiency. A rich nation can afford at times to be somewhat inefficient if this inefficiency preserves wants or values that would be destroyed by asking for the utmost in efficiency. It may be more efficient to string power lines between poles rather than to place them underground, to put a transmission line through a Civil War battlefield rather than around it, to put a super highway through a wilderness area rather than around it, or to put former slum dwellers in unlivable 15-storied tenement buildings rather than in livable low-lying

---

[12]Ayres, Clarence E., *The Theory of Economic Progress*, 1944, p. 208.

garden apartments—but in an affluent society these efficiencies in the opinion of many protest groups are not worth the price in human dis-amenities.

The difference between the conventional view of economics as a narrow study of economic decision-making and the neoinstitutionalist view of economics as a broad study of the evolving goal-directed economic system is also the difference between a short-run view and a long-run view of the economic system. Gunnar Myrdal has severely criticized conventional economists on the ground that they are nearsighted and without a long-range view of the development of the industrial system. He tells us in the *Challenge to Affluence* that among "the things that have not changed in America and specifically in Washington during different administrations is . . . a general tendency to nearsightedness among both politicians and [economic] experts. . . . There are today an astonishing number of people in the United States who can offhand give a detailed and comprehensive analysis in quantitative terms of what is just now happening [in the business world], how all important economic indices have recently been moving, and how they are likely to move months ahead. Not only the President and Congress but also leaders in business are left without that intellectualized vision of what the future holds in store in regard to economic development in more general terms. But such a vision is needed for rational decision [-making]. . . . It is difficult to avoid the reflection that the neglect by government agencies as well as by American universities and other research institutions of the long range aspects of the American economy as a whole and the undue concentration on short-range issues . . . on timeless and by any standards less important terminological questions and unworldly [theoretical] constructs . . . all this is partly responsible for the failure of . . . economists to disseminate more economic understanding among the American people."[13]

When the economist takes a long view of the economy, he necessarily views the economy as an evolving system. The question then arises, can one develop a theory of the evolving economic system? The answer of Ayres, Galbraith and Myrdal to this question is that the evolving industrial system can be explained with the aid of the concept of the logic of the process of industrialization. The neoinstitutionalists would be the first to say that, while there are no universal economic laws governing the course of industrialization, the process of industrialization is not a haphazard, utterly random process which follows no discernible path. The neoinstitutionalists assert that there is a logic or pattern running through the process of industrialization. Clark Kerr has explained in *Industrialism and the Industrial Man* that there is a "pure logic of the industrial process" which reveals the inherent tendencies of this process. Kerr goes on to explain that: "Given the character of science and technology and the requirements inherent in modern methods of production and distribution," we may

[13]Myrdal, Gunnar, *Challenge to Affluence*, 1962, pp. 87-88.

deduce the likely characteristics and path of the evolving industrial system.[14] To the neoinstitutionalist, if not to the conventional economist, the general features of the process of industrialization are clear. These features constitute a pattern or logic through which all mature industrial nations have passed or are passing. The logic of the process of industrialization points in the direction of an urbanized society, a decline of the free competitive market, the rise of a large public sector, the separation of the managers and the managed, the emergence of conflicting economic power groups, the elevation of natural science over social science, and the development of the government as an agent mediating among conflicting economic power groups and providing guidance for the evolving economy.

The concept of the logic of the process of industrialization lies between the universal laws of pure economics and mere description. It is an explanatory device that finds a place for both quantitative and qualitative factors in explaining the nature and functioning of the modern industrial system. Conventional economists have no place in their analyses for the concept of the logic of industrialization, because by definition they exclude from economic analysis all consideration of the impact of technological change on the structure and functioning of the economy. They agree with Lionel Robbins who states that "Ends as such do not form part of this subject-matter [of economics]. Nor does the technical and social environment."[15]

The technological explosion works its way out very largely through the operations of the economic system; yet the conventional economists pay little attention to how this explosion is affecting both the economic decision-making process and the larger total economic process. The conventional economist can sit idly by without explaining how the technological revolution of the past few decades further urbanizes our society, clogs our roads and air lanes, pollutes our air and water, upsets the balance of nature, unites the nation with ribbons of concrete, dangerously raises the noise level of our environment, and fills our houses with a vast array of gadgets limited in number and variety only by the fertile and highly paid imagination of those in charge of the research and development departments of our large business corporations.

One of the major issues of today is who will harness the technological explosion, the large industrial corporation or the public as represented by the government? Who will plan the flow of technological change spurred on by scientific research, who will make certain that adequate account is taken of the social costs of technological progress, and how will the benefits of the technological revolution be shared? Will the contributions of scientific research be used largely to meet the commercial objectives of

[14]Kerr, Clark; Dunlop, John T.; Harbison, Frederick H.; and Myers, Charles A., *Industrialism and Industrial Man*, 1960, p. 33.

[15]Robbins, Lionel, *An Essay on the Nature and Significance of Economic Science*, Second Edition, 1935, p. 38.

industry or the welfare objectives of the general public? According to Galbraith, Ayres, Myrdal and other neoinstitutionalists modern industrial technology points in the direction of some form of national economic planning. Technology is a cultural imperative or "compulsion" that gives shape or pattern to the process of industrialization. As Galbraith puts it, "Technology, under all circumstances, leads to planning; in its higher manifestations it may put the problems of planning beyond the reach of the industrial firm."[16] In the opinion of the neoinstitutionalists it is no longer a question of planning or not planning, but what kind of planning and who will direct the planning. The neoinstitutionalists assert that it is up to economists to explain to the public the consequences of the alternatives of planning by private industry, or of planning by the government in cooperation with the nation's economic interest groups. Not much can be expected with regard to these issues from conventional economists, because their absorbing interest in the economics of decision-making prevents their viewing the economy as an evolving system, and also prevents their developing the long and comprehensive view necessary for analyzing the problems of a guided industrial society.

Simplistic conventional economics leads to simplistic economic policy proposals. When one looks at the superficiality of conventional economic analysis and all the important and complicating economic factors that it leaves out of account, it is not surprising that some conventional economists propose to solve our basic economic problems, as would Professor Milton Friedman and other monetarists, by simply making adjustments in the nation's supply of money relative to the changing size of the gross national product, while other simplists, the proponents of the so-called "new economics," propose to solve the same problems by simply altering tax rates in a countercyclical manner. The long, non-simplistic view of the economy held by the neoinstitutionalists suggests to them that complicated economic problems can probably be solved only in complicated ways. According to the neoinstitutionalists the "new economics" of the Kennedy and Johnson Administration can never successfully handle the long-term goals problem, because its main attention is on the employment and growth rates of tomorrow, not on the long-term national goals of the future. No one denies that full employment and rapid economic growth are important, short-run goals, but more important questions are full employment and rapid economic growth for what? It does not seem very rational to develop a finely-tuned economic engine without asking where it is going—without asking whether it is on the low road to commercialized affluence or on the high road to what Ayres calls a "reasonable society."

The industrialization process has not yet come to an end. We are now moving from an advanced industrial society to a post-industrial society. In the opinion of the neoinstitutionalists we are now entering a post-industrial era in which the economic power of the large industrial corporations

---

[16]Galbraith, John Kenneth, *Industrial State*, p. 20.

is being challenged by what George Kennan describes as "protest groups" which spearhead the development of public opinion and unite the weak economic interest groups. In the post-industrial society of the future the guidance of the economy will come less from the big business sector and more from the nation's educational, scientific, and artistic groups as well as from aroused citizens in general. The basic problem is, how will national priorities be determined in the post-industrial society? Before this problem can be met satisfactorily, new institutional arrangements will have to be made. We will have to substitute a new participatory democracy for our current outmoded ballot-box type of democracy which may have been adequate for the nineteenth century but which is obviously unable to cope with the problems raised by a technological society. It is now necessary to bring together representatives of all economic interest groups for the joint consideration of what should be the nation's economic and social priorities. Much progress along this line has been made in Western Europe where the United Kingdom has its National Economic Development Council, the Netherlands its Economic and Social Council, and Sweden, France, Belgium and other countries their similar joint councils.

There is no major nation so ill prepared as the United States to cope with the problem of determining national economic and social priorities. Although the Employment Act of 1946 opens the doors to the possibility of joint consultation by representatives from major economic interest groups, the Council of Economic Advisers under all administrations has consistently refused to provide for any such joint consultation, preferring to approach each interest group, if at all, on a separate basis. Consequently, national priority determination in the United States has become a running contest between the Office of the President with his troika or quadriad of governmental advisers and the Congress. The group that should provide a bridge between the President and the Congress, namely the presidential cabinet, is conspicuous for its docility and the infrequency of its meetings. The Congress has no adequate way of comparing and analyzing the nation's total resources and total needs, since, unlike most legislative bodies in Western Europe, it does not have presented to it for its consideration any annual and long-term national economic budgets of the kind recommended by Gerhard Colm, Gunnar Myrdal, Adolph Lowe, and François Perroux. In this connection the Congress does not lack the power to determine national priorities. What it does lack is an effective way of determining these priorities.

The New York *Times* recently reported that President-elect Nixon had said that national priorities are determined in the White House. This is a gross and misleading oversimplification of the national priorites problem. In fact national priorities are determined in part in the White House, but also in the Congress, in the large business enterprises, in the trade unions, increasingly in the ghettos, and elsewhere. Each economic interest group is out more or less on its own to advocate the acceptance of its own goals

16

as something worthy of high priority consideration. But there are no well-established institutional arrangements for getting these various competing economic interest groups together for joint consultation with regard to the determination of national priorities. What we have in operation today in the United States is the outmoded advocacy concept of national priority determination which provides no adequate method of communication between the many economic interest groups at the bottom and the Congress at the top. This is an archaic way of determination national priorities that is more appropriate to the nineteenth than to the twentieth century. The neoinstitutionalists point out that the national priority determining process needs to be modernized, and related more effectively to the needs of our emerging participatory democracy. The lag between our political institutions and the rapidly changing industrial technology will have to be eliminated, before we can succeed in domesticating the technological revolution and in planning for the achievement of a life of high quality.

We can anticipate three criticisms levelled against neoinstitutional economies by conventional economists. The standard bearers of conventional economics will assert (1) that the neoinstitutionalists have made no theoretical contributions, (2) that, in assigning an imperative or compulsive character to industrial technology, the neoinstitutionalists are guilty of the sin of technological determinism, and (3) that the neoinstitutionalists, by raising the issue of wants, goals, or values, have become bogged down in normative considerations and so cannot qualify as scientists. These criticisms have been presented many times in the past, and will doubtlessly be dredged up again. If the conventional economists wish to continue to deny the validity of the concept of the logic of the process of industrialization, if they wish to deny that industrial technology is an imperative or compulsive force having much to do with the structure and functioning of our evolving industrial society, if they wish to deny that existing economic wants or goals of individuals and groups may be treated as scientific data, they are quite free to do so. But in the opinion of the neoinstitutionalists the conventional economists can do so only at the cost of keeping standard economics narrow and irrelevant with respect to much that is significant in the modern economic world.

I would like to conclude this discussion of neoinstitutionalism, the only significant academic economics of dissent in my opinion, by saying that we need both economic technicians or specialists and also what the Union for Radical Political Economists—an organization made up largely of disturbed graduate students in economics in our most prestigious universities of the northeast and far west—has described as "economic social scientists." I am fully aware of the important progress made in recent years in developing the theory and practice of economic decision-making. I am well aware of the contributions along the lines of econometric model building, linear programming, game theory, cost-benefit analysis, cost effectiveness studies, sampling theory and techniques, input-output analysis, and welfare economics with its emphasis on Paretian optimality. While this progress in the field of economic decision making has enabled us to manage ourselves more efficiently, it does not tell us whether we are moving toward Paradise or Purgatory.

While I would certainly not close the door on economic technicians, I would say that these specialists are not the best prepared to present economics as a social science in written form or on the lecture platform to the general public, or to young students who are coming for the first time to the study of economics. Also, it is my position that the general public and the political and other leaders of public opinion should see economics not through the eyes of the economic technician, but through the eyes of the economist as a social scientist.

What the neoinstitutionalists object to is not so much what is found in our widely used standard economics textbooks, but rather to what is left out of them. It was to meet these deficiencies in conventional economics that Galbraith wrote *The Affluent Society* and *The New Industrial State;* that Myrdal wrote the *Challenge to Affluence* and *Beyond the Welfare State;* and that Ayres wrote *The Theory of Economic Progress* and *Toward a Reasonable Society.* On a more popular level the Michael Harringtons, Vance Packards, William H. Whytes, David Bazelons, Bernard Nossiters, and Rachel Carsons have sought to offset the irrelevance of conventional economics by showing the public how the quality of economic life is being lowered in this age of affluence. Without these and many other economic dissenters whom I have not mentioned, economics would be still more of an irrelevant science than it now is—that is to say, irrelevant not to economic decision-making, but to issues relating to the creation and achievement of private and public economic wants, without a discussion of which economic decision-making becomes a routine without much social significance.

I would not like to close this discussion on a somewhat sour note. Neoinstitutionalists are by nature pessimistic optimists. While they are pessimistic about the immediate future, they are nevertheless sustained by a deep optimism with regard to the long-run possibility of making economics a social science that is highly relevant to the major issues not only of our time, but also of the emerging future. It is my conviction, and I believe the conviction of those unconventional economists whom I have called neoinstitutionalists, that economics will increasingly come to have more concern with what people think is the Good Society, and less concern with efficiently making decisions but never asking what the decisions are really about.

THE NATURE AND SIGNIFICANCE OF INSTITUTIONAL ECONOMICS

K. William Kapp † *

'I see the tasks of social sciences to discover what kinds of order actually do exist in the whole range of the behavior of human beings; what kind of functional relationships between different parts of culture exist in space and over time, and what functionally more useful kinds of order can be created.' R. S. Lynd, *Knowledge for What?*, 1939, pp. 125/126.

'The failure of the social sciences to think through and to integrate their several responsibilities for the common problem of relating the analysis of parts to the analysis of the whole constitutes one of the major lags crippling their utility as human tools of knowledge ...', *Ibid.*, p. 15.

I. INTRODUCTION

Robert Lynd's critical diagnosis of the crippling situation of the social sciences in the thirties was echoed later by Schumpeter's statement that the social sciences have steadily grown apart 'until by now the modal economist and the modal sociologist know little and care less about what the other does, each preferring to use, respectively,

* Editors' note: Professor K. William Kapp died unexpectedly on 10th April 1976 whilst taking part in a seminar of the 'Inter University' at Dubrovnik, Yugoslavia. He was born on 27th October 1910 in Königsberg and studied economics and law in Berlin, Geneva and London. Between 1938 and 1965 he taught at several American and Asian universities, then from 1965 to 1975 he was full professor of political economy at the University of Basle. Among his most well known books are 'History of Economic Thought' (1949) with his wife Lore Kapp, 'The Social Costs of Private Enterprise' (1950), 'Toward a Science of Man' (1961) and 'Hindu Culture, Economic Development and Economic Planning in India' (1963). Several of his many articles appeared in 'Kyklos'.

University of Basel, Switzerland. Paper presented at the Symposium on Economics and Sociology: Towards an Integration, Faculteit der Economische Wetenschappen, Rijkuniversitaet, Groningen (Holland), Sept. 9–11, 1975.

K. WILLIAM KAPP

a primitive sociology and a primitive economics of his own to accepting one anothers' professional results – a state of things that was and is not improved by mutual vituperation'[1].

In fact, neo-classical[2] economics has tended increasingly to develop into a self-contained body of knowledge which has become more and more isolated from other social sciences and analytical systems. This has been brought about by the influence of several inter-related tendencies and orientations which cannot be examined here as thoroughly as would be desirable. No doubt, the mathematization and formalization of economic theory have played a predominant role. So has a methodological individualism which can be traced back to the origins of our discipline. Equally important is the long tradition of reasoning by analogy to mechanics and the related search for levels of stable equilibrium, as well as the implicitly normative insistence that economic theory is concerned with the explication of the logic of rational action under conditions of scarcity or, as LIONEL ROBBINS, following Ph. WICKSTEED, put it, with a particular type or 'form' of human conduct: the study of 'human behavior as a relationship between ends and means which have alternative uses'[3].

Under the influence of these orientations conventional economic theory has defined its subject-matter and the scope of its analysis in a rather narrow way and has convinced its practitioners that it is possible and useful to distinguish between 'economic' and 'non-economic' factors or aspects of social processes. Concrete economic systems or processes are thus believed to be adequately represented as isolated, self-contained and self-sustaining, closed mechanical processes with definable boundaries.

While it is true that individual economists who laid the foundation

1. JOSEPH A. SCHUMPETER, *History of Economic Analysis*, New York, Oxford University Press, 1955, p. 26/27.

2. The term 'neo-classical' is used here in a broad sense including standard micro- and macro-economics.

3. LIONEL ROBBINS, *The Nature and Significance of Economic Science*, London, Macmillan & Co., 1932, p. 16. WICKSTEED had pointed out that 'there is no occasion to define the economic motive, or the psychology of the economic man, for economics study a type of relation, not a type of motive and the psychological law that dominates economics dominates life'. Ph. WICKSTEED, 'The Scope and Method of Political Economy in the Light of the Marginal Theory of Value and Distribution', *Economic Journal*, Vol. 24 (1914), p. 10.

THE NATURE OF INSTITUTIONAL ECONOMICS

of neo-classical analysis have repeatedly and explicitly warned against any belief in the 'self-sufficiency' of neo-classical analysis particularly for the formulation of practical policies[4] the mainstream of neo-classicism has not heeded these warnings and has instead insisted on the autonomy and greater specialization of economic analysis if not its systematic isolation from other social sciences. A few illustrations may suffice to illustrate this point. SCHUMPETER denied the relevance of psychology for economic theorizing by stating, without qualifications and apparently with approval, that 'economists have never allowed their analysis to be influenced by psychologists of their time, but have always framed for themselves such assumptions about psychical processes as they have thought it desirable to make'[5]. DUESENBERY who rediscovered what he called the (Veblenian) demonstration effect defended the neglect of psychology 'as a deliberate attempt to sidestep the tasks of making psychological assumptions ... [which] has the advantage that it allows one to avoid getting out on a psychological limb which may collapse at any moment'[6]. Other neo-classical economists were even more explicit in rejecting attempts to relate economic analysis to other social disciplines. Thus, in opposing the trend toward interdisciplinary studies at American universities, G.J. STIGLER dissented by stating categorically that the royal road of efficiency in intellectual as in economic life is specialism – not interdisciplinary work[7].

These attitudes together with the orientations outlined above have tended to push conventional economic theory more and more into the direction of a formal, self-contained, closed mechanical analytical system and have prevented the assimilation of new perspectives and

4. Thus WICKSTEED stated explicitly 'that the economic machine is constructed and moved by individuals for individual ends, and that its social effect is incidental ...', 'that the market does not tell us in any fruitful sense what are the "national", "social" and "collective" wants' ..., that 'economic laws must not be sought and cannot be found on the properly economic field ...', that 'to recognize this will be to humanize economics ...', and 'that economics must be the handmaid of sociology', PHILIP H. WICKSTEED, *op. cit.*, pp. 11/12.

5. JOSEPH A. SCHUMPETER, *op. cit.*, p. 27.

6. J.S. DUESENBERY, *Income, Savings and the Theory of Consumers' Behavior*, Cambridge, Harvard University Press, 1949, p. 15.

7. G.J. STIGLER, 'Specialism: A Dissenting Opinion', *AAUP Bulletin 37 (Am. Ass. of University Professors)*, 1951/52, p. 651.

K. WILLIAM KAPP

new paradigms developed by other disciplines. In fact, we seem to be witnessing to-day the extension of the neo-classical theoretical framework to such fields as the analysis of political behavior, public choice, and decision-making in general. While this development may be regarded by some as a move in the direction of interdisciplinarity it carries with it the dangers of a new kind of reductionism of social analysis to neo-classicism. It is not too late that social scientists and sociologists in particular take a critical position toward this kind of 'academic imperialism'[8].

II. INSTITUTIONAL ECONOMICS

Dissatisfaction with the 'mechanics of utility and self-interest'[9] and the narrow scope of conventional economics manifested itself very early; in fact, criticism has never ceased and is to-day stronger than ever. As always in times of economic and social crisis 'normal' economic theory is under attack and is criticized for its inability to provide an appropriate analytical framework for the diagnosis of the problems and the formulation of more adequate criteria, policies and remedies designed to cope with increasing internal and international disorganisation, environmental disruption, stagnation and inflation as well as unemployment, conflicts over terms of trade, *etc.*

The critique has always been directed against the scope and methodological preconceptions inherent in the equilibrium approach. This holds true for the historical school; it applies to MARX (with some qualifications) and to institutional economics the origins of which go back to the early critics of classical economics. What these critics have in common is the denial that economic processes (of production, distribution, and reproduction) can be adequately understood and analysed as closed, *i.e.* self-contained and self-sustaining systems isolated from a social and physical 'environment' of which the economic system is a part and from which it receives important inputs and with which it is related through manifold reciprocal inter-

8. BRIAN M. BARRY, *Sociologists, Economists and Democracy*, London, Collier Macmillan Ltd., 1970.

9. The words are those of W. STANLEY JEVONS, see his *Theory of Political Economy*, 2nd edition, London, Macmillan, 1879, p. 23.

212

THE NATURE OF INSTITUTIONAL ECONOMICS

dependencies. In other words, the critics have always considered the economy as an open system in continuous dynamic interaction with a more comprehensive social and political as well as physical system from which economic processes receive important organising (and disorganising) impulses and upon which they exert their own negative and positive influences. In addition to denying the self-contained and self-sustaining character of economic processes and by stressing the open character of economic systems the critics have challenged above all the belief in the mechanical and self-regulating character of economic processes. They have questioned the search for levels of partial and total equilibrium within an artificially closed system; they have refused to accept the view that economic analysis must confine itself to the study of a particular type or form of behavior; that the best method of studying complex phenomena is to separate the parts and study them one by one[10], and that specialism is the royal road to efficiency in social analysis. In short, the critics have always been more or less open to other social and natural sciences. This applies particularly to institutional economists.

In fact, institutional economics has always aimed at a coherent representation of economic processes within and as part of a complex social system and their interaction. Institutionalists have endeavored to make explicit the relationships and the reciprocal interaction of the parts with one another and with the 'whole'. Long before structuralism and functionalism appeared on the academic horizon institutionalists have placed this reciprocal interaction in the center of their theoretical investigations. Institutionalists have found it problematical and indeed unacceptable to draw classificatory distinctions between so-called economic and non-economic factors and between economic and social processes. In order to illustrate these important characteristics of institutional economics let me first contrast ROBBINS' definition of economics with GRUCHY's characterisation of institutional economics. According to GRUCHY economics is concerned with 'the study of the structure and functioning of the *evolving* field of human relations which is concerned with the provision of material goods and services for the satisfaction of human wants. [...] it is the study of the changing patterns of cultural rela-

10. VILFREDO PARETO, *Traité de Sociologie Générale*, Lausanne, Librairie Payot, 1917, p. 17.

K. WILLIAM KAPP

tions which deals with the creation and disposal of scarce material goods and services by individuals and *groups* in the light of their private and *public* aims'[11]. Hence, whereas the neo-classical definition selects rational human conduct as a criterion GRUCHY makes it clear that economics is concerned with a much broader range of problems, namely the interdependencies of a great number of variables within a dynamic process of human and socio-cultural (interpersonal) relations resulting from changing modes of production, distribution and social reproduction. Not a particular *form* of behavior serves as the criterion of differentiation of economic analysis and determines its scope and approach but rather a particular set of interconnected dynamic problems which arise in the satisfaction of individual needs and public objectives.

In fact, the institutional approach focusses attention on the evolution of social systems and social processes. The analysis of the factors which provide the dynamic elements of these evolutionary processes has been in the center of institutional economics. Thus innovations, science and technologies as well as conflicts of interests, power and coercion in economic and social life have therefore always been included in their investigations. The central role of science, technology and innovations found an early expression in VEBLEN's *Theory of Business Enterprise* (1904). 'The material framework of modern civilization is the industrial system, and the directing force which animates this framework is business enterprise [...]. This modern economic organization of the "Capitalistic System" or "Modern Industrial System" so-called, its characteristic features, and at the same time, the forces by virtue of which it dominates modern culture, are the machine process and investment for a profit[12].' Innovation, technology and domination of economic processes by the machine process set the pace for the rest of the industrial system and distinguish the present situation from all previous forms of economic organizations and civilizations. The aim of institutional economics is 'a theory of business enterprise [...] sufficiently full to show in what manner business methods and business principles, in

11. A. G. GRUCHY, *Modern Economic Thought*, New York, Prentice Hall, 1947, pp. 550, 552 (emphasis added).

12. THORSTEIN VEBLEN, *The Theory of Business Enterprise*, New York, Charles Scribner's Sons, 1904, p. 1.

THE NATURE OF INSTITUTIONAL ECONOMICS

conjunction with the mechanical industry, influence the modern cultural situation'[13].

In addition, VEBLEN's theory of business enterprise laid the foundation for the analysis of economic instability and business fluctuations with their cumulative processes of investment based upon credit and the pervasive creation of debts, the generation of demand and employment and the inflation of all monetary values.

The preoccupation with the role of conflict, power and coercion is an intellectual heritage which, in America, antedates MARX and goes back to the Federalists and their European mentors prior to the American Revolution; early American institutionalists like VEBLEN and COMMONS have reformulated and integrated this heritage into their analysis of 'vested interests', absentee ownership, the economic role of the state, the legal foundations of capitalism, the importance of collective and political bargaining, public utility regulations and the analysis of collusion between financial, industrial and political power. In short, the problems raised by the industrial military complex and the 'power elite' have not been neglected in institutional economics.

In harmony with their early critique of the classical preconceptions and particularly the mechanics of self-interests developed by neo-classical utility, price and equilibrium theory, institutional economists have from the very beginning been sceptical of market prices in terms of which business enterprise tends to measure its performance and efficiency in utilizing scarce resources, *i.e.* of the criteria which price theory has accepted and legitimized, at least until quite recently, as criteria of optimal decision-making and as indicators of economic rationality in general. No wonder, therefore, that institutional economists were among the first who have called attention to and have analysed in considerable detail the social costs of production, long before the latter found a sudden and belated recognition in the current discussion of the increasing environmental and ecological disruption (including the exhaustion of non-renewable stock resources) with its serious threats to social reproduction and the quality of individual and social life. Unlike positive economics,

13. *Ibid.*, p.21. For an account of the emergence of innovations and new technologies, *cf.* VEBLEN's *Instinct of Workmanship and the State of The Industrial Arts,* New York 1914.

K. WILLIAM KAPP

institutional economists have not hesitated to use the results of their inquiries as the basis of a critique of existing institutions and the *status quo*.

Equally significant have been the contributions of institutionalists to the analysis of underdevelopment (and development) and the persistence of increasing disparities not only between rich and poor countries but also within each of these two groups. MYRDAL's seminal studies of underdevelopment in South East Asia just as his earlier work on race problems in America are the outstanding examples of an institutional analysis which has overcome the conventional concentration on 'economic' variables such as savings and investment, employment, money, interest rates and GNP. MYRDAL and others have shown the true dimension and complexity of the persistent problems of poverty and underdevelopment and their relation to institutions, the soft state, the fundamental issue of the relationships between man and land including land-tenure relationships[14], the population-resources relationship, illiteracy, the low level and an appropriate content of education, poor health and nutrition, prescientific knowledge of techniques, traditional attitudes, value systems, class, caste and kinship systems, and, last but not least, the domination effect (PERROUX) and center-periphery problem (GALTUNG) with its dramatic effects on the terms of trade. All these problems neo-classical theory had pushed more or less aside; to-day (1976) they can no longer be ignored for the simple reason that the countries of the Third World have begun to insist upon a new world economic order. No analysis in purely economic terms which abstracts from these institutional factors is able to come to terms with the circular interdependencies between these factors and the cumulative causal interaction which delay and arrest the process of development.

The preoccupation with problems of the kind outlined above gives institutional economics its scope and shows why there have always existed points of contact with other social and natural sciences including sociology, social anthropology, political science and ecology.

Needless to add that sociologists, social anthropologists and political scientists have contributed in no small measure to our under-

14. ERICH JACOBY (with CHARLOTTE JACOBY), *Man and Land*, London, André Deutsch, 1971.

216

THE NATURE OF INSTITUTIONAL ECONOMICS

standing of such important elements of the development process as the analysis of caste, kinship and religion, factions and class conflict in traditional village life, attitudes and responses to innovation and modernization, economic motivation in traditional rural societies and socio-cultural evolution in general. However, in contrast to institutional economists these other social scientists have found it difficult, until quite recently, 'to think in terms of planning for national development. They are still laboring with finding out how people live and survive, and they are regularly, different from other economists, dealing with only segments of the national society and also mostly focussing their work on certain problems that have traditionally been at the center of their attention like *e. g.* caste in India. They have seldom attempted systematically to lay bare the circular causation between all conditions in a society they are studying[15].'

III. THE PRINCIPLE OF INTERLOCKING INTERDEPENDENCIES WITHIN A PROCESS OF CUMULATIVE CAUSATION AS A NEW THEORETICAL FRAMEWORK FOR THE SOLUTION OF CONCRETE PROBLEMS

With MYRDAL's formulation of the principle of circular causation we finally arrive at the core of institutional economics which sets it apart from earlier and contemporary non-institutionalist approaches and particularly from mechanistic equilibrium analysis. For, 'the principle of interlocking circular interdependencies within a process of cumulative causation'[16] is at the same time a new theoretical framework which rejects and replaces the traditional equilibrium framework and an analytical tool which permits the solution of concrete problems (*i.e.* of problematical, indeterminate situations) which have, so far, remained anomalies which could not be adequately accounted for in terms of the traditional 'disciplinary matrix'[17].

15. GUNNAR MYRDAL, *The Unity of the Social Sciences*, Plenory Address to the *Society of Applied Anthropology*, Amsterdam, March 21, 1975 (ms), p. 12.

16. GUNNAR MYRDAL, *Economic Theory and Underdeveloped Regions*, London, Gerald Duckworth & Co., 1957, p. 23.

17. I am using here THOMAS KUHN's *new* terminus instead of his earlier 'paradigm'. Following MARGARET MASTERMAN, KUHN now identifies the growth

K. WILLIAM KAPP

The principle of interlocking circular interdependencies within a process of cumulative causation has a long history. It played an important role in MALTHUS' analysis of the growth and decline of populations. THÜNEN advanced an early version of it when he stated that the manual worker cannot rise into the class of enterpreneurs because he lacks the necessary schooling since his wages are low which, in turn, is due to the fact that the poor have higher reproduction rates and hence the supply of labor is almost always higher than the demand, and consequently wages tend towards the subsistence level[18]. MARX was the first to stress the fundamental reciprocal interaction between 'productive forces' and 'production relations' and the ideological superstructure. VEBLEN developed and used the principle of circular interdependencies of a number of factors within a process of cumulative causation in connection with his analysis of the function of the leisure class, the role of technology and credit particularly in connection with his explanation of the business cycle and the inflation of all monetary values; and so did KNUT WICKSEL, within a narrower market framework, in his account of the inflationary expansion of credit resulting from a deviation of the money (market) interest rate from the natural, real rate of interest[19].

However, it was left to MYRDAL to develop the principle of inter-

---

of knowledge with 'framework breaking' whereby the 'traditional' framework of analysis for problems solving (disciplinary matrix) is rejected *and* replaced by another set of ordered elements capable of 'solving' or accounting for what remained unexplained by the former: 'an artifact which transforms problems to puzzles and enables them to be solved even in the absence of an adequate body of theory'. THOMAS KUHN, Reflections on my Critics, in: IMRE LAKATOS and ALAN MUSGRAVE (Eds.), *Criticism and the Growth of Knowledge*, Cambridge, at the University Press, 1970, p. 273. *Cf.* also MARGARET MASTERMAN, *The Nature of a Paradigm, Ibid.*, pp. 59–90.

18. JOHANN H. VON THÜNEN, *Der Isolierte Staat* (1850), Jena, Gustav Fischer, 1910, pp. 440/441.

19. The neo-classical theoretical framework of general equilibrium or total interdependence of all prices in a market economy is of course also a case of mutual interlocking interdependencies. However, in contrast to VEBLEN and MYRDAL, the neo-classical framework postulates an isolated closed analytical model with self-equilibrating tendencies. Similarly the 'multiplier' or the 'accelerator' are cases of cumulative interdependencies even though the relationships referred to are conceived in a narrow mechanical and deterministic fashion.

THE NATURE OF INSTITUTIONAL ECONOMICS

locking interdependencies within a process of cumulative causation in a systematic way, and to have shown its significance and its implications as an alternative analytical framework for the entire field of social relations. He has done this in a continuous critical confrontation with the closed system of neo-classical equilibrium analysis, its hidden political or normative elements and in his life-long preoccupation with concrete and persistent problems such as race discrimination in America, international disparities, and the intractable problems of underdevelopment and poverty in Asia. In dealing with these problems MYRDAL has developed a new explanatory theoretical framework which consist of a matrix of ordered and specified elements of social conditions which, in their reciprocal interdependencies, can be shown to influence the evolution and transformation of social processes. As an exemplary illustration we choose the relationship between developed and underdeveloped countries and the interpretation of the process of development and underdevelopment. The problems to be accounted for are the empirically observed disparities and the persistence of development differentials between 'rich' and 'poor' countries or regions. Both rich and poor regions are characterized by a number of specific conditions which can be classified or categorized in different ways. MYRDAL considers the following conditions as relevant for the analysis and interpretation of the process of underdevelopment: *Productivity* (output/worker; income/population); *conditions of production* (techniques, scale, capital intensity, savings and investment, social overhead, labor utilization and employment); *levels of living* (nutrition, housing, hygiene, medical attention, education and training, literacy and income distribution); *attitudes* to production, work and living (discipline, punctuality, prejudice, apathy, world outlooks, religion, absence of birth control, *etc.*); *institutions* (man-land relations, tenure conditions, market structures, class, caste and kinship systems, structure of national and local government and administration, *etc.*) and *policies and legislation* (the 'soft state', lack of law enforcement, taxation, mobilization of actual and potential surplus). Needless to say, this does not represent a complete list of possible relevant factors and conditions; moreover, they may have to be classified in a different manner depending upon problems and regions to be investigated. However, the important point is that, among all the conditions, there

K. WILLIAM KAPP

exists a causal relationship, and this relationship is to a large extent, but not always, of a circular character. In other words, the principle of circular interdependencies postulates a mutual responsiveness, *i.e.* a capacity of the different conditions to react upon changes of one or several elements. It is this circular and cumulative interaction which shapes the dynamics of the system which institutional analysis has to elucidate and to determine. In addition, it is essential to study the specific circular interrelations between the different factors and conditions before it will be possible to define objectives, to develop appropriate criteria of choice, and to make decisions with regard to long-run strategies as well as specific developmental policies. For, the formulation of such strategies and policies will require detailed, regional and local empirical studies designed to ascertain the concrete relationships between the different endogenous factors and conditions including their responsiveness to one another as well as the possible time lags and, in some cases, the lack of responsiveness of one or several of them to induced changes initiated by policy measures[20].

In other words, only by ascertaining the interaction and responsiveness of productivity and conditions of production to changes of the level of living, institutions and policy measures, is it possible to arrive at reasonable judgments as to the possible effects and outcomes of alternative policies, investments, and legislative action, as for instance agrarian reforms, new techniques, *etc.* In this sense, we believe that it is justified to regard the principle of interlocking circular interdependencies within a process of cumulative causation as the 'disciplinary matrix' which provides institutional economists with a new tool for the identification and ordering of the relevant elements in the study of socio-economic processes in their immensely diversified and changing complexity. More than this, the principle enables institutionalists (and other social scientists) to transform problematical situations and unsolved open problems (as for instance increasing disparities within and between 'rich' and 'poor' regions) into 'puzzles' which can be solved even when a complete theory and the precise knowledge as to the 'coefficients of interaction' are not (yet) available. As a matter of fact, this is precisely what the principle of

---

20. Gunnar Myrdal, *The Unity of the Social Sciences, op. cit.*, p. 6.

THE NATURE OF INSTITUTIONAL ECONOMICS

circular interdependencies has made possible not only with regard to the 'diagnostic' identification of relevant factors and conditions with regard to the problem of underdevelopment, but also with respect to the specification of possible measures and priorities required to deal with them.

One thing deserves special emphasis before turning to other matters. This is the question of the boundaries of the system and hence the question of the limits of the analysis. In other words, how far and how wide have we to extend the net of our investigations? A general but perhaps not entirely satisfactory answer is that all factors which can be shown to have a possible influence on the process or problem under investigation will have to be included regardless of whether or not this transcends the borderlines between traditional academic disciplines. In a more fundamental sense, the answer to the question as to the boundary of the system and hence to the factors to be included depends on the nature of the problem and the purpose of the investigation. Social Costs, environmental disruption, the increase of oil prices, and the emerging scarcities of non-renewable resources force economists to realize that economic processes depend upon a continuous exchange of energy and matter between the economy and nature and that available and accessible matter-energy is continuously and irreversibly transformed and partly dissipated into unavailable energy (increasing entropy). Therefore, an adequate and complete analytical description of economic processes cannot be obtained by the analysis of closed system (*e.g.* circulatory processes of production and consumption or systems of partial and total equilibrium, *etc.*) but calls for a representation of what the process needs in the form of input and what it does to man's environment by the emission of pollutants and the disposal of waste material. In other words, what is called for is a specification of the inputs required (and available), of the outputs including wastes disposed into the environment; the energy required (and available) for the transformation process as well as the resulting qualitative changes in time and space. I am listing these points not in order to suggest that institutional economics has already solved these problems but rather in order to call attention to the wide gap which exists between economic reality and economic models currently used for the theoretical representation

K. WILLIAM KAPP

of economic processes. In short, the question of the boundary of the system raises much more fundamental problems than is usually believed; it includes the problem of the relevant time horizon or, more precisely, the question of the appropriate long-run time schedules of the inputs and outputs to be considered[21]. One thing, however, should be clear from the foregoing observations: the existing borderlines between traditional disciplines are to-day the most important obstacles to an adequate analytical treatment of economic and social processes. This is the essential point of MYRDAL's dictum: there are no economic (or, for that matter, sociological) problems; there are only problems and they are all complex. In fact, MYRDAL recently made the point that since research must be focussed on specific problems which are all composite and mixed, 'borderlines between our traditional disciplines should be transgressed systematically'[22].

The central significance of the principle of circular interdependencies and cumulative causation derives from the fact that it abandons and, in fact explicitly rejects the notion of stable equilibrium as a misleading and unwarranted analogy to mechanics. From the perspective of mechanics everything is treated as a pendular movement where changes produce their counterbalancing forces and where production merely becomes a process of transformation under the influence of a maximization rule[23]. 'Actually, the economic process is not an isolated, self-sustaining process. It cannot go on without a continuous exchange which alters the environment in a cumulative way and without being, in its turn, influenced by these alterations[24].'

In short, economic processes can be understood and must be represented for analytical purposes as radically open systems which

21. '[...] where we draw the abstract boundary, what duration we consider, and what qualitative spectrum we use for classifying the elements of the process depend on the particular purpose of the student, and by and large on the science in point'. NICHOLAS GEORGESCU-ROEGEN, 'Energy and Economic Myths', *Southern Economic Journal*, Vol. 41 (1975), 3, p. 350.

22. GUNNAR MYRDAL, *The Unity of the Social Sciences, op. cit.*, p. 15.

23. 'To equate the economic process with a mechanical analogue implies [...] the myth that the economic process is a circular merry-go-round which cannot possibly affect the environment of matter and energy in any way'. GEORGESCU-ROEGEN, *op. cit.*, p. 350.

24. *Ibid.*, p. 348.

THE NATURE OF INSTITUTIONAL ECONOMICS

exchange energy and matter with the environment in the course of which qualitative changes take place both with respect to the environment and the process itself. That is to say, socio-economic processes move in a definite direction and this direction needs to be ascertained[25].

However, even if we could get away from the fundamental fact of entropy the analogy to mechanics with the notion of stable equilibrium would still be problematical and usually misleading for the analysis of contemporary social conditions. For, these conditions are no longer, if they ever were, characterized by the interaction of a great number of more or less equal units in perfect competition none of which exert a dominating influence on the direction of the process and its outcome (*e.g.* prices, quantities produced and sold, inputs chosen, technologies adopted, and locations selected). Exchanges between dominating and dominated units, give rise to unequal exchanges and unequal terms of trade and to a choice of inputs, technologies and locations which are bound to result in self-reinforcing movements and an unequal distribution of income, growing disparities and polarization. In short, in the normal course of exchange relations between dominating and dominated units, between 'center' and 'periphery', between 'growth poles' and dependent economies there is no assurance that inequalities and domination will cease or 'backwash' effects will be compensated by expansionary 'spread' effects.

Under these circumstances, it becomes clear why the new theoretical framework of circular interdependence and cumulative causation is justified to reject the analogy to mechanics with its notion of stable equilibrium as a paradigm for problem solving in the social sciences. In fact, the new paradigm assumes that 'the system is by itself not moving towards any sort of balance between forces, but is constantly on the move away from such a situation. In the normal case a change does not call for countervailing changes but, instead, supporting changes, which move the system in the same direction as the first change but much further. Because of such circular cau-

25. 'Actual phenomena move in a definite direction and involve qualitative change. This is the lesson of thermodynamics [...] (*i.e.* the law of increasing entropy or the continuous dissipation of available energy into unavailable energy).' *Ibid.*, pp. 351/352.

K. WILLIAM KAPP

sation a social process tends to become cumulative and often to gather speed at an accelerating rate'[26]. The principle does not prejudge the direction of the cumulative response nor the final outcome. In fact, it does *not* imply only 'vicious' circles. In other words, the response of the system to an endogenous or exogenous change such as deliberately planned exogenous impulses may either reinforce, retard or reverse the process; hence there is room for a variety of possibilities of interdependencies[27].

Moreover, the principle of cumulative causation and circular interdependencies offers a logical explanation why, under certain conditions, relatively 'small' changes are capable of bringing about comparatively 'big' effects or transformations in socio-economic as well as ecological processes. Once the conditions for cumulative processes (either upward or downward) exist in a particular system a relatively small additional impulse can act as an 'evocator' of substantial, non-linear and even 'jump-like' transformations particularly when certain limits or thresholds of tolerance are reached. Good examples for such disproportionalities between cause and effect can be found in the field of air and water pollution where critical limits of the carrying capacity of the environment may be reached or exceeded by small additional emissions of pollutants. Needless to add the principle of the disproportionality between cause and effect is not confined to environmental disruption. It applies also to socio-economic as well as to biological processes as it does to chemico-physical reactions.

Before concluding these considerations let me come back to the problem of the precision and completeness of our knowledge regarding cumulative causation and circular interdependencies of a great number of conditions. I have already referred to 'coefficients of interaction' of relevant variables, to possible time lags, and even to the total non-responsiveness of one or several of the relevant conditions to induced changes. Institutional economists are not opposed to precise and quantitative knowledge; on the contrary, they were among the first to call for and insist upon the quantification of

---

26. GUNNAR MYRDAL, *Economic Theory and Underdeveloped Regions, op. cit.*, p. 13.
27. GUNNAR MYRDAL, *Asian Drama*, Vol. III, New York, Pantheon Books, 1968, p. 1859.

THE NATURE OF INSTITUTIONAL ECONOMICS

relevant relationships between variables in scientific investigations[28]. They have insisted on precise concept formations as well as on detailed and disaggregated empirical and quantitative statistical studies of all important factors and their interaction irrespective of conventional borderlines between academic disciplines with a view to filling the gaps of our knowledge. But, unlike those who are interested in quantification and precision out of a 'quest for certainty' and a search for precise and purely formal solutions of frequently esoteric problems, institutionalists have remained aware of and have warned against the tendency 'to overlook the imperfection of our knowledge and to pretend to precise knowledge which does not stand scrutiny' and serve no rational purpose[29]. While the ideal scientific solution of a problem may be, as MYRDAL indicated, to formulate 'an interconnected set of quantitative equations, describing the movement – and the internal changes – of the system under the various influences which are at work'[30] such a quantitative formulation is to-day, as MYRDAL also pointed out, far beyond the horizon. Moreover, I doubt that we possess or will ever possess the data and the type of mathematics needed for the quantitative formulation of mutual circular interdependencies and thus for a precise expression of coefficients of interaction. In any event, it would be questionable if not illogical to require, or to make action dependent upon, a degree of quantitative precision of our knowledge which may be neither attainable nor necessary for the formulation of public policies.

IV. SOME PRACTICAL IMPLICATIONS OF THE PRINCIPLE
OF CIRCULAR INTERDEPENDENCIES

In rejecting the mechanistic equilibrium approach as false and misleading and by stressing the importance of the principle of circular causation institutionalists do not argue that the situation is hopeless. While it is true that institutionalists regard circular causation, dis-

28. *Cf.* W. E. MITCHELL's work on business cycles and his programmatic article, 'Quantitative Analysis in Economic Analysis', *The American Economic Review*, Vol. 15 (1925), March. MYRDAL was one of the founder members of the Econometric Society.

29. GUNNAR MYRDAL, *The Unity of the Social Sciences, op. cit.*, p. 6.

30. GUNNAR MYRDAL, *Economic Theory and Underdeveloped Regions, op. cit.*, p. 19.

K. WILLIAM KAPP

ruption, disparities and disequilibria as 'normal' tendencies they also regard these tendencies as the main determinants of the dynamics of the system, both evolutionary and cataclysmic[31]. At the same time, it is these dynamic tendencies towards disequilibrium which provide the main impulse for attempts at remedying, channelling and controlling social and economic processes by deliberate policy measures with a view to maintaining social reproduction.

What should be the specific policy objectives of such measures? How will they be determined? How can they be defined? Which criteria need to be used? These are some of the central questions with which institutionalists will have to concern themselves. They have only begun to deal with these problems and it would be too much to expect that a large measure of agreement has been reached, except at the most general level. MYRDAL, in his studies of underdevelopment, speaks of modernization ideals and economic integration as goals of policies designed to guide the process of development planning with a view to moving the entire social system 'upwards'[32].

Others have argued that balanced growth be considered as a

31. W. F. WERTHEIM, *Evolution and Revolution*, Harmondsworth, Penguin Books, 1974, p. 9.

32. MYRDAL's modernization ideals are the basic and explicit value premises underlying the development effort; they include social and economic equalization, greater rationality, improved levels of living, including nutrition, health and housing, rise of productivity, new institutions, attitudes and motivations including the liberation from all notions of fatalism and 'destiny', national consolidation, self-reliance. These ideals have been criticized as eurocentric and 'Western' in character (*cf*. CLIFFORD GEERTZ, MYRDAL's Mythology – 'Modernism and the Third World', *Encounter*, Vol. 33 (1969), 1, pp. 26–34.) While this may be so, it is at least worth noting that they represent positive values for influential groups in some of the underdeveloped countries and that they were even shared by a man like GANDHI: 'The young Indian must come round to a rational and objective view of material advancement. He must be able and willing to tear himself away from his family ties; flout customs and traditions; put economic welfare before cow worship; think in terms of farm and factory output rather than in terms of gold and silver ornaments; spend on tools and training rather than on temples and ceremonials; work with the low caste rather than starve with the high caste; think of the future rather than of the past; concentrate on material gains rather than dwell on kismet (destiny). These are extremely difficult changes to envisage in the Hindu social structure and ideas. But they seem unavoidable'. D. K. RANGNEKAR, *Poverty and Capital Development in India*, London, Oxford University Press, 1958, p. 81, quoted from MYRDAL, Asian Drama I, *op. cit.*, p. 62, fn.

THE NATURE OF INSTITUTIONAL ECONOMICS

general objective of policy measures particularly in developed countries. This advances us only in so far as it stresses the need to look for, and to develop appropriate criteria and definitions of states of dynamic equilibria which should be the basis for the formulation of the specific goals and objectives of all our strategies and policies in a world in which tendencies toward disequilibrium are typical and prevailing whereas conditions of equilibrium and balance are transitory and provisional. In this sense and in so far as unbalance and disequilibrium endanger social reproduction and hence human life and survival, the analysis of disequilibria and the search for dynamic states of balance as policy objectives may indeed be said to be complementary. The latter presupposes the former.

However, I would go one step further. The search for and hence the formulation of conditions of admittedly transitory balance and equilibrium will have to be guided not only by a critical and diagnostic identification of the full range of relevant variables, their circular interaction and their logical (probable) outcome but by fundamental and explicit value premises. For to avoid value judgments in the field of practical action in an effort of maintaining one's alleged objectivity is nothing but an evasion of the basic problems inherent in policy formulation. In order to contribute to the latter social inquiry must go beyond a 'positive' analysis of the interaction of relevant variables; it will have to assess critically the outcome of social processes *in the absence* of deliberate social action and, in the light of such a critical evaluation of reality, contribute to what may be called the formulation of possible and desirable states of dynamic balances or processes as goals of social policies and social development. The creative formulation of possible and 'desirable Futures' (OZBEKHAN) goes far beyond anything that has thus far been undertaken by social analysis. Institutionalists are certainly not the only ones who have something to contribute to these new tasks. They bring to it perhaps a more thorough understanding than other social scientists, of the relevant circular interdependencies which determine the outcome of action or inaction. My own view is that possible and desirable Futures need to be defined with reference not only to general objectives of modernization, but with respect to more specific requirements defined in terms of essential or basic human and collective needs and the minimization of human suffering.

227

K. WILLIAM KAPP

In fact, what is essential, perhaps more than anything else, are new fundamental principles for the determination of social goals and for the formulation of our public policies. Such basic principles must be 'operational', *i.e.* they must not remain vague and ambiguous like the utilitarian principle of maximizing happiness but must be capable of being translated into criteria of action and into quantifiable indicators of performance. Not maximization of pleasure, but the satisfaction of basic human needs or the minimization of human suffering seems to me to constitute such a first principle which could guide practical policies and serve as a yardstick of social efficiency. For, unlike happiness and welfare 'human suffering is utterly concrete [...]. To wipe out hunger and sickness, unemployment and poverty, illiteracy and ignorance can give rise to practical political action'[33] on a national and international scale. It is this 'inverted utilitarianism' which has been suggested as the first principle which must be our value premise to-day and in the future if we want to come to terms with the problems of social and ecological disruption as well as growing national and international disparities, inflation, unemployment, poverty, and last but not least with the threat to world peace.

In this context, I do not consider it as my task to outline the full implications of such a new normative approach to social analysis and social action. Suffice it to say, however, that what would be involved is a basic re-orientation of social analysis which ultimately will have to find expression in a reversal of our previous epistemological attitudes and thought processes: Many of the factors which we have so far accepted as given (even if only as parameters) as for example individual preferences, the state of technology, the principle of 'investment for profit' (as VEBLEN used to say) will have to be considered as dependent variables which need to be adapted and modified in accordance with the new value premises of minimizing suffering and providing the means for the gratification of basic human needs and the maintenance of essential economic, social and ecological balance[34].

33. GUNNAR ADLER-KARLSSON, 'Inverted Utilitarianism or a New Way of Life in Developed Countries', *Symposium on a New International Economic Order*, The Hague, May 23–24, 1975, p. 68.
34. For evidence that the practical and political implications of such a re-

THE NATURE OF INSTITUTIONAL ECONOMICS

V. CONCLUSIONS

I hope to have demonstrated that institutional economists have provided more than a rational critique of the scope and method of traditional economics. They have shown the trans-disciplinary character of our problems, and they have considerably broadened the scope of socio-economic analysis. Above all, they have provided an alternative analytical framework for the explication of the circular interdependencies within a process of cumulative causation which provides economists and other social scientists with a tool for the solution of theoretical and practical problems.

The principle of cumulative causation does not reflect a static view of interdependencies giving rise to a stabilization of the *status quo* within a given form of social organization. The principle does not rule out conflict, tension, contradiction, change, and transformation; on the contrary. Furthermore, the active factors in circular interdependence include both subjective and objective elements: common ideas, valuations, ideologies and institutions as well as techniques, and 'production relations'. While the principle refuses to attribute exclusive or primary importance to one or the other set of factors in circular interaction, it does not rule out the possibility that either one or the other set of factors may exert a predominant or decisive influence with either positive or negative effects. What the principle rejects as futile is any search for a primary cause.

In this as in other respects, institutionalists have indeed followed the lead of the problems with which they are concerned. This does not preclude specialization nor does it call for expert familiarity of

orientation are being investigated, *cf*. in addition to MYRDAL's writings, IGNACY SACHS, 'La crise dans les stratégies de développement: Vers l'identification de nouveaux objectifs', OECD, Séminaire: Sciences, Technologie et Développement dans un Monde en Mutation, Paris 1975. UNEP, The Cocoyac-Declaration, Development Dialogue, 1974, No. 2, pp. 88–96. 'What Now – Another Development', *The 1975 Dag Hammarskjöld Report*, prepared on the occasion of the 7th Special Session of the United Nations General Assembly. HASAN OZBEKHAN, *Technology and Man's Future* (ms), Santa Barbara 1965. K. WILLIAM KAPP, 'Umweltkrise und Nationalökonomie', *Schweizerische Zeitschrift für Volkswirtschaft und Statistik*, Vol. 108 (1972), 3, pp. 231–249.

K. WILLIAM KAPP

the results of all disciplines. It means, however, as C. WRIGHT MILLS put it in another context, that a social scientist will have to be 'familiar enough with the materials and perspectives of other disciplines to use them in clarifying the problems that concern him'[35]. It does not mean that a social scientist needs to master everything and all fields.

The relevant boundaries of the limits of social inquiry differ depending upon the problems under discussion. In any event, in view of the cumulative circular interdependencies which link the economy to the environment and the resource base and hence to the interests of future generations economic processes cannot be adequately described without reference to a time horizon: that is to say, without reference to the time schedule of inputs in relation to scarce available resources, and the direction of the qualitative changes which the use of energy and matter as well as the disposal of waste have upon the environment and hence on economic processes and the well-being of future generations. It is this concern for a longer time horizon and for the complex interdependencies of actual social phenomena and processes moving in a definite direction with possibly irreversible qualitative changes and, last but not least, the rejection and the replacement of the mechanical analogy by the principle of circular causation which gives modern institutionalism, what I venture to call its modern character and its transdisciplinary scope.

SUMMARY

Critics of traditional economic theory have always denied the closed character of economic systems. They have stressed instead the open character of economic processes and have challenged above all the belief in their self-regulatory tendencies. They have rejected the belief in the dogma of the 'mechanics of self interest' and the conviction that specialism is the royal road to efficiency in scientific analysis as well as in production. However, institutional economists have not only provided a rational critique of the traditional scope and method of mainstream economics; they have advanced an analytical framework for the explication of the circular interdependencies within a process of cumulative causation – a framework which gives them a powerful tool not only for the ordering of relevant factors in the analysis of socio-economic processes but also for the formulation

35. C. WRIGHT MILLS, *Sociological Imagination*, New York, 1959, p. 142.

THE NATURE OF INSTITUTIONAL ECONOMICS

and 'solution' of theoretical and practical problems. As such MYRDAL's principle of circular interdependencies can be regarded a new paradigm for a new approach to socio-economic analysis. Institutional economics aims at a normative system of knowledge which calls for explicit value premises of a preliminary and hypothetical nature. Instead of the vague utilitarian principle of maximizing 'pleasure' the author regards the satisfaction of basic human needs and the minimization of human suffering as the first moral principle and at the same time as a yardstick of social rationality which he considers as urgently needed in an era of environmental disruption and national and international socio-economic disorganization.

ZUSAMMENFASSUNG

Kritiker der Wirtschaftswissenschaft haben seit jeher die Annahme «geschlossener» wirtschaftlicher Prozesse in Frage gestellt und haben demgegenüber den offenen Charakter ökonomischer Systeme betont, wobei sie gleichzeitig die Annahme einer quasi-automatischen Selbstregulierung als Dogma einer «Mechanik des Selbstinteresses» ablehnten. Sie haben ebenso die Ansicht abgelehnt, dass Spezialisierung die Voraussetzung zur Effizienz der Sozialforschung wie in der Produktion darstellt. Institutionelle Ökonomen von VEBLEN bis MYRDAL haben neben einer rationalen Kritik der methodologischen Grundlagen der traditionellen Ökonomie ein alternatives Erklärungsprinzip für die Erfassung der zirkulären Interdependenzen innerhalb eines Prozesses kumulativer Verursachung entwickelt – ein Prinzip, das ihnen ein wichtiges Werkzeug sowohl für die Ordnung relevanter Faktoren als auch für die Formulierung und Lösung relevanter theoretischer und praktischer Probleme bietet. MYRDAL's Prinzip der zirkulären Interdependenz mit kumulativer Verursachung kann in diesem Sinne als ein Paradigma für eine Erneuerung der Sozialwissenschaften angesehen werden. Die institutionelle Ökonomie strebt ein normatives System des sozialwissenschaftlichen Denkens an, das mit expliziten Wertprämissen hypothetischer Natur arbeitet. Anstelle des vagen utilitaristischen Prinzips der Maximierung von '*pleasure*', das heisst eines subjektivischen Glücksempfindens, plädiert der Verfasser für die Befriedigung existentieller Grundbedürfnisse und der Minimisierung menschlichen Leidens als ein moralischer Imperativ der gleichzeitig als konkreter Massstab gesellschaftlicher Rationalität von grundsätzlicher Relevanz im Zeitalter der Umweltzerstörung und nationaler und internationaler sozialer Disorganisation dienen kann.

RÉSUMÉ

Ceux qui critiquent la théorie économique traditionnelle ont toujours nié le caractère fermé des systèmes économiques. Ils insistent au contraire sur le caractère ouvert des processus économiques et contestent en particulier la croyance en leur tendance auto-régulatrice. Ils ne croient pas non plus au dogme des «mécanismes

K. WILLIAM KAPP

de l'intérêt personnel» et rejettent l'idée que la spécialisation est la voie royale vers l'efficacité, tant dans le domaine de l'analyse scientifique que dans celui de la production. Pourtant, les économistes institutionnalistes n'ont pas seulement élaboré une critique rationnelle des buts et méthodes de l'économie tradition-nelle; ils ont aussi proposé un outil analytique pour l'explication des interdépen-dances circulaires à l'intérieur d'un processus de causalité cumulative – outil fort utile, non seulement pour la classification des facteurs appropriés à l'analyse des processus socio-économiques, mais aussi pour la formulation et la «résolution» de problèmes théoriques et pratiques. Ainsi, le principe des interdépendances circulaires de MYRDAL peut être considéré comme un nouveau paradigme pour une approche nouvelle de l'analyse socio-économique. L'économie institution-naliste cherche à être un système de connaissance normatif qui exige comme hypothèses préliminaires des jugements de valeur explicites. Au vague principe utilitariste de la maximisation du 'plaisir', l'auteur oppose la satisfaction des besoins humains élémentaires et la minimisation de la souffrance humaine; il en fait à la fois la norme et le premier principe d'une rationalité sociale dont le besoin se fait pressant dans une époque de destruction de l'environnement et de désorganisation socio-économique sur le plan national et international.

[7]

IN DEFENSE OF INSTITUTIONAL ECONOMICS*

K. William Kapp

Summary

Against the background of a definition of institutional economics and in the light of the traditional critique directed against it the author outlines the main preoccupations and major contributions of institutional economics in America and Europe. The paper then proceeds to demonstrate the specific usefulness of the institutional approach to the study of underdeveloped economies viewed as social systems marked by circular interdependencies which the traditional study of economic processes ignores and is incapable of incorporating within its theoretical framework.

The author concludes that institutional economics needs not so much a defence as a systematization and calls for a more assertative stand to be taken by institutionalists in developed and underdeveloped countries.

The task which I have set myself today is to throw some light on the nature and significance of institutional economics; to show its major preoccupations and its methodological procedures; to indicate how it differs from alternative approaches to economic analysis. And finally to point to the contributions it can make to the study of economic development.

Parenthetically I should perhaps mention that American institutionalists have abandoned the term "Institutional Economics" in favor of "Evolutionary Economics" in their desire to stress the fact that they are concerned above all with the dynamic character of economic processes and systems including problems of economic development and underdevelopment.[1]

1. Toward a Definition of Institutional Economics

Perhaps you expect first a precise definition of institutional or evolutionary economics; such a definition has been formulated. It contrasts sharply with that of pure economics which Lionel Robbins advanced as far back as 1932. You will no doubt recall that Robbins defined economics as the study of a particular form of behavior, namely human conduct under the influence of scarcity or, as he also expressed it, the study of "human behavior as a relationship between ends and scarce means which have alternative uses".[2] In contrast with this definition of economic science which I think characterizes very well the prevailing preoccupations of many economists, institutional economics has been defined as "the study of

---

* Paper presented at the Institute for International Economic Studies, University of Stockholm, on September 27th 1967.

[1] In fact, American institutionalists have recently founded an Association of Evolutionary Economics with a membership of more than seven hundred. Cf. also David Hamilton, "Why is Institutional Economics not Institutional", *American Journal of Economics and Sociology*, Vol. 21, No. 3, 1962, pp. 309–318.

[2] Lionel Robbins, *The Nature and Significance of Economic Science*, London 1932, p. 16.

the structure and functioning of the evolving field of human relations which is concerned with the provision of material goods and services for the satisfaction of human wants." ... [it is] "the study of the changing patterns of cultural relations which deal with the creation and disposal of scarce material goods and services by individuals and *groups* in the light of their private and *public* aims."[3]

The contrast between this and Robbins' definition of economics is obvious and needs hardly any emphasis. Whereas Robbins selects a particular form of behavior and insists that we define the subject matter of economics with reference to scarcity and rational conduct, the definition of institutional economics focusses on the study of the structure and functioning of an *evolving* system of human or cultural relations, and includes explicitly in addition to individual behavior and individual wants, the consideration of *group* behavior and *public* aims. In other words, institutional economics is not confined to the study and explication of deliberate rational behavior, or to use Jevons' felicitous phrase, to "the mechanics of self-interest and utility," but includes also other forms of behavior such as traditional behavior patterns of individuals and groups—i.e. patterns which derive their relative stability and uniformity from the fact that they have become institutionalized. While the Robbinsian definition in effect enthrones *homo oeconomicus* institutional economics replaces the concept of the economic man by something which we may call the "institutional man". Both these conceptions are, of course, abstractions—but whereas the former is constructed by isolating and accentuating one conceivable aspect of human behavior, the latter is derived from observation of concrete behavior patterns and leaves room for the consideration of different forms of behavior in different societies. Indeed, institutional economics rejects the thesis that economic science must confine its theoretical analysis to the study of rational human conduct.[4]

In this context you may also ask what are "institutions"? I shall make no attempt to offer a satisfactory definition of institutions because to do so would call for a philosophical or rather an anthropological inquiry into the mutual relationship of man and culture, which it would be foolhardy to attempt within the time at our disposal. However, let me say at least that the concept of institution in this context does not refer to legal forms of organization as for instance, to use a primitive example, the Federal Reserve System; the term is to be understood rather [2] as referring to stabilized forms of behavior, habits of thought and conduct including group habits and behavior patterns which have been developed in, and are taken over from the past and are enduring in the present. Needless to add that institutions understood in this fashion have their origin in the nature of man and are human and social achievements. And yet, as more or less stabilized forms of behavior they tend to assume an autonomy of their own and mould human conduct. For Veblen it was, therefore, axiomatic that institutional behavior patterns may be more or less out of date at any given point of time.

Having thus attempted to offer a definition of what I am supposed to defend let me point out immediately that I am not a great believer in definitions of this

[3] A. G. Gruchy, *Modern Economic Thought*, New York 1947, pp. 550, 552.
[4] In fact, there are some economists who hold the view that the tendency of using formal rationality as the exclusive perspective for the study of human behavior has unduly narrowed the scope of economic inquiry and that the assumption of rationality should be dropped from economics as a permissible assumption. Arthur Schweitzer, *The Method of Social Economics*, (mimeographed and privately circulated) p. 48, see also pp. 16–17.

kind. For definitions of a particular discipline or a field of study are rarely as informative as they claim to be; frequently they remain vague and their usefulness is at best limited. In fact they may be positively harmful, particularly if they are used as a pseudo-scientific justification for the convenient practice of considering evidence against particular conclusions as irrelevant or inadmissable on the ground that it falls outside the proper scope of the discipline. Even more harmful is the practice of using such definitions as an instrument to channel research into one direction only or, whether consciously or unconsciously, to suppress evidence altogether. For this reason I believe that definitions of the nature and scope of a particular field of study acquire their full meaning and precision only as our acquaintance with the problems under study expands.

2. The Critique of Institutional Economics

Having thus sketched the nature and scope of institutional economics, it is doubtless high time to proceed to its defense. For you probably have already thought of several reservations against a type of economics which does not confine itself to the "mechanics of self-interest and utility" and claims as its province no less than the study of the structure and functioning of the evolving field of human relations concerned with the provision of material goods and services for the satisfaction of human wants. You may, for example, regard institutional economics rather as a kind of sociology or anthropology. Or, you may say that anybody who undertakes such an ambitious program of study reaches for the moon and will not be able to go beyond empirical studies describing perhaps this or that aspect of socio-economic reality without ever being able to achieve a generalized analysis and explication of economic phenomena. This indeed has been the major criticism advanced against institutional economics. Indeed, institutionalists have been called naive empiricists who are said to have no clear realization that the crux of all science is a combination of theory and observation with a view to their ultimate confrontation.

[3]   Let me admit that this line of criticism has had some validity particularly during the earlier stages of the development of institutionalism. However, as I shall endeavor to show, it is not *generally* valid—it did *not* apply to Veblen—nor does it to institutionalists of a more recent vintage. Closely connected with this critique is a second line of argument frequently advanced against institutional economics: namely that it is a collection of apparently unconnected ideas and doctrines which cannot claim any logical consistency of its basic theories. In other words, it is argued that institutional economics lacks the character of a systematic body of thought in the sense of a framework of concepts and propositions logically related to one another. To this point I shall come back in my concluding remarks.

Institutional economics have also been attacked on the ground that despite their persistent criticism of utility and price analysis they have not been able to develop any alternative theory of price formation. Here I would say that the critics of institutionalism are in the peculiar position of a person who uses his own standards of theoretical excellence as a criterion for the evaluation of alternative forms of generalizations. It is as if a fortune teller whose crystal gazing you criticize as a method of predicting the future tells you that you have no better way of doing it. Actually we have today alternatives to the conventional theory of price—

alternatives which have discarded the maximization hypothesis and are orientated toward an institutional approach. In fact, there are several hypotheses such as the desire to increase or, in other instances, to maintain the share of the market, the maximization of turnover, or even the domination principle of Perroux, which are institutional in character.[5]

Similarly the rate of savings and investments has been explained in the light of institutionalized behavior. Thus what an economy saves and invests is not determined simply by the level of income but also by what individuals and groups as members of a given society consider as essential or non-essential consumption. If a society regards expenditures for ceremonial purposes, or for the maintenance of rank and status, or for the conduct of war as essential, this obviously has an influence on the rate of savings and investments. In short, whether a nation has an investible surplus—over and above the actual cost of producing the goods and services required for the satisfaction of essential needs—is not only a function of its income but also of its institutionalized value structure which thus plays an important role in determining the proportion of outlays used for productive invest-
[4] ments or for non-productive purposes, and hence of the size of the national product. In fact, many institutional economics would take the position that not only in traditional societies but also in modern economies the decision to invest increasingly precedes and determines the act and the volume and therefore, the rate of saving. It needs hardly to be added that this way of looking at saving and investment implies a specific theory of capital formation which throws a very different light on the scarcity of capital and the problem of development in underdeveloped areas than do most traditional theories of capital.[6]

3. Main Preoccupations and Major Contributions of Institutional Economics

It is important to emphasize first that institutionalism starts from a basis of dissent— i.e. a common critique of the conventional wisdom, to use the well-known term of Galbraith. I shall not enter into a detailed discussion of this dissent but will confine myself rather to two observations about its general direction and significance. In this respect, it is perhaps not sufficiently realized that American pragmatism

[5] It should perhaps be added that institutional economists have not been particularly interested in the question of prices of particular commodities or price relations in general. This does not mean that they are without an explanation of relative prices. Why a Cadillac should sell for a higher price than a Volkswagen is certainly not an unimportant problem and doubless "supply" and "demand" are useful concepts to account for these differences. However, the institutionalist would not be satisfied to derive these fundamental categories from axioms of rational conduct, marginal rates of substitution and static production functions but would push the analysis beyond supply and demand by inquiring into the factors of market power and market domination including high pressure salesmanship and would point out that goods and services also derive their relative importance from the fact that they serve as symbols of rank and status. Cf. J. S. Gambs, *Beyond Supply and Demand—A Reappraisal of Institutional Economics*, New York 1946.
[6] On Veblen's highly original theory of capital see Thorstein Veblen, On the Nature of Capital—The Productivity of Capital Goods, *The Quarterly Journal of Economics*, Vol. XXII, 1908 and Vol. XXIII, 1909. See also Thorstein Veblen, *The Vested Interests and the Common Man*, New York 1919, esp. pp. 35–64.

and particularly Charles Peirce and John Dewey have left their mark on American Institutionalism and especially on Veblen. I shall mention here only two major epistemological insights:

1. That scientific inquiry always proceeds within a cultural matrix—in other words, all theorizing operates within a framework of preconceptions which is not of our own making but is taken over from society—a whole apparatus of concepts and categories within which individual thinking is compelled to move.[7] These inherited preconceptions which are at the root of all our knowledge—including our scientific knowledge—need to be made explicit, and must be held up for critical examination. In fact, any improvement of our scientific knowledge presupposes such critical awareness.[8]

2. A second contribution of American pragmatism to institutional economics is its scepticism toward any quest for certainty. This scepticism questions the widespread belief that social processes move toward a pre-established and determinate end—a fixed telos; instead of this teleological bias pragmatists stress indeterminacy and uncertainty as basic characteristics of all processes, including and particularly social processes. The critical genius of Veblen accepted these tenets of American pragmatism. In fact, Veblen started his career as an economist and social scientist

[5] with a series of inquiries into what he called the "preconceptions" of classical, neo-classical, marxist and historical economics.[9] But he went also beyond pragmatism by emphasizing again and again the "ineradicable propensity of the human mind for self-delusion"[10] and he never tired to focus attention on the patterns of social irrationality existing behind a front of formal rationality imputed to small segments of social processes as for example the price system.

No other American dissenter with the exception of Galbraith today has carried the systematic critique of conventional economic theory as far as Veblen—a critique which in Europe has been voiced with equal conviction by Myrdal's earlier analysis of the hidden normative elements of classical and neo-classical economics and, more recently by Hans Albert in Germany.[11] I do not intend to give a detailed

---

[7] John Dewey, *Logic*: The Theory of Inquiry, New York 1938, p. 487 and F. M. Cornford, *From Religion to Philosophy*. Torchbook ed., New York 1957 (original edition 1912), p. 45.

[8] I admit that such a critical attitude may not be sufficient but it is a first and essential step without which we cannot hope to improve our scientific procedures and formulations. Critique in this sense is therefore an essential part of scientific analysis.

[9] Thorstein Veblen, The Preconceptions of Economic Science, *The Quarterly Journal of Economics*, Vol. XIII, July 1899; The Socialist Economics of Karl Marx, *The Quarterly Journal of Economics*, Vol. XX, August 1906; The Limitations of Marginal Utility, *The Quarterly Journal of Economics*, Vol. XVIII, 1909; see also Veblen's earlier article Why is Economics not an Evolutionary Science? *The Quarterly Journal of Economics*, Vol. XII, July 1898.

[10] Louis Schneider, *The Freudian Psychology and Veblen's Social Theory*, New York 1948, p. 55.

[11] Gunnar Myrdal, Das politische Element in der nationalökonomischen Doktrinbildung, Berlin 1932, and Hans Albert, Dans Ende der Wohlfahrtsökonomik, *Gewerkschaftliche Monatshefte*, January 1958, pp. 33–36 and Die Problematik der ökonomischen Perspektive, *Zeitschrift für die gesamte Staatswissenschaft*, 1961, cf. also Sidney Schoeffler, *The Failures of Economics: A Diagnostic Study*, Cambridge 1955.

account of this critique not because I consider it unimportant but because it is well known, even though conventional theory has tended to ignore or to neutralize it by introducing new assumptions and definitions.

I shall dwell at greater length on the second characteristic of institutional economics i.e. its common way of looking at the structure and functioning of economic systems and economic processes. This common perspective which unifies institutional economics and differentiates it from the conventional theory is based on the conviction that economic systems are open and dynamic systems and must be treated as such by our conceptual theoretical frameworks. Let me try to make this point clear. The economy has, of course, long been viewed as a *system* of production and distribution. In fact, to have done so is the particular achievement of macro- and micro-economic analysis from the Physiocrats to Adam Smith, Marx, the Neo-Classicists and the Keynesian and Post-Keynesian model builders. Their models and particularly today's macro-economic growth models are meant to be conceptual representations of *economic systems* with specific determinate relationships between a few variables. As theoretical representations they make use and frequently consist of nothing else but algebraic functions i.e. a set of relations between numbers or ratios or coefficients. But consider for a moment how many factors are assumed to be given or are kept constant i.e. treated as parameters: there is first the factor population; then the state of knowledge and of the industrial arts (technology); the tastes, preferences and behavior of consumers; the conduct [6] of entrepreneurs, the distribution of power between different social groups (such as employers' and labor organizations, or classes, castes, landlords and tenants), all of these and more are treated as data or are held deliberately constant. In fact, it would be no exaggeration to say, that the entire social and institutional system is simply taken as constant; in other words, for analytical purposes the economy is viewed as a closed system. In the economics of the model building variety we select so few interrelationships and treat so many variables as "constants" that our students probably have not the faintest idea as to which and how many factors have been deliberately left out. I am sometimes wondering whether the model builders themselves are fully aware of these omissions. For many of them, and certainly for most of the average students of theoretical economics society seems either hardly to exist or has become a synonym for a set of variables kept constant or outside the analysis.

Now, from the viewpoint of an institutional economist this tendency of systematically isolating the economic system from the social system, even if only for purposes of analysis, constitutes much more than a neglect of many of the factors which have an ascertainable effect on the outcome of economic processes. Indeed, this deliberate concentration on two or three keyrelationships treated moreover under specific assumptions or simply axioms as to human behavior which individuals in a particular social system may or may not follow—does indeed make possible the use of a quantitative mathematical treatment and facilitates the search for determinate levels of stable equilibrium but it is a form of loose theoretization based upon concepts which have no clear empirical counterpart—a procedure which most institutionalists would regard as a misuse of the method of simplification and abstraction. In fact they consider this procedure not only as a misuse of theoretical analysis but as a potentially dangerous trivialization of the use of reason which is rapidly making of economics a technique rather than a social science. They take this position *not* because they are naive empiricists interested only in an ideographic description of particular events or because they are hostile to theory or fail to appreciate the importance of abstraction, measurement and quantification,[12] but because they consider the economic system as part of a more inclusive comprehensive social system with which the economic process is interrelated by numerous channels and from which it receives some of its most important impulses and inhibitions [7] in ascertainable ways and with ascertainable effects. I shall come back to this matter in connection with my observations on institutional economics as a kind of social systems analysis with particular reference to underdeveloped areas. Here I shall push on immediately to the third common characteristic of institutional economics: namely its main working hypothesis for the study of economic processes.

Institutionalists interested in the analysis of the economic system viewed as part of a social system need not only specific concepts and categories but, as every scientist, a theoretical framework capable of conceptually representing in a generalizing and yet relevant and adequate fashion the various elements which in their interaction constitute the unit of investigation. Whereas traditional economics uses the concept and the theory of stable equilibrium as an instrument of analysis in its study of small segments of isolated subsystems (as for instance supply and demand[13]) institutional economists use the hypothesis of circular causation as an analytical instrument which they regard as particularly appropriate for the analysis of complex and dynamic systems. This principle is of course an outgrowth and a logical consequence of the institutionalists' perspective which views economic processes as a complex of elements in mutual interaction. The particular usefulness of the hypothesis of circular causation also stems from the fact that institutional economics is interested primarily in the analysis of the dynamics of economic processes including the development process and the analysis of structural changes. In fact, there is probably no institutionalist who has not shown some impatience with the traditional preoccupation with problems of economic statics to which the widespread use of the equilibrium concept and the search for levels of stable equilibria have given rise. Indeed, I have a hunch that most institutionalists would question

---

[12] It would be erroneous to believe that institutionalists are opposed to measurement and quantification. In fact, they called from the very beginning for greater precision and measurement of economic observations particularly in national income and business cycle analysis. But they rarely lost sight of the difficulties and the proximate character of most measurements of socio-economic phenomena. Good illustrations are Veblen's early suggestions as to how to measure and account for what he called with Adam Smith the "annual production" or the productivity of the industrial process and the "disposable net margin" on the one hand, cf. The *Vested Interests and the Common Man*, op. cit. p. 48 and W. C. Mitchell's plea for a quantitative analysis of the business cycle on the other; cf. W. C. Mitchell, Quantitative Analysis in Economic Theory, in *The American Economic Review*, Vol. XV, No. 1, pp. 1–12. On the need for measurement see also Arthur Spiethoff, *Die wirtschaftlichen Wechsellagen*, Vols. 1 and 2, Tübingen–Zürich, 1955.

[13]Institutionalists do not deny that for the analysis of small segments of deliberately closed systems the concepts of stable equilibrium and disequilibrium may have their usefulness. However, they have repeatedly pointed out that equilibrium analysis has an apparently inevitable tendency of making economic analysis itself static or of confining such analysis to processes which are self-correcting with the additional danger that evidence to the contrary may be overlooked or suppressed.

the theoretical usefulness of the distinction of statics and dynamics—both as a classificatory scheme and as categories of social analysis.[14] They would with E. Lindahl regard static theory at best as a special and highly complex tool hardly appropriate as a point of departure for the development of a general dynamic theory which they consider to be the logical starting point for social analysis.[15] Moreover, most institutional economists would probably take the position that variables change discontinuously and that even our empirical and statistical observations are not continuous but refer only to a particular period or point in time.[16]

[8]   As an analytical instrument the principle of circular causation seems to be of Scandinavian origin—if you include Veblen in this context among the Scandinavians. Both Veblen's *Theory of Business Enterprise* which coincides roughly in time with Wicksell's analysis of the influence of credit and the interest rate on the price level use a principle of circular causation. Ever since, this principle has played an important role in economic analysis particularly in business cycle and macroeconomic analysis. (I need only refer to the accelerator, the multiplier, the study of speculation and inventory accumulation etc.) However, whereas these applications of the principle consider only a relatively narrow set of variables viewed often in a rather mechanical interrelationship with one another, it is in the hands of institutionalists and particularly since Myrdal's systematic exposition of its methodological foundations and practical implications in his *American Dilemma* (1944) that the principle of cumulative causation has assumed its present comprehensive form in which it includes not only socalled economic variables but at the same time the frequently powerful social and political elements operative in a social system. In Stockholm it is perhaps superfluous to enter into a more detailed discussion of this central hypothesis of institutional economics. I shall come back to it, however, in connection with my discussion of institutional economics as a kind of social system analysis.

In short, then, we may say that institutional economics is marked by three major characteristics:

1 a common critique of the preconceptions and hidden normative elements of traditional economic analysis;
2 a common view of the economic process as an open system and as part of a broader socio-cultural network of relationships;
3 a common acceptance of the principle of circular causation as the main hypothesis for the explanation of dynamic economic processes including the process of underdevelopment and development.

While I regard these three elements as the central distinguishing characteristics of institutionalism my discussion would be incomplete if I did not mention, however briefly, several additional features which are integral parts of institutional economics. Among these I would list

a. a pervasive concern with the role and significance of conflict, coercion and power in economic and social life;

---

[14] Th. W. Adorno, Static and Dynamic as Sociological Categories, *Diogenes*, No. 33, 1961.
[15] E. Lindahl, *Studies in the Theory of Money and Banking*, London 1939, pp. 31–35.
[16] W. J. Baumol, *Economic Dynamics*, New York 1951, p. 123.

b. a rejection of price or market values as exclusive indices of individual and social welfare and as criteria of the efficiency of allocation and the "optimality" of decision-making in general;

c. an early and persistent interest in problems of instability as characteristic of an economy of business enterprise dominated by modern technology;

d. a continuous preoccupation with the problems raised by the phenomena of social costs and social benefits or, what the conventional theory—appropriating a term of Marshall—likes to call somewhat innocently "externalities" or external economies and diseconomies;

[9]

e. an early and systematic recognition of the central role which science and technology play as determinants of the productivity of human labor and capital goods and as dynamic factors of development; and, last but not least

f. a commitment to a critical analysis of the quality of individual and social life in a technical civilization in terms of such explicit values as the elimination of poverty, the equalization of opportunities regardless of race, color and creed, the maintenance of peace and democratic rule.

The concern with the role of conflict and coercion and power in economic life is in America an intellectual heritage which dates back to the Federalists and their European mentors. Among institutionalists the voices of dissent against the tendency of conventional economic analysis to ignore the influence and frequently central significance of conflict, domination and power in economic processes are associated with such names as Veblen, Commons, and Galbraith. Veblen's early *Theory of the Leisure Class* and his later concept of "vested interests" runs parallel with Commons' analysis of the role of power in economic life, of the role of the state, his later studies of the legal foundations of capitalism, his preoccupation with collective bargaining and public utility regulations which lead directly to the doctrines of countervailing power of Galbraith in his *American Capitalism*. Only François Perroux[17], it seems to me, has carried the systematic analysis of power and domination beyond the level of generality which it had reached in the writings of American institutionalists.

In harmony with their critique of the preconceptions and normative elements of neo-classical utility and price theory institutional economists have always shown a healthy scepticism towards those criteria in term of which business likes to evaluate its own success and efficiency of allocating scarce resources and in term of which traditional price theory also tends to ascertain the rationality and "optimality" of economic decisions. Institutionalists were among those earlier dissenters who pointed to such social costs as the destruction of the ecological balance, air and water pollution and similar harmful effects of private economic activities which tend to be shifted to third persons or to society as a whole. They analyzed relatively early the increasing significance of technology and overhead costs, the threat of excess and unused capacity and the resulting trend toward high pressure salesmanship, built-in obsolescence of consumer's goods and the pressure toward "unproductive" consumption in affluent societies. It seems to me that none of these increasingly

---

[17] Francois Perroux, The Domination Effect, *Social Research*, Vol. 17, 2 June 1950, pp. 188–206 and *L'Economie du XXe Siècle*, Paris 1964.

significant phenomena can be adequately accommodated by the traditional theory for example by putting them in Marshall's conceptual box of "externalities".

[10] Because most institutional economists share the value premises of the Age of Reason, they have rarely found it possible to confine themselves to a positivistic analysis of given conditions or an uncritical acceptance of the *status quo*. On the contrary, they have invariably felt it necessary to raise the question of the quality and the rationality of human and social life in a technical civilization. Indeed, institutional economists, unlike positive economists, are convinced that as social scientists commited to certain values they have a responsibility to indicate when and in which way socio-economic processes may endanger human values and human life.[18] In this sense I would not hestiate to characterize institutional economics as working within the tradition of a rational humanism which takes its stand for the preservation of human life and the full development of the human personality (Maslow) without any invidious reservations, whether conscious or unconscious, relating to class, color, creed or nationality.

4. Institutional Economics and the Development Process in Underdeveloped Areas

Having thus far identified the major preoccupations of institutional economics, I shall, in conclusion, try to indicate the institutional approach by a brief analysis of its potential contributions to the study of the development process in underdeveloped areas. I ought to warn you, however, that this part of my presentation reflects rather my own view as to the potentialities of institutionalism and no institutionalist living or dead should be blamed for its shortcomings.

Let me start with some of the more successful examples of economic development in recent times as illustrated by the cases of Japan, the Soviet Union and Israel. In each of these instances the discerning social scientist will soon discover that relatively high rates of capital formation and output-capital ratios and hence rates of economic growth can be accounted for only in terms of a complex interaction of economic and socio-cultural factors and powerful political elements. In short, the economic development process received some of its most important impulses from the social and political system; in other words the economic system was anything but isolated. Let me single out the highly exceptional and yet particularly instructive case of Israel. Its national and external political environment can hardly be said to have been favorable to economic development. And yet, "nowhere else in the Middle East and nowhere among the presently 'underdeveloped nations' can there be found a combination of cultural values, institutions, and linkages so conducive to rapid economic growth."[19] The cultural values in the case of Israel have included such important attitudes as "*nationalism*, based upon a burning sense of historical wrongs that have been suffered ... and the biblical vision of a return [11] to a "Holy Land" ... *instrumental activism*, the attitude that people can change the world instead of having to accept a predestined order; and *collectivism*, in

[18] C. E. Ayres, *Towards a Reasonable Society: The Values of Industrial Civilization*, Austin 1961.
[19] B. M. Gross, Planning as Crisis Management, Preface to Benjamin Akzin and Yehezkel Dror, *Israel-High Pressure Planning*, Syracuse 1966, reprinted in *Mitteilungen der List Gesellschaft*, Fasc. 6, Nr. 1, 1967, p. 18.

the sense of an orientation toward group action . . . rather than purely individual activity. The institutional structure of the Jewish community in Israel . . . has included a remarkable set of powerful trade unions, political parties, pressure groups and economic enterprises. . . . Finally, the country has enjoyed organized support from a large number of Jews in other countries—support that has evidenced itself not only in direct assistance but also in favorable action by the governments of these countries."[20]

A similar interaction of cultural values, institutions and economic factor although not necessarily of the same character and content can be identified in the case of Japan[21] and the Soviet Union as well as other Soviet-type economies. Conversely, the much less rapid rate of growth in some of the Arab countries, in India, Indonesia and many others can be accounted for in terms of institutionalized traditional value orientations and social arrangements which either may not give sufficient support to the development effort or may actually delay or even inhibit the process of development.

These factual conditions and their interpretation lead me to the conclusion that instead of viewing the development process as an isolated *economic* system, it would be more appropriate to view it, particularly in traditional societies, from the very outset as part of a complex social system with various components in mutual or circular interaction.

Anybody who has had first hand experience with traditional societies has been impressed not only by the fundamental differences between *their* social systems and those of modern societies but also by the high degree of internal coherence of their patterns of ideas, values, and their Socio-political arrangements. Their patterns of motivation, their attitudes, knowledge, technology, the power system and the kinship system *do* represent more or less organized entities. Let me be specific: Fatalistic or even animistic world views support disbeliefs in opportunities for improvements: they are correlated with pre-scientific systems of knowledge and a technology which account for the relatively low productivity of labor and capital goods in farming thereby making it necessary to retain a high percentage of the population in agricultural production in order to provide the necessary agricultural products. This in turn reinforces and perpetuates a power system of which the prevailing land tenancy relations are only the most obvious manifestations. This power system affects not only the distribution of the national product; it also limits the internal purchasing power, restricts the extent of domestic markets for manufactured products and accounts for the absence of sufficiently strong incentives for modernization. Add to this power system a pattern of traditional values which

[12] attribute considerable importance to expenditures for ceremonial, ostentatious and national prestige or even war purposes and you will find the reason why the domestic rate of saving and investment remains inadequate or why the nation's potential investible surplus is not adequately mobilized and utilized for productive purposes. At the same time the still relatively high death rate, together with the household

---

[20] Ibid., p. 18.
[21] Takekazu Ogura, ed., *Agricultural Development in Modern Japan*, Tokyo, Japan FAO Association, 1963 and Tobata, S. ed., *The Modernization of Japan*, Vol. I, Tokyo, The Institute of Asian Economic Affairs, 1966.

or peasant character[22] of the agricultural sector, and probably other factors related to traditional patterns of values and attitudes continue to put a premium on the maintenance of an extended family system which favors high fertility.[23]

Of course, all this sounds like the famous vicious circle and, indeed it is precisely this. But it is at the same time an illustration of the institutional or social system character of the process of underdevelopment and development. It illustrates the impact of the process of circular causation on economic development; it suggests a framework of analysis which does *not* single out one or two factors as the primary causes of the process.

As far as the theoretical representation of the process of circular causation is concerned, I agree with Myrdal that "the ideal solution would be to formulate the functional relationships between the various parts in the form of an inter-connected set of equations describing the movement—and the internal changes—of the system studied under the various influences which are at work in it."[24] I doubt, however, that the type of mathematics needed for the formulation of equations and coefficients describing the relationships of the process of mutual interaction of the various subsystems in a social system is yet at hand.[25] Moreover, I doubt, as Myrdal incidentally also does, that we will be able, in the foreseeable future, to acquire the complete and quantitative information required for a representation of the fundamental relationship in the form of an interconnected set of equations describing the structure and the internal changes of a social system. However, even without such complete and precise knowledge the institutional approach can contri-bute a good deal not only to the diagnosis but also to the planning of the development process. Even explanations in principle of the nature of relevant relationships or the general direction of the possible changes can be of considerable importance. One thing seems to me to be certain: any search for a primary cause of development must be regarded as futile—as futile indeed as the conventional concentration on the rate of investment as the determining factor of development. Instead, what
13] is needed, and all one can hope for, is to be able to identify derisive strategic factors, i.e. factors which can be more easily influenced than others and are them-selves capable of changing the pattern of interaction in the direction of economic development. My own hunch is that improvements in technology, in land use and tenancy relations, measures designed to reduce inequalities of opportunities, tech-niques to control the birth rate, improvement in education and public administration offer such possibilities of change and as such constitute strategic factors. There

---

[22] In Chajanov's sense of the term. Cf. A. V. Chajanov, *The Theory of Peasant Economy*, New York, 1966.

[23] Kingsley Davis, Institutional Patterns Favouring High Fertility in Underdeveloped Areas, *Eugenics Quarterly*, Vol. 2, No. 1 March 1955, pp. 33–39 reprinted in Lyle W. Shanon, *Underdeveloped Areas*, New York 1957, pp. 88–95.

[24] Gunnar Myrdal, *Economic Theory and Under-Developed Regions*, London 1957, p. 19.

[25] Certainly the mathematics of the calculus and of differential equations which are adequate for the description of tendencies towards stable equilibria offer no solution to the analytical description of the process of circular or inextricable interdependencies "where cause and effect interweave", as Pareto called it. See V. Pareto, On the Economic Phenomenon—A Reply to Benedetto Croce, reprinted in *International Economic Papers*, No. 3, New York, 1953, p. 185.

may be others which an empirical study of specific social systems in concrete societies may be able to identify.

Social systems do attain states of relative constancy in which the system as a whole does not change its character. In fact, this constancy may be a state of stagnation in which even stimulating impulses (as for example new techniques) may be counteracted by the inhibitory effects of institutions, cultural values, attitudes, power systems and other elements. However, such states of constancy are no guarantee against the emergence of disturbances. In fact, the very inertia of the system may create disturbances such as population pressures and famines. It is under the pressure of such disturbances that social systems may be compelled to change and to adapt themselves by producing new institutional arrangements. In fact, such adaptations seem to me to be the *prerequisite* of change and development. In other words, social systems have a dynamics;[26] they are in process in the course of which there emerge internal tensions and conflicts between different components of the system. While extreme forms of conflict may destroy a social system—other conflicts and internal tensions tend to set in motion the essential dialectical process through which a creative adaptation of the system to new conditions may take place. Let me add, however, that this is not a simple teleological three step dialectics of thesis, antithesis and synthesis as envisioned by Hegel and Marx, but a much more complex dialectical process with more than one conceivable outcome.

In short, it seems to me that the institutionalist's view of the development process as a social system with several components in circular interaction could provide an alternative to the conventional approach to the study of economic development. Not only does it offer an explanation for many failures of particular development projects and plans but, properly interpreted, could also yield pragmatic indicators for a more successful planning of such projects and of development efforts in general. An illustration may serve to make this point clear. Preindustrial societies with traditional forms of agriculture, land-tenancy systems, and rates of population growth between 3 and 4 per cent are facing formidable problems the full complexity of which can be grasped only in terms of a social system approach. For, all indications point to the conclusion that given their knowledge and technology (as reflected in the available capital goods such as plant and animal varieties and their agricultural

[14] techniques), given their climatic and soil condition, given their inherited land-tenancy systems as well as credit and marketing organization, given their rates of increase of the number of persons seeking employment, these traditional economies have by and large exhausted the range of their economically profitable investment opportunities in the field of agriculture. Therefore, neither the reliance on private profit incentives, nor the improvement of present marketing and market structures nor the provision of a better infrastructure (irrigation systems, roads etc.), nor institutional reforms, nor even the simple transfer of the highly sophisticated western agricultural methods and technology *taken separately* can be expected to be sufficient or effective. Viewed as a process of circular interdependencies economic underdevelopment can be overcome only by a combination of specific measures designed

---

[26] On the dynamics of social systems see the pertinent observations of B. M Gross, *The State of the Nation—Social Systems Accounting* (Social Science Paperbacks) London 1966, pp. 30–33.

to bring about the modernization of a traditional agricultural society. The following steps may offer a way out of the dilemma: 1) the development of an agricultural technology by creating new varieties of plans (and animal stock) which under the specific climatic and natural conditions of particular regions would make it possible to overcome the present stagnation of yields per acre: 2) the widespread diffusion of the technical knowledge required to make use of and protect these new capital goods, 3) the choice—as far as possible—of labor intensive methods of cultivation, 4) measures of land reform in the most comprehensive sense of the term, 5) the creation of the strategic infrastructure including the provision of a dependable supply of water as well as transport and distribution facilities and 6) the reform of the present agricultural tax system. I shall mention the necessary industrialization of the economy only in passing despite its obvious importance as a means to reduce the dependence on imports and to provide opportunities for useful employment for the increasing army of unemployed. In short, by stressing the mutual interaction of a complex of components, the social system approach to economic development not only induces us to stay closer to the "facts" but will help us to develop workable indicators for a more adequate strategy of development planning than any conventional theory formulated in terms of purely economic variables.

Before concluding these observations it may be useful to raise briefly the question of the relationship between institutional economics and the conventional model approach to the study of economic processes. It may be argued that both approaches stress the system character of the economy. Both identify a number of components of a given situation and aim at a conceptual representation of interrelationships. In this general sense, there are of course similarities between the two approaches which stem from the fact that all science is interested in identifying the relevant components of a "problematical" situation and to show that and how these components "hang together". However, the fact remains that the institutional approach, unlike the conventional model approach, considers the economy from the very outset as a part of a larger sociocultural entity, a fact which calls—as we have [15] pointed out—for special categories, concepts and theories.

Nevertheless, it might still be argued that the whole difference between the institutional and the model approach to the study of economic development boils down to a broadening of the framework of analysis and the incorporation of additional variables and additional sets of equation into the model. Take for instance the various consistency models which relate the rate of growth (g) with the rate of capital formation (α) and the average rate of productivity of investments (β) i.e. the marginal output-capital ratio. No one will deny the formal, tautological correctness of the relationship $g = \alpha \times \beta$ under given conditions of techniques, skills, attitudes and knowledge and other factors which, at any given time determine the rate of investment and the productivity of labor and capital goods. The institutionalist may indeed be said to be concerned with the analysis of these latter factors which influence the rate of capital formation, the average productivity and hence the rate of growth. He raises questions which the conventional model builder does not raise. In this sense it is indeed possible to say that he broadens the framework of analysis. This way of interpreting the relationship between institutional economics and the construction of models would not be objectionable if the functional relationship which exists between the many components which make α and β what they are, could actually be expressed in the form of algebraic functions. I have indicated why I believe that this solution will escape us at least for the foreseeable future. We have neither the mathematics nor the needed factual knowledge and measurements of the relevant relations.

There is one additional reason which makes it problematical to incorporate the institutional approach into the traditional growth models or vice versa. Consistency models operate with such aggregates as savings, investments, capital formation, productivity of investment or for that matter with productive capacity, employment, unemployment and underemployment. These aggregates may have a precise, ascertainable and hence measurable content in the reality of market economies. In non-market, traditional economies savings and investments as well as productivity and employment and particularly underemployment are much less easily determinable.

The institutionalist is convinced that the indeterminacy and the lack of precision are only partly the result of gaps in our knowledge about the relevant causal relations. They constitute rather an inescapable residuum of indeterminacy which has its basis in the factual conditions, and is inherent in the inextricable interdependencies and the lack of homogeneous human valuations.[27] The attempt to overcome this inescapable indeterminacy by formulating concepts with greater precision than is justified by the factual conditions would be evidence not of logical clarity but [16] of logical error and of hidden bias—i.e. a kind of loose thinking which is detrimental to scientific analysis. These considerations concerning the inescapable indeterminacy of many aggregate concepts and measurements used in models of the conventional variety raise serious questions not only with regard to their relevance and adequacy but also with regard to the alleged compatibility of the institutional approach and of conventional Wisdom.

5. Summary and Conclusions

I hope to have succeeded not only in defending institutional economics against its critics but also to have shown that institutionalism offers a way out of the present impasse into which our discipline has been led by a misuse of abstraction from social reality. Far from reflecting a naive empiricism and far from any hostility to theorizing, institutionalism views the economy as an open system the analysis of which calls for new categories, concepts and perspectives which must be found outside the conventional apparatus of static and teleological theories. Thus institutionalists have developed, as an alternative to the concept and the theory of stable equilibrium, the principle of circular causation as a basic theoretical framework in terms of which it is possible to arrive at a generalized explication and understanding of the *modus operandi* of complex open social systems including their structural changes.

In addition, institutionalists have been preoccupied with such unorthodox issues as the role of conflict, coercion and power in economic life; they are doubtful about market prices as an index of individual and social welfare and as criteria

---

[27] On this whole problem see Gunner Myrdal, "Valued Loaded" Concepts, in H. Hegeland (ed.), *Money, Growth and Methodology*, Essays in Honor of J. Åkerman, Lund 1962, pp. 273–275 and Paul Streeten, The Use and Abuse of Models in Development Planning, in *The Teaching of Development Economics* (eds. Kurt Martin and John Knapp), London 1967, pp. 60–65.

of substantive efficiency in allocating scarce resources; they have explored the phenomena of social costs and they have placed major emphasis on the role which science, shared knowledge and technology play as determinants of the productivity of human labor and capital goods and, finally, they are committed to a critical analysis of the quality of individual and social life in a technical civilization.

It seems to me that institutional economics needs not so much a defense as a systematization. For if the critics of institutional economics are wrong in regarding it as hostile to theory, they are correct in pointing out that institutionalism is not yet a systematic body of thought. I do not think that either the nature of the subject matter or gaps in our knowledge make such a systematization impossible. It may be due rather to the fact that as dissenters institutionalists have been preoccupied with a host of issues and have certainly not written the kind of massive textbooks which end to systematize and to perpetuate a dominant school. While this may have protected them against a premature dogmatization of their ideas, it has laid them open to a partially legitimate questioning of the coherence of their concepts and theories. I think that the time is ripe for a systematization of institutional economic thought.

[17]   Apart from this, one of the most urgent needs for institutional economists today is to overcome their relative isolation. Instead of withdrawing into the lonely position of the dissenter they will have to work together in closer contact not only with one another but also with other social scientists because they will have to know more of what is known in related social disciplines than the pure economist.

Above all, they must not permit the weight of the conventional wisdom to silence them. While they must maintain an appropriate humility before the manifold problems and their complexity—this humility does not justify an undue defensiveness about their position and their work. For even if some of their conclusions may remain imprecise it is better to have imprecise or approximate answers to the right questions than to have precise answers to the wrong questions.[28] I would go even one step further. I think that the time has come for institutionalists in developed and underdeveloped countries to unite and to become more assertative than the majority of institutional economists, with few notable exceptions, have been in the past. They need not shout or become strident in their arguments, but they [18] should not mumble.[29]

[28] Peter Wiles, *The Political Economy of Communism*, Cambridge 1962, pp. 246–247
[29] D.F. Dowd, On Veblen, Mills and the Decline and Criticism, *Dissent* (Winter, 1964), p. 37.

[8]

Jei *JOURNAL OF ECONOMIC ISSUES*
Vol. XV   No. 3   September 1981

The Compulsive Shift to
Institutional Analysis

Marc R. Tool

Over the last half-century, the pervasive grip of the Marshallian/Hicksian orthodoxy on the minds and hearts of an increasing number of economists and policy makers appears to have relaxed, despite, perhaps, desires to the contrary. Untoward and pervasive events and circumstances have produced successive and urgent demands for divergent and more relevant social, political, and economic policy responses. The Great Depression was the forcing bed for the Keynesian revolutionary formulations. World War II required the advent of aggregate integrative planning and control of a war economy. The conspicuous emergence of the post colonial Third World generated an ambitious, and at times heretical, quest to invoke and accelerate growth and development in poor countries. The domestic concern to reactivate the economy and make war on poverty in the 1960s led to the use and refinement of Keynesian-based "fine tuning" demand management and to an attack on structural malfunctions in the economy. The convulsive and worsening instability of concurrent unemployment and inflation, especially in the last decade, has forced attentive theorists and policy framers out of habitual views into what is for them new, unfamiliar, and uncharted areas of the unconventional and the unorthodox.

It is a contention of this article that the aforementioned events and

The author is Professor of Economics, California State University, Sacramento. This article is a shortened version of the Presidential Address delivered to the Association for Institutional Thought, Albuquerque, New Mexico, April 1980.

circumstances, among others, and the scholarly and analytical efforts prompted thereby have been, and are now, contributing to a profound paradigm shift in political economy. The economists' abiding commitment to develop and apply theory that is relevant, directly or indirectly, to the great issues and problems of the day is driving economists out of orthodoxy and into other positions. Some of these are similar to or compatible with the positions institutional theorists (Thorstein Veblen, John Dewey, Clarence Ayres, Gardiner Means, and so forth) have been evolving over this century. The shift is compulsive in the sense that the necessity of claiming pertinence to crucial problems of the day compels movement out of and beyond the mainstream conventional wisdom. The shift does not appear to be intended to engineer a premeditated change in paradigm. The departures from orthodoxy that are noted here usually are seen as nothing more than corrections in or addenda to orthodoxy.

Many have observed the disjunction among those economists who proclaim their commitment to neoclassical orthodoxy and the market mentality, but who ignore, compromise, or subvert that commitment when they come to deliberate on and recommend public economic policy. The rigor and rationality of the orthodox model and the efficiency of unfettered market forces often are extolled in principle by the same individuals who recommend policies that manipulate markets, money stocks, prices, and income flows, that is, manage the economic process to produce consequences they favor. These overt acts are sometimes rationalized as generating consequences comparable to what would have occurred had there been competitive markets. And in the advocacy of, or the acquiescence in, such policy shifts, positivist economists become practicing normativists, that is, they are engaged in deciding what proper policy ought to be.

The fact of the disjunction can hardly be in dispute. The position developed here acknowledges that contradictory posture and suggests that the shift is not merely away from orthodoxy, but is generally in the direction of institutional thought.[1] Will we, a decade or so hence, hear all economists proclaim they are institutionalists? Perhaps not, but intellectual honesty and consistency might recommend such an assertion. If the selected cases herein discussed turn out to be representative of the whole, institutionalism may well become the successor to neoclassical orthodoxy, although probably under another name.

What follows are examples of compulsive shifts to congruency or correspondence with institutional analysis. Three primary areas of inquiry and focus have been chosen: the Keynesian revolution and contribution; the "stagflation" crises and responses thereto; and methodological and psychological erosions in and departures from orthodoxy. We must be content with indicative instances; we cannot presume definitiveness.

The Keynesian Revolution

John Maynard Keynes concluded the Preface to *The General Theory* by saying: "The composition of this book has been for the author a long struggle of escape . . . from habitual modes of thought and expression."[2] Those "habitual modes" were, of course, the postulates, principles, and policy recommendations of classical and neoclassical theory in which he was trained. Keynes acknowledged his struggle to escape from the smothering embrace of orthodoxy; he appeared unaware that his shift in "modes of thought and expression" was in significant degree in the direction of the Veblen-Dewey-Ayres tradition in institutional economics.[3] Students of his career know well that his "struggle of escape" did not begin with the writing of *The General Theory*; it is reflected in virtually all of his published work from World War I onward.

For present purposes, attention is invited to four foci of convergence of Keynes's thought and institutional analysis: method and scope of inquiry, concern with institutional adjustment, focus on political economy, and instrumental value theory.

Method and Scope

Keynes's approach to inquiry was a self-conscious concern to formulate theory, or revisions of theory, to guide conduct in problematic situations. The question of relevance never arose; it was obvious to him that relevance derives from the applicability of analysis to real problems. Keynes was no ivory tower resident and no pursuer of esoteric knowledge. As do institutionalists who follow Dewey, Keynes perceived the inescapable necessity of employing both deductive and inductive modes of reasoning. He castigated David Ricardo and gave accolades to Thomas Malthus because the former failed to grasp and the latter recognized the limitations of a deductive bias. Although Ricardo provided theory that he and his peers perceived as relevant to his day, he offered only the deductive half of the methodological loaf. Malthus identified the insufficiency; Keynes recognized its historic significance. "Ricardo . . . by turning his back so completely on Malthus's ideas, constrained the subject for a full hundred years in an artificial groove."[4]

Keynes did not dichotomize theory and fact; for him, there was no divorcement between pure and applied theory. He, as do the institutionalists, sought theory that actually explained observed phenomena. With, and only with, improved understanding, predictive judgments *might* be advanced. His analytical grasp was sufficiently firm and extensive to permit him, for example, accurately to warn of the economic consequences of the reparation settlements after World War I and to anticipate social unrest following Great Britain's return to the gold standard in the 1920s.

As with imaginative scholars generally, Keynes was prepared to create or modify intellectual tools or constructs (for example, the marginal efficiency of capital[5]) or to adapt theorems (such as the investment multiplier) as the formulations and refinements of his analysis required. His inquiry into the areas of his interests was open ended and nondoctrinaire.

In scope, Keynes's *General Theory* is not, of course, a general theory of the economic process for which Veblen called.[6] But it is a general theory of the determinants of the level of real income. That is, Keynes sought to identify and to explore interrelations of all of the major causal elements that determine the level of production. As Gladys Meyers Foster has suggested, Keynes's theory of real income determination, although less inclusive, does not materially contradict the more general theory of the economic process of the institutionalists.[7] Indeed, with the further development of each, they may be expected to move toward congruency.

Moreover, Keynes did not delimit the reach of his inquiry *a priori*. He sought determinants within and without orthodoxy as mandated by his overriding concern to understand the actual determinants of real problems. Although, with the advantage of hindsight, Keynes's positions in *The General Theory* may at times appear inadequate, he nevertheless did extend the scope of his analysis to include psychological expectations as behavioral determinants. And although he acknowledged the fact of profit motive, he recognized that it is an acquired, not an inherent or natural, trait.[8] In addition, as is explored below, Keynes abandoned the traditional divorcement and antagonism of the public and private sectors (politics and economics) and formulated a heretical theory recommending continuing political participation in the economic process in the pursuit of full employment.

Keynes clearly set off his own inquiry mode from that of formal mechanistic model builders: "The object of our analysis is, not to provide a machine or method of blind manipulation, which will furnish an infallible answer, but to provide ourselves with an organized and orderly method of thinking out particular problems."[9]

Keynes's focus was on expectations and uncertainties, not on predictions and certitudes. The latter reflect a mechanical focus for which mathematical precision is sought; the former are amenable to analysis and perhaps to modification or management, but they are not precisely pre-dictable. The diversity and complexity of actual determinants preclude dependence upon simplistic model building and linear "rationality."[10]

Institutional Adjustment

Keynes applied, although he evidently did not formulate, a distinction used by institutionalists between economic function and economic struc-ture—between the process or flow of real income and the institutional arrangements through which it is accomplished. As with the institutional-ists and with Karl Polanyi,[11] Keynes's work reflects the recognition that continuity in the provision of the material means of life must be sustained (at times, restored) and that prescriptive and proscriptive patterns of correlated behavior (institutions) must be modified in order for that to occur. The economic function is and must be continuous and develop-mental; the institutional structure is and must be discontinuous and re-placemental at points of disjunction or breakdown.[12]

Keynes unequivocally acknowledged that problems cannot be resolved without institutional adjustment, even though he did not present a theory of institutional adjustment as such. For Keynes, institutions were inven-tions of the human intellect created for specific tasks. Recall that in *The General Theory* he was prepared to see the retention of some of the cap-italist institutional structure because, as he saw it, it was *not* the source or locus of the problem of depression. That which *was* identified in his theory as problematic structure (high interest rates, low inducements to private investment, laissez-faire attitudes, patterns of inequality of income distribution, role of the renter) would require modification or abandon-ment if the removal of involuntary unemployment were to be achieved.

In accord with institutionalists, Keynes neither identified nor recom-mended institutions that are allegedly natural (therefore "given" and in-vulnerable to adjustment), divinely sanctioned, or mandated by doctri-naire ideology. He did not take institutions as fixed; they are products of discretionary acts of usually identifiable persons. Keynes did aspire to be among those who recommend structural change, however.

Putting the matter another way, Keynes's mode of inquiry and views of institutional change appear not to be vulnerable to the charges Veblen made against late-nineteenth-century neoclassicism. Veblen described orthodoxy as exhibiting characteristics of teleology, tautology, taxonomy, and hedonism, all of which were pre-Darwinian in origin and unaccep-table.[13] Keynes's position does not rest on the presumption that the econ-omy is a natural order teleologically working out its own inherent and natural "ends." His running attack on laissez-faire makes this clear. Keynes's analysis does not tautologically reaffirm the assumptions and structure with which it begins. "Its assumptions and its fundamental determinants as well as the patterns of causation which it sets forth are subject to evidential verification and correction. And its conclusions are not simply the validation of its assumptions."[14] Keynes's overall position manifests recognition of the economic process in an historical and cultural setting; the analysis is not taxonomically static and status quo reinforcing, even though his theory of income and employment is sometimes characterized as short-run, static analysis. Finally, Keynes's writing acknowledges the fact of hedonistic self-serving and profit maximization, but, as noted above, such motivations and attitudes are simply cultural facts, not natural and inherent attributes or traits of persons. And they do not constitute the meaning of "rationality." Perhaps there is more "daylight" between Keynes and the orthodox theorists than has been thought.

Political Economy

Throughout Keynes's long career as public servant, scholar-teacher, and theorist, he attempted to write the epitaph for laissez-faire. As with such institutionalists as Veblen, Dewey, John R. Commons, Wesley Mitchell, Means, Ayres, Gunnar Myrdal, and J. K. Galbraith, among others, Keynes at no time accepted the dichotomous separation of the public and private sectors. In *The End of Laissez Faire*, he sought to repudiate the tenets that support laissez-faire and this orthodox separation. "Let us clear from the ground," he urged, "the metaphysical or general principles upon which, from time to time, *laissez-faire* has been founded. It is *not* true that individuals possess a prescriptive natural liberty in their economic activities. There is *no* compact conferring perpetual rights on those who Have or on those who Acquire. The world is *not* so governed from above that private and social interest always coincide. . . . It is *not* a correct deduction from the Principles of Economics that enlightened self-interest always operates in the public interest. . . . Experience does *not* show that individuals, when they make up a social unit, are always less clear-sighted than when they act separately."[15] An institutionalist will find little to fault in the foregoing.

Returning to the language of Jeremy Bentham, but rejecting Bentham's view that governments are necessarily "pernicious," Keynes suggested that "perhaps the chief task of Economists at this hour is to distinguish afresh the *Agenda* of Government from the *Non-Agenda*; and the com-

panion task of Politics is to devise forms of Government within a Democracy which shall be capable of accomplishing the *Agenda*."[16] Clearly
implied is the idea that the functions or tasks of government, *including*
its involvement (not "intrusion") in the economy, must continuously
be revised in response to emergent problems. Keynes's "agenda" is neither
formally given (as in socialism) nor delimited or proscribed (as in capitalism). Government need not be a threat; it might be a promise. The
government's role is emergent and evolving as a source and site of institutional adjustment.

Keynes's biographer, Roy Harrod, suggests that Keynes's life-long interest in reform efforts began when he was still an undergraduate at
Cambridge: "The view asserted to be Liberal was assuredly Maynard's
throughout his life. He believed that distress in all its forms should not
go unheeded. He believed that, by care and pains, all our social evils,
distressed areas, unemployment and the rest, could be abolished. He believed in planning and contriving."[17]

Consistent with this view, in *The General Theory* Keynes recognized
the probable need for "the State" to accept responsibility for invoking
"central controls" in order to help establish "an aggregate volume of output corresponding to full employment, as nearly as practicable."[18]
Keynes's analysis anticipates a private sector shortfall in generating sufficient consumption and investment spending to provide full employment.
He suggested that the propensity to consume might be enhanced through
public policy. He expected, and accepted the prospect, that the state will
increasingly find it necessary to socialize investment. In the closing pages
of *The General Theory*, his suggested or implied reforms go farther—to
the contemplated "euthanasia of the rentier" and a reduction in the degree
of inequality of income distribution.[19] In a moderately favorable comment
on Friedrich von Hayek's *The Road to Serfdom*, Keynes nevertheless
suggested the desirability and need for economic planning.[20] He supported
the Beveridge Plan for the introduction of comprehensive social services
in post–World War II Great Britain.[21] Accordingly, for Keynes, although
the economic and political processes are distinguishable, they are not
separable. Analysis must encompass political economy. Political policy
is often addressed to the revamping of economic institutions.

Instrumental Value Theory

To suggest that Keynesian theory incorporates a de facto and unan-
nounced shift from the utility value principle of orthodoxy to an instrumental theory of social value commensurate with that which emerges from

the institutionalists Veblen, Dewey, Ayres, and J. Fagg Foster is to offer an atypical but profoundly significant inference.[22] It is the burden here to demonstrate that Keynes was a practicing normativist, not a positivist, to note value positions to which he evidently did not or would not subscribe, and to show the extent to which he actually employed the instrumental value principle of the institutionalists. For present purposes, that principle is identified as "the continuity of human life and the noninvidious re-creation of community through the instrumental use of knowledge."[23]

That Keynes was a practicing normativist needs little defense or elaboration. Virtually all his academic and public life was devoted to the formulation and application of theory to permit or facilitate the resolution of real problems. Accordingly, he distinguished in scores of settings a difference between what is and what ought to be. Of course, it is both logically and operationally *impossible* to distinguish between the two without *applying* a criterion of judgment—a social value principle. Since Keynes's career is replete with policy recommendations for substantive institutional adjustment—revision of the Versailles treaty, scaling down of reparations, abandonment of the gold standard, invocation of compensatory fiscal policy, introduction of a deferred income scheme during World War II,[24] establishment of the World Bank and the International Monetary Fund—he is indeed a practicing, de facto normativist.

Moreover, as Dudley Dillard has recently shown, there is extensive similarity between Veblen and Keynes in a number of areas.[25] Central to Dillard is the substantial commonality in their respective monetary theories of production. Of more immediate interest here is the related matter of Keynes's tacit acceptance of the Veblenian distinction as a judgmental premise.[26] Says Dillard: "Keynes's categories, Industry and Finance, are cognates of Veblen's Industrial and Pecuniary Employments."[27] For each, industrial activity is normatively approved; financial or pecuniary activity is normatively disapproved. Differing forms of the Veblenian distinction permeate all of Veblen's writings;[28] a comparable distinction permeates Keynes's writings, for he "remained critical of speculation, the gold standard, policies of the Bank of England, and the rentier, or absentee owners."[29]

The convergence of the tacit value theories of Keynes and Veblen is also revealed in their similar concepts of economic waste. Keynes's statement about filling "old bottles with banknotes," burying "them at suitable depths," and leaving them "to private enterprise on well tried principles of laissez faire to dig up" is in contrast to his observation that it would "be more sensible to build houses and the like"; he is making an ethical judgment on economic activity. Keynes's references to the "virtues" of "pyramid building" and the search for precious metals in ancient Egypt and his satirization of investment decision making as the counterpart of playing Old Maid also imply normative assessment of behavior.[30] Similarly, Veblen's *Theory of the Leisure Class* is replete with examples of waste, especially among the elite in the form of "conspicuous consumption," "invidious display," and the like. Such practices, he observed, are emulated by others.[31]

That Keynes's thought and conduct reflected rejection of a variety of noninstrumental criteria may also be inferred with a minimum of defense. First, Keynes was no conservative; he did not use what is as a criterion of what ought to be. Second, despite undergraduate contact with G. E. Moore, Keynes did not share Moore's view that the "good" is and must be "indefinable."[32] Third, Keynes did not make normative use of the competitive model. His willingness to recommend or allow for the continuance of some capitalist institutions (distributive arrangements, private property, and so forth) is to be judged by his provisional acceptance of their then current performance, not on some *a priori* basis of their naturalness or inevitable efficiency. He did not presume that departures from the competitive market are "bad" per se and that closer approximations are necessarily "good." Fourth, he seemed not to use pecuniary criteria in identifying what ought to be. Profit maximization is not necessarily a success indicator. "There is no clear evidence from experience," he argued, "that investment policy which is socially advantageous coincides with that which is most profitable."[33] Price, as such, is not a measure of economic worth. Fifth, Keynes, although himself from what many might call an elitist background, appeared not to use class, status, wealth, rank, position, or ancestry as criteria of appraisal. Sixth, his frequent denigrative comments on authoritarian politics obviously implied his unwillingness to permit the achievement and use of coercive power as the meaning or measure of what ought to be. Finally, human differences of sex, creed, color, and the like, were not given a definitive or discriminatory standing and converted into judgmental determinants of structural change in Keynes's work.

Keynes's tacit acceptance of instrumental value theory is implicit in his rejection of the foregoing noninstrumental and anti-instrumental criteria. These rejected criteria would be characterized as "invidious" by Veblen or "ceremonial" by Ayres.[34] In reference to the instrumental value principle as identified above, "the continuity of human life" is reflected in Keynes's career-long quest for genuine solutions to real problems and situations that threatened continuity. Examples of such threats include pervasive and extensive involuntary unemployment, economic determi-

nants of warfare, the effect of domestic instability on international harmony, monetary determinants of economic instability, and the like. The
"noninvidious re-creation of community" is implied by Keynes's specific
unwillingness to be deferential to the discriminatory use of wealth, economic power, self-aggrandizement, rentier status, and so forth, in deciding
whose interests matter or count. Indeed, his opening sentence of the last
chapter of *The General Theory* (on social philosophy) asserts that "the
outstanding faults of the economic society in which we live are its failure
to provide for full employment and its arbitrary and inequitable distribution of wealth and income."[35] Communities are factionated and demoral-
ized by extensive and continuing unemployment and substantial maldis-
tribution of income and wealth.

Finally, "the instrumental use of knowledge" is manifested in Keynes's
creative mauling and modification of orthodoxy in his pursuit of a credible theory of real income determination. Other areas of orthodoxy not
deemed problematic were left unaddressed. Keynes developed new knowledge and modified and adapted old knowledge in order to achieve more
definitive understanding. He engaged in conceptual tool and idea combining activities in his area of interest, reflecting Ayres's view of the
cumulative growth of knowledge.[36] Keynes's theory building tacitly reflects the awareness that "instrumental" addresses the appropriateness,
fitness, and relevance of the conceptual tool in its role and capacity of
explaining phenomena. "Instrumental use" implies both functional pertinence and normative admissibility. Two illustrations are the relevance
and use of both the bacterial theory of disease for public health measures
and the Keynesian theory of income determination for compensatory,
economic stabilization measures. Keynes made instrumental use of knowledge.

The foregoing suggests that with reference to method of inquiry, institutional adjustment, political economy, and tacit employment of instrumental value theory, Keynes was, if inadvertently, engaged in moving
from orthodox neoclassicism in the direction of institutional analysis.

Stagflation

The chronic inflation and concurrent unemployment of the 1970s—
stagflation—continues into the 1980s. Economists remain substantially
engaged in an almost ten-year agonized soul-searching over this unorthodox aberration as the profession seeks to modify theory and alter policy
recommendations to sustain its credibility and usefulness. This pursuit
of the relevant has led some macro-theorists and national policy advisers

to formulate analyses and changes in policy that reflect a shift not only from orthodoxy but also, inadvertently, toward correspondence to, if not congruity with, elements of institutional theory. The following observations concerning the views of some macro-theorists are indicative of this shift.

Walter Heller's Presidential Address to the American Economic Association, "What's Right with Economics,"[37] brought the agonies and the issues into focus in the mid-1970s. He described the efforts of economists to revise both their models and their recommendations to bring them into accord with realities of the day. In the course of his commentary, he pointed the direction for a substantial break from orthodoxy by identifying three different sources of inflation. One is the familiar excess demand argument. A second is the price-wage-price spiral. A third is the "external-shock or special-sector" or "commodity-price surges."[38] The first responds to conventional (since Keynes) monetary-fiscal pressure. The second responds "more reluctantly" to such constraints. "The third is highly resistent to demand management measures."[39] Moreover, the third generates the most adverse consequences. Both the second and the third forms of inflation compel economists to breach orthodoxy and begin to address the locus and use of economic power in wage and price setting and its inflationary consequences; some institutionalists have long argued for this approach.[40]

Among others, the late Arthur Okun's analyses make even more obvious than Heller's comments the approaching correspondence with institutional thought. Over the last few years, Okun moved closer to institutional thought in at least three areas: market pricing, economic power, and implicit value theory.[41]

Market Pricing

Okun and others recognized well that mainstream orthodoxy is no longer the general theory of the economic process. The major part of that conventional general theory (following Alfred Marshall) in effect prescribed a myopic and normative focus on market pricing under competitive conditions to foster efficient allocation of scarce means among alternative and unlimited ends. Elements of Keynes's views (after the exorcising of threatening corollaries and heresies) were wedded to this tradition by Paul Samuelson as the postwar "grand synthesis." It is this Marshall-Keynes orthodoxy that is disintegrating, and stagflation is providing the eroding wave action. The "new problem [of stagflation] requires the additional help of new remedies, which of necessity are unconventional and unproved," said Okun. "We cannot count on our current policies to pull us out of the stagflation swamp. The evidence of recent years has accumulated and become overwhelming. . . . The time has come to face the likelihood that we have a losing hand and to deal a new one."[42] Conventional theory simply does not permit an adequate analysis of the concurrent crises of unemployment and inflation.

For Okun, the central heretical fact was that most prices and wages are not set in competitive "organized auction markets" where supply and demand theory applies. This is but "a small and shrinking sector of the U.S. economy. . . . Most of our economy is dominated by cost-oriented prices and equity-oriented wages. Most prices are set by sellers whose principal concern is to maintain customers and market share over the long run. . . . Prices are set to exceed costs by a percentage markup that displays only minor variations over the business cycle."[43] Sellers do not merely respond to a price set by the market; they administer price as an overt decision subject to whatever constraints are operative at the time.

Joan Robinson has recently come to a similar conclusion. After observing that it is "rare for the 'free play of market forces' to be entirely free," she goes on to describe how "manufacturers set prices for themselves" by employing the "full cost principle."[44] This principle connotes discretionary control over prices, which are set to cover all costs plus a profit margin at whatever the market will bear.

Similarly, wages do not move up and down as markets adjust supplies of workers to the fluctuating demand of employers. The latter set wages with long-term interests in mind. According to Okun, "the key to wage decisions in both union and nonunion areas is the common long-run interest of skilled workers and employers in maintaining their job relationships. Employers make investments in a trained, reliable, and loyal work force as well as in plant and equipment. They know that if they curbed wages stringently in a slump, they would pay heavily for that strategy with swollen quit rates during the next period of prosperity. Thus, during recession and slack periods, nonunion firms with workers on layoff and queues of eager job applicants find it worthwhile to raise the wages of their workers, in order to protect their longer term personnel relationships."[45] More recently, Okun elaborated this theme with a defense of "the theory of implicit contracts" and the concept of "the invisible handshake."[46]

The point has recently been made even more directly and unequivocally by Gardner Ackley. In the context of examining the redistributive effects of inflation, Ackley asserts: "In modern economies almost all wages and the bulk of all prices are 'administered' rather than market clearing. They change only periodically, through discrete decisions made by individuals or groups that possess varying degrees of market power (and hold particular price level expectations). Those who decide are applying their particular 'policies'—practical rules of thumb, usually reflecting some concept of 'equity.' "[47] When Ackley considers the inflationary implications of this institutional characteristic, he comes strikingly close to a theory of "administered inflation" as developed by Gardiner Means and others of the institutional school.[48] Continues Ackley: "Some of us believe that an important force making our economy so inflation prone is the ability of many organized groups in our society to obtain—through market or political action—changes in relative prices that are expected to be favorable to them, although these expectations are repeatedly frustrated through the delayed rise in other prices."[49]

Economic Power

Once the shift is made from the presumption that the normal case is market pricing to the recognition of the omnipresence of administered pricing, a substantially new approach to economic analysis is required. The inquiry focus has been transformed from determining approaches to or departures from a market equilibrium to examining the locus and use of economic power, with special reference to pricing power in both the product and factor markets. The latter, of course, has been a major research interest of institutional economists for a very long time.[50]

Having tacitly acknowledged that wage-price (or better, price-wage-price) spirals are the prime stimulus to inflation and that they are a product of discretionary acts by persons and groups holding economic power, Okun, Ackley, and others have perforce been prompted to recommend policy shifts, institutional adjustments, to constrain the fragmented and self-serving use of such pricing power to achieve a differential advantage over the rest of the economy. Okun's major proposal was "the development of a tax-based incomes policy [TIP] that would reward compliance or penalize noncompliance with the [nationally established price and wage] guidelines. The social interest in wage and price restraint can better be pursued by providing market-line incentives through the tax system than by relying on voluntary appeals or rigid mandatory rules."[51] More recently, he recommended "sweetening the kitty" for those who comply with wage price guidelines by extending to them significantly expanded tax writeoff privileges through accelerated depreciation allowances.[52]

To complement this tax-based incomes policy, Okun advocated federal cost-reducing initiatives and most cautious use of fiscal and monetary restraint.[53] His wariness about the latter was grounded in the contention that "the nation squanders about $200 billion of real production and roughly 5 million worker-years of jobs for every point that it reduces the inflation rate" through heavily restrictive monetary and fiscal policy.[54]

Okun was also aware that what Heller called "external-shock or special-sector" or "commodity-price surges" induced inflationary pressure. The classic case is obviously the OPEC generated increase in petroleum prices over the last decade. As Okun argued, "a jump in the price of any major product raises the price level and indeed the inflation rate."[55] Since, in his view, this inflationary influence operated as an excise tax imposed on the U.S. consumer, the institutional adjustment needed was to "neutralize" the effects by "cuts in state sales taxes or in federal payroll taxes on employers."[56]

Although space does not permit a critique either of the adequacy of Okun's theory of inflation or of the virtues of his recommended structural changes, the foregoing does unequivocally demonstrate that Okun, Ackley, and others recognize that the problem of stagflation is a product not of impersonal market forces but of overt discretionary acts. And the consequences of such decisions must be channeled sufficiently to bring them into conformity with what Okun called "the social interest." As a de facto institutionalist in this context, then, he acknowledged the need for creative institutional adjustments (policy shifts) to move toward a solution. Okun thought that pecuniary incentives of a tax-based incomes policy would have a substantial effect and, accordingly, rejected mandatory controls on political and other grounds. Some institutionalists are not so sanguine about the outcome and suggest the probable need for selective (major prices only) and permanent mandatory controls over prices.[57] If major prices were to be controlled, the need for wage controls might not arise on the supposition that wages tend to follow, not lead, prices.

Implicit Value Theory

Implicit with Okun, as it was with Keynes, was a shift in the criteria of judgment on the basis of which problems were identified and some institutional adjustments were chosen over others. Throughout these papers of Okun's, he was concerned fundamentally with continuity in the flow of real income to the community at large. The continuing and accelerating inflation coupled with substantial, if not rising, unemployment clearly threaten that continuity and, accordingly, civil peace. Okun was an instrumentalist in this regard.

Moreover, Okun made no special reference in these papers to maximized utility, individual or collective. There was no elevation of particular institutions to a normative status or criterion. He offered no apologia for an elitist power system; he did not discriminate against some economic interests in deference to others. Okun was a practicing normativist. He was tacitly employing the instrumental theory of social value much of the time. In his efforts to rethink the theory of inflation, he was seeking new knowledge of inflation's actual determinants and was engaged in incorporating the substance and implications of such knowledge into his policy recommendations. He shifted direction and focus, but he probably would not have identified himself as an institutionalist.

Human Nature and Motivation

The erosion of the credibility and usefulness of orthodoxy and the drift to institutional thought is reflected not only in a fresh assessment of the Keynesian revolution and in the compulsive scramble to understand stagflation determinants, but also in the gradual crumbling of philosophical and psychological underpinnings of mainstream orthodoxy. Space constraints preclude a full view of the latter, but the curtains can be parted sufficiently to obtain a glimpse of the departures from micro orthodoxy in theories of human nature and motivation that have been emerging recently from some individuals intimately familiar with traditional theory. Brief consideration will be given to Harvey Leibenstein's X-efficiency thesis and to Herbert Simon's decision theory.

As a prologue, it will be useful to recall the pervasive and continuing attack of institutionalists on the psychological assumptions of orthodoxy, an attack that began with Veblen's characterization in *The Place of Science*: "The hedonistic conception of man is that of a lightening calculator of pleasures and pains who oscillates like a homogeneous globule of desire of happiness under the impulse of stimuli that shift him about the area, but leave him intact. He has neither antecedent nor consequent. He is an isolated, definitive human datum."[58] Although references to "hedonism" have mostly vanished from economic discourse, this view of people as egoistic (hedonistic), rationalistic, quietistic, and atomistic organisms remains implicit (and at times explicit) in conventional micro theory.[59] The orthodox perception of people as utility and/or profit maximizers (Marshall and others) or as individuals who have preferences that can be rationally ordered (Hicks and others) rests in large part upon the submerged methodological and psychological individualism alluded to above. Institutionalists and instrumentalists have for nearly a century sought to

584   Marc R. Tool

displace this truncated and archaic view of human nature with a perception of man as a producer and product of culture, as one whose attitudes, beliefs, and behavioral modes are acquired, and, as one who is a continuously emergent agent-actor engaged in learning, valuing, and choosing.[60] Let us consider the institutional drift of Leibenstein and Simon.

Harvey Leibenstein's cautious "dissatisfaction with contemporary micro economics" and its psychological base emerged from his "attempts to understand the processes of economic development of developing countries" and from his personal experience with the operators of business firms.[61] As tools of analysis, the utility maximizing or optimizing assumptions seemed "inappropriate for the understanding of the problem at hand."[62] Leibenstein evidently confronted both the disjunction of traditional theory and observed fact and the questionable relevance of traditional views. Methodologically, Leibenstein is questioning the wisdom of *starting* inquiry with, say, an assumption of profit maximization. Instead, inquiry should be focused on the nature and intensity of individual motives, among which one may find profit maximization. The assumption is converted into a question. With regard to the latter, institutionalists would applaud.

Insufficiently considered in orthodox micro theory, argues Leibenstein, is the analysis of effort. He argues that research be directed to an examination of "effort, and the effort decision." While reward aspects are of interest, monetary rewards are not "the only elements that determine effort decisions."[63] Leibenstein is also aware of the logical futility and the analytical sterility of presuming that *all* behavior is guided by utility maximization.

In distinguishing between the allocative efficiency of conventional micro theory and the X-efficiency of his revised formulation, Leibenstein broadens the concept of motivation to consider other determinants of effort left unaddressed by orthodoxy. X-efficiency refers to the latter. In the study of particular areas of productivity, long-run supply determinants, and oligopolistic and quasi-oligopolistic enterprise, the dependence on the conventional theory "can lead to serious errors."[64] Orthodoxy becomes a special case, "an extreme variant," not the general case.[65]

Leibenstein's fundamental psychological postulate follows: "We assume that basically an individual effects a compromise between his desire to do as he pleases and internalized standards of behavior acquired through background and environment. Thus, we assume that individuals are influenced by others and that their psychology requires them to strike a balance between conflicting desires."[66] People thus employ a "selective rationality" in the context of their emergence from the interaction with other persons and their environment.

An exploration and appraisal of X-efficiency is beyond the scope of this article, but some generalized observations are feasible concerning Leibenstein's shift from orthodoxy. (1) Only individuals have motives; firms and organizations do not. (2) Economic motives are matters to be examined; they are not pecuniary or hedonistic motives to be assumed at the outset of inquiry. (3) Motivations for economic behavior are acquired; people are both conditioned beings and learning organisms. (4) Rationality is broadened to focus on choice and constraints casually perceived. (5) Motivations are complex; they are not simplistic or linear. (6) The nature and extent of effort are socially and individually determined; the character and intensity of effort may not be assumed *a priori*.

An institutionalist could join Leibenstein in his identification of the limitations of the psychological creed of orthodoxy. An institutionalist could also support the substance of the foregoing observations. Leibenstein's departure from orthodoxy is clear enough. "The existence of X-efficiency," he insists, "implies that except in extreme cases firms do not minimize costs, maximize profits, or optimize the rate of technological change."[67] What is not so clear in Liebenstein's work is the extent to which he recognizes, as does an institutionalist, the subversive effect of the foregoing on orthodoxy's continuing claims to general theory status and mainstream standing.

Nobelist Herbert Simon and others who work in the area of "decision theory" are also raising profound and significant questions concerning the adequacy of psychological assumptions in orthodox theory. Simon questions the realism of orthodox analyses of choice behavior. "The axiomatization of utility and probability after World War II," he writes, was an effort to determine whether or not "people behaved in choice situations so as to maximize subjective expected utility (SEU)." The results were virtually conclusive that "SEU theory does not provide a good prediction —not even a good approximation—of actual behavior."[68]

What Simon makes clear is that the rejection and refutation of the psychological postulates of conventional theory have "to do with the substance of the decisions, and not just the process by which they are reached. It is not that people do not go through the calculations that would be required to reach the SEU decision— neoclassical thought has never claimed they did. What has been shown is that they do not even behave *as if* they had carried out those calculations, and that result is a direct refutation of the neoclassical assumptions."[69]

Simon's disaffection with orthodox maximizing and optimizing postulates is both specific and extensive. Factual support for the postulates is lacking. "Evidence that consumers actually distribute their purchases in such a way as to maximize their utilities, and hence equate marginal utilities, is nonexistent. . . . The observed data make it exceedingly doubtful that the cost curves are in fact generally U-shaped. Specific phenomena requiring a theory of profit or utility maximization for their explanation . . . simply have not been observed in aggregate data."[70]

Drawing initial inspiration from some early work of John R. Commons and Chester I. Barnard,[71] Simon seeks a behavioral theory of the firm to replace the neoclassical theory of the firm. He seeks premises regarding decision behavior that are descriptively credible and empirically demonstrable. He recommends the analogy of evolutionary biology in place of physics in formulating decision theory. He wishes not only quantitative information but also bases for qualitative judgments. He would displace maximizing and optimizing postulates with the concept of satisficing. For the ungrounded assumptions of perfect rationality, he would offer the demonstrable principle of bounded rationality. For Simon, rationality is always "bounded" because people are not omniscient. The complexity of situations and problems is so great that no person or group can know all the alternatives, avoid uncertainty about exogenous influences, or calculate major outcomes with complete confidence.[72]

Simon's bounded rationality implies a deliberative process in decision making; if the alternatives are not provided *a priori*, a search must be undertaken to identify them. The individual is an information generator, an information processor, and an information assessor. The decision maker is in quest of accessible, satisfactory choices, not maximizing or optimizing ones. He replaces "abstract, global goals with tangible subgoals,"[73] progress toward which can be evidentially confirmed. In organizations, decision responsibilities may be fragmented and specialized when communications and authority permit. In such fashion, the referential content of bounded rationality is provided. Simon concludes by saying that "we do understand today many of the mechanisms of human rational choice. We do know how the information processing system called Man, faced with complexity beyond his ken, uses his information processing capacities to seek out alternatives, to calculate consequences, to resolve uncertainties, and thereby—sometimes, not always—to find ways of action that are sufficient unto the day, that satisfice."[74]

From the institutionalist's perspective, Simon's decision theory may still fall substantially short of the theory of human nature and motivation incorporated in the general theory of institutional economics, but in its critique of the *a priori* (and now hidden) hedonism of orthodoxy, it is to be commended. In addition, Simon should draw accolades for the methodological shifts from orthodoxy he recommends and for his recognition of the limits to and constraints on choice making.

But most important is his recognition of the human organism as being perpetually engaged in a learning process. Man is a deliberative agent; he makes choices; he is educable. A person is transformed both by the activity of making choices and by the consequences then experienced and appraised. The theory of bounded rationality may not yet be a critique and reconstruction sufficient to upend traditional micro theory, but it is philosophically, psychologically, and methodologically a major step in the direction of positions held by institutionalists.

Simon and the decision theorists seem unaware, however, that sooner or later their inquiry into choice behavior must directly confront the question of choice criteria—value standards in terms of which choices are made. When *that* Rubicon is crossed, the normative aspects of economic inquiry can be moved by them into the agenda of priority concerns that their significance warrants.[75] Then Simon and others will have additional and conclusive grounds for a total abandonment of the neoclassical utility maximizing and optimizing theories of economic motivation.

Conclusion

There are other instances of departures from orthodoxy that move in the direction of institutional thought. A provisional agenda might well include the four noted below. First, an examination is needed of the theory and practice of democratizing the work site with industrial democracy, models of a participatory economy, job power, and the like. Dewey's democratic theory applies to nongovernmental as well as governmental institutions.[76] Second, it is possible to expand vastly the scope of inquiry in theories of economic growth and development as reflected in the writings of Albert Hirschman and others.[77] Hirschman's theory of "reform-mongering" has substantial, but not total, common content with the institutionalists' theory of institutional adjustment. Third, the area of environmental inquiry and the problems of pollution, ecological deterioration, and destruction offer a rich field, particularly as to how these force consideration of an environmental ethic to displace the pecuniary and utility maximizing criteria of conventional analysis.[78] Even the benefit-cost analyses that retain dependence on ethical relativism in this area must be expected eventually to give way to counterpart formulations of the instrumental social value theory. Fourth, there should be an investigation of the development and economic power role of transnational and multi-national corporations that moves beyond conventional "market mentality" orientations to consideration of multiple goals and strategic concerns of these "private industrial governments."[79] At issue in part is a concern for holding economic power accountable by those affected by such power, as institutionalists have long favored. The agenda, of course, could be extended.

All are aware that "one robin does not make a spring" and that the examples cited may not be sufficiently persuasive or representative to generate conviction that "a compulsive shift to institutional analysis" is in fact under way. Claims of proof are doubtless premature; suggestions of drift and indicative shift are not premature. Years ago, Dewey reminded us that it is not the number of cases marshaled that proves the point, but whether or not those cited can be shown to be representative. Such a demonstration can only be suggested here. The hope is that readers will wish to make their own assessments and, perhaps, extensions.

Notes

1. For purposes of this article, the referent for "institutional thought" will be, unless otherwise indicated, the author's formulation of a synthesis of the neoinstitutionalist position in *The Discretionary Economy: A Normative Theory of Political Economy* (Santa Monica: Goodyear Publishing Co., 1979).
2. Keynes, *The General Theory of Employment, Interest and Money* (New York: Harcourt Brace, 1936), p. viii.
3. On Keynes and the institutionalists, see Dudley Dillard, *The Economics of John Maynard Keynes* (New York: Prentice Hall, 1948), especially chapter 12; Allan G. Gruchy, "Keynes and the Institutionalists: Some Similarities," and "Keynes and the Institutionalists: Some Contrasts," in *Economic Theory in Review*, edited by C. Lawrence Christenson (Bloomington: Indiana University Press, 1949), pp. 96–126; Gladys Myers Foster, "Some Institutional Aspects of Keynesian Economics," an unpublished graduate paper presented to C. E. Ayres, January 1950, pp. 1–57; J. Fagg Foster, "Understandings and Misunderstandings of Keynesian Economics," a paper presented at the Annual Meeting of the Association for Evolutionary Economics, San Francisco, California, December 1966 (later published in *Rivista Internazionale di Scienze Economiche e Commerciali* 15, no. 12 [1968]: 1234–44); Richard X. Chase, "Keynes and U.S. Keynesianism: A Lack of Historical Perspective and the Decline of the New Economics," *Journal of Economic Issues* 11 (September 1975): 441–70; R. X. Chase, "The Failure of American Keynesianism," *Challenge* 19 (March-April 1976): 43–51; Wallace C. Peterson, "Institutionalism, Keynes, and the Real World," *Challenge* 20

(May-June 1977): 22–32; W. C. Peterson, "Financial Instability and Economic Concentration," a paper presented to the Western Social Science Association, Denver, Colorado, April 1978, pp. 1–26; and Dudley Dillard, "A Monetary Theory of Production: Keynes and the Institutionalists," *Journal of Economic Issues* 14 (June 1980): 255–73.

4. John Maynard Keynes, *Essays in Biography* (New York: Horizon Press, 1951 [1933]), p. 103.

5. F. Gregory Hayden suggests that John R. Commons, in *Legal Foundations of Capitalism* (Madison: University of Wisconsin Press, 1959 [1924]) is concerned with pecuniary expectations in a manner somewhat anticipatory of Keynes's MEC; see, for example, Commons, *Legal Foundations*, pp. 166–67.

6. "There is the economic life process still in great measure awaiting theoretical formulation." Thorstein Veblen, *The Place of Science in Modern Civilization* (New York: Russell & Russell, 1961 [1919]), p. 70.

7. G. M. Foster, "Some Institutional Aspects," pp. 32, 52, and passim.

8. Keynes, *General Theory*, p. 374.

9. Ibid., p. 297.

10. On "explanation" versus "prediction," see Harvey Leibenstein, *Beyond Economic Man* (Cambridge, Mass.: Harvard University Press, 1976), pp. 12–17.

11. See Karl Polanyi, *The Great Transformation* (New York: Rinehart & Company, 1957), passim. Also see J. Ron Stanfield, "The Institutional Economics of Karl Polanyi," *Journal of Economic Issues* 14 (September 1980): 599 and passim.

12. The distinction comes from the lectures of J. Fagg Foster at the University of Denver.

13. Veblen, *Place of Science*, passim.

14. J. F. Foster, "Understandings and Misunderstandings," p. 11.

15. John Maynard Keynes, *The End of Laissez Faire* (London: Hogarth Press, 1926), pp. 39–40 (emphasis in original).

16. Ibid., pp. 40–41 (emphasis in original).

17. Roy F. Harrod, *The Life of John Maynard Keynes* (New York: Harcourt, Brace, 1951), p. 192.

18. Keynes, *General Theory*, pp. 378–79.

19. Ibid., pp. 95, 324–25, 373–78, 164, 376, and 372–73.

20. Harrod, *Keynes*, p. 436.

21. Ibid., p. 535.

22. Marc R. Tool, "A Social Value Theory in Neoinstitutional Economics," *Journal of Economic Issues* 11 (December 1977): 823–46.

23. Tool, *Discretionary Economy*, p. 293.

24. John Maynard Keynes, *How to Pay for the War* (New York: Harcourt, Brace, 1940).

25. Dillard, "Monetary Theory of Production."

26. Tool, "Social Value Theory," p. 827.

27. Dillard, "Monetary Theory of Production," p. 267.

28. Tool, "Social Value Theory," p. 827.

29. Dillard, "Monetary Theory of Production," p. 267.

30. Keynes, *General Theory*, pp. 129, 131, 155–56.

590   Marc R. Tool

31. Veblen, *The Theory of the Leisure Class* (New York: Modern Library, 1934 [1899]), passim.
32. Harrod, *Keynes,* p. 75.
33. Keynes, *General Theory*, p. 157.
34. Tool, "Social Value Theory," pp. 827, 835.
35. Keynes, *General Theory*, p. 372.
36. Clarence Ayres, *Theory of Economic Progress* (Kalamazoo, Mi.: New Issues Press, 1978 [1944]), chapter 6.
37. *American Economic Review* 65 (March 1975): 1–26.
38. Ibid., p. 21.
39. Ibid.
40. See, for example, the following by Gardiner C. Means: *Administrative Inflation and Public Policy* (Washington, D.C.: Anderson Kramer Associates, 1959); "Pricing Power and the Public Interest," in *Administered Prices: A Compendium on Public Policy*, U.S. Senate, Committee on the Judiciary, Subcommittee on Antitrust and Monopoly (Washington, D.C.: U.S. Government Printing Office, 1963), pp. 213–39; "The Administered-Price Thesis Reconfirmed," *American Economic Review* 62 (June 1972): 292–306; and "Simultaneous Inflation and Unemployment: A Challenge to Theory and Policy," in *The Roots of Inflation* (New York: Burt Franklin & Co., 1975). See also John M. Blair, "Inflation in the United States: A Short-Run Target Return Model," in ibid.
41. Arthur M. Okun, "The Great Stagflation Swamp," *Brookings Bulletin* 14 (Fall 1977): 1–7; A. M. Okun and George L. Perry, "New Ways to Slow Inflation," *Brookings Bulletin* 15 (Summer 1978): 1–3; A. M. Okun, "An Efficient Strategy to Combat Inflation," *Brookings Bulletin* 15 (Spring 1979): 1–5; and A. M. Okun, "The Invisible Handshake and the Inflationary Process," *Challenge* 22 (January-February 1980): 5–12.
42. Okun, "Stagflation Swamp," pp. 7 and 5.
43. Okun, "Efficient Strategy," p. 2.
44. Joan Robinson, "Solving the Stagflation Puzzle," *Challenge* 22 (November-December 1979): 42.
45. Okun, "Efficient Strategy," p. 2.
46. Okun, "Invisible Handshake," pp. 1–12.
47. Gardner Ackley, "The Costs of Inflation," *American Economic Review* 68 (May 1978): 150.
48. See Means, "Simultaneous Inflation," and other sources cited in note 40 above.
49. Ackley, "Costs of Inflation," p. 150.
50. See, for example, Walton H. Hamilton, Mark Adams, and Irene Till, *Price and Policies* (New York: McGraw-Hill, 1938); and John M. Blair, *Economic Concentration* (New York: Harcourt, Brace Jovanovich, 1972).
51. Okun, "Efficient Strategy," p. 5. See also Lester Thurow, "Towards a U.S. Incomes Policy: Strategy and Tactics," *ADA World* (June-July 1978): 7, 9, 11, and 37. The original tax based incomes policy proposal was formulated by Henry C. Wallich and Sidney Weintraub in "A Tax-Based Incomes Policy," *Journal of Economic Issues* 5 (June 1971): 1–19.

Further consideration of TIP is provided by Laurence S. Seidman, "Would Tax Shifting Undermine the Tax-Based Incomes Policy?" *Journal of Economic Issues* 12 (September 1978): 647–76. See also Michael P. Claudon and Richard R. Cornwall, eds., *An Incomes Policy for the United States* (Boston: Martinus Nijhoff, 1981).

52. Okun, "Invisible Handshake," p. 11.
53. Okun, "Efficient Strategy," p. 4.
54. Ibid.
55. Okun, "Invisible Handshake," p. 10.
56. Ibid., p. 11.
57. John Kenneth Galbraith, "Social Balance and the Tax Revolt," Plenary Address, Southwestern Social Science Association, Fort Worth, Texas, 29 March 1979. The present author shares this view.
58. Veblen, *Place of Science*, p. 73.
59. Harry K. Girvetz, *The Evolution of Liberalism* (New York: Collier Books, 1963), pp. 27–47.
60. This literature includes the following: John Dewey, *Human Nature and Conduct* (New York: Modern Library, 1922); Wesley Clair Mitchell, *The Backward Art of Spending Money* (New York: Augustus Kelley, 1950 [1937]), pp. 149–202 and passim; John M. Gambs, *Beyond Supply and Demand* (Westport, Conn.: Greenwood Press, 1976 [1946]), chapter 3; Ayres, *Theory of Economic Progress*, chapter 5 and passim; David Hamilton, *Evolutionary Economics* (Albuquerque: University of New Mexico Press, 1970), chapter 3 and passim; and Tool, *Discretionary Economy*, chapter 3.
61. Leibenstein, *Economic Man*, p. viii; see also his "X-Efficiency: From Concept to Theory," *Challenge* 22 (September-October 1979): 13–22.
62. Leibenstein, *Economic Man*, p. viii.
63. Ibid., p. 7.
64. Ibid., p. 9.
65. Ibid., p. 71.
66. Ibid.
67. Ibid., p. 95.
68. Herbert A. Simon, "Rational Decision Making in Business Organizations," *American Economic Review* 69 (September 1979): 506.
69. Ibid., p. 507 (emphasis in original).
70. Ibid., pp. 496 and 497.
71. Ibid., pp. 499–500. See John R. Commons, *Institutional Economics* (Madison: University of Wisconsin Press, 1961 [1934]); and Chester I. Barnard, *The Functions of the Executive* (Cambridge, Mass.: Harvard University Press, 1938).
72. Ibid., p. 502.
73. Ibid., p. 501.
74. Ibid., p. 511.
75. In this connection, see also Kenneth Arrow, "The Limitations of the Profit Motive," in *New Challenges to the Role of Profit*, edited by Benjamin M. Friedman (Lexington: D. C. Heath, 1978).
76. David Jenkins, *Job Power* (New York: Penguin Books, 1974); also see

592   Marc R. Tool

Theodore Geiger, "The Movement for Industrial Democracy in Western
Europe," *Challenge* 22 (May-June 1979): 14–21.

77. Albert O. Hirschman, *Journeys toward Progress* (New York: 20th Century Fund, 1963), and *Exit, Voice, and Loyalty* (Cambridge, Mass.: Harvard University Press, 1970).

78. See, for example, Aldo Leopold, *A Sand County Almanac* (New York:
Sierra Club/Ballantine, 1970).

79. See, for example, Richard J. Barnet and Ronald E. Muller, *Global
Reach: The Power of the Multinational Corporations* (New York: Simon
& Schuster, 1974).

Part II
Leading Figures

[9]

The
American Economic Review

Vol. XXV DECEMBER, 1935 No. 4

COMMONS ON INSTITUTIONAL ECONOMICS

Institutional Economics is a militant sage's summing up of his lifetime's thinking. Despite the author's disavowal of discoveries, it is a highly original book—the product of a stubbornly independent mind, developed by intense strivings with problems of social behavior. Happily that mind has given an account of itself: *Myself,* by John R. Commons, reveals the author's personality and sketches his rich experience. Readers will get more profit and more pleasure from the nine-hundred page treatise if they start with the two-hundred page autobiography.[1]

I

As a boy John Commons found difficulty in acquiring knowledge at second hand from school books. His was not a docile mind; he could not cram for examinations. Always he had to find out facts for himself and to think out the relations among his findings. As a college instructor he failed when he tried to give systematic courses. He was essentially an investigator; an investigator who observed man's theories as carefully as he observed their actions. He talked with people of all sorts and he ransacked libraries. The theories collected from books required as much working over as the theories collected from conversations; both sets had to be thought out afresh to find what they really meant. All the materials and products of this smelting process—the formulation of his problems, the facts and theories that he observed, the interpretations that he offered, the solutions that he found— came to bear the imprint of John R. Commons.

That compound of scepticism and curiosity was the son of a Quaker father whose family had left North Carolina because they hated slavery and of a Presbyterian mother whose family came from Vermont. The two met on the Ohio-Indiana line where John Rogers was born in 1862 and named after the martyr burned in "Bloody Mary's" reign. The elder John Commons developed a discursive interest in the world at large. He read Shakespeare, Darwin and Herbert Spencer; he drifted away from the Quaker assembly, talked politics endlessly and acquired by swapping a country newspaper which he could not make pay. The family responsibilities fell

---

[1] *Institutional Economics, Its Place in Political Economy,* John R. Commons, New York, Macmillan, 1934, pp. xiv, 921. *Myself,* John R. Commons, New York, Macmillan, 1934, pp. x, 201.

to the strict Puritan mother, who had graduated from Oberlin College and who wished to make her eldest son a minister. With that ambition she sent John to Oberlin when he was twenty, following the next year with her two younger children and taking boarders to pay for their education. The boys had picked up printing in their father's shop and supplemented the family income by setting type both in term times and during vacations. The double burden of study and earning overtaxed John's strength. He suffered nervous breakdowns, took six years to graduate and had a poor record at that. But he won the confidence of his teachers.

A thousand-dollar loan from two Oberlin trustees made possible graduate work at Johns Hopkins. There the youth met Richard T. Ely and learned that economics might include much more than the deductive analysis he had been taught in Oberlin. But his academic work did not prosper. Failure in a history examination spoiled his chances of a fellowship, a third year of study and a doctor's degree. Yet his teachers again showed faith in the ultimate success of this unconventional student, and got him an instructorship at Wesleyan. Another failure resulted. His effort to teach in the standard fashion satisfied no one, and Commons was dropped at the end of the year. That did not dismay him, for he had learned to teach in his own way; thereafter he used whatever he happened to be investigating as material for his classes, "regardless of logical sequence in a course of lectures."

Oberlin took him back for a year; he passed on to Indiana for three and then to Syracuse for four years. At Syracuse he taught anthropology, criminology, charity organization, taxation, political economy and municipal government. He took his students into the field and learned with them a surprising variety of things about contemporary life. But he also acquired the reputation of being a "radical." Chancellor Day told him that expected contributors refused gifts to Syracuse because he taught there. The trustees did not discharge him; they quietly abolished his chair. In public the Chancellor "bewailed the loss of one of their ablest and most popular professors." Commons drew two inferences: "It was not religion, it was capitalism, that governed Christian colleges." Wealth had a double meaning, *"holding* something useful for one's own use and exchange," and *"withholding* from others what they need but do not own."

Never again did he seek an academic position. To meet his craving for first-hand investigation and to give his family a meager support, research jobs turned up one after another. George H. Shibley, a bimetallist with money, financed Commons and N. I. Stone while they compiled a weekly index number of prices at wholesale covering a long stretch of years. The first figures were published in July, 1900. Prices were falling and the index made good campaign material for Bryan. But the decline stopped in August. Shibley telegraphed that the figures must be wrong. Commons and Stone could find no error. In the first week of September the index rose and

Shibley cancelled the contract within twenty-four hours. That mattered little; for E. Dana Durand asked Commons to finish a report on immigration for the United States Industrial Commission, and later to help in preparing the *Final Report.* This job brought close associations with Marxian socialists, with a flamboyant capitalist who hated the Standard Oil Company, and with an able staff of investigators, whom Commons calls the first "brain trust." Next, Ralph M. Easley took him into the National Civic Federation —that well-meant attempt to solve social problems by getting the leaders of capital and labor to sit down together. Easley dealt with capital through Marcus A. Hanna; Commons dealt with labor through the chiefs of great unions. In 1903 the Department of Labor gave him four helpers to investigate the restrictions and regulations of output by capital and labor. This was the last of his casual jobs; for Professor Ely had been "working up" a position for him at the University of Wisconsin, and in the summer of 1904 Commons came into his own.

Seldom have a man and an opportunity been better mated. Under the leadership of Governor LaFollette, Wisconsin was ready to experiment with social legislation. The state expected the university to serve the people in more ways than by giving college educations to a limited number of its sons and daughters. Commons had learned much about the cantankerous nature of man, the frictions and the wastes of modern life. He thought that the pursuit of self-interest produced efficient coöperation only when some social authority existed to judge and to enforce proper practices. What practices are proper in different types of transactions must be found out by studying practical experience. What forms and powers the judging and enforcing authority should have also depend upon the type of transaction. To produce satisfactory coöperation, both the practices and the social authorities should develop with changes in economic conditions. Like the Wisconsin "progressives," Commons wanted "to save capitalism by making it good" (*Myself,* p. 143). He was tireless in finding facts, he was ingenious in inventing devices, he knew how to deal with men of different occupations and prejudices. In short, he was admirably fitted to become a designer of social legislation for a "progressive" party.

The story of Professor Commons's contribution to the social legislation of his state is too long to tell. He drafted the civil service law in 1904-5; helped to shape the extension of public-utility regulation into the municipal and inter-urban field; got himself investigated by the Progressives for promoting a small-loan law that authorized interest at $3\frac{1}{2}$ per cent a month; suggested the Wisconsin Industrial Commission, served two years as one of the commissioners, and capped his service with the Wisconsin Unemployment Reserves law of 1932. Meanwhile he had shared in the National Civic Federation's study of municipal ownership in Great Britain and America, in the Pittsburgh Survey of 1906, in the United States Industrial

Relations Commission of 1913-15, and in the Pittsburgh-plus case of 1923. He had taken up monetary problems after the war and collaborated with Congressman Strong in preparing a banking bill that aimed at stabilizing prices. Also he had trained graduate students year after year by making them participate in his successive investigations. With the help of several co-workers he had compiled *A Documentary History of American Industrial Society* in ten volumes and written a *History of Labour in the United States* in two volumes to which a third will be added this year. Besides his books published before going to Wisconsin, *The Distribution of Wealth, Social Reform and the Church,* and *Proportional Representation,* he had written six volumes dealing with various aspects of industrial problems, a learned treatise upon the *Legal Foundations of Capitalism,* and two dozen papers in technical journals.

Such in brief was Professor Commons's preparation for writing *Institutional Economics.* Few indeed are the men who combine intimate and varied experiences in practical affairs with so much experience in using ideas.

II

The fundamental convictions which Commons drew from experience were that men are mutually dependent creatures who must coöperate with one another; that the scarcity of goods gives rise to private property and to conflicts of individual interests; that collective action is necessary to decide these conflicts and to create a new harmony of interests, or to establish at least the modicum of order required for coöperation.

Collective control, then, is essential to economic life. It is exercised by the sovereign, primarily through the courts. Such control is found in all societies, though in a well-ordered state it works so unobtrusively most of the time that economic theorists have given it scant attention.

It follows that the unit of economic investigation must be a unit that combines the three constituents of dependence, conflict and order established by social control. This unit is a *transaction.*

Transactions . . . are not the "exchange of commodities," in the physical sense of "delivery," they are the alienation and acquisition, between individuals, of the *rights* of future ownership of physical things, as determined by the collective working rules of society (*Institutional Economics,* p. 58).

There are three types of transactions. Economists have concentrated their attention upon one type only, bargaining transactions, and have simplified unduly their presentation even of that type. In a bargain there are never just two parties exchanging goods; always in the background influencing the bargain and sometimes coming into the foreground, are a second potential buyer, a second potential seller, and a ruling authority ready to decide disputes. In the second type, managerial transactions, there are three parties: a legal superior giving orders to a legal inferior—for example, a factory superintendent and a foreman, or a foreman and a laborer, or a sheriff and a citizen—plus the controlling authority in the background. Also in the third type, rationing transactions, there are three parties—a superior, an inferior and a court—but here the superior is a collective body or its official spokesman prorating burdens or benefits among inferiors. Examples are a government apportioning taxes, a trade union collecting dues from and making disbursements to its members, the directors of a corporation levying assessments upon the stockholders or declaring dividends.

These three units of activity exhaust all the activities of the science of economics. Bargaining transactions *transfer ownership* of wealth by voluntary agreement between legal equals. Managerial transactions *create wealth* by commands of legal superiors. Rationing transactions apportion the burdens and benefits of wealth creation by the *dictation* of legal superiors (p. 68).

The three types of transactions are brought together in a larger unit of economic investigation which is called a *going concern.*

A going concern is a joint expectation of beneficial bargaining, managerial and rationing transactions, kept together by "working rules" and by control of the changeable strategic or "limiting" factors which are expected to control the others (p. 58).
It is these going concerns, with the working rules that keep them agoing, all the way from the family, the corporation, the trade union, the trade association, up to the state itself, that we name Institutions. . . . we may define an institution as Collective Action in Control of Individual Action (p. 69).

All the activities of going concerns look to the future.

. . . the persuasions or coercions of bargaining transactions, the commands and obedience of managerial transactions, and the arguments and pleadings of rationing transactions . . . will ultimately determine production and consumption. In these negotiations and decisions, which are of the essence of institutional economics, it is always *future* production and *future* consumption that are at stake, because the negotiations determine the legal control which must precede physical control (p. 7).

This conception of economic activities carries with it psychological conceptions different from those with which most economists have worked. Man is an active creature who forms plans and strives to carry them out. His mind-body is

a *creative* agency looking towards the future and manipulating the external world and other people in view of expected consequences (p. 17).

The mind is an "organizer of impressions." It

does not wait for impressions, it is continually looking for them, breaking them up into parts, and reconstructing them into new feelings. Those new feelings are . . . active beliefs reaching forward for future action. It is this relation of the part to the whole and of the past experience to future expectations that becomes the psychology of our transactions and going concerns (p. 153).

Repetition of similar experiences makes it possible to test different modes of action by trial and error, to select those modes that seem most satisfactory, and to test ideas about physical phenomena or human behavior. From repetition arise habits and customs which conserve the lessons of past experience and provide a basis for future expectations.

Habit is repetition by one person. Custom is repetition by the continuing group of changing persons. It has a coercive effect on individuals . . . (p. 155).

Among the most significant of customs are those investigated by economics, the working rules laid down by collective action for the conduct of the transactions among individuals belonging to going concerns.

These I take to be the basic ideas of institutional economics according to Professor Commons.

III

Had some other man grasped these ideas vividly he might have contented himself with working out a logical treatise having little reference to the history of institutions or the evolution of economic doctrines. Not so our indefatigable investigator. To him institutional economics is an evolutionary science. It

consists partly in going back through the court decisions of several hundred years, wherein collective action, not only by legislation but also by common-law decisions interpreting the legislation (culminating in the common-law method of the Supreme Court of the United States), takes over, by means of these decisions, the customs of business or labor, and enforces or restrains individual action, wherever it seems to the Court favorable or unfavorable to the public interest and private rights . . . [It] consists in going back through the writings of economists from John Locke to the Twentieth Century, to discover wherein they have or have not introduced collective action (p. 5).

The first of these laborious tasks was performed in *Legal Foundations of Capitalism*, published in 1924; the second is performed in *Institutional Economics* published a decade later. Since the two books should be read together, I must recall the content of the first before dealing more fully with the second.[2]

IV

Capitalism evolved slowly out of feudalism by the rise of novel practices, the exfoliation of concepts, and the formulation of new working rules by the courts, which judged what practices were beneficial under changing conditions and devised ways of legalizing them.

Under William the Conqueror, the king's property was not distinguished from his sovereignty; there were local customs on every manor, but there was no common law of the realm; the tenants of the king and the villeins

[2] For a less condensed statement, see "Commons on the Legal Foundations of Capitalism" by the present writer, *American Economic Review*, June, 1924, vol. xiv, pp. 240-253.

on a manor owed personal services to their lords; use values dominated economic life; there was little exchanging and that little was mainly by barter. All these conditions had to undergo fundamental changes before there could come into being a system of "production for the use of others and acquisition for the use of self."

The idea of property in land was gradually separated from the idea of sovereignty by commuting the obligation of rendering military service to the king into the obligation of making money payments to him. The king substituted his own army for the retainers of his tenants and made his sovereign power indisputable; but the tenant got a clear title to his land and could buy or sell as he saw fit. By sending his circuit judges to hold court in the counties, Henry II laid the basis for the common law; for the king's court could take cases out of the manorial courts and refuse to recognize local customs of which they disapproved. Commutation of labor dues into money payments helped to clarify and standardize the rights of the small man; it gave him control over his own time and a wider range of choice. When prices rose in the sixteenth century, new courts were created to which even villeins had access; and these courts adopted the rule that the landlord could not alter at will the customs by which lands were held. Money proved a solvent of ideas and an instrument of economic liberty in these humbler dealings as well as in the dealings of the king with his magnates.

Meanwhile capitalism was getting its start among the traders and later among the artisans of the towns which were for a time "islands of money economy in a sea of barter." The gilds secured charters from feudal superiors, largely by purchase, and were empowered to make and enforce their own working rules. But their increasing power brought the gilds into conflict with the common law. Late in the sixteenth century the king's courts ventured to condemn by-laws that established monopolies, even though the by-laws rested upon charters granted by the crown. Later the courts took over the constructive task of working out common rules of fair competition and enforcement of contracts. The promissory note was legalized; the law of copyright and of patents recognized that property rights covered not only physical things but also expected profits from business dealings. Common law that deals with physical things and punishes after the event was supplemented by equity that deals with intangible values and commands, before the event, the actions on which values depend.

These gradual achievements of English law were taken over by the American courts, though Professor Commons thinks that the lag between changes in business practice and changes in legal theory has been longer in the younger country. Not until about 1900 did our Supreme Court definitely recognize intangible property. And one important type of bargain still lacks a satisfactory set of working rules. Labor is not a commodity or a promise; the laborer is free to quit at will and the employer to lay him off at any time. The courts could not maintain the personal liberty of the worker if they assimilated the wage contract with other contracts. The legally anomalous position in which that contract stands has been made more anomalous still by the intervention of trade unions, which have thrust themselves as third parties between employer and employee.

Apparently a "new equity" is needed—an equity that will protect the job as the older equity protected the business (*Legal Foundations of Capitalism*, p. 307).

Of this development Professor Commons could descry merely the beginnings in 1924 as the courts in their deliberate fashion were taking cognizance of the practices that were developing in dealings between employers and organized labor.

V

What *Legal Foundations of Capitalism* essays to do for court decisions, *Institutional Economics* essays to do for economic concepts. Professor Commons can see nothing new in his analysis.

Everything herein can be found in the work of outstanding economists for two hundred years. It is only a somewhat different point of view (*Institutional Economics*, p. 8). The problem now is not to create a different kind of economics —"institutional" economics—divorced from preceding schools, but how to give to collective action, in all its varieties, its due place throughout economic theory (p. 5).
Each idea here incorporated is traced back to its originator, and then the successive modifications of that idea are developed and the earlier double or treble meanings of the idea are separated, until each, as a single meaning, is combined with the others in what I conceive to be the Science of Political Economy as it is developing since the last Great War (preface).

It is this attempt to make institutional economics a history of the exfoliation of theoretical concepts that makes the book so long, so formidable to the layman, and so difficult to summarize. The advantage of this mode of treatment is that

every student of political economy repeats in his own mind the historical evolution of the schools, and a study of the history of economic theory is not an academic curiosity—it is a recapitulation of the evolution of our own thinking (p. 260).

Doubtless the candid reader will agree that he began "his working life as a Mercantilist" and arrived at more penetrating insights by degrees. But he may not now attach much importance to his early errors, and a book that recapitulates the tortuous process of his own thinking may tax his patience. He may feel that the ripe scholar who writes this book has much in common with the young instructor who failed when he tried to give a systematic course of lectures at Wesleyan in 1890. But the discursive writer of today is also the teacher who became keenly stimulating when he began to make his students participate in his own investigations. That is the opportunity which Professor Commons offers in *Institutional Economics*. The reader must do his own systematizing of the rich materials put before him; but the result will amply reward the effort.

VI

Starting with Locke's *Essay concerning Human Understanding*, Commons traces the conception of the mind as a recipient of sensations and an organizer of ideas, through Hume's distintegrating scepticism, to the "scientific" pragmatism of Charles S. Pierce and the pragmatic ethics of John Dewey. On parallel lines, he traces the concepts of the interdependence of men, the conflict of individual interests, and the basis of social order from Locke's *Two Treatises on Civil Government*, through the writings of Hume, Quesnay, Adam Smith, Blackstone and Bentham, to the idea of "reasonable value" worked out by the Supreme Court of the United States. He sets forth the "intellectualist fallacy" committed by the "Eighteenth Century Age of Reason," which he contrasts with the "Age of Passion and Stupidity" proclaimed by Malthus. For his own part, Commons follows Malthus rather than the ruling dynasts from Smith and Bentham to Herbert Spencer. But he prefers to speak of

Custom . . . instead of passion and stupidity, in order to avoid invidious reflections and to allow for a slow infiltration of reason provoked by uncomfortable experiences (p. 846).

Efficiency and Scarcity have a chapter to themselves as well as many casual passages before and after.

Scarcity is primarily distinguishable as power over others, and efficiency as power over nature (p. 387).

The conflict between engineering and business centers in the difference between these inseparables. Efficiency is the theme of engineering economics, which deals with the relations of man to nature, with the physical input and output of industrial processes, with use values. Scarcity is the theme of institutional economics, which deals with the relations of man to man, with pecuniary outgo and income, with scarcity values. Smith and Ricardo took wants for granted and explained values by scarcity; but the former traced scarcity to man's reluctance to undergo labor-pain, while the latter traced scarcity to the limitations of labor-power. The Austrians eliminated both labor-pain and labor-power as causes of scarcity by assuming that man has attained a "pleasure economy"; they made the diminishing intensity of consumer wants the decisive variable.

Marshall coördinated the two schools by introducing the relativistic concept of changing ratios between . . . the quantities wanted by consumers (buyers) and the quantities supplied by producers (sellers) —both of which were variable independently on their own account (p. 386).

This familiar interpretation of the evolution of value theory is intertwined with an analysis of the concept of wealth. From John Locke to Alfred Marshall that term carried a double meaning: physical objects and their ownership. It was tacitly assumed that everything valuable is owned, that ownership varies exactly with the quantities of materials owned, that production can be identified with selling and consumption with buying, that exchange is both a transfer of physical objects and a transfer of legal control. Observation of actual processes shows the inaccuracy of these assumptions. Ownership, in the economically important sense of value owned, varies with prices as well as with quantities of materials; producers do not always succeed in selling; there are transfers of legal control without transfer of physical objects. Hence institutional economics must improve upon the organization of orthodox economics. It must incorporate the theory of money and credit in its discussion of value. It must make the theory of business cycles an integral part of its account of modern processes, trying to show how difficulties in selling at remunerative prices prevent men from producing as large a national dividend as technology and natural resources make possible. So also, institutional economics must supplement the concept of corporeal property by the concepts of incorporeal property or negotiable debts, and intangible property or "the right to fix prices by withholding from others what they need but do not own" (p. 3).

Still another variable that institutional economics must recognize is the principle of futurity, separable in thought, but inseparable in fact, from the principles of scarcity and efficiency.

The concept of Time, in economic science distinguished from physical science, has shifted from the *past* time of classical and communistic theory, into the *present* time of hedonistic theory, until it is becoming the *future* time of waiting, risking, purpose, and planning. These are the problems of Futurity, another economic "force," not found in the physical sciences, but nevertheless approximately measurable in all the diversities of reasonable value (p. 389).

The long chapter on futurity starts with debts. The large significance of that theme Professor Commons sets forth in a characteristic passage:

When the science of Political Economy began to emerge in the Eighteenth Century, it fell in line with the theory, then dominant, of an original state of liberty and rationality of human beings. . . . These theories of liberty and rationality accomplished extraordinary results in overthrowing absolute monarchies, abolishing slavery, and establishing universal education. But it was not because they were historically true—it was because they set up ideals for the future. Historically it is more accurate to say that the bulk of mankind lived in a state of unreleasable debts, and that liberty came by gradually substituting releasable debts. And historically it is more accurate to say, as Malthus said, that man is originally a being of passion and stupidity for whom liberty and reason are a matter of the slow evolution of moral character and the discipline enforced by government (p. 390).

Prior to the sixteenth century, only landlords and wealthy people could make contracts that the common-law courts would enforce. Merchants based their deals with one another on "parol" contracts. As trade expanded in volume and grew impersonal, it became necessary to give these contracts legal standing. The lawyers accomplished that desideratum very simply: they assumed that the person who received goods did so with intent to pay, and so virtually accepted a debt which he must discharge—a rule that still suffices to establish obligations between brokers on stock exchanges. The next step was to make merchants' debts, now legally enforceable, also negotiable. The foundation of the law of negotiable instruments was laid in the seventeenth century. Thus "incorporeal" property in the form of debts had become a factor of considerable consequence in economic life before Adam Smith was born. But the classical economists were so much concerned with material goods, so intent upon showing that money and all that sprang from it was a mere instrument of convenience, that they paid little attention to these legal claims of one set of people upon property in the hands of a second set. It remained for the lawyer-economist H. D. MacLeod in 1856 to recognize that "a debt is a saleable commodity" and to analyze the relationship of the debt market to commodity markets.

This insight into a neglected problem proved extraordinarily stimulating, and gave rise to much of the acutest analysis of later decades.

Sidgwick's distinction of the money market and capital market (1883) ; Wicksell's world debt-paying community (1898) ; Cassel's scarcity of waiting (1903) ; Knapp's release of debt (1905) ; Hawtrey's creation of debt (1919) ; and Fisher's over-indebtedness and depressions (1932) . . . were all developed out of MacLeod's writings (p. 396).

Commons's critical exposition of these ideas leads to a discussion of how "banker capitalism" can be made to function steadily. Left to itself, this form of economic organization tends to run now faster, now slower, in a rough rhythm. Business activity depends upon the prospects of profits as seen by business men and gathers speed when these prospects are deemed bright. If the profits anticipated are to be realized, consumers must be able to buy the goods produced for them and to pay prices that include a margin above cost. But consumers' demands are limited by the money incomes they have already received, mainly from business enterprises, as wages, rent, interest or profits. Business demands, on the other hand, are limited by the indefinite quantity of purchasing power that may be created for them outright, or transferred from savings, by the banks. And the banks, like the borrowing business men, keep their eyes fixed upon future profits. Thus,

The institution of credit is the biggest factor which enables the business man to buy *more* when prices are rising, whereas the consumer buys *less* when prices are rising; and the institution of credit is the biggest factor which *compels* the business man to buy *less* when prices are falling, whereas the consumer, since he does not do business on future sales, buys *more* when prices have fallen (p. 560).

I think that these statements concerning the cyclical behavior of consumers' purchases are inaccurate; but let that pass. Professor Commons is certainly right in bringing all the factors mentioned into the business-cycle problem. He goes on to demonstrate admirably that the profit margins, on which so much depends, are very narrow.

If any one of the cost prices rises one or two per cent, the margin for profit may be reduced 10 to 30 times as much (p. 587).

It seems, then, that the working of the whole system can be altered by making minor changes in any of the many costs of doing business. This fact points the way toward a possible social control over business cycles.

Wicksell taught that central-bank discount rates are the most promising instrument to use for this purpose. To make that instrument effective, he proposed "world-wide monopolistic concerted action of central banks." Experience has shown that this mode of control, while effective in checking booms, is not effective in relieving severe depressions.

With the modern very narrow margins for profit, very few industries could continue on a world-wide bank rate of 10 per cent, whereas it is obvious that a bank rate as low as one per cent could not, of itself, stimulate an inflation of prices, if risk is unfavorable (p. 610).

The risk-discount, to which Irving Fisher has called attention, "is the most important factor in present valuation" (p. 609). It declines in the expansion phase of business cycles and rises in the contraction phase. Bank rates can be put high enough to offset the fall of risk-discounts during booms, but not low enough to offset the rise of risk-discounts during depressions.

Hence, a more direct method of control must be resorted to, if we are to have managed revivals.

In order to create the *consumer demand,* on which business depends for sales, the government itself must create the new money and go completely over the head of the entire banking system by paying it out directly to the unemployed, either as relief or for construction of public works, as it does in times of war. Besides, this new money must also go to the farmers, the business establishments, and practically all enterprises, as well as to wage-earners, for it is all of them together that make up the total of consumer demand (pp. 589, 590).

"Reasonable value," like scarcity, efficiency and futurity, crops up for discussion in many earlier passages and then has a chapter all its own. To Commons, reasonable value is a theory of intangible property developed by the Supreme Court of the United States since 1890. Its characteristic features are made clear by contrasts with the rival theory of intangible property developed about the same time by Thorstein Veblen.

Veblen took as the source of his materials the testimony of industrial and financial magnates before the United States Industrial Commission of 1901 (p. 649).

He found that these men were using a concept of property unrecognized by economists, namely, the present value of their future bargaining power. Through their legal control over the means of production, the captains of industry were able to prevent the community from producing goods except on terms profitable to themselves, and through the financial markets they could capitalize their prospects of profits, thus exploiting the community in years to come.

But during the years when Veblen was developing his scientific analysis of what the greater business men were doing, the Supreme Court was attacking the problem in a purposive fashion. The Court recognized property rights in prospective profits, but gradually developed criteria for judging what profits a corporation might be allowed to expect—criteria that are summed up in its doctrine of reasonable value.

The court was beginning to distinguish, as Veblen did not,

between good-will and privilege, good-will being the reasonable exercise of the power to withhold, and privilege being the unreasonable exercise of that power (p. 673).

. . . the administrative machinery for research in ascertaining reasonable value . . . did not begin until the powers of the Interstate Commerce Commission were extended in 1908, followed by hundreds of state commissions on fair competition, reasonable discriminations, and reasonable values, as well as by industrial commissions after 1911, the latter to ascertain reasonable relations in the conflicts of capital and labor.

Also, the movement towards scientific management had only just begun [when Veblen was doing his pioneer work], and a professional class devoted to ascertaining and installing reasonable conditions in all the parts of managerial transactions had not yet begun to find itself.

Other applications of the principles of intangible property, especially the stabilization of prices, had not yet even been thought of, much less the administrative machinery to be devised (*sic*) (p. 676).

Since the war, considerable progress has been made in these various directions and Commons expects the future to bring higher standards of what is reasonable in bargaining, managerial and rationing transactions, and more effective social control for enforcing reasonable practices.

He draws a lesson for economics from the two theories of intangible property. It ought to take the constructive, purposive attitude of the courts in its explanation of institutional growth, instead of the purely objective attitude of physical science that was professed by Veblen.[3]

[3] In this connection, Professor Commons becomes momentarily confused. Veblen, he says, considered that science is "matter-of-fact" science, arising from the modern inventions of machinery, wherein the scientist eliminates all of the older ideas of purpose or "animism" contained in the concepts of alchemy, or divination, and adopts merely the ideas of "consecutive change," or "process," which has no "causation" and no "final end" or "purpose."

If this is so [Commons comments], then there is no science of human nature. Science becames only the physical sciences (p. 654).

He proceeds to argue that institutional economics is concerned precisely with human

The reason is not that the economist should be more keen to "do good" than a physical-chemist, but that the problems of social behavior contain elements not present in problems of physical chemistry. The "Will-in-action, guided by purpose and expectation" (p. 648), is a cardinal factor in the behavior of all individuals, including Supreme Court justices. In so far as action is purposive, causation runs from the future back to the present; not from the past forward to the present. One cannot understand what men do, if he treats them as he would treat molecules, leaving their expectations, valuations and purposes out of account. Concepts like reasonable value play as definite a rôle in shaping institutions as does the difference between the cultural incidence of machine tending and money making, which Veblen taught us to see. Even if the economist remains an aloof spectator of social processes, with no itch to modify them, he must not leave human purposes out of his explanations.

John Commons is both a theorist and a reformer—like Adam Smith, Malthus and Ricardo. And it is the reformer who winds up the chapter on reasonable value as follows:

The theory of reasonable value may be summarized, in its pragmatic application, as a theory of social progress by means of personality controlled, liberated, and expanded by collective action. It is not individualism, it is institutionalized personality. Its tacit or habitual assumptions are the continuance of the capitalist system based on private property and profits. It is fitted to a Malthusian concept of human nature, starting from the passion, stupidity, and ignorance whereby mankind does the opposite of what reason and rationality would prescribe, and ending in an admiration for the individual who, by initiative, persistence, taking risks, and assuming obligations to others, rises to leadership.

Unregulated profit-seeking drags the conscientious down towards the level of the least conscientious; yet a considerable minority is always above that level, no matter how high it may have been raised by collective action. These indicate the possibility of progress.

The problem, then, is the limited one of investigating the working rules of collective action which bring reluctant individuals up to, not an impracticable

---

purposes as summed up in "worldly wisdom"—a mental attitude which Veblen regards as "at cross-purposes with the disinterested scientific spirit."

Of course, Veblen did not conceive human beings as devoid of purpose. Commons himself presently recognizes that the "instinct of workmanship" brings purpose into the foreground of behavior (p. 661). That was not the only instinct with which Veblen endowed mankind, and all instincts are purposive. His chief criticism of hedonism is that it pictures men as passive creatures, controlled by the pleasure-pain forces which impinge upon them.

What Veblen was driving at is that science assumes no purposes in "nature," or in "the course of events" outside of man. In dealing with human behavior, he tries to give an account of human purposes in terms of an evolutionary process of natural selection. For those purposes are an evolutionary product and so can be explained in the same fashion as man's opposable thumb. The scientist should refrain, so far as is possible for such a purposeful creature as man, from mixing his own purposes into his explanations of cumulative changes in the purposes of others. That rule of intellectual honesty Commons accepts in principle and practices with indifferent success, like Veblen and the rest of us.

ideal, but a reasonable idealism, because it is already demonstrated to be practicable by the progressive minority under existing conditions. . . .

If the profit-motive, in the field of economics, can be enlisted in the program of social welfare, then a dynamic factor, more constructive than all others, is enlisted. It is an appeal to the business man to get rich by making others rich, and, if he does not respond, then to appeal to collective action (*sic*) (pp. 874, 875).

Commons is by no means certain, however, that the courts, industrial commissions, scientific managers, monetary reformers and their colleagues will succeed in saving capitalism by making it good. He devotes his last chapter to the characteristics and prospects of the three forms of economic organization that dominate the world today—capitalism, fascism and communism. What the future holds in store he makes no pretense of knowing. Nor is he sure which form of organization is to be preferred by the mass of mankind.

. . . it is doubtful whether, under modern conditions, a decision can be reached as to which is the better public policy—the Communism of Russia, the Fascism of Italy, or the Banker Capitalism of the United States. In the two European systems . . . liberty is suppressed and the intellectuals . . . are eliminated. not merely because they are physically suppressed but because individual originality and genius cannot thrive in a nation of fear.

Yet these are a small fraction of the population. The overwhelming majority are manual and clerical workers. . . . To them liberty is an illusion under institutions which demoralize them on the upturn of prices, pauperize them on the downturn, and coerce them by lack of jobs. They do not miss liberty if Communism or Fascism gives them security at low wages.

Likewise with the personal thrift which became the basis of . . . small capitalism. . . . The inflation and deflation of a twentieth-century Banker civilization scrapes off the cream of that individual proprietorship which hitherto had induced individual wage-earners and farmers to save, to economize, to take the risks which they had a chance to surmount, and to maintain the American Republic. . . .

If these thrifty individuals are eliminated from the capitalist civilization by becoming a proletariat of wage and salary earners, then it is probable that, for the overwhelming majority, a communist or fascist dictatorship may be preferable to American Banker Capitalism. It will, no doubt. promptly eliminate academic liberty and a free press, but meanwhile the economists have, for the time being, a new equipment of experimental laboratories on three grand scales, in Russia, Italy and America, for a rough and tumble testing of their classical, hedonistic, and institutional theories (p. 903).

VII

One of the chief services that Professor Commons's treatise performs is to clarify the relations of "institutional economics" to what for lack of a better term is called "orthodox economics." The institutional type is often conceived to be a rival of and would-be substitute for the types of theory that derive from Ricardo, Menger, or Walras. The leading institutionalists may be partly responsible for that misapprehension. MacLeod, whom Commons names the "originator" of institutional economics (p. 399), was an acrid controversialist, and Veblen explained the preconceptions that had prevented economics from becoming an evolutionary science as cultural lags. But whether one accepts Veblen's concept of an institution as a widely prevalent habit of thought, or Commons's concept that an institution is "collective action in control of individual action," he must acknowledge that the earlier masters of economic theory dealt with institutions at length. Certainly the mercantilism that Adam Smith condemned was an institution, or complex of institutions, on either definition, and so also was the "simple and obvious system of natural liberty" that Adam Smith praised; for his discussion of the duties of the sovereign makes it clear that there must be collective control over individual action even under a policy of laissez faire. The philosophical radicals talked explicitly about "bad institutions," showed marked ingenuity in devising paper schemes for "good institutions" and influenced powerfully the institutional development of England for three generations. Perhaps no other economist has stressed the importance of institutions in human history more incisively than did John Stuart Mill in his discussion of distribution. It certainly is not the choice of institutions as subject matter that differentiates "institutional" from other types of economics. The day must be close at hand when critics will begin to proclaim that economics has always been "institutional."

What did mark off Veblen's work from that of his predecessors was concentration upon the evolution of institutions, and the application to that problem of a fresh conception of human nature. Adam Smith, the philosophical radicals and later economists had analyzed the workings of contemporary institutions, had shown how these workings promoted or obstructed public welfare as they conceived it, and had argued that the bad institutions should be abolished to make way for good ones. Institutional change to them meant a process of "reform," based upon rational insight. In this respect I do not see that MacLeod differed as an institutionalist from Mill. Karl Marx is a fitter candidate for nomination as the "originator" of the later type of institutional economics; for he focused his attention upon the process of institutional change. But Marx retained substantially the conception of human nature that the philosophical radicals had elaborated, and his notion of institutional evolution reeked of Hegel's metaphysics.

Veblen was the first economist to present institutional evolution in terms of natural selection, and his conception of human nature derived from Darwin and William James, not from Bentham. To him the proper way to explain existing institutions was in terms of the cumulative changes in ways of making a living. He took that factor to be of chief importance in forming the habits of thought prevailing in successive generations, because most men and women spend more of their time in getting a living than in any other activity. When he thought about the workings of contemporary institutions, his interest centered in the changes that these great social habits are now undergoing. He was not concerned with the quasi-mechanical details of price determination, after demand schedules and supply schedules had been assumed. To him the significant problems of value were hidden from sight in these formal schedules. He asked, for example, why men desire obviously expensive goods and accomplishments however much discomfort their display may impose, and how a species of animals that owes its primacy to work can form the habit of thinking labor irksome.

Great as was the service that Veblen rendered by studying the evolution of institutions, it is clear that this theme does not constitute the whole of economics. The problems treated by orthodox theory are genuine problems, and the two sets of discussions should be put into such form that everyone can see how they supplement each another. For example, Veblen's analysis of the cultural incidence of the machine process and of business traffic takes for granted knowledge of how prices are fixed and of the bearing of prices upon the distribution of income. Every scheme of institutions has an implicit logic of its own, and it is not less important to know what that logic is than to know how the institutions came into being and what they are becoming. When Veblen's friend H. J. Davenport defined economics as the science that treats phenomena from the standpoint of price, and insisted that it must be written "from the private and acquisitive point of view," he was elaborating the logic of pecuniary institutions in much the same way that Euclid elaborated the logic of ideas about space. Though Davenport explicitly ruled cultural evolution out of economics, he was contributing toward the understanding of one set of institutions.

Professor Commons, as an institutionalist, takes this catholic point of view. Let me quote again one of his most characteristic statements:

The problem now is not to create a different kind of economics—"institutional" economics—divorced from preceding schools, but how to give to collective action, in all its varieties, its due place throughout economic theory (p. 5).

Collective action, like Veblen's widely prevalent habits of thought, is the product of cumulative changes, and Commons studies its historical evolution with care; but he finds no difficulty in fitting the ideas of "orthodox" economists into his framework. On the contrary, the evolving ideas of economic theorists help him to elucidate the evolution of collective action. Study of institutional change taught him, as it had taught Veblen, to eschew the intellectualist fallacy; but Commons found the traits of human nature that are basic for his purposes summed up by Malthus. Veblen took a whimsical pleasure in making orthodox economics appear in the light of his work-a-day world as airy rationalizings, spun from conceptions that live below the threshold of consciousness and that wither in the light of common day. Commons goes to the opposite extreme. Having spent a lifetime in trying to get men to coöperate in his reforms, he is temperamentally inclined to minimize the element of novelty in his thinking and to magnify the insight of his predecessors.

VIII

No man can cover the field of institutional economics, however keen his insight and however persistent his industry. Commons's largest contribution to our knowledge concerns a specific form of collective control over individual action—that exercised by the courts. As he points out, this field Veblen did not cultivate. *Legal Foundations of Capitalism* is one of the most suggestive contributions to social history made in this generation. Repeating what is needful from the earlier volume, *Institutional Economics* sets forth the stellar rôle that judicial process plays in the present scheme of things in the United States. To perform that task thoroughly, Professor Commons has to clear the way by sketching men's developing conception of human nature, and the gradual discovery that social coöperation rests, not upon a divinely appointed or a "natural" harmony of interests, but upon a state of order that men learn to establish among themselves. This order must control the conflicts among individuals arising from the scarcity of goods, and it must provide for the organized coöperation indispensable to efficiency. The individuals whose clashing interests must be controlled and whose mutual interdependence must be organized are creatures of passion and stupidity, but creatures who can plan. In their planning, expectations of the future are the controlling factor. These expectations gradually come to be the dominant form of property, the center of clashing interests and the crux of interdependence. At this stage of institutional evolution, the courts are forced to develop a doctrine of reasonable value that includes the "principles" of scarcity, efficiency and futurity in a scheme of collective control adapted to the rapidly changing needs of the day.

This brief summary of the theme, and even the fuller statements in the preceding pages, show only the skeleton of a living book. It shares the vitality of the author's career. His interest in economics has the driving force that characterized the work of Malthus and Ricardo and that declined as "political economy" turned into an academic discipline. *Institutional Economics* is the fitting crown of a real investigator's life, and it should be an incitement to other investigators to follow the various leads that Professor Commons has given.

WESLEY C. MITCHELL

Columbia University

[10]

THORSTEIN VEBLEN'S ECONOMIC SYSTEM

DONALD A. WALKER*

*This study provides a foundation for an understanding of
Veblen's economics by displaying its various parts as components of a system, and analyzing and evaluating them. An
examination is made of Veblen's views on the subject-matter of
economics, his general theory of economic change, his theory
of economic change under capitalism, and his prediction of
the end of capitalism, under the emergence of a new economic
order. It is shown that he constructed a highly general theory
economic change that was scientific in character, but that
in dealing with capitalism he wrote primarily as a social
philosopher and ideologist.*

Twenty-two years ago A. W. Coats (1954, p. 529) observed that
although there had been a growth in the literature concerned with
Veblen's contributions to social thought there existed no comparable
body of studies dealing with his contributions to economics. Coats felt
that the time was ripe for building such a literature, and he analyzed
Veblen's methodology in order to provide a background for it. Nevertheless, since 1954 there has been no more than a handful of articles on
special aspects of Veblen's economics (Hansen 1964; Spengler 1972;
Leathers and Evans 1973; O'Donnell 1973), and only one that deals with
a variety of his economic subjects. The latter was written by Sowell
(1967), who adopted the approach of examining one topic after another,
offering an incisive evaluation of each. A few books and a collection of
essays on Veblen have appeared in the last twenty years, but rather than
concentrating upon his economic doctrines they have been concerned in
a diffuse and episodic way with his ideas in a variety of disciplines, or
have reviewed his philosophical and methodological ideas, or have
attempted to deal with his background, to place him in the context
of American culture, and to discuss his psychological peculiarities
(Rosenberg 1956; Dobriansky 1957; Dowd 1958; Dowd 1964; Qualey
1968; Seckler 1975). Many articles have been written on Veblen's sociological ideas, but those contributions, which appear in a number of his
major essays and in much of *The Theory of the Leisure Class*, are not the
concern of the present paper.

In short, Coats's observation is still true. There is no study in the past
literature that shows the economic system that Veblen constructed,
perhaps because of the difficulty of discerning its outlines in the many

---

*Indiana University of Pennsylvania.

pages of his verbose and discursive works.[1] Veblen himself never provided an outline of it, nor even considered it explicitly as a subject. The present study therefore has the principal objective of contributing to a foundation for an understanding of his economics by displaying its various parts as components of a system. A secondary objective is to add to the analysis and evaluation of his ideas.

It is not necessary to show the development of Veblen's system, because although he added to it, and changed a few of its minor features, he did not modify its basic structure. The contradictions in his theories generally appear in the same book, rather than being the result of an evolution of his thought. The study is limited to a direct examination of his views, and does not consider their many sources, or compare him with other writers, or relate his work to its times, although it provides materials that are necessary for such types of inquiries.[2]

An appropriate level of generality has been found to present without superficiality all the elements of Veblen's system within the confines of an article. In certain respects the treatment of his work is intentionally brief. Veblen's views on human nature, for example, and his theories regarding the three instincts that he identified, have been discussed at great length in the existing literature. These familiar topics must be mentioned here in order to present his complete system, but there is no necessity to repeat the exhaustive exposition and criticism that they have frequently received elsewhere.

This paper is the outcome of reflecting upon Veblen intermittently over a period of twenty-four years, ever since the time that I became Clarence Ayres's graduate student and assistant, and was therefore introduced to Veblen's work — I should say not merely introduced, but, inevitably, steeped in and saturated with it. I promised myself that some day I would try to assess Ayres's arguments that Veblen had discovered the essential workings of the economy, and I hope that I have been able to formulate a balanced view of the matter. The stimulus that has motivated me to undertake the study at this particular time is the special interest that is given to Veblen's work by the continuing problems of unemployment and business fluctuations. Veblen asserted that these problems are caused by businessmen's search for profits at the expense of industrial efficiency. An examination of his work therefore affords an opportunity to evaluate a timely and important thesis.

I. VEBLEN'S VIEWS ON THE SUBJECT-MATTER OF ECONOMIC SCIENCE

Veblen's system deals with the subject-matter that he identified as the

---

1. In an article entitled "The Unity of Veblen's Theoretical System," Anderson (1933) concentrated on Veblen's quasi-anthropological system of past states of culture, not on his economic doctrines.

2. In many respects Veblen's work has been related to its times by Dorfman's (1934) superlative book. See also Walker (1978).

proper study of the economist, in which respect he was in disagreement with his orthodox contemporaries. His main objection to their work was not directly that their method or metaphysics or psychological theory was wrong, but that they were concerned with a range of problems that is irrelevant for understanding the modern industrial economy (Veblen 1919a, pp. 240-41). Veblen invariably qualified his infrequent praise of the neoclassical economists by stating that their work was commendable only in relation to its aims, postulates, and frame of reference, and those, he felt, were of little value (ibid., pp. 239-44).[3] By directing their attention to such narrow questions as the properties of marginal utility, whether rent can be regarded as interest, or interest as rent, and whether capital is a fund or a flow, they failed to take cognizance of the facts of "everyday traffic and growth and change," or of the "stupendous sweep of events in the market place" (Veblen 1973, pp. 563-64). To understand the modern economy, Veblen felt that it was necessary to understand the fundamental characteristics of humanity that have affected the development of civilization over past centuries, and to view the present-day economy as a phase in an evolutionary development.

Veblen argued that economics should be an evolutionary science, by which he meant that economic action should be its subject matter, rather than the material objects that were the principal concern of other economists (Veblen 1919a, p. 72). Instead of examining static equilibrium, economists should analyze the endless process of cumulative causation that the economy is undergoing, and should therefore study the dynamic principles of genesis, growth, and proliferation (ibid., p. 177). Instead of viewing the economy as constituted of an unchanging set of institutions, economists should follow the genetic approach, whereby they would examine not the purposes but the emergence and modification through time of economic institutions (ibid., pp. 124, 240, 267). Regarding the changes in these institutions and in culture generally, Veblen believed that there is no meliorative tendency (ibid., p. 229), no secular trend of any kind, nor a final state of economic organization (ibid., p. 436). Of course, he was not able to offer any scientific verification of these metaphysical opinions and normative judgments.

Veblen had two definitions of economics, each of which emphasizes different aspects of economic studies. First, he asserted that economics should be studied from the point of view of what it contributes to an understanding of the totality of behavior. It should be a study of the impact of economic activities upon culture, "an inquiry into cultural or institutional development as affected by economic exigencies or by the economic interest of . . . men . . ." (ibid., p. 173), a study of "the manner and degree in which the economic interest creatively shapes the general

---

3. Clarence Ayres (1944, p. 11) wrote that Veblen "dismissed price analysis altogether as a pre-Darwinian taxonomy," and referred to his "contempt for price theory."

scheme of life" (ibid., p. 177). This definition deals exclusively with the effects of economic conditions on culture in general, and it is so all-encompassing that it cannot serve as a guide. It embraces all aspects of human life, and calls for a type of study that is so highly inter-disciplinary that it can hardly be called economics. Of course, there are many interdisciplinary studies that examine the impact of special economic activities and conditions upon particular aspects of life, such as religion, politics, war, and crime. Indeed, Veblen's own study of private enterprise emphasizes the impact of business on cultural growth "apart from what is of immediate economic interest," and in this respect, like much of his work, "belongs rather in the field of the sociologist" (Veblen 1904, p. vi). Such studies are valuable in a variety of respects, but it must be recognized that they are only of indirect use in solving many economic problems.

Perhaps realizing the deficiencies of his first definition, Veblen also suggested a narrower scope for economic studies, and proposed that the discipline should study general cultural conditions insofar as they affect economic behavior, rather than the other way around: "In so far as the inquiry is economic science, specifically, the attention will converge upon the scheme of material life and will take in other phases of civilization only in their correlation with the scheme of material civilization" (Veblen 1919a, p. 241). The study of the scheme of material life is the study of "the sequence of change in the methods of doing things, — the methods of dealing with the material means of life" (ibid.. p. 71). Thus Veblen appeared to believe that economic science should concentrate on the technological developments that have occurred in the processes of making a living. In further explanation of his definition, however, he shifted his emphasis so as to interpret *methods of doing things* as *economic institutions* (ibid., pp. 71-72). When taken as items in the scheme of life, even productive goods, he asserted somewhat obscurely, "are, substantially, prevalent habits of thought" (ibid., p. 71). Material civilization, he wrote, "is a scheme of institutions" (ibid., p. 241), and therefore economics should develop "a theory of a cumulative sequence of economic institutions . . ." (ibid., p. 77).

Veblen's second definition of economics, which is the one to which he adhered in the construction of his economic system, does indicate an interesting and worthwhile aspect of the discipline, but it excludes a great many important matters. The difficulty with pronouncements like Veblen's is that brief statements about what economics ought to be display the opinions of the writer rather than provide a description of what economics actually is, and they are either so general as to be barren of content, or so narrow as to exclude much of the discipline and to cause sight to be lost of the diversity of the subject matter. Economics has undergone such a growth of content and scope, and in detailed respects such an enrichment of analytical and quantitative methods, that there is no brief way to describe it. In part, economics is the study of the way that the economy is affected by cultural and social conditions; in part it is the study of ways of making a living, both technological and institutional; but it is also concerned with the analysis of narrowly technical economic phenomena. Veblen not only neglected the latter, he directed attention away from many important problems by his opinion that price theory is not a valuable part of the discipline, whereas in fact some of the central concerns of economics are matters such as the determination of output prices, techniques of optimization, and the process of allocation of resources.

II. VEBLEN'S GENERAL THEORY OF ECONOMIC CHANGE

Exemplifying the approach that he advocated in his discussion of the subject matter of economics, Veblen's economic system is a theory of economic change over long periods of time, which examines the influence of methods of making a living upon the economic order and upon other aspects of culture. Veblen had a general theory of the process by which he thought all economies evolve, and a theory of capitalism that was intended to display it as a special case of the operation of the forces identified by his general theory.

Veblen's general theory proceeds through a number of different stages, and is sufficiently complicated to be worth outlining in advance. First, Veblen sought for a dominant factor that influences human behavior, and concluded that it is habits of thought. Second, he inquired into the origin of traditional habits of thought, and found it to lie in instinctive behavior. Third, he took up the question of how new habits of thought come into being, and concluded they are caused by developments of technology. Fourth, he considered how technological change occurs, and concluded that it results from a basic instinctive drive. Veblen emerged with the thesis that there are antiquated habits of thought which support the traditional organization of economic life, including the position of a dominant group, and that there are new habits of thought which tend to undermine the old patterns of economic organization, and thus lead to changes in the economic order.

The foundation of Veblen's theory of economic change is his theory of human nature. This was a mixture of behaviorism, the doctrines of William James, and an instinct and habit psychology. Veblen believed that mankind is always engaged in purposive behavior (Veblen 1914, pp. 3-4). Economic action, intelligence, and human life in general are teleological "in the sense that men always and everywhere seek to do something" (Veblen 1919a, p. 75; and see ibid., p. 5). The "prime movers" which establish the purposes of behavior and thereby condition the life of the species are "the instinctive proclivities and tropismatic aptitudes with which the species is typically endowed" (Veblen 1914, p. 1).

Veblen therefore simultaneously criticized the orthodox economists for their teleological interpretation of economic behavior, and argued that human behavior is purposive (Veblen 1919a, pp. 238-39). Without noting the further contradiction, he also wrote that humanity is guided in large part by habits and tropisms (Veblen 1914, p. 1), rather than by rational considerations and calculations, that social and economic change is strictly determinate and essentially mechanical, and that society as a whole is in the grip of blind and impersonal evolutionary forces over which it has no control (Veblen 1919a, p. 436).

Veblen believed that behavior is dominated by habits of thought. It is a reflection of the vagueness of his concept of habits of thoughts that after stressing that they are institutions (ibid., p. 239; Veblen 1923, p. 101, n. 1), he wrote that "institutions are an outgrowth of habit" (Veblen 1919a, p. 241; and see ibid., p. 243). Habits of thought are manifested in myths, superstitution, metaphysical theories, usage, customs, canons of conduct, and principles of right and propriety (Veblen 1914, p. 49; Veblen 1919b, pp. 3-7). The organization of society is based upon and supported by habits of thought, which constitute a complex of beliefs that buttress the special privileges and economic domination of a particular group, such as the war lords during the "barbarian era," and the nobility and clergy during the feudal era.

Veblen then took up the problem of the origins of traditional habits of thought, and hence of the origins of traditional patterns of behavior and of traditional economic institutions. One major answer that social scientists have given to questions about the sources of civilization is that *omnis cultura ex cultura*, that previous culture is the matrix of change, that the individual is formed by society and not the other way around. Marx, for example, believed that religion, customs, and principles of right and propriety are devised at the behest of the economically dominant class in order to maintain their superior position, which is an explanation in terms of a cultural process. By contrast, Veblen was driven by the turn-of-the-century quest for certainty, which in cultural inquiries was manifested by the desire to establish the foundations of cultural phenomena upon simple ultimate elements of which culture could be regarded as a derivative product. At each critical point in the development of his system, therefore, Veblen tried to base it upon innate biological properties.

The habits of thought that were formed in pre-industrial ages, and that through lags in cultural change have survived into the present, resulted, Veblen asserted, from the action of instincts. "Under the impulsion of a given instinctive propensity, a given line of behaviour becomes habitual and so is installed by use and wont as a principle of conduct" which is then handed on by tradition (Veblen 1914, p. 50; and see ibid., p. 49). Veblen did not explain the process by which instincts result in the formation of habits, and he rendered his proposition difficult to test and his theory dubious by stating that habits enter into the formation of instincts: "All instinctive behaviour is subject to development and hence to modification by habit" (ibid., p. 38). This modification, according to Veblen, does not always take a desirable form. The aims of instincts are in some respects perverted and distorted by the contaminating influence of bad habitual behavior (ibid., pp. 51 ff.).

Veblen's theory has a number of deficiencies. First, it provides no explanation of how habits affect instincts, or of how instincts, which in his view are essentially good, can result in the formation of what he regarded as bad habits of thought. Second, his theory is untestable, since it is framed in such a way that it is consistent with any behavior. For example, if behavior is workmanlike, it displays the operation of the instinct of workmanship. If behavior is unworkmanlike, as in the case of Veblen's businessmen, it is because the instinct of workmanship is distorted or contaminated. Third, since the theory of instincts is itself an unsatisfactory explanation of human behavior it is not surprising that Veblen failed to demonstrate that instincts are responsible for the creation of institutions, and that he fell into the practice of using the word "instinct" as a synonym for "behavioral pattern," thereby abandoning the notion of instincts as an explanatory principle.

Veblen's procedure is evident in his treatment of the institution of private property. He asserted that it is an institution, and hence results from the operation of instinctive drives, and is indeed the most important of the "time-warped preconceptions — or superstitions" that have been handed down from an alien past (Veblen 1917, p. 363), but his account of the emergence of the institution described it as a matter-of-fact cultural phenomenon. In his early work, Veblen argued that property began as booty held as trophies of a successful raid, and that it started with the ownership of persons, primarily women (Veblen 1899, pp. 22-28, 53; Veblen 1934, pp. 46-48). This does not imply that Veblen was demonstrating that property is the result of a warlike instinct, because predatory behavior is not itself instinctive in his work. Such behavior was, he asserted, unknown in a long previous era of peaceful savagery (Veblen 1914, pp. 100-102). Subsequently Veblen emphasized that the evolution of private property was made possible "in all cases . . . as a consequence of an appreciable advance in the industrial arts" (ibid., p. 157). It had its origins in the peaceful savage era, after technological advances made land usable for agriculture and established the special fertility and hence desirability of certain pieces of land (ibid., pp. 150-52, 161). Religious leaders may then have claimed a right to the exclusive ownership of some of the best land. A military hierarchy arose in the course of the continual warfare of the barbarian era, and the war lords appropriated much of the booty (ibid., pp. 157-66; Veblen 1915, p. 167). This account has serious defects (Anderson 1933, p. 609), but the point of interest here is that it explains the present-day institution of property as an outcome of

the character of previous culture, not as a superstition generated
by innate instinctive drives.

The next matter to consider is Veblen's theory of how habits of thought
undergo change. They are inherently static, but they are unstable and
"necessarily vary incontinently with the passage of time" (Veblen 1915,
p. 5). In explanation of why they vary, Veblen wrote in more than one
place that there is an endogenous process within institutions that produces change in the rest of life: the "unremitting changes and adaptations
that go forward in the scheme of institutions, legal and customary, unre-
mittingly induce new habits of work and of thought in the community,
and so they continually instill new principles of conduct ..." (Veblen
1914, p. 17; and see ibid., p. 19). This view, however, clearly contradicts
the central thesis of his theory, and in contrast to it, in his main explanation of economic change Veblen argued that new habits of thought result
from the emergence of new ways of making a living, which are in turn the
result of technological change (Veblen 1904, pp. 322-24; Veblen 1914,
pp. 147-48; Veblen 1923, pp. 42-43). Institutions are static and resist
change; new institutions are formed as the result of the dynamic impact
of technology.

The question then arises as to how technological change can occur, a
question that is made more difficult by the supposition that humanity is
in the grip of old habits of mind. As in his theory of habit formation,
Veblen sought some factor more fundamental than culture that would
explain the development of technology, and once again asserted that it
occurs because of the operation of humanity's biological constitution.
Veblen postulated the existence of three instincts which interact to cause
technological change. The instinct of workmanship is the desire to
perform efficiently the activities that fulfill the goals set by the other
instincts (Veblen 1914, pp. 25-37 and passim; Veblen 1934, pp. 78-96).
It speeds and aids technological change. A second instinct is the bent of
idle curiosity (Veblen 1914, pp. 85-89; Veblen 1919a, pp. 6 ff.). "Idle
curiosity" is an inappropriate term for conveying an important part of
Veblen's meaning. He did not mean that the curiosity is idle or aimless,
but that it operates only if there is surplus energy after the satisfaction of
essential needs; and he meant that humanity is motivated by a desire to
discover knowledge independently of the desire for material gain and of
any utilitarian aim (Veblen 1914, pp. 86-88). The operation of the instinct
of idle curiosity results in some useless information, but it is also
the source of the new basic knowledge upon which the instinct of workmanship draws to produce practical innovations (ibid., pp. 87-88). The
third instinct is the parental bent, which is the urge to care for the welfare
of others. It reinforces the instinct of workmanship in the pursuit
of efficiency (ibid., pp. 25-27, 48, 89-91).

Humanity's instinctive drives therefore result in continuous technological change, and that is the basic factor which causes and shapes

the growth of culture: "The facts of technological use and wont are fundamental and definitive ..." (ibid., p. vii). New technology foments change by generating new habits of thought, which lead to new economic and social arrangements. The impact of technology upon institutions is made through a process of conditioning that occurs in the activities of making a living, where the cultural incidence of technological change is focused. In pre-industrial centuries the techniques of making a living contributed to the development of superstition and to the elaboration of the notion of a divinely ordained social and economic structure, but in the modern era the character of the machine process generates matter-of-fact habits of mind. "In proportion as a given line of employment has more of the character of a machine process and less of the character of handicraft, the matter-of-fact training which it gives is more pronounced" (Veblen 1904, p. 322; and see Veblen 1919a, pp. 50-55, 62-64). Veblen therefore destroyed the consistency of his discussion of habit formation by abandoning his explanation in terms of instinctive behavior when he considered the emergence of new habits. Although technological progress in his system is a result of instinctive behavior, the activity of undertaking such change does not itself generate new habits of mind. In Veblen's theory they are not formed in the course of the continual exercise of an instinct, but as a consequence of the impact on the human constitution of the external conditions of the machine process (Veblen 1904, pp. 322-23).

The material basis of existence has always been characterized by obvious causal sequences and mechanical processes, and in the past most of life was spent in trying to earn a living. Why then was humanity not conditioned by the matter-of-fact nature of earning a living before the industrial revolution, and how was it possible for superstitious habits of mind to emerge in the course of undertaking economic activities? How did the structure of religious ideas, folklore, myth, and customs get its start? Why would humanity, faced with the matter-of-fact environment of our physical world, begin to imagine an unseen world of spirits, devils, and gods? Veblen's extracultural explanation argues that an anthropomorphizing tendency leads the worker to impute a workmanlike propensity to the objects involved in making a living when they are manipulated directly in a handicraft process of production. The anthropomorphizing tendency is a property of the way that the human intellect works; it is an instinctive way of perceiving things. Since human activity in the course of making a living is teleological, the objects used in that process are assumed to be similarly motivated (Veblen 1914, 52-61). The animistic imputations lead the worker into methods and expedients that are inefficient, but that are nevertheless perpetuated. Over time the imputed notions may "grow into a developed animistic system and come to the dignity of myth, and ultimately of theology" (ibid., p. 62). Clearly this explanation asserts little more than that the reason for anthropomorphization is that humanity has an anthropomorphizing tendency.

After pursuing the various foregoing lines of reasoning, Veblen emerged with a theory of economic change that divided the history of civilization into an older era dominated by traditional habits of thought that developed as a consequence of the manner of making a living prior to the advent of the industrial revolution, and the beginning of a new era initiated by the growth of the machine process. The traditional institutions were engendered in previous generations by past material conditions, and they are necessarily out-of-date insofar as technology and ways of getting a living have changed (Veblen 1923, pp. 207-208). Habits of thought are induced by workday conditions, so the new habits are "enforced by the current technological scheme," and reflect the "working logic of the current state of the industrial arts . . ." (Veblen 1918, p. 4). "The new terms of workday knowledge and belief, which do not conform to the ancient canons, go to enforce and stabilize new canons and standards, of a character alien to the traditional point of view," (Veblen 1919b, p. 9).

Consequently, the old and the new habits of thought are in conflict across the entire spectrum of economic behavior (Veblen 1914, pp. 148-49). Those who are under the influence of the old habits of thought, including both those who benefit from them and those who do not, resist the social, legal, and economic changes that grow from the new habits that are produced by changes in the state of the industrial arts (Veblen 1917, pp. 363-66; Veblen 1919b, pp. 18-23). The old habits are inimical to a rational conduct of economic life; they are "at cross purposes with serviceability and the sense of workmanship" (Veblen 1914, p. 50); and the history of their struggle with efficiency provides many examples of "the triumph of imbecile institutions over life and culture . . ." (ibid., p. 25). Thus there is a conflict that arises from the "discrepancy between the current conditions of life and the received rules which govern the conduct of life . . ." (Veblen 1923, p. 208).

III. VEBLEN'S THEORY OF ECONOMIC CHANGE UNDER CAPITALISM

The form that the conflict takes in modern Western society is the outcome of the activities and interests of five main economic groups: absentee owners, businessmen, technicians, workers, and champions of the archaic principles of conduct.

Owners and Businessmen. The class of owners has been created as a distinct group, Veblen wrote, by the separation of ownership from control which results from the corporate form of business organization (Veblen 1904, pp. 174-75). Because of this statement he has frequently been credited with anticipating the work of Berle and Means (Sowell 1967, p. 196; Veblen 1973, pp. 278-79, 321-22), but in actuality Veblen's view of the matter is different from the modern theory, and cannot be said to constitute a coherent position. We would say that ownership and control are often separate functions in corporations because stock ownership is often absentee ownership. A small minority of stockholders, who may be executives of the corporation, may have a sufficiently large percentage of the stock to exercise control; or control may be in the hands of the executives because stock ownership is diffused, and because of the powers and self-perpetuating character of the jobs that they hold. Veblen argued, however, that owners are the possessors of tangible property, whereas control over business is exercised by managers in proportion as they own the common stock and other intangible property of the business (Veblen 1904, pp. 174-75, 266-67). In Veblen's theory, therefore, ownership and control are not separated, since those who own businesses are the controllers of them.

In fact, although Veblen had written that absentee owners do not have control of their businesses, he subsequently stated explicitly that they do: "The control of . . . industrial powers, and the decision as to what, when, and how much work shall be done by them, is vested in the absentee owners of the country's resources. And these owners and their business agents go into this work of directing and restraining the work in hand . . ." (Veblen 1923, p. 210). Veblen also defined absentee ownership as "ownership of means in excess of what the owner can make use of, personally and without help" (ibid., p. 12), an extremely broad definition that has no direct implications for the question of whether ownership and control are separated in the modern corporation or in other proprietory forms.

Owners and businessmen are the beneficiaries of the scheme of habits of thought formed during the eighteenth century, the natural rights scheme of contract, individualism, security of possessions, and above all, of ownership (Veblen 1904, pp. 380-81; Veblen 1919b, pp. 18-23). Businessmen make money for the absentee owners and are the guardians of their vested interests, although the objectives of the two groups do not always coincide because businessmen are not directly interested in the efficient operation of industrial property (Veblen 1904, p. 176; Veblen 1921, pp. 125-26; Veblen 1973, p. 521). They have in fact become progressively less interested in industrial processes, which reflects the displacement of the nineteenth century captain of industry as the dominant type of businessman by the corporate financial expert, and his displacement in turn by the banker or financier (Veblen 1919b, pp. 42-45; Veblen 1923, pp. 110-13, 231-32, 256-57). Financiers are interested only in money, which they seek by manipulations that were frankly incomprehensible to Veblen: "The 'money power' comes in as a . . . pecuniarily trained factor, with ever increasing force and incisiveness, to muddle the whole situation mysteriously and irretrievably . . ." (Veblen 1914, p. 347).

Businessmen are conditioned by their competitive mode of life. Even their criteria of the efficiency and worth of a person are pecuniary (ibid., p. 349). In Veblen's work they are exaggerated caricatures of the same economic man that Veblen criticized as a fiction created by orthodox economists. Businessmen spend their time trying to maximize their pecuniary gains, which they do with limitless rapacity, by force and fraud. The "whole duty" of the businessman is to make money (Veblen 1923, p. 211), so he operates with "an eye single to the net gain . . ." (ibid., p. 217). This is the fundamental weakness of the capitalistic economy, Veblen argued, because the goal of making money is in conflict with industrial pursuits, which are aimed at the efficient production of commodities. To make money, businessmen disrupt the orderly process of production by competitive strategems and maneuvers, and by restricting output in order to raise prices (Veblen 1904, pp. 261-62; Veblen 1919b, p. 100). They waste resources by conducting sales promotion campaigns, by producing "superfluities and spurious goods," and by "systematic dislocation, sabotage and duplication" (Veblen 1921, p. 108; and see Veblen 1919b, p. 100; Veblen 1921, pp. 1-26; Veblen 1923, pp. 215-20). "The prevalence of . . . business enterprise . . . is perhaps the most serious obstacle which the pecuniary culture opposes to the advance in workmanship" (Veblen 1914, p. 350).

Veblen's treatment of business reflects his view that the productive process is confined to activities on the workshop floor, and to the technological activities that link different enterprises and markets. His attention was focused on things that he could see: the man at the machine, the physical transformation of materials; and he neglected many matters that are not directly engineering activities but that are also part of the technological process of producing goods, such as financial control and personnel management. Many of the procedures for accomplishing managerial functions are affected by the economic and legal institutions of the particular society in which they are undertaken. Veblen supposed, however, that capitalism was wholly responsible for the existence of the procedures rather than for their particular form. Furthermore, in assuming that making money is the only motive of businessmen, Veblen neglected to recognize that business executives are also driven by a desire to achieve productive efficiency and to encourage the growth of their firms. These are ways of making money, but they are also ways in which businessmen increase their power and prestige, obtain a sense of accomplishment, and satisfy a desire for workmanlike efficiency.

Veblen did not understand that productive efficiency can be defined only in economic and not in technological terms. The distinction between business and industry, between pecuniary and technological criteria, is false as presented by Veblen. He believed that pecuniary criteria of efficiency lead to wastefulness, and that there is a true and good technological rule for determining the optimum level of output of every firm, the rule that output should be maximized, that plant and equipment should be operated at maximum capacity (Veblen 1904, passim; Veblen 1919b, pp. 92-93, 113; Veblen 1921, pp. 9-10, 121; Veblen 1923, p. 10). In actuality the optimum volume of output and the optimum technique of production, under socialism as well as capitalism, are determined by the economic condition of profit maximization, which transcends engineering relationships and the physical process of producing output. The economic problem of how much to produce of any commodity emerges when the question of allocating resources among alternative uses is raised, and cannot be solved or even posed on the grounds of the technological properties of production. Even business policies that are damaging to economic efficiency, such as the restriction of output that can occur under collusive oligopoly agreements, must have their deleterious effects measured by the use of a value standard, and are identified by comparison with optima that are pecuniarily determined.

It has often been recognized that Veblen correctly pointed out an area of inefficiency in his criticisms of salesmanship, advertising expenses, and other wastes of imperfect competition, and he deserves great credit for the forcefulness of his critique of such activities. Nevertheless, his generalizations went beyond what the data could support. He seized upon examples of financial manipulation and fraud, upon colorful incidents from the careers of the robber barons, and formed the absurd proposition that all business behavior is destructive to the economy.

Veblen then proceeded to identify the consequences of businessmen's behavior. Their pecuniary motivation, he argued, is the cause of depressions. This theme, manifested by each of his propositions about economic fluctuations, is the single element which lends some degree of unity and coherence to his work on the topic, for his propositions are not analytically complete, nor are they consistent internally or with each other, nor is any empirical evidence presented in support of them.

One major characteristic of the capitalist economy, Veblen asserted, is the unprofitability of older enterprises. Technological changes enable capital goods to be produced at lower cost, thus lowering the cost of production of commodities. As the cost of production falls, competition between businesses results in a fall in the price of output. Businesses which do not have the new capital goods have relatively high costs, and cannot make adequate profits at the lower prices set by new and rejuvenated firms (Veblen 1904, pp. 228-30). Furthermore, businesses tend to become overcapitalized during a period of prosperity. During an ensuing period of lower prices for their products, the interest that they have to pay and their other liabilities become excessive in relation to earnings, their profits are eliminated, and they are forced into bankruptcy (ibid., pp. 99-176, 200-203, 222-27; and see Veblen 1921, pp. 14-15).

Another major characteristic of capitalism is that businessmen systematically tend to overproduce. They issue unnecessarily large amounts of securities, because, for reasons that Veblen does not explain, a large nominal capital yields large net gains (Veblen 1923, pp. 90-96). Excessive capitalization, however, ultimately leads to "an excess of goods . . . above what is expedient on pecuniary grounds, — above what there is an effective demand for at prices that will repay the cost of production of the goods and leave something appreciable over as a profit" (Veblen 1904, pp. 216-17). The result of overproduction is cut-throat competition, depressed prices, and losses (ibid., pp. 257-58; Veblen 1923, pp. 90-91; Veblen 1973, p. 521). In work written prior to the creation of the Federal Reserve System, Veblen stated that when lenders observe this situation they cut off lines of credit, precipitating a liquidity crisis and a series of bankruptcies (Veblen 1904, pp. 191-93). Veblen also expressed the contradictory opinion that businessmen have eliminated overproduction by purposely creating habitual unemployment and restricting output (Veblen 1919b, pp. 93-100; Veblen 1921, pp. 3-13), and denied on theoretical grounds that overproduction is possible: "General overproduction . . . is a contradiction in terms. Aggregate supply is aggregate demand" (Veblen 1934, p. 104).[4]

One reason for Veblen's obscurity on the issue of overproduction was his lack of comprehension of the economics of the firm and of the workings of finance. topics on which his statements were sometimes ridiculous: "The funded value of the productive goods in question," he wrote, "should be competent, through the introduction of credit relations, to pay for, and therefore to capitalize, these goods in the form of increased industrial equipment" (Veblen 1973, p. 519). A second reason was that he did not give sufficiently sustained attention to the problem to make up his mind on it. The overproduction thesis — a thesis that has been central to the work of most heterodox economists since the time of Malthus, and one which is of such critical structural importance that every economist should know whether he believes it to be true or false — was not of great significance to Veblen. He was not interested in analytical problems of a purely economic nature. On the question of the details of the operation of a capitalistic economy, his objectives were polemic, not scientific. If in one context he could turn some clever phrases against businessmen by asserting that they restrict the level of output so that there is no overproduction, then he would do so. If in another context he thought it striking and iconoclastic to allege that the nature of business leads to overproduction, then he would follow that course. The inconsistency of his positions troubled him not at all.

4. Thus he led different writers of great ability to dissimilar perceptions of the position that he held. Sweezy (1958, p. 27), for example, stated that Veblen "habitually and naively" assumed that Say's Law operates "in the extreme form in which total income is automatically spent and remains constant over time," despite the incompatibility with it of many of the processes that he described. On the other hand. Sowell (1967, p. 187) wrote that Veblen was, like Keynes, unimpressed with Say's Law, treating it as an identity.

Veblen's opinions on the nature of depression and prosperity are similarly difficult to reconcile. Sometimes he asserted that depressions are characterized by "an appreciable curtailment of industry" (ibid., 1904, p. 191), but he also argued that a depression is "mainly, a readjustment of values," a change of ownership, "rather than a destruction of wealth or a serious reduction of the aggregate productiveness of industry as measured in goods" (Veblen 1934, pp. 112-13; see also Veblen 1904, pp. 185, 191). To Veblen, normal times were not much different from booms in regard to the volume of output: "In brisk times there is likely to be something in the way of a competitive increase in the volume of output, but in ordinary times such an effect is not likely to be observed" (Veblen 1923, p. 94). Depressions, he explained, are primarily "a psychological fact" (Veblen 1934, p. 112), "a malady of the affections of the business men" (Veblen 1904, p. 241). In Veblen's opinion the control of credit by private banks and the operations of the Federal Reserve System have almost eliminated liquidity crises and have "virtually done away with . . . fluctuations of prosperity and depression" (Veblen 1923, pp. 91-92; and see ibid., pp. 219, 369-71).

Veblen had a separate opinion about the secular level of prices in the nineteenth century. Modern machine processes are so productive that businesses during that century engaged in vigorous competition to sell their output, thus lowering prices to levels at which profits could not be made, which is the condition that Veblen frequently described as depression. Over the large part of the economy in which competitive forces were at work, prices were ordinarily at unprofitable levels. The condition of "chronic depression, more or less pronounced," was "normal to business under the fully developed regime of the machine industry (Veblen 1904, p. 234; and see ibid., p. 255).

The view that modern competitive industry results in unprofitably low prices led Veblen to his theory of the secular trend of output. Businessmen have open to them two ways of remedying the condition of depressed prices. The first is by increasing consumption in order to use up the products of industry without creating increased capacity. Driven by the desire to emulate each other, businessmen and owners engage in conspicuous consumption (Veblen 1899, pp. 22-34, 68-101), but nevertheless they cannot enable consumption to become large enough to maintain product prices (Veblen 1904, pp. 255-58, 264). Modern industry is too productive, and income is too unequally distributed. The income that goes to productive individuals, that is, to workers, is determined by the minimum that is necessary to induce them to work, while most of the national income — at least seventy per cent — goes to businessmen (Veblen 1973, p. 566). People with high incomes waste a lot, but they are committed to the desirability of saving and investment, and therefore do not consume enough, while their investments add further to productive capacity (Veblen 1904, pp. 255-58).

Since consumption cannot be increased sufficiently, a second course adopted by businessmen is to retard production to a rate less than that which is needed for current consumption, thus enabling product prices to be maintained (Veblen 1919b, pp. 91-101; Veblen 1921, pp. 9, 42; Veblen 1923, pp. 415-17). Organized labor performs the same function to a lesser degree by withdrawing efficiency for the purpose of maintaining wages (Veblen 1923, pp. 412-15). The businessman's aim of restricting output is achieved by business coalitions, because they reduce cut-throat competition. "Thorough going coalition" would eliminate fluctuations of prices and output entirely (Veblen 1904, pp. 258-63), but the total elimination of competition is very difficult. Even in industries in which there is a high degree of concentration, price wars sometimes occur (ibid., p. 264). Nevertheless, the degree of concentration has been increasing (Veblen 1919b, p. 107), and, in Veblen's opinion, the old era of competitive underselling, the reasonably free competitive system of production and sales, "is a past phase" that ended sometime toward the close of the nineteenth century (Veblen 1923, p. 98). The new system is primarily one in which business coalitions engage in non-price competition and follow a policy of curtailing output in order to maintain prices and thereby to make profits (Veblen 1919b, pp. 91-113; Veblen 1923, p. 99). As the degree of concentration becomes more pronounced, the tendency to restrict output will become more extreme, and over time there will be a "progressive shrinkage of the available means of life" (Veblen 1923, p. 445; and see ibid., pp. 421-23).

Veblen thus presented a picture of a twentieth-century economy that is subject to short-run fluctuations of prices of diminishing amplitude, and to slight fluctuations of output that are damped around a depressed and falling secular trend. Most of the time Veblen clearly believed that business fluctuations were not an important problem, a view shown to be mistaken by the historical record before, during, and after his life. On the other hand, he also expressed the contradictory opinion that conflicts between labor and management would generate "frequent and substantial oscillations" of output "below the ordinary level," and that these would cause the downward trend (ibid., p. 423). This opinion is an oversimplification of the complex reality of business fluctuations, which cannot be attributed to conflicts between labor and management, or to any other single cause. Different fluctuations often have different causes, and the importance of any single factor varies over time. The lower turning point is ordinarily the result of the combined action of several different causes, and the upper turning point is generated by several others. On the matter of the declining secular trend of output Veblen never equivocated, but in that regard his prejudice against business once again interfered with his ability to understand the economy, and he predicted the opposite of what occurred. It is evident with respect to Veblen's views on both business fluctuations and the secular trend that he did not have an integrated theory of the level of economic activity, which explains why his work on the topic is confused in its general conceptual characteristics and disorganized in its detailed expression.

Technicians and Workers. Technicians, a brief name for a group that includes engineers and industrial experts, perform a complicated economic role in Veblen's system. They are motivated by a desire for monetary gain, which leads them to pursue pecuniary principles of efficiency, by which Veblen meant principles of industrial inefficiency (Veblen 1914, p. 346). Their loyalties are with the owners and businessmen, but their industrial functions are ultimately subversive of the system of business enterprise.

Technicians are important, Veblen observed, because they keep the industrial machinery in operation (Veblen 1921, p. 136). Businessmen, preoccupied with pecuniary matters, have become incapable of understanding the increasingly complex process of production, so the technicians have progressively taken over more of the industrial functions of management (Veblen 1914, p. 345; Veblen 1923, pp. 105-7, 254-59). Businessmen are still in authority, but their inability to exercise their responsibility competently prevents the attainment of efficiency (Veblen 1914, pp. 345-48, 351; Veblen 1923, pp. 259-61). This does not offend the technicians. Their pecuniary motivations lead them to cooperate willingly with the businessmen in limiting the productiveness of the industrial system (Veblen 1921, p. 135). In Veblen's work the technicians are capitalist lackeys, "a harmless and docile sort, well fed on the whole. and somewhat placidly content . . . , unreservedly doing job-work for the Vested Interests" (ibid., p. 135). Their aid would be necessary in directing the planned economy that Veblen advocated as a replacement for capitalism, but he did not believe that the technicians have any wish to assume that function (ibid., pp. 135-69).[5]

Technicians are also important because they are responsible for most of the technological progress that occurs (Veblen 1923, pp. 263-80), and are therefore unwittingly the source of much of the process of cultural change. Veblen did not have an explanation of how they initiate technological improvements, either in regard to inventions or to the innovative activity of adapting them to the production of commodities and incorporating the changes into the economic system. His account of technological change is largely confined to the observations that technological knowledge is a collective possession of the community, and that contributions to it are made by individuals who are endowed with strong instincts of workmanship and idle curiosity (Veblen 1914, pp. 103-12).

---

5. Veblen's opinions on the desirable future role of the technicians are expressed in the closing pages of *The Engineers and the Price System*, which in it utopian tone, and in the stridency of its advocacy of a particular form of economic order, is not characteristic of the mainstream of his thought.

One wonders how Veblen thought that technological innovation occurs. He wrote that "technicians are forever occupied with contriving new ways and means" designed to increase output (Veblen 1923, p. 230), whereas absentee owners "decide summarily what and how much is not to be done" (ibid., p. 260), and businessmen are indifferent or hostile to industrial efficiency and technological change (Veblen 1904, pp. 27-29; Veblen 1923, pp. 106-9). Did Veblen believe, then, that technicians think of new industrial processes and products in their off-hours, and install the innovations in secret behind the backs of the businessmen? Whatever the sources and motivation of basic research and invention, the adoption of new technology, whether occurring in established firms or in the course of the creation of new ones, is so clearly the businessman's decision that Veblen's view is inexplicable except by reference to his emotional bias against business.

Unskilled workers in Veblen's system are frequently described as "the underlying population" (Veblen 1921, pp. 115, 117; Veblen 1923, p. 6), an amorphous, passive, and anonymous mass; but skilled workers are the immediate instruments of change in the organization of economic life, because their habits of thought are undergoing modification (Veblen 1904, p. 349; Veblen 1914, p. 343). Veblen's discussion of how new habits are formed in the modern era includes both workers and technicians. Technological progress has created the industrial age in which the transformation of commodities is dominated by machine processes. Material inputs are subjected to an impersonal mechanical sequence of operations, each of which has an obvious causal connection with the preceding and following parts of the process. Participation by workers and technicians in these operations subjects them to the "intellectual and spiritual training of the machine . . ." (Veblen 1904, p. 323), induces them by occupational conditioning to think in the impersonal terms of causal sequences, and leads them to adopt scientific impersonality and mechanistic criteria in evaluating propositions of all sorts (ibid., pp. 322-24; Veblen 1923, pp. 254-55). The machine discipline, "with its spiritual concomitant — workday ideals and scepticism of what is only conventionally valid—" (Veblen 1904, p. 323), "runs counter to the habit of thinking in conventional, anthropomorphic terms" (ibid., p. 322). Workers and technicians become progressively "addicted to the mechanistic logic of the inorganic sciences and more intolerant of all those conventional truths and amenities that lie beyond the borders of tangible fact" (Veblen 1923, p. 254; and see Veblen 1919b, p. 40). They are trained into materialistic iconoclasm, lose faith in conventional standards of certainty (Veblen 1904, pp. 322, 352), and come to disbelieve "any proposition that cannot be stated convincingly in terms of . . . mechanistic logic" (Veblen 1917, p. 362).

The immediate consequence of the adoption of mechanistic logic for the economic organization of society is that the domination of the natural rights philosophy is weakened. Although the technicians do not react by opposing their masters, the workers begin to question the traditional metaphysical bases of justification of economic institutions (Veblen 1904, p. 327; Veblen 1914, p. 343). They become critical of specific economic and social arrangements, such as the distribution of income, the existence of privileged classes, the economic and legal domination of businessmen, and, Veblen insisted, the desirability of thrift and even the family (Veblen 1904, ch. 9, ch. 10).

Most significant of all, the workers no longer regard the institution of private property as sacrosanct. They are "losing the instinct of individual ownership"; the acquisition of property is in some respects "ceasing to appeal to them" (ibid., p. 327; and see ibid., p. 351). Furthermore, Veblen argued, they are beginning to disregard the property rights of owners, impelled not only by their changing habits of thought but also by their economic interests. The worker is prevented from attaining wealth because the "rights of ownership and investment uniformly work to his material detriment . . ." (Veblen 1917, p. 364), and this sharpens his antagonism to the capitalist system. Economic conflict in the modern era is therefore generated between the workers, who have new habits of thought, and owners and businessmen, who have older habits of thought. The technicians also adopt the new habits of thought, but they do not experience the additional element of economic deprivation that would bring them into opposition with the wealthy classes. In Veblen's system, therefore, the development of new habits of thought is necessary but not sufficient to bring about change, and his efforts to differentiate his system from Marx's (Veblen 1919a, pp. 415-17) were consequently partially unsuccessful in regard to the question of the causes of class conflict.

Veblen wrote in one place that the conflict is thus far almost wholly negative and destructive in its results (Veblen 1914, p. 343). Workers are becoming willing to confiscate property without compensating the owners, and to eliminate a distribution of income based on property ownership (Veblen 1904, pp. 338-43), but they have not as yet taken the initiative to achieve constructive alternatives to the received institutions (Veblen 1914, p. 343). Elsewhere, however, Veblen expounded a theory of the emergence of a new economic order, expressing repeatedly the view that the new habits of thought are leading the workers to develop forms of economic life in replacement of the institutions of the natural rights system. The organization that will have the most important role in fomenting social change is the labor union (Veblen 1904, pp. 327-28)— local and national unions, not the A.F. of L., precluded as it was from radical action by its devotion to selfish material interests (Veblen 1921, p. 88). Labor unions have developed along with the growth of machine industry. Creations of the modern era, they are inherently opposed to the dogmas formed in pre-industrial times and therefore direct their policies against the natural rights of property and pecuniary contract (Veblen

1904, pp. 328-30).

The economic order that will result from union activity, if it is left unchecked, is socialism (ibid., pp. 331, 353-57). Partly this will occur because of the characteristics of labor leaders. Mechanical processes induce a socialistic or iconoclastic inclination in those who, because of their special mechanical aptitude, are thrown into prominence among the ranks of workers, and who are most capable of revolutionary socialism (ibid., pp. 348-53). As socialists they concentrate primarily upon the reconstruction of economic institutions (ibid., p. 355), contending that the existing ones are "unfit for the work of the future" (ibid., p. 338).

There are elements of undeniable truth in Veblen's speculations. The machine process does have a great impact on society; workers have become liberated from the conviction that the rights of property are divinely ordained; unions do express opposition to the prerogatives claimed by business management. These, however, are obvious features of our century, and although Veblen observed them and gave vigorous expression to their characterization, it cannot be maintained that he had equal success in explaining their origins, discovering their interrelations, or discerning their future course. The last two hundred years has shown that working with machines does not in itself necessarily diminish superstition, or alter principles of right and propriety, or lead to the adoption of scientific reasoning processes in the mind of the workers. To account for the modification of attitudes, the secularization of thought, and the growth of rationality over the last two hundred years, it is more satisfactory to refer to the increase of scientific knowledge about humanity and the physical universe, and its widespread dissemination through public education.

In view of the materialistic inclinations of workers and unions during his own time, Veblen's account of their emerging attitudes reveals the degree of self-delusion into which he was led by projecting his personal opinions onto the subjects of his examination. The majority of workers in the Western world are interested in material gain. It was Veblen, not the workers, who disliked the institution of private property. It was Veblen, not the workers, who questioned the value of solvency, the family, and other bourgeois ideals. As for labor unions, there is no single way of life or set of goals or economic system to which they are led by some transcendental logic of the machine process (McNulty 1973, p. 474). American unions follow the principles of business unionship, and are firm supporters of the principle of pecuniary contract. A number of European unions have socialistic objectives, but many do not, and although a few American union leaders may be socialists, it is an uncontrovertible fact that many decades after Veblen's prediction socialistic American unions do not exist.

IV. THE END OF CAPITALISM AND THE EMERGENCE OF A NEW ECONOMIC ORDER

Veblen expressed the opinion that there are two possible courses of economic change, both of which lead to the end of the price system and business enterprise. The first is the course by which the forces of technological development and economic self-interest are leading the workers to reach toward socialism. Although arguments will continue to be made in favor of the status quo, business principles cannot win against the cultural effects of the machine process (Veblen 1904, p. 375). Unions will lay the groundwork for the formation of the new order, but the transition to socialism will not be peaceful. There will be a growth of antagonism "between those who own and those who do not," and an eventual violent cleavage will occur (Veblen 1917, p. 365). Owners and businessmen will almost certainly lose a contest of force with the workers, in which case some variety of socialism will emerge in the course of the post-revolutionary reconstruction (Veblen 1904, p. 337; Veblen 1917, pp. 364-66). The mechanistic logic of the machine process will therefore prevail, and "the price-system and its attendant business enterprise will yield and pass out" (Veblen 1917, p. 366).

The second possibility is that there will be a halt to the trend toward rationality and matter-of-factness. The development by the worker of new habits of thought, and the consequent attacks on property and private enterprise, can be avoided by a reversion to the institutions of the barbaric phase of Western civilization (Veblen 1915, p. 236). This can be achieved by adopting the prescriptions of the champions of the archaic principles of conduct, the final group that Veblen introduced into his system.

The champions of the archaic principles are the clergy, the military, politicians, lawyers, civil servants, and men of fashion (Veblen 1904, p. 321). A diverse collection of people, but linked in their freedom from direct employment within the system of business enterprise, they uphold the "ancient virtues of allegiance, piety, servility, graded dignity, class prerogative, and prescriptive authority . . ." (ibid., p. 393). Extolling the advantages of an ancient war-like culture, they seek the restoration of a system based on "absolute government, dynastic politics, devolution of rights and honors, ecclesiastical authority, and popular submission and squalor" (ibid., p. 394).

Owners and businessmen are beginning to embrace the views of the champions of the archaic principles, believing that to do so will strengthen the domination of business interests, and will lead to the adoption of imperialistic policies for purposes of commercial gain (ibid., pp. 394, 398-99; Veblen 1923, pp. 442-44). The pursuit of national glory and the development of a militaristic frame of mind will permit the creation of hostile relations with other nations, which will make it possible to place the country on a war footing (Veblen 1917, pp. 366-

67). This will enable the development of the apparatus of a police state, with surveillance of public and private life, repressive policies, and a consequent control of ideas and behavior (Veblen 1904, pp. 391-99). In this way owners and businessmen will try to achieve a continuation of their political and economic domination.

Nevertheless, Veblen went on to argue, if the policies of the champions of the archaic principles are adopted, business will become the victim of the ideology that it has nurtured. The archaic philosophy, reactionary rather than conservative, is more consistent with the barbarian past from which it springs than with a society based on the doctrine of natural rights. While not explicitly opposed to the interests of owners and businessmen, the champions of archaic principles articulate a structure of belief and practice that entails a neglect of business interests through an emphasis upon patriotism and national aggrandizement rather than profits (ibid., pp. 394-95). "Natural rights cannot be reinstated by a recourse to warlike habits and a coercive government . . ." (ibid., p. 376). Militaristic adventures and the archaic scheme of culture are un-businesslike and anti-materialistic, and they lead, through a course that Veblen left unexplained, to "a decline of business enterprise itself" (ibid., p. 400; and see ibid.. p. 399). In other writings on the topic, however, Veblen contradicted this thesis by stating that placing the country on a war footing and preserving the rights of ownership by force of arms would enable the retention of the price system and the pecuniary scheme of business (Veblen 1917, pp. 366-67; Veblen 1923, pp. 444-45).

To provide empirical evidence in support of an evaluation of Veblen's understanding of the currents of economic and political life in Western civilization would require an effort of research and exposition beyond the scope of this study. Here it is possible only to make a few comments about his major postulates.

Veblen asserted repeatedly that technology is fundamental and definitive in forming the character of a culture, and that this would be exemplified in the modern era by the destruction of the domination of the owners by the machine process, but then he took the position that it is equally probable that the effects of modern industry will be counteracted by an opposing movement which will overwhelm its disintegrative impact. Similarly, early in his work Veblen had indicated uncertainty as to whether old habits of thought would be displaced by new ones (Veblen 1914, p. 25). His hypotheses about the future therefore show that he never decided whether there is a dominant force in the determination of the character of culture and the economic order, and consequently his predictions about economic and cultural change ultimately dissolve into uncertainty.

Although Veblen must have seemed almost prescient in regard to the experience of Europe during the nineteen thirties, there has not been a subsequent movement toward fascism. In many countries there are signs of an increasing democratization, a growth of individual freedom, and a shift of attitudes against what are conceived to be the vested interests, the archaic virtues, and the militaristic, imperialistic, and authoritarian state. Wars seem to have encouraged rather than counteracted such a shift of attitudes. On the other hand, most Western countries have not become purely socialistic either. The alternatives which Veblen did not foresee, and with which his formulations are not consistent, are the mixed economy of private enterprise and government intervention that has actually evolved in the U.S., and the similar system, mixed also with government ownership, that has evolved in most other Western countries.

Veblen's conviction that the price system would disappear under socialism does not make sense. Prices are inherent in the activity of exchange that accompanies the division of labor and the specialization of production within different plants, and an explicit price mechanism is increasingly used as an allocative device in socialist countries. Business principles, in the sense of pecuniary evaluations of cost and benefits, far from diminishing in their use, have been extended to the operations of governmental units and non-profit institutions in the U.S. and elsewhere.

V. CONCLUSION

Veblen formulated a general system which rests upon an instinct and habit theory of human behavior, and upon the dynamic principle of technological change that alters ways of making a living and consequently generates conflict and evolution in the scheme of economic institutions. He applied his theory to the special case of change under capitalism, portraying a conflict between the institutions of the system of natural rights and the institutions that result from the impact of the modern machine process. Veblen's general economic system and the out-lines of his theory of capitalistic change are his principal contributions in the field of economics. They provide a number of suggestive insights, but in some respects they are marred by contradictions and in some respects they are incomplete.

Veblen's theory of capitalism is weakened by two major defects. First, it is deficient in its analysis of technical economic problems. It does not contain an adequate theory of output, employment, and the allocation and pricing of resources. The lack of such a theory limited Veblen's ability to understand the American economy, and so also did his prejudice against business, his impatience with orthodox economic analysis in general, and his unfamiliarity with finance. His comments on capitalism were therefore in many ways inaccurate as a description of the economy of his own time, and naturally in most respects they do not describe the economy of the present.

Second, Veblen's theory of capitalism is permeated with normative elements. Veblen thought scientifically when he constructed his general system of economic behavior, and there are scientific aspects to his treatment of capitalism, but when he considered the latter topic he was primarily animated by normative convictions, and wrote as a publicist, a shaper of attitudes, a social philosopher and ideologist. During Veblen's era there was a widespread acceptance of the idea of the primacy of business interests, and a consequent tendency to judge economic issues which had many dimensions in favor of business property rights alone. Veblen challenged that tendency. In doing so he used various circumlocutions, pretending to be a neutral observer, describing different forms of behavior as efficient or inefficient rather than as good or bad, but nevertheless his work on the system of business enterprise was primarily a judgment on it. To a considerable extent the objectives of his critique have been achieved, for which he was unquestionably in part responsible (Dorfman 1958; Veblen 1973, pp. 5-326; Walker 1978). Veblen helped to liberate the minds of his readers from the prevailing set of values, and his writings still provide a useful stimulus to thought and inquiry in the field of the evaluation of business behavior.

REFERENCES

Anderson, Karl L., "The Unity of Veblen's Theoretical System," *Quarterly Journal of Economics*, August 1933, *47*, 598-626.

Ayres, Clarence E., *The Theory of Economic Progress*, University of North Carolina Press, Chapel Hill, 1944.

Coats, A. W., "The Influence of Veblen's Methodology," *Journal of Political Economy*, December 1954, *62*, 529-37.

Dobriansky, Lev. E., *Veblenism, A New Critique*, Public Affairs Press, Washington, 1957.

Dorfman, Joseph, "Veblen Centenary Round Table; Source and Impact of Veblen," *American Economic Review*, Supplement, May 1958, *48*, 1-10.

_____ , *Thorstein Veblen and His America*, 1934. Reprint, Augustus M. Kelley, New York, 1961.

Dowd, Douglas F., ed., *Thorstein Veblen: A Critical Reappraisal*, Cornell University Press, Ithaca, 1958.

_____ , *Thorstein Veblen*, Washington Square Press, New York, 1966.

Hansen, Niles M., "Weber and Veblen on Economic Development," *Kyklos*, fasc. 3, 1964, *17*, 447-69.

Leathers, Charles G., and Evans, John S., "Thorstein Veblen and the New Industrial State," *History of Political Economy*, Fall 1973, *5*, 420-37.

McNulty, Paul J., "Hoxie's Economics in Retrospect: The Making and Unmaking of a Veblenian," *History of Political Economy*, Fall 1973, *5*, 449-84.

O'Donnell, L. A., "Rationalism, Capitalism, and the Entrepreneur: The Views of Veblen and Schumpeter," *History of Political Economy*, Spring 1973, *5*, 199-214.

Qualey, Carlton C., *Thorstein Veblen*, Columbia University Press, New York, 1968.

Rosenberg, Bernard, *The Values of Veblen, A Critical Reappraisal*, Public Affairs Press, Washington, 1956.

Seckler, David, *Thorstein Veblen and the Institutionalists: A Study in the Social Philosophy of Economics*, Colorado Associated University Press, Boulder, 1975.

Sowell, Thomas, "The Evolutionary Economics of Thorstein Veblen," *Oxford Economic Papers*, New Series, July 1967, *1*, 177-98.

Spengler, Joseph, "Veblen on Population and Resources," *Social Science Quarterly*, March 1972, 52, 861-78.

Sweezy, Paul M., "Veblen's Critique of the American Economy," *American Economic Review*, Supplement, May 1958, 48, 21-29.

Veblen, Thorstein, *The Theory of the Leisure Class*, 1899. Reprint. B. W. Huebsch, New York, 1918.

_____ , *The Theory of Business Enterprise*, 1904. Reprint, Charles Scribner's Sons, New York, 1932.

_____ , *The Instinct of Workmanship*, 1914. Reprint, The Viking Press, New York, 1946.

_____ , *Imperial Germany and the Industrial Revolution*. 1915. Reprint, Augustus M. Kelley, New York, 1964.

_____ , *An Inquiry Into the Nature of Peace and the Terms of Its Perpetuation*, 1917. Reprint, Augustus M. Kelley, New York. 1964.

_____ , *The Higher Learning in America*, 1918. Reprint. Sagamore Press, New York, 1957.

_____ , *The Place of Science in Modern Civilization*. 1919a. Reprint, Russell and Russell, New York, 1961.

_____ , *The Vested Interests and the Common Man*. 1919b. Reprint, Augustus M. Kelley, New York, 1964.

_____ , *The Engineers and the Price System*, 1921. Reprint, Augustus M. Kelley, New York, 1965.

_____ , *Absentee Ownership and Business Enterprise in Recent Times*. 1923. Reprint, The Viking Press, New York, 1954.

_____ , *Essays in Our Changing Order*, 1934. Reprint. The Viking Press, New York, 1954.

_____ , *Essays, Reviews, and Reports: Previously Uncollected Writings*, edited and with an introduction, *New Light on Veblen*, by Joseph Dorfman. Augustus M. Kelley. Clifton, 1973.

Walker, Donald A., "New Light on Veblen's Work and Influence," *American Journal of Economics and Sociology*, 1978, forthcoming.

[11]

THE DEVELOPMENT OF CLARENCE AYRES'S THEORETICAL INSTITUTIONALISM

WILLIAM BREIT
University of Virginia

T HE DEATH OF CLARENCE EDWIN AYRES ON JULY 24, 1972, WHICH FOL-
lowed by only a few months the demise of his long-time friend and
adversary, Frank H. Knight, has left economics without a philosopher in the grand manner. For what was significant about Ayres as an
economist was his also being a social philosopher of the first chop. From
the day he broke into print in the professional literature of economics in
1918,[1] until the last full statement of his position in 1967,[2] he stood in direct
opposition to the snarling narrowness and scholastic certainties that characterize much of economic thinking. In 1917 Ayres received a Ph.D. in
philosophy from the University of Chicago with a dissertation on "The
Nature of the Relationship Between Ethics and Economics." It was a topic
that remained his central concern although his precise views and position
shifted considerably over his professional lifetime.

After leaving Chicago, Ayres started his full-time teaching career as an
instructor at Amherst College. While there he was an apprentice teacher
under the redoubtable Walton Hamilton, the economist and legal scholar
who, among other contributions, was to coin the term "Institutionalism" to
describe the way of thinking of which Ayres later became the chief exemp-
lar in the post World War II period. Hamilton was to play a large role in
Ayres's career. The young Ayres was Hamilton's assistant in the conduct
of his course, "Social and Economic Institutions." And it was under his
tutelage that Ayres reacted against the orthodox opinions of the economic
Establishment of that time. Ayres himself told the story:

> I had been "properly" brought up, as most undergraduates still are; and
> as Professor Hamilton discoursed to Amherst freshmen . . . I began to
> wonder when he was going to get around to unfolding to these freshmen
> such basic ideas as "marginal utility." Finally I mustered up my courage
> to ask him, and through the 44 years that have since elapsed I have never
> forgotten the gleam of amusement in his eyes as he replied, "I'd do so at
> once if only I understood them myself!" Like Henny-Penny, I felt the
> heavens falling, for already I had conceived a tremendous admiration for
> the mental processes of this extraordinary young professor. Could it be that
> all the elaborate analytical apparatus of marginal analysis was actually with-
> out meaning?[3]

[1] C. E. Ayres, "The Function and Problems of Economic Theory," *Journal of Political Economy*, 26 (Jan., 1918), pp. 69–90.
[2] C. E. Ayres, "The Theory of Institutional Adjustment," *Institutional Adjustment*
(Austin, University of Texas Press, 1967).
[3] C. E. Ayres, *Toward a Reasonable Society* (Austin: University of Texas Press,
1961), pp. 27–28.

To Ayres the answer was, and remained, "It could." Marginal analysis, the keystone of neoclassical and modern economic thought, was rejected by Ayres then and there, and he was to spend the rest of his life in search for a new framework and approach within which to understand the economic forces that were shaping Western civilization.

Ayres early showed a talent for inspiring students. Among the pupils he influenced at Amherst was Talcott Parsons. Later at Reed College, where Ayres spent 1923 to 1924 in educational experimentation, he was to stimulate the interest of Joseph Dorfman in the ideas of Thorstein Veblen. Ayres's suggestions were to bear fruit some years later when Dorfman submitted his dissertation to Columbia University which became the first full-length definitive study of that brooding genius of Institutional economics, published as *Thorstein Veblen and His America*.[4]

At Reed Ayres met the girl who was to become his second wife and one of the most important influences in his life. Gwendolen Jane was a young artist, a portrait painter, who was an ardent admirer of Cezanne and the post-impressionists. Ayres already was keenly interested in music. (At Brown University, where he was an undergraduate, he had sung in the Glee Club, and he was proficient at the piano and cello). He taught Gwen much of what he knew about music; she talked to him about painting. His deep appreciation of both music and painting and their place in the "technological continuum" were to become familiar themes to his students and readers of later years. The wife of a professor of English who was at Reed College while Ayres was there has recently reminisced about her impressions of the young professor:

> Clarence had such a brilliant mind. Everything sparkled when he was around the college. I remember him and Scotty (chemistry) egging each other on from prank to prank. He accompanied us regularly on our hikes usually to the Columbia river gorge. His mind was so alive and brilliant up to the last letter.

It was Ayres's good fortune to have been both a scholar in the cloistered academy and a toiler in the world of journalism. In 1924 he became an associate editor of the *New Republic*. At the time it was one of the premier intellectual organs in the country. The editor was Herbert Croly and along with Ayres the small editorial board consisted of men such as John Dewey, Alvin Johnson and R. H. Tawney. From across the ocean one of its most frequent contributors was John Maynard Keynes. A more formidable posse of intelligentsia would be hard to imagine!

Ayres's contributions from June 8, 1924, when he put in his first appearance, until September 2, 1925, when he resigned to do serious work on his first book, covered a staggering range of topics. He was as at home discussing Freud's theory of the Oedipus complex as he was in describing the pure essence of Joseph Conrad's literary contributions. The love of

---

[4] Joseph Dorfman, *Thorstein Veblen and His America* (New York: The Viking Press, 1934).

Conrad survived Ayres's whole career and every student of his was infected with a similar enthusiasm for that great literary phenomenon. Ayres's appreciation of Conrad's legacy in 1924 could be taken as a summary statement of one of Ayres's own major themes which came out of his study of economic development: "a sense of the complexity of human life, of the unpredictability of human motives, of the overwhelming significance of the massive impersonal forces of nature and of civilization moving obscurely in the background."[5] Besides *belles lettres*, Ayres was an acerbic commentator on theology, sociology, politics, education and, of course, music. The experience of having to read so much in such a variety of fields gave to Ayres a rare understanding of the significance of man's intellectual endeavors. From his training in philosophy, he was struck by what he conceived to be the essential unity of all knowledge.

After he left the *New Republic*, he sought a place where he could reflect on his ideas. A ranch south of Deming, New Mexico, seemed to be an ideal spot for him to write and for Gwen to paint. During the three years he was there he completed his first two books. In the fall of 1928, he went to Madison, Wisconsin to join Alexander Meiklejohn in the Experimental College of the University of Wisconsin, and in the summer of 1930, he taught at New York University. In New York, his old mentor and friend, Walton Hamilton, put him in touch with the University of Texas, which was looking for a professor to fill the place of Dr. Max Handman. The economic historian was visiting for what was to have been a year at Ann Arbor, but decided not to return to Texas. Ayres was offered, and he accepted, a permanent position on the Texas faculty. It was to be a long and fruitful association.

SCIENCE AND CEREMONY

When Ayres arrived in Austin as Professor of Economics, he had two books on social philosophy to his credit. They were, in a sense, companion volumes. Both works demonstrated Ayres's youthful mastery of the vast literature of the history of science, technology, and social institutions. There was much about religion in both of them and the style is interwoven with abundant biblical quotations and word-plays on scriptural verse. This fascination with religion is indicated by their titles. The first was *Science: The False Messiah*,[6] the second, *Holier Than Thou: The Way of the Righteous*.[7] An interest in religion is not surprising for a young man whose father was a Baptist minister and whose mother, before her marriage, had been a Christian missionary in China where she started a church school. The young Clarence was raised in the fear of the Lord, and the importance of the supernatural was deeply impressed upon him as a child.

---

[5] C. E. Ayres, "Nostr'omo," *New Republic* (Aug. 27, 1924), p. 391.
[6] C. E. Ayres, *Science: The False Messiah* (Indianapolis: Bobbs-Merrill, 1927).
[7] C. E. Ayres, *Holier Than Thou: The Way of the Righteous* (Indianapolis: Bobbs-Merrill, 1929).

As James Buchanan has pointed out, a reaction against religious orthodoxy can be an essential ingredient in one's intellectual development since, having rejected it, the less rigid dogmas encountered in the world of scholarship become easy prey.

Science: The False Messiah attacked one of the most cherished of beliefs of that emancipated generation of which Ayres was so solidly a member: that science is the salvation of Western Civilization. Science, Ayres argued, is merely folklore. That is, it consists of a set of beliefs which are nothing more than particular conceptions which people agree upon.[8] So the truths of science are established in the same manner as the truths of folklore, and have no more significance. Moreover, science does not have anything to do with the real problems of living. The mystery of the forces which rule our lives can never be solved by science. To such questions science can only be indifferent. Since human life is all mystery, religion still reigns supreme as a guide to meaningful living.

In this work, Ayres made a sharp distinction between science and industrial technology. It is the instruments of precision-machines which have given rise to modern science. So science depends on invention, and invention in turn derives its power from the penetrating force of technical innovations.

But the rapid growth of technology has undermined traditional values and beliefs. No aspect of life has been exempt from its insidious influence: religion, manners, customs, morals, and the class structure. The most cherished beliefs of civilization are being dissolved by technological change, and science is being used to fill the vacuum. Thus scientists have become the new priestly class: feared, revered and given immense power. They are believed endowed with mystic potency and seen as paragons of virtue with white robes and gleaming test-tubes. But this conception of the scientist must be shattered. Scientists, says Ayres, are motivated by self-interest and in that respect are no different from anybody else. The idea of the scientific superman guided only by an inspiration to improve the conditions of life for his fellow man was stupidly naive. The institutional structure of science leads them to honesty, not the fact that they are superior moral beings. The bookkeeper who adds a column of figures upward and downward in the hope of finding mistakes does so not out of any unusual devotion to the truth, but out of fear of being detected in error by the accountant. But the demonstrations of scientists are also checked and so they have as great a personal stake in being careful and honest as anyone can ever have in anything.

> This is what all the peculiar virtues of the scientist amount to; they are the ordinary acts of ordinary men magnified ten thousand times by the projecting lens of fame. Not that a very able scientist is the precise equivalent of a very ordinary bookkeeper in the skill and effect with which he does his

[8] Ayres's view is similar to the concept of "shared paradigms" in the work of Thomas S. Kuhn. See *The Structure of Scientific Revolutions* (Chicago: University of Chicago Press, 1962).

stuff. An able man is by definition rather abler than an unable man. But to suppose that a scientist is more alert than a prize-fighter, or more observant than a painter, or more rigorous than a grammarian or more ingenious than a woman in pursuit of a husband, is to think nonsense.[9]

Because of their ostensible superiority scientists are being relegated to the seats of the mighty where they make arrogant pronouncements as self-appointed priests. Ayres ends his book with a warning: When scientists become the accepted rulers of society, they may attempt to put down dissenters who attempt to rectify their formulae with persecution as bad as any theological or political tyranny.

But Ayres's book was much more than a *caveat* against science. For it contained a theory of social change that Ayres was to use with a great effect in his later works. In this volume Ayres recognized the immense importance of industrial technology in transforming the life-styles and values of civilization. The connection between machines and morality, between science and values, intrigued Ayres from his earliest writings and remained the most important single conception that he held of change and progress throughout his scholarly career. What was missing from *Science: The False Messiah* was only a theory of value. It remained for John Dewey's instrumental logic to provide the missing link.

Ayres's second book, *Holier Than Thou*, is concerned less with the growth of technology and its devastating effect on civilization than with the structure of the beliefs themselves that were undergoing modification. In this study he was interested in the ideas and behavior patterns that men have and the processes by which they acquired them. By what route do otherwise sensible people come to believe their strange conceptions of right living and behave in the curious ways they behave? The book's approach was strongly influenced by Thorstein Veblen's dissection of the folkways and mores of the leisure class society. The point of departure was a discussion of Veblen's hypothesis concerning the rapid alteration of styles in dress. Each style, argued Veblen, is a revolt against the atrocious ugliness of each preceding style. Since each style is ruled by the same principles that guided all its predecessors it must express the same canons of invidious display and conspicuous waste. But these are not esthetic canons and so a fresh atrocity is committed no more tolerable than its predecessor. It is, therefore, just as transient.

To this theory Ayres proposed two objections. (1) There is no absolute standard of good taste to which a satisfactory style might approximate,

---

[9] Ayres, *Science: The False Messiah*, pp. 255–256. Ayres's analysis of the institutional constraints of science leading to honest behavior on the part of its practitioners is supported by the work of Gordon Tullock: "Apparently the basic reason for scientists' strict adherence to scientific standards arises not from any moral superiority, but from the social situation in which they find themselves. It is not that scientists are more honest than other men; it is that they are more carefully watched." *The Organization of Inquiry* (Durham: Duke University Press, 1966), pp. 130–135, quote on page 132.

and (2) it is not necessary to posit a revolt of taste to account for the alternation of styles. For the rapidity of succession in styles depends on the speed with which the poor can emulate the clothing and other social gestures of the rich. But this depends on technology. So the technological revolution in our way of life is the main cause of style changes since it is technology which determines the rate of speed with which styles can be aped. This is true in raiment as well as morals.

The remainder of the book is an attempt to drive home the point that, just as there is no absolute standard of esthetic excellence, so too there is no absolute standard of righteousness. What is right and wrong, good and bad, is wholly a matter of tradition and custom. Moreover, very few individuals can rise above the moral parochialism of their respective cultures. But scattered individuals are cast up and become the moral strays, the men without a country, citizens of the world: "They are the material from whom the heroes and the martyrs of our history have been drawn, and their strange, partially emancipated fate at least serves to throw into relief that righteousness in which the majority of the human race is at all times perforce content to grope."[10]

Ayres then brings in his Veblenian weapon of the dichotomy between ceremonial and technological behavior, which in *Holier Than Thou* is rendered as a clash between habit and intelligence. Man has a fatally restless temperament and an incurable itch for innovation. (Veblen had called this "idle curiosity.") At the same time he is a creature of order and habit. Man is addicted both to social order and to revolution. "Civilization is bounded on one side by machinery and on the other by decorum; and human behavior oscillates between the two poles, positive and negative."[11] At this point Ayres for the first time shows a glimmering of the theory of value which he borrowed from John Dewey, and which is largely absent, at least in any explicit form in Veblen's writings. It is stated so well and so explicitly early in his works, that it is worth quoting:

> What we mean by truth—the kind of truth that is no respecter of persons and will be uttered though the heavens fall—is instrumental truth. It is derived from our tools and instruments. It is tested by the standard of "consistency" which is nothing more or less than a principle of mechanics. If things fit together and work smoothly without friction, they are consistent, true, mechanically efficient. The object of such truth is to get things done.[12]

In illustration of instrumental logic Ayres gave an example of a housewife baking a cake. Her conversation may be one long uninterrupted stream of buncombe, but she is also interested in truth as indicated by her experimental testing of the recipe and her careful scrutiny of the eggs before adding them to the dough. So the dichotomy between decorum and experimentation permeates all of our attitudes. Notwithstanding his earlier

[10] Ayres, *Holier Than Thou*, pp. 18–19.
[11] *Ibid.*, p. 40.
[12] *Ibid.*

assertion that there is no objective standard for testing our values, Ayres does detect an instrumental basis to the mores. Thus, for example, he argues that prohibiting workmen from drinking on the job makes instrumental sense. Steel workers building skyscrapers ride huge beams swung out over space from enormous heights. A rum barrel is not a safe companion for the people who control the derricks. For this reason, sobriety is a prerequisite to the proper functioning of a modern industrial enterprise. This means that prohibiting the drinking of alcoholic beverages is in many instances sensible from the point of view of the smooth workings of modern society. This is the meaning of the instrumental approach to value and Ayres stated it very lucidly in this 1929 volume. Still Ayres did not yet see that this argument undermined the chief theme of the book which was that there is no standard of right and wrong behavior that is not wholly a matter of custom and tradition, differing from society to society. What Ayres had done with his examples of the housewife baking a cake and the workmen constructing a modern skyscraper was to lay the foundation for a trans-cultural theory of value based on instrumental logic. He was to more fully develop this notion 15 years later in his magnum opus *The Theory of Economic Progress*[13] and bring it to complete maturity in his *Toward a Reasonable Society*[14] after more than three decades of further study and reflection. But in *Holier Than Thou* the idea is in embryonic form so very delicate that it is aborted almost at the moment of conception. For to Ayres in 1929, the world of increasing machines growing at an exponential rate was appalling. "What good does it do us to be mechanical, beyond covering the face of the earth with second-hand automobiles?" he asked. This is a lament worthy of Ezra J. Mishan in his highly-acclaimed *The Costs of Economic Growth* published in 1967. Neither Ayres in 1929—nor Mishan in 1967—fully accepted the instrumental theory of valuation. To Ayres, mechanical technology and science cannot teach people to think or solve any important problems. There is no cultural or moral meaning to it. "Science never tells us what to do. Whenever we imagine that it has told us what things mean we are just mistaken."[15] His concluding chapter titled "No More Crusades" ends the whole work on a cynical note. The hold of custom and tradition is all-powerful and will prevail. For those sophisticated few who come fully to realize that their most cherished beliefs are nothing but culture-bound conceptions with no transcendent meaning or significance there is some consolation in feeling superior to the uneducated and in realizing that "nothing matters much." One can then direct one's contempt not at the preposterous beliefs and ridiculous rites of one's fellow men, but at "the parasites of civilization—reformers, crusaders, holy men, archbishops, grand dukes and presidents—who live by propagating those beliefs and so exploit the common

[13] C. E. Ayres, *The Theory of Economic Progress* (Chapel Hill: University of North Carolina Press, 1944).

[14] Ayres, *Toward a Reasonable Society*.

[15] Ayres, *Holier Than Thou*, p. 144.

man's devotion." And although the fate of the universe and the progress of civilization must be "left to the shysters" it is well to remember that what matters most in human life is little things: "meat and potatoes for dinner, the young lady across the way, the conditions of the crop. . . . The most important thing in life is the struggle to make two carrots grow where one has grown before, or to make a sentence bear some resemblance to what is in one's head. . . ."[16] The know-how involved in "growing carrots" and writing effective sentences was far more important than Ayres was willing to admit in 1929, since he had not yet placed such things in the "value continuum." It is for this reason that both early works were more indebted to Veblen than to Dewey. Nevertheless the seeds of the instrumental concept of value were already planted. They were to reach full flower only after Ayres completed his system of thought which was to give a theoretical structure to institutional economics. The foundation stone of that structure is to be found in the most unlikely quarter: in a biography of a great nineteenth century biologist.

DARWINISM AND CULTURE

The first book Ayres published at Texas was a sprightly yet profound work of scholarship, a life of Thomas Henry Huxley.[17] The book is directly related to the theoretical system that Ayres was to construct for institutional economics. The book was "entertaining" and "racy" as the dust jacket blurb pointed out. The character of Huxley was sketched with painstaking attention to detail and with drama. The high spot of the biography is the historic scene at Oxford on the momentous occasion before the British Association for the Advancement of Science when Samuel Wilberforce, Bishop of Oxford, debated Thomas Huxley on Darwin's theory of evolution. When the bishop solicitously inquired whether the young scientist supposed himself to be descended from an ape on the side of his grandmother or his grandfather, Ayres tells what ensued with great dramatic effect:

> The audience quivered; but Huxley turned to Sir Benjamin Brodie . . . and emphatically striking his hand upon his knee, exclaimed in a whisper, "The Lord hath delivered him into my hands!" Then, leaving Sir Benjamin in a daze, Huxley slowly and deliberately arose: a slight, tall figure, stern and pale, very quiet and very grave; young, cool, quiet, scientific, he began to speak. He rehearsed the bishop's arguments and riddled them. He examined his facts, exhibiting with perfect lucidity his ignorance and folly. And then he delivered his famous counter-stroke, the upshot of which is that as ancestors apes are preferable to bishops. The science of this point is dubious, but as farce and delivered as Huxley delivered it, there could be no doubt: it spitted Soapy Sam with incomparable éclat. The hostile audience was staggered; a great commotion followed; Lady Brewster fainted.[18]

[16] *Ibid.*, p. 240.
[17] Clarence Ayres, *Huxley* (New York: W. W. Norton, 1932).
[18] *Ibid.*, p. 51.

This is Ayres's writing style at its best. Notwithstanding such excitement and keen wit displayed on almost every page, the royalties on the book were small. The Great Depression was underway, and 1932 was a bad year for best sellers. But the book remained Ayres's favorite piece of writing, and he requested that Gwendolen read it to him the year before his death when, his eyesight failing, he was unable to do much reading himself. From the point of view of social philosophy, the real significance of the Huxley book was its analysis of the implications of Darwin's theory and the role that Huxley played in spelling them out.

For Ayres showed that Huxley was the true author of the range of ideas known as "Darwinism." That is, Huxley could lay claim to having originated the theory of human descent from anthropoid stock. This is true even though anthropoid descent is logically implicit in the Darwinian theory of general development. Of course, Darwin's theory was implicit in evolutionary theory developed before his own time, and going clear back to Greek philosophy. According to Ayres, the real issue is whether Darwin understood, stated and attempted to impress on Huxley the theory of man's descent from anthropoids. Darwin's work was almost exclusively focused on the general theory of species development including the biological mechanisms responsible for that development. Huxley's concern, on the other hand, was entirely focused upon man's relation to the anthropoids and the significance of that relationship for the interpretation of human concerns. Darwin was timid enough to suppress any discussion of human descent which could prejudice the acceptance of his theory of development. It was Ayres's highly original contention that Darwin never understood the inevitable corollaries of human evolution, while Huxley clearly did. Ayres's words on this subject are important, not only for a full appreciation of the significance of Huxley's work, but for an understanding of the contributions that Ayres was to make to economic theory:

> Evolution, we are told, is affecting an intellectual revolution in modern society. Its incidence is incalculably great upon every department of thought and so even upon the structure of civilization itself. The civilization of men who know themselves to be super-apes . . . is bound to be different from that of men who believe themselves to be fallen angels. But what evolution is it that is permeating modern thought in this fashion? It is, I have ventured to think, Huxleyism—the implications which Huxley was so determined, and Darwin so reluctant, to acknowledge. Huxley did not spin the idea from his own insides while hanging intellectually in mid-air. Perhaps he did after all only draw certain inevitable conclusions from the general theory of evolution. What I mean to suggest is that he did draw conclusions and, if the modern world is any index, important ones. Indeed, I am not at all sure that what chiefly concerns the modern world is not precisely Huxley's too inevitable conclusions.[19]

Huxley's development of Darwin's implications was used by Ayres in the construction of his theoretical institutionalism. Darwinism was the first

[19] *Ibid.*, pp. 241–242.

block in this structure, for it was crucial in undermining faith in the received doctrine. One of Thorstein Veblen's main strictures had been that traditional economic thought was pre-Darwinian. But, as was so often the case, Veblen was magnificently vague as to what this criticism entailed. Indeed, Frank Knight, in an exchange of amenities with Ayres in the mid-nineteen thirties, could complain that when Veblen claimed to be Darwinian, "I cannot find anything in particular that he could reasonably have meant by this claim nor [can] any of my students who have worked on the problem."[20]

What Veblen meant by the claim is not entirely clear. But Ayres's interpretation takes the Huxley viewpoint, to wit, that man is a super-ape, not a fallen angel. And this arrays man along with all the other species as an animal, not divinely created with certain likes and dislikes, but a natural phenomenon. Classical economics had a natural order conception of the universe, a doctrine of very ancient and honorable lineage. In the eighteenth century, it permeated philosophical writings on the rights of man, reaching its most stirring expression in Thomas Jefferson's Declaration of Independence. That man had "unalienable" rights, that he was endowed with them by his creator—this was part of the best reasoning of enlightened men, Jefferson no less than Adam Smith, and led classical economics to suppose that human nature is antecedent to the economic system. To Adam Smith, the "propensity to truck, barter and exchange" is antecedent to the division of labor to which it gives rise, eventuating in the creation of balanced market forces. But Darwin and Huxley asserted the doctrine of natural selection diametrically opposed to the doctrine of special creation. Such Darwinian thinking rejects the notion of the inherent propensities of man and of the invisible hand.

What Ayres added to this conception of Darwinism was the anthropologists' concept of culture. One of the great intellectual advances was the recognition of human behavior as social behavior shaped by the system of existing behavior patterns. The concept of culture is related to Darwinism because the obvious question raised by the latter is answered by the former. If man's likes and dislikes and his sense of right and wrong are not divinely instituted, then where do they come from? The question raised by Darwinism is answered by the concept of culture. What man approves and disapproves is determined by a body of behavior patterns having a continuous existence of its own. Human beings are different from other animals in the obvious ways they are different because humans are social animals with a continuous culture.

With these tools Ayres had most of the equipment needed to construct his institutional economic theory. The analysis of Huxley provided the first stone, the anthropologists' concept of culture provided the second. His earlier work *Science: the False Messiah* showed Ayres's profound understanding of the pervasive influence of technology in transforming society;

[20] Frank H. Knight, "Intellectual Confusion on Morals and Economics," *International Journal of Ethics*, 45 (Jan., 1935), p. 209.

Holier Than Thou indicated his appreciation of the rigidity and past-bindingness of institutions. It remained only for Ayres to incorporate Dewey's instrumental value theory to provide the last building block for a theoretical institutional economics. All of this came together in 1944 in the book that was to make Ayres the leading exponent of institutional economics in his lifetime, *The Theory of Economic Progress.*[21]

THE AYRESIAN SYSTEM

The Theory of Economic Progress, as its title implies, is a treatment of the forces which have shaped the development of the economy. It is a theoretical work in which a bold and sweeping explanation is given of the economic development of the Western World isolating those factors which accelerate development and those which impede it. The book is rich in erudition and insight, urbanity and wit, and no short summary can do it justice. In essence its theme is that human skills and the tools by which they are exercised are logically inseparable; that the term "technology" must be understood to include all human activities involving the use of all sorts of tools; and that our present age of scientific enlightenment and artistic achievement is intelligible only if we see that the simplest striking stones of primeval man, the fire built around a tree to fell it, written language, books, the symbols of mathematics and the language of poets involve tools and instruments all related to each other by the same developmental process. The tool-using process is thus broadly conceived. It is precisely this surging force growing at an exponential rate which is responsible for the enormous changes in the welfare of the human race over its lifetime. What is really involved in this thesis is a shifting of attention from men to tools; a realization that the key force making for increasing benefits to mankind derives not from an increase in human genius but from the fact that the technological process is one of accessible and objective instruments. These instruments are capable of combination. Ayres

[21] To bring together the inchoate and amorphous ideas that constituted institutional economics and systematize them into a genuine theoretical framework involved a *tour de force*. The Ayres-Knight dispute in the pages of the *International Journal of Ethics* indicated that adherents of neoclassical economics like Knight could make little sense of the loose-jointed doctrines of institutionalism. Ayres admitted the deficiency at the time. Veblen himself had lamented that, "There is the economic life process still in great measure awaiting theoretical formulation." Ayres used this statement as the motto of his 1944 volume. But glimpses of his system could be found in two earlier essays "The Gospel of Technology," *American Philosophy Today and Tomorrow* (New York: Lee Furman, 1935); and "The Significance of Economic Planning," *Development of Collective Enterprise* (Lawrence: University of Kansas Press, 1943). But the first complete exposition of his views is in *The Theory of Economic Progress*. His one effort between *Huxley* and the former volume was *The Problem of Economic Order* (New York: Farrar and Rinehart, Inc., 1938), a small book inspired by the Great Depression and concerned chiefly with the industrial revolution and economic growth combined with some underconsumptionist feelings about the causes and cures of the 1930's stagnation. But it was not the major theoretical work that *The Theory of Economic Progress* was to be, and its best insights were incorporated into the latter study.

does not thereby deny that individuals play a role in the process. But the point is that the answer to the conundrum of increasingly rapid progress lies in the tools themselves. All tools are related to each other in the sense that the earlier ones make the later ones possible. The existence of different tools and instruments defines the possibility of their combination into new artifacts. The individual is the agent of combination—it is he who sees the possibility of putting the tools together into new and innovative forms. But the process of change is best understood on the cultural level, since the more plentiful the tools become, the greater is the possibility of recombination. That is why technological advance occurs more rapidly as we go onward.

But there is another side of the story of economic progress. For there are forces hostile to development which Ayres summarizes under the rubric, "ceremonial" behavior. In his later work, *Toward a Reasonable Society*, Ayres showed that the symbolic process of which tool-using is one manifestation, also gives rise to fanciful behavior completely contradictory to the technological process. The ceremonial, myth and status aspect of human behavior derives from the same symbolic process that gave rise to technological development. But the authoritarian, taboo-ridden, emotion-fraught aspect of life is static by its very nature. The binding force of any established institution derives from its past, and is part of tribal legend. Ayres was more fully to develop this aspect of his dichotomy in his paper "The Theory of Institutional Adjustment" which he prepared for a conference in his honor in 1965.[22] In this last major contribution he stressed the importance of the Freudian revolution in providing the explanation for the intensity with which people hold their various beliefs and adhere to their traditional way of life. The emotional conditioning of the whole community to supernaturalism is what binds together status systems, legends and ceremonial activities. But this institutional coherence is in process of destruction. For the Freudian revolution is demythologizing modern culture and the institutionalizing process is in consequence being short-circuited. The root cause of superstition which is the chief enemy of technological progress is being shriveled by modern psychopathology with consequences we cannot yet foresee:

> This is truly cataclysmic. If it is true . . . that the myths, ceremonies, mores, and status systems which make up the institutional sysems of all peoples are themselves welded together and shackled upon their peoples by a community-wide process of emotional conditioning to supernaturalism, then the short-circuiting of that welding current, which is the inevitable consequence of technological progress and its accompaniment of intellectual sophistication, means that the whole institutional complex is coming apart at the seams.[23]

To Ayres, the way out of this total disintegration is to devise new organizational forms, to pragmatically develop organizational arts to match,

---

[22] Ayres, "The Theory of Institutional Adjustment."
[23] *Ibid.*, p. 11.

rather than contradict, our science and technology. For to Ayres the question of whether we should go ever onward is answered by the process itself. Technology broadly conceived involves trans-cultural values altogether different from those beliefs deriving from superstition. Whereas superstitions vary from culture to culture and in all cases are past-binding, the values deriving from technology are progressive and are so recognized by all peoples. A sharp knife is preferred to a dull knife in all cultures in order to perform efficiently the task of cutting, and the values generated by the technological process are shared values, understandable and acceptable to all peoples everywhere. This is Dewey's meaning of the technological value continuum, but never was it put to better use than at Ayres's hands. That is why those who see in Ayres only a disciple of Dewey and Veblen miss the main point. In his articulation of some of their positions and in having the vision to synthesize some of their insights with his own understanding of economic history, Ayres left them miles behind. His Veblen was no longer anyone else's Veblen and his Dewey was no longer the Dewey of pragmatic philosophy. Ayres emphasized those elements in each man's work that best suited his own purpose and temperament, re-creating both of them in his own image.

WHAT HATH AYRES WROUGHT?

In spite of Ayres's skill in exposition and his immense power to explain the complex processes of economic history, he was too unorthodox to succeed in making much impression on the economic Establishment of his day.[24] He was denied the presidency of the American Economic Association when many men of lesser attainments were given this honor. Ayres accepted this neglect without any sign of bitterness. He was a philosopher among the Philistines, and he knew it.[25]

[24] Ayres's work has only recently received detailed treatment. See Allan G. Gruchy, "The Instrumental Economics of Clarence E. Ayres," *Contemporary Economic Thought: The Contribution of Neo-Institutional Economics* (Clifton: Augustus M. Kelley, 1972). His work on economic development was discussed in an "unpremeditated symposium" in the pages of this journal, June, 1960, with articles by Benjamin Higgins, Manuel Gottlieb, Jack E. Robertson and William C. Frederick. Ayres responded with an article of his own, later reprinted with an introduction by Coldwell Daniel, III, and a discussion by Ayres himself in the March, 1970, anniversary issue of the *Social Science Quarterly*. A short and rather unsatisfactory account of Ayres's views can be found in Ben B. Seligman, *Main Currents in Modern Economics* (Glencoe: The Free Press, 1962), pp. 239–240.

[25] I believe that Ayres did himself a disservice in beginning *Theory of Economic Progress* with an attack on neoclassical price theory. Ayres was not at his best in discussing technical economic theory which he was always too impatient to fully master, and it was easy for first-rate price theorists to show that the natural order mentality which could explain the *origin* of classical and and neoclassical economic thought had nothing to do with the *validity* of these doctrines. The real issue is whether theories of economic behavior based on unrealistic and fanciful assumptions yield better predictions than alternative theories. The attractiveness of neoclassical price theory lies precisely in its success in isolating the correct elements in diverse situations to which it is applied and thus it yields better predictions than any proposed alternatives. But Ayres

Although economics today is going through some paroxysms of discontent, it cannot be safely stated that Ayres is the author of that malaise or that his way of thinking will prevail. Never before has orthodoxy been under so much fire, and from the highest mountaintops. John Kenneth Galbraith's criticisms of the irrelevance of much of economics echoes Ayres's sentiments some 20 years previously. But Ayres, alas, launched his salvos from the University of Texas, not from Harvard. A shot from the banks of the Charles can be heard around the world; from the banks of the Colorado its sound might penetrate the Red River. There is much snobbery in academic circles and Ayres doubtless fell victim to it. To the end he remained apart and almost alone.

But if the principle of comparative advantage were applied to the allocation of college faculties, Ayres's move to Texas would doubtless prove that the market had achieved blissful optimality. As a teacher *par excellence* he introduced scores of southwestern plowboys to a sophisticated culture to which they could not have aspired outside of the eastern seaboard. "For a day in thy courts is better than a thousand" said the infallible psalmist, and one semester with Ayres was an education in itself. It usually took the second semester to sort and formulate the ideas he exposed in the first: the relationship between Bach's equal temperament tuning and Darwinian evolution, the essential similarities between Byzantine, Gothic and modern architectural styles, the origin and significance of the word "serendipity," the relative merits of Damascus versus modern steel, the technical intricacies of Vavilov's theory of the hybridization of crop plants, the origin of the term "barbarian," the contributions of the Buddhist religion to the art of printing. . . . But was there nothing about consumer equilibrium in an Edgeworth-Bowley box? Then so much the better! Such exhausted and sterile exercises tried his patience. To Ayres economics was not merely a device for improving the mind, but a wholly magnificent adventure. The young Texans who followed him emancipated themselves from what Wesley Mitchell called "the subtle tyranny of circumstance." At his hands economics shed its dismalness and became provocative and exciting.

---

never found it in his heart to identify the tools of price theory on the technological side of his dichotomy, to recognize that they are neutral instruments of analysis which, like nuclear energy or a hammer, can be put to any use, good or ill, depending, as Ayres might have put it, on the persistence of technological or ceremonial elements in the thinking of the users. Moreover, in the new foreword which he wrote for the paperback reprint of the *Theory of Economic Progress* in 1962, he came close to admitting that he had made a tactical mistake. The decisive issue, he noted, was not price theory as such, but neoclassicism's misconception of the nature of the economic system itself. He did not go on to say, as he should have, that microeconomics might be a useful tool in getting a clearer understanding of the *correct* conception of the economy. Because many economists were "put off" by Ayres's unjustified strictures on price theory, they ignored the important contributions to the theory of economic development that he made much earlier than anyone else. For this reason Ayres's influence has probably been greater outside the economic canon. C. Wright Mills, Marion Levy, Talcott Parsons: all were Ayres's students at one time, although not disciples in the usual sense.

[12]

THE INSTITUTIONALIST ECONOMIC THEORIES OF CLARENCE AYRES

DONALD A. WALKER*

This paper creates a synthesis of Ayres's views, drawing them together from his many publications, and displaying his work as an intellectual system. His work is also evaluated, with the conclusion that his basic distinction between institutional and technological behavior is not tenable, but that he made some contributions of lasting value in his elaboration of institutionalist theory. In particular, he demonstrated the necessity for a recognition of the cultural and technological environment within which economic behavior occurs, he argued persuasively in favor of an interdisciplinary approach, and he contributed to the analysis of the process of technological change.

Twenty-seven years ago I entered the University of Texas as a graduate student in economics, and studied under Clarence Ayres, eventually becoming his assistant, with a little desk in his office at which I graded what seemed like thousands of papers on Veblenesque topics. I listened to him in and out of class with deep interest. He had actually met Veblen, shaken his hand, conversed with him, and for this and for other reasons was in an incontestable position of moral authority to be the one who should hand forward the torch of Veblenian lore. The true doctrine of institutionalism was expounded by Ayres in a sort of evangelical camp-meeting atmosphere, replete with Veblen and Dewey as angels, and price theorists as devils. Generating such an atmosphere was something that Ayres could do really well. He was a superb teacher in the sense of a person who could change the entire world outlook of his students, and exercise an enduring influence upon them.

I sat through Ayres's lectures in his popular undergraduate course, Introduction to Social Science. The room would be filled with the most unpromising human material imaginable for the sort of purposes that Ayres had — backcountry students from the small towns and ranches of Texas, rich students from Dallas and Houston. Most of them were conservative or reactionary in their social and economic views; most of them were initially supremely indifferent to the issues that agitated Ayres. Yet he would work his magic on them, and by the end of a single semester he would have them ready to leap out into the real world and to start tearing down the old institutions, ready to begin immediately with building a new society free of ceremony, superstition, and myth. Ayres's objectives required him to cover a wide territory. He stimulated his classes to think about such questions as the relation between economic doctrines and

*Indiana University of Pennsylvania.

religion, the impact of the West on underdeveloped countries, the nature of mathematics, the philosophy of science, and the significance of primitive taboos in relation to modern society. Students who previously perceived the world in wholly conventional ways would start writing papers about "societal stasis" and "instrumentalist interaction," full of neologisms and muddled theorizing about social change and the dynamics of technological progress. Even those who remained in disagreement with him would find that their structure of attitudes had undergone alterations — had been turned upside down. It was a marvelous performance.

The problem to be considered here is the content of that performance, which is an interesting question, because Ayres was Veblen's most creative and theoretically-inclined intellectual descendant, and one of the most important advocates of institutionalism during the years since the Great Depression. The matters that concerned Ayres can be divided into four major categories: a critique of orthodox theory, his institutionalist alternative, his policy proposals, and various philosophical aspects of his theory of value that transcend his treatment of economic values. The first and third of these topics have been explored elsewhere;[1] the fourth is more a matter of epistemology, metaphysics, and aesthetics than economics; and the second topic is the subject of the present study. The paper does not consider the sources of Ayres's ideas, nor their relation to his times. It is concerned with the presentation of his theories in their mature form, not with their evolution.[2] Some of them assumed that from as early as the 1930s, and most of them were fully developed by the early 1950s, but subsequently there were some modifications of his attitudes and analyses, and account will be taken of these. Unlike other studies of Ayres's work, the present one displays it as an intellectual system. Instead of taking an isolated aspect of it, or dealing with a variety of his ideas in a piecemeal fashion, a synthesis of his views is created by drawing them together from his many publications.[3] The study is therefore written on a level of generality that enables an exposition of the entire range of his theoretical institutionalist ideas with superficiality in a single article. The paper also has the objective of evaluating his theories to determine whether he left a legacy of ideas in his constructive work that should be preserved as part of economic science.

1. See Walker 1978a and Walker 1980. Ayres's use of Keynesian theory, including his underconsumptionism, is covered in the former of these two references.

2. The most important source of Ayres's institutionalism has been examined recently by Walker (1977). A treatment of the evolution of Ayres's ideas has been given by Breit (1973), and Breit and Culbertson (1976) have provided an excellent account of Ayres's life.

3. With one exception the essays collected in the volume edited by Breit and Culbertson (1976) are nominally concerned with some particular aspect of Ayres's thought — nominally, because the essays are too brief to be considered adequate studies of their topics, and because several of them pay only cursory attention to Ayres and are devoted instead to the authors' own interests. The exception is an essay by Coats, which deals with a variety of Ayres's ideas, but does not display them as components of a system of thought. Coats offers the essay as an interim assessment, and in fact it is neither complete nor definitive in a number of important respects (Walker 1978b).

I. TECHNOLOGY AND INSTITUTIONS

In Ayres's theory there are two distinguishable types of cultural activity that are involved in economic behavior: the tool-using or technological system of activities through which commodities are made, and the ceremonial use of tools and of their products undertaken with the aim of establishing distinctions of status. The first problem for institutionalist economics, Ayres asserted, is to analyze the technological system of activities with particular reference to Western industrialization. With their attitudes formed by the classical tradition, economists have tried to attribute the process of industrialization and the resulting economic progress to Western institutions such as business enterprise, the market, democracy, puritanism, private property, the state, and the church (Ayres 1944, pp. 177, 185). Ayres argued, in contrast, that "there is no such thing as an institution (or set of institutions), that is 'appropriate' to a given technology in any but a negative sense" (ibid., p. 187). He was horrified by Schumpeter's opinion that modern science and culture are by-products of the institutional system of capitalism and manifestations of the capitalist spirit of rationalist individualism, and scandalized by his assertion that industrialization is primarily attributable to the leadership of great men of affairs. Ayres called this "an astonishing farrago," blindly neglecting all the other factors involved in cultural development, and disregarding the entire product of scholarship in such fields as the history of science and the history of the various arts (Ayres 1943a, p. 299). Schumpeter — "a perfect clinical picture of capitalist astigmatism" — did not take account of the most important force in civilization (ibid., p. 301).

That force, Ayres maintained, is the growth of technology. He was obsessed by the importance of technology because he regarded it as the agent of social change, the dynamic force by which the achievements of industrial society have been made possible, and by which institutions, human nature, and civilization in general have been shaped (Ayres 1951, p. 51). Technology has been responsible for Western industrialization and economic development, and therefore institutionalists want an explanation of "human nature (working, buying, consuming, investing, and so forth) as an expression of the social order (institutions and technology)" (Ayres 1936, p. 235). Such an explanation requires, among other things, a theory of how technological change occurs, and Ayres therefore proceeded to develop one. Scientific progress and technological change, he argued, are dependent upon the use of instruments, including formulas, tools, and industrial and scientific processes. Technology is itself constituted of instruments. Instruments have an objective existence, so they can be sent from one location to another; they can be transmitted from one person to another; and they can be juxtaposed in different ways. The result is "the virtual inevitability of combinations occurring once their components have been brought into existence and have been so

widely distributed as to be generally juxtaposed" (Ayres 1960a, p. 47).
New technology is the consequence of the combination of previously
existing devices and ideas.

In elaborating upon this thesis, Ayres revealed himself to be a technological determinist, despite his disclaimers and qualifications. He
believed that technological change is largely a self-generating process,
resulting not from human motivations, such as the desire for fame or
material wealth, but from "the serendipity of the laboratory and the
machine shop . . . And what is serendipity but idle curiosity, the free
play of the inquiring mind?" (Ayres 1964, p. 58). Indeed, Ayres maintained, motivations may impede technological change: "Excessive
preoccupation of any kind — pious, financial, uxorious, or even professional — is inimical to the 'free play' of the imagination in the course
of which combinations somehow occur" (Ayres 1944, p. 117). The thesis
expressed in many places in his work is that the process of technological
change is impelled by its own internal momentum and historical necessity, so that machinery and instruments breed more machinery and
instruments. Although all technological combining is affected by human
intelligence, the accumulation of knowledge and skills occurs because
they are objectified in tools and symbols, and "the developmental character of technology is implicit not in the skill-faculty of the human individual but in the character of tools." Since the artifacts that are put
together are physical objects, "the coexistence of these objects constitutes
a possibility of combination which transcends the acts of any individual.
It is in this sense that inventions seem 'bound' to occur. Granted a
working steam engine, the steam-propelled locomotive was bound to
follow" (ibid., pp. 112, 115-116).

It follows from the combinatorial principle that technology can
develop at a progressively more rapid rate as the available number of
devices and ideas grows (Ayres 1938, pp. 13-14; Ayres 1953, pp. 282-
83; Ayres 1960a, pp. 46-48; Ayres 1961, pp. 80-93), but the rate of
development also depends on the rigidity or flexibility of the society's
institutions. These exercise an influence upon the directions that technology takes, promoting some and inhibiting others, and in some societies
halting technological change altogether (Ayres 1967a, pp. 171-72). All
that can be said in favor of the role played by the institutions of Western
Europe with respect to industrialization is that they were permissive
because they were not deeply entrenched (Ayres, 1944, p. 177). Europe
was a frontier society that inherited thousands of years of accumulated
Mediterranean technology, and that was then, with the end of the Roman
occupation, liberated from an alien institutional domination (Ayres 1961,
pp. 178-79; Ayres 1967b, p. 8). Thus Europe was free of the encrusted
traditions that would have inhibited technological development, and
proceeded to develop, although not in all cases to originate, a series of
fundamental inventions, such as printing, gunpowder, the astrolabe, the

compass, the use of zero, and other innovations which laid the groundwork for the industrial revolution (Ayres 1938, pp. 15-17; Ayres 1961,
p. 180). Furthermore, the growth of world trade stimulated the development of towns in the medieval period. Since they were not part of the
manorial feudal society, they were even freer than that society from inhibitory institutions, and it was therefore easy for them to become centers
of technological experimentations. As a result of regional and global
trade the towns also became centers of cultural cross-fertilization, which
provided a powerful stimulus to new technological combinations. Thus
the development of towns assured the occurrence of the industrial revolution and the economic growth of which it was a part (Ayres 1944, pp.
146-47).

Ayres concluded that economic development in the West has not been
due to the market system. "The productive powers of industrial society
have grown not because of the institutions of capitalism but in spite of
them" (Ayres 1943c, p. 166). The diverse commodities that merchants
sell are not generated by the market but are instead the results of modern
science and technology (Ayres 1961, pp. 6-7). It was technology that
enabled the development of the market, because, Ayres wrote in a sentence that contradicts his thesis, technological specialization is possible
"only if the various specialists exchange their products" (ibid., p. 24).

There is a great deal of truth in Ayres's account of the reasons for
technological change. The combinatorial character of technology and
cultural cross-fertilization are unquestionably important in explaining
the rapidity of technological innovation, and Ayres's assertion of the
importance of industrialization and hence of economic development is
obviously true. Nevertheless, he was not convincing in his argument that
the motivations of individuals are of much less importance in promoting
growth than the characteristics of tools and scientific concepts. Contemporary economic historians believe that "economic growth or the
lack of it is obviously a consequence of the incentive structure which
influences choices with respect to children, savings, and productive
activity" (North 1976, p. 462), and the incentive structure is an institutional phenomenon, not part of the machine process. Economic development in the West has been the outcome of a complex interaction of
motives, incentives, technological change, institutions, and economic
development itself. The truth of this observation was ultimately given
some degree of recognition by Ayres, for he noted explicitly the importance of motives when he stated that it "was the vigorous, shrewd, and
persistent efforts of the historical middle class to get ahead that broke
down the feudal system" (Ayres 1961, p. 190; and see 1967a, p. 174),
even though he insisted that the very existence of the middle class was the
result of the industrial revolution (Ayres 1948, p. 225). Furthermore,
he unwittingly subscribed on occasion to the view that business motivations played an important part in the process of Western industrialization,

as when he observed that engaging in world trade was a central activity of the medieval towns and the crucial factor in their development.

Ayres then turned from the study of technology to an examination of the character and impact of institutions, advocating that the study of them be substituted in place of the eternal subject-matter of an economy of wants, satisfactions, and prices (Ayres 1936, p. 234). Writing in the manner that was fashionable in the 1930s and '40s among sociologists and anthropologists, Ayres's mode of interpretation of modern Western culture was to view it in the light of the behavior of pre-industrial societies, seeking parallels between our current practices and the more explicit ceremonial observances of primitive peoples. The study of institutions is important, he argued, because an understanding of myth and superstition, of totem and taboo, enables us to explain social, economic, and political phenomena, and because institutions are impediments to technological change and economic development (Ayres 1953, p. 280).

In order to understand the institutional aspect of life, Ayres observed, it is necessary to analyze ceremonial behavior, by which he did not have reference to mere ceremonies, but to the non-technological behavior that establishes differences in rank by conferring status through ritual (Ayres 1952. pp. 42-46). Behavioristic psychology, which is espoused by institutionalism, demonstrates that human nature is not inborn, but is the outcome of conditions such as society's aspirations, systems of belief, and conceptions of the universe and human life (Ayre 1951, p. 49). These beliefs are required for the maintenance of the social system, because to doubt their validity is to challenge the social order. Institutions inculcate the idea that the structure of society is sanctioned by the higher powers, and guide the behavior of the members of the community, forming a body of culture that is received from the past and handed on by a process of indoctrination that continues throughout the life of each person (Ayres 1953. p. 281; Ayres 1961, pp. 100-101).

The mores of society, which define what is right and wrong for a person in a given station in life, are believed to have their appropriateness demonstrated by physical consequences, but although distinctions of ceremonial status mimic differences in technological competence, they do not often rest on merit. In actuality, ceremonial behavior is thought to have authenticity because it derives from and is oriented toward the past, in which nothing can be changed. Thus the institutional patterns of society are legitimized by earlier institutions, of which they retain as much as circumstances permit. Institutions are therefore archaic, static, and lack the organizational fluidity that is necessary for technological progress (Ayres 1952, pp. 49-50; Ayres 1961, pp. 30-31, 126, 134-137). Institutions are not only highly resistant to change, they also "limit and circumscribe technological activities at every turn" (Ayres 1960a, p. 49). "The superstitions, taboos, and tradition-encrusted status systems of all peoples work at cross-purposes with the technological process" (ibid.).

Since they derive from the past, Ayres maintained, institutions are not invented to deal with new challenges. Western society, for example, did not invent institutions that were better adapted to the needs of an evolving commercial and industrial society. The institutions that were thrown into prominence had their origin in previous ones. For instance, the rules of chattel transfer were inherited from the feudal period (Ayres 1944, pp. 196-97), and the security of modern property rights is derived from earlier practices in regard to ownership. The idea of the inviolability of the urban home is an extension of the notion of the rights of the feudal castle, a notion which is also perpetuated by the prerogatives that are claimed by the modern corporation (Ayres 1938, pp. 22-24; Ayres 1960a, p. 51; Ayres 1967a, pp. 173-74).

In Ayres's theory of social and economic change, the impact of science and technology tends to diminish the scope of institutional behavior. Scientific knowledge undermines myth and superstition, and the behavioral patterns necessitated by machine technology break down ceremonial distinctions of status. These processes do not necessarily occur, and, indeed, have not occurred in most societies most of the time, and it remains to be seen whether technology will ultimately prevail over ceremonial behavior in the West. Nevertheless, our society has thus far followed a clear pattern of progress, manifested by the process of industrialization and the increasing technological complexity that it displays (Ayres 1944, pp. 123-24; 175-76), and as a result our basic institutions have been weakened and modified. For example, the family has been diminished in importance by the factory system, which took industry out of the home, and authority and status are being replaced by efficient teamwork in the operation of the home. Technology has also been transforming the institutional characteristics of business. The development of specialized business equipment and machinery, the growth of technology in such areas as communications and transportation, and the necessity for related skills, have enabled a managerial group to take power at the expense of the authority of the owners (ibid., pp. 186, 188, 198-99). In government also, the growth of managerial technology "has overshadowed the ancient sanctions of sovereignty," and, indeed, throughout society there has been "the elaboration of administrative techniques along distinctively instrumental lines, and the gradual atrophy of whatever institutional considerations of rank and power fail to take this line" (ibid., pp. 200, 201; and see Ayres 1952, pp. 58-59).

Technological change has also altered the concept of property. The development of industry and commerce caused the increased importance of chattel property relative to land, as a result of which the legal conditions of chattel transfer have come to supersede the conditions of land transfer (Ayres, 1944, p. 196). Technological development has led to the growth of large corporations, resulting in a definition of property as "a fractional share of an undifferentiated mass of assets" (Ayres 1960a, p. 51). Nevertheless, despite the influence of technology, property is still sacrosanct, "still a matter of ceremonially determined rights the sanction of which derives from the legendary past." Like all institutions, Ayres thought in 1944, private property, the structure of economic power that is based upon it, and its legendary background, the theory of capitalism, are impediments to economic progress (Ayres 1944, pp. 201, 202).

Ayres did not establish his case regarding the conflict of technology and institutions by his brief examples and sketchy historical references, and during his entire career he felt that he had to controvert the allegation that some institutions contribute to the viability of society, and stimulate technological change and economic development. If it is true that some institutions stem from the same sources of human inventiveness as science and technology, and are manifestations of a dynamic endogenous social process which contributes to social survival and economic growth, then it is impossible to accept the difference in function that Ayres postulated between technological activities and institutions, and the basis of his entire system collapses. In order to meet this problem and to be able to assert that "the Veblenian antithesis" (Ayres 1958, p. 27) exists, he therefore tried to locate its source in the biological characteristics of human beings, just as Veblen had done in the case of his theory of instincts (Walker 1977, p. 218). To establish that a dichotomy between technological and institutional behavior is an outcome of our physical processes would be to furnish unambiguous and unchallengeable evidence of its existence and of its permeation of all cultures at all times. Although Ayres frequently pointed out that "all human proclivities, propensities, and wants, however fully 'internalized' they have become and however natural-seeming they may therefore be, have in fact been formed through a culturally developmental process" (Ayres 1958, p. 26), and although he emphasized that the behavioral patterns that Veblen called instincts are "wholly cultural" (ibid., p. 29), he did not apply that analysis to what he regarded as the organic basis of the Veblenian antithesis.

In 1956 Ayres expressed his viewpoint to me in the following way:

> Primitive man does of course make mentalistic assumptions. Just as a matter of communication strategy I would avoid calling them that — just yet. For the mentalism that is still endemic is of course a survival of primitive supernaturalism. Why does primitive man do so? Why ask? Because *omnis cultura ex cultura* isn't a cloture to all further investigation. Why do zoological investigations continue, notwithstanding the universal acceptance of the doctrine *omne vivum ex vive*? Granted that culture is *sui generis*: doesn't the question still remain, what sort of genus is it, and how did that genus evolve?
>
> I think so. But most particularly I think the differentiation of the

technological from the ceremonial (or institutional) aspects of culture
won't stand up as a fiat: in the beginning was culture, and culture
was bipolar. What does this mean? How come? I think Veblen's
"instinct" [his perception of the existence of a problem] was sound.
To get his idea of workmanship established he had to face the question, How come? He tried to do so by attributing it to instinct, an
attribution which seemed to make sense then, but doesn't now. So
then, now what? The question has to be faced. I may be muffing it
too; but it's a good try! (Ayres 1956, p. 2).

Ayres's initial speculation was that "the whole ceremonial behavior
function by which human beings have made so much trouble for themselves throughout the ages is an *organically inevitable* joint-product of
the same evolutionary process, the same refinement of the nervous (and
perhaps endocrine) system which makes speech and tool-using possible"
(Ayres 1944, p. 173; italics added). He later came to identify that process
more precisely as the formation and use of symbols, which, he argued,
enable our technological progress, but also permit us to imagine the nonexistent and hence to create myths, legends, and superstitions (Ayres
1961, pp. 31, 95-99, 101-102). "Through the fallacy of imputation the
symbols by virtue of which man has accomplished his wonders have been
endowed with a wonder-working magic potency. It is the sense of magic
potency which inspires all superstition and all magic" (ibid., p. 95). Imputation inevitably leads to reification, a process in which the belief that
the symbol has personality leads to belief in the actual existence of the
forces or beings symbolized. The fact that names can be used even if they
make reference to imaginary things creates the presumption that they
exist, a presumption that is reinforced by the emotional force with which
the symbols are charged (ibid., pp. 97-99, 139-62). Symbols are used to
spin legends and myths which support the existing structure of society
and its status relations, and the process of emotional conditioning to
supernaturalism in which the entire community participates results in
the maintenance of those institutional patterns of belief and behavior
(Ayres 1967b, p. 11).

In the forceful and articulate passage that he wrote in 1956 Ayres was
in fact presuming the point at issue. He started with the assumption that
culture is bipolar, asserting that humanity not only performs technologically efficient operations but also develops and then clings to behavioral patterns that are detrimental to it, and he thereby created for
himself the intractable problem of accounting for how such a curious
bipolarity could possibly have originated. His solution is open to the fatal
criticism that a biological function can never provide more than a non-
specific foundation for a behavioral pattern. The specific qualities of
human behavior depend upon cultural influences that direct, express,
and give precise character to the results of our biological capabilities.
Suppose it is granted that language is symbolic, a theory that some but

not all linguists and philosophers accept. The question then arises as to why some symbolization is mythopoeic. It is obvious that many people in our culture are not imbued with superstitions, nor devotees of ceremonial behavior, nor believers in ritualistically sanctioned status or social organization. Indeed, on one occasion Ayres denied his own thesis regarding symbolization (Ayres 1952, p. 47), and elsewhere as will be seen, he argued that modern Western civilization is no longer creating and sustaining myths and ceremonial behavior. Consequently, the answer to the foregoing question must be that if some symbolization is mythopoeic, it is because of cultural influences. Since all culture does not manifest ceremonialism, the symbolic process does not inevitably result in ceremonialism, and the Veblenian antithesis is therefore not an inherent feature of that process.

The use of language and ritual for the purpose of transmitting myths, elaborating superstitions, maintaining aspects of a social order, and supporting distinctions of status is undeniable, and it is also undeniable that some ceremonialism may have deleterious effects, but that does not prove that all institutions are static and harmful in their impact on cultural and economic development. Walton Hamilton, Ayres's friend and forever mentor, recognized this when he wrote, in an analysis that goes far beyond Ayres's in its richness and subtlety, that institutions are imperfect means of achieving order and attaining objectives. Both chance and purposeful intent enter into their creation. Dynamically evolving structures, their "identity through the impact of idea upon circumstance and the rebound of circumstance upon idea is forever being remade" (Hamilton 1932, p. 89). An institution is

> a folkway, always new yet ever old, directive and responsive, a spur to and a check upon change, a creature of means and a master of ends. It is in social organization an instrument, a challenge and a hazard; in its wake come order and disorder, fulfillment, aimlessness and frustration. The arrangements of community life alike set the stage for and take up the shock of what man does and what he leaves undone. Institutions and human actions, complements and antitheses, are forever remaking each other in the endless drama of the social process (ibid.).

Many traditional practices are valuable for society and useful in generating technological change and economic development. The beliefs and practices constituting the institution of private property are an example of this truth. Similarly, the market, which includes many institutional patterns of behavior, stimulates the modification of business practices, induces technological change, and undermines and disposes of organizations and ways of behaving that have outlived their usefulness. It cannot even be shown that the static features of institutions are all undesirable, inasmuch as many institutions draw upon past practices that have been found useful in coping with the problems of life, utilizing the solutions that have been learned through hard experience. Institutions thereby moderate or avoid the chaos that might ensue from the intemperate adoption of untried modes of organization and behavior.

An institution may include elements of past practices but may nevertheless be a useful invention, and, indeed, the same combinatorial principle that Ayres observed to be at work in the development of new technology is operative in the development of institutions. New institutions are created by the combination of previous practices. Ayres himself wrote that technological innovation created and established the institutions of capitalism (Ayres 1944, p. 154), thus unintentionally conceding that useful institutions are invented and that institutions are not exclusively remnants of the past, except perhaps in the sense that everything is. In his later work, Ayres verged upon adopting the position that institutions can aid economic development. Although he reiterated the view that they are never invented for that purpose (Ayres 1967c, p. 6), he nevertheless wrote that "much is to be said to the credit of the institution of property. Its extraordinary flexibility has suited the requirements of industrial revolution to an extraordinary degree" (Ayres 1968, p. 343). Institutions and technology, he wrote, "overlie each other and interpenetrate, condition, and *complement* each other" (Ayres 1953, p. 283, italics added). Again, he explained that exchange is possible only if buyers have security in the ownership of purchased property, and if sellers have the right of free disposal. "These rights, and the legal system that defined them, were the institutional foundation on which the industrial economy was built. They provided the motivation that impelled common men to build the modern world" (Ayres 1967a, p. 174). Such statements amount to an abandonment of much of the sharpness of Ayres's distinction between institutional and technological behavior. His position thus became closer to the reasonable view that there are some institutions — like private property — that have aided economic growth, and others — like the belief that a large number of offspring is desirable — that in some countries have impeded growth.

Traditional practices, many of them reinforced and legitimized by ceremony, frequently preserve valuable qualities of social, political, and economic life. As John Stuart Mill pointed out regarding transactions, agreements, the distribution of income, and political rights:

> Custom is the most powerful protector of the weak against the strong; their sole protector where there are no laws or government adequate to the purpose. Custom is a barrier which, even in the most oppressed condition of mankind, tyranny is forced in some degree to respect . . Every relaxation of . . . [the law of the strongest] . . . has a tendency to become a custom, and every custom to become a right (Mill 1862, vol. 1, p. 307).

Thus there is no ultimate distinction between technological and institutional behavior in the sense that only the former promotes economic development and is beneficial and that the latter always impedes development and is deleterious. Technology and institutions should not be separated and regarded as antitheses. Technology is just one of the many aspects of society, and to adopt Ayres's attitude of regarding it "as *causing* the progress of society is as mistaken as to suggest that the growth of a university is caused by the growth of its buildings" (Frankel 1976, p. 68).

Finally, it must be observed that Ayres was frequently obscure in his writings on institutions, and that much of what he wrote on the topic was irrelevant for the objective he was presumably trying to pursue, namely, an understanding of the modern economy. He dealt with the elaboration of myths, with the ceremonial conception of life that regards personality as a mystic potency, and remarked upon how that potency can be diminished by transgressions of taboos, upon how primitive peoples believe that human personality can be projected into inanimate objects, etc. etc. (Ayres 1944, pp. 165-68; Ayres 1961, pp. 126-37), but, in actuality, myths and superstitions have little to do with the formulation of a theory of the economic system of a modern Western country. Anthropologists now acknowledge that the problems, patterns of behavior, and cultural characteristics of contemporary industrial society are, in most respects, quite different from those of primitive communities. Even Ayres came to recognize that the importance in the Western world of myth, superstition, and ceremonial behavior is far less than was represented in his earlier works. In his last major statement on institutions, he observed that modern intellectual sophistication, scientific attitudes, and especially the development of psychopathology have made clear that the emotional intensity surrounding superstitious beliefs is not supernatural in origin, a realization that has "laid bare and shriveled up the root cause of superstition itself" (Ayres 1967b, p. 11; and see ibid., pp. 10-15). The institutionalizing process has therefore been short-circuited in Western society, and that is why its traditional institutions are disintegrating and new ones are not being created (ibid., p. 16).

II. VALUE

The treatment given here of Ayres's theory of value is confined to those aspects of it that are directly relevant to his institutionalist economics, and therefore excludes the extended exposition and analysis that could be undertaken of many of the sociological, historical, aesthetic, epistemological, and metaphysical aspects of his theory. Ayres regarded himself as showing the relevance of John Dewey's value theory to economics (Ayres 1943b, p. 477; Ayres 1961, pp. 29-30), arguing that economics is concerned with values in the sense of what is morally and ethically good or bad. That was the position taken in his doctoral dissertation (Ayres 1918a),[4] and in all his subsequent work. It was a logical necessity for Ayres to construct a theory of what is good and what is bad. He recognized that social values are incorporated in and expressed by institutions. He believed that institutional behavior detracts from the viability of society and impedes its economic progress, in other words, that institutional behavior is harmful or worthless. Consequently, he believed that institutional values are harmful or worthless, and he wanted to provide an intellectual rationalization for his opinion. That objective entails the necessity of formulating a theory of what is truly valuable in order to have a standard by which to define and identify the false values.

It has commonly been supposed, Ayres maintained, that the mores of society determine all distinctions of good and bad, but in fact there are two sets of values. One of these derives from technological processes, which are the true sources of value regarding economic matters. Ayres's reasoning with respect to economic value is, first, that the condition which defines what is truly valuable is whether the action or object contributes to the activity of making a living. That activity is instrumentally organized, so society depends upon its technology. Every economic decision is a judgment about what will contribute most to the efficiency of the technological system on which life depends. "The criterion of every economic judgment is 'keeping the machines running'" (Ayres 1944, p. 223). Whatever contributes to the efficiency of the technological system is therefore economically valuable and whatever hinders it is deleterious (ibid., pp. 222-23). Thus it is not the experience of consumption that determines economic value, but the activities that are part of the endless continuum of production and consumption, and those in turn are part of the whole life process (Ayres 1943b, p. 479). Second, the technological operations that are employed in the activities of making a living are the same in all societies. For example, the functioning of a tractor, Ayres believed, is the same regardless of whether it is used on a Russian *kolkhoz* or on an American family farm. As a result, the values that are derived from technological operations are the same regardless of the institutional structure in which they are undertaken. The general agreement over these values derives from the uniformities of nature, as manifest in the uniform behavior of the tools and materials with which all peoples operate" (Ayres 1959, p. 10). Science-and-technology "contains within itself a criterion both of truth and of value that is the same for all ages, all peoples, and all cultures" (Ayres 1961, pp. 51-52; and see Ayres 1952, p. 26).

In Ayres's opinion, the values that are based on the technological life process are genuine and good. "The term 'good' has clear and definite meaning only with reference to the ongoing life process of humanity,"

4. A chapter of Ayres's dissertation was published in the *Journal of Political Economy* (Ayres 1918b).

which is a causal process, and genuine values derive their meaning from knowledge of demonstrated cause-and-effect processes (ibid., p. 18). This is not, Ayres argued, an exhortation that we should adopt the view that technologically derived values are true and good, but a statement of fact. To say that an event is good actually does and always has meant that it contributes to the life process of humanity (ibid., p. 17). "Doing-and-knowing, science-and-technology, is the real life process of mankind. This is the process from which modern industrial civilization has resulted, and it is the process in terms of which men have always judged things good and bad, and actions right and wrong" (ibid., p. 15). Science and technology are not value free; they are the matrix from which all genuine values derive. The "continuous instrumental-technological process itself provides the standard of judgment both of truth and error and of good and bad" (ibid., p. 29). Inasmuch as "moral judgments are judgments of causal relationships" (Ayres 1958, p. 35), and since all human interests are embraced by the values that are based on the technological life process, they are moral values, not merely judgments of efficiency (Ayres 1961, pp. 8-9).

The second set of values is based upon institutional patterns of belief and behavior, and therefore differs from society to society. Institutional values are supported by superstitions and fantasies in which imagined causes have imaginary effects, so the values which derive their meaning from such processes are pseudo values (Ayres 1961, pp. 17-21). Ayres became increasingly dogmatic in his insistence that culturally relative values are false. He wrote of "values which are true and rational and those which are irrational and false" (ibid., p. 85). "We must be prepared to declare, without fear and without scorn, that nothing but science is true or meaningful" (Ayres 1949, pp. 58-59), which implies that "insofar as a people's values derive from mores they are founded upon falsehood" (Ayres 1961, p. 125). Ayres therefore rejected moral agnosticism, as indicated by his assertion that there are true values which are objectively determined, and he rejected cultural relativism, as indicated by his views that there are true values which are the same for all cultures, and that values which are peculiar to particular cultures are false (Ayres 1949, pp. 55-63; Ayres 1952, pp. 19-20; Ayres 1957, pp. 116-25).

In answer to the criticism that consumption and not the maintenance of our machines is the purpose of economic activity, Ayres responded that we should abandon the means-end dualism in the light of which consumption is identified as an end (Ayres 1944, pp. 224-25). He was not, he argued, substituting the end of maintaining the machines in place of consumption, not emphasizing the importance of machines at the expense of human life. He believed in value as the fuller realization of our potentialities as human beings, as the creative achievements of the human spirit, and so forth, but he insisted that the technological continuum is what gives meaning to those phrases. Technological progress is not "meaningless apart from ends"; on the contrary, it is the locus of meaning (Ayres 1943b, p. 479). Living is doing, and doing is the life process, which involves the whole vast range of tools and skills and know-how (Ayres 1945, pp. 938-39). The use of technology is "co-extensive with life itself, identical with the existence and continuance of the species, and it is the locus of value because of this integral continuity" (Ayres 1944, p. 225).

According to Ayres, progress is the development of technology and the accompanying diminution of superstition and ceremonially invested status, or, more generally, the displacement of institutional by technological values. Such a displacement can be precisely defined as progress, because the locus of value is the objective technological process. Since true values are objectively knowable, progress is also knowable and attainable (Ayres 1944, p. 231). Technological development has created the industrial way of life, and it is good, since it has brought affluence and knowledge and rationality (Ayres 1961, pp. 15-16). Ayres denied that the advancement of technology is responsible for increasing human misery through enabling the invention of terrible devices for making war. "In saying that atomic fission is 'a good thing,' notwithstanding its use in bombing Hiroshima and Nagasaki, we are voicing the same judgment we make when we say that the discovery by primeval man of the principle of the stone ax was a good thing notwithstanding its use also as a weapon. Both judgments are valid, since both invoke the longrun onward march of civilization" (Ayres 1966, p. 88). Advancing technology makes a better life possible, whereas the misuse of technology to cause suffering, wars, and other varieties of social disorder results from the misdirection of technology by institutionally determined objectives (Ayre 1944, pp. 242-43). Ayres came to lump together and to describe as institutional phenomena every undesirable type of condition and behavior: "coercion, injustice, inequality, ignorance, and superstition" (Ayres 1943c, p. 162).

In evaluating Ayres's theory of economic value, it should first be observed that his sequences of statements on value have the external trappings of reasoned discourse; they are sprinkled with words like "therefore" and "consequently"; but in fact what he presented as conclusions do not follow from his assumptions. When stripped of their grammatical connectives and stylistic ambience, his statements are revealed as disjointed expressions rather than as forming a coherent whole. His writings on the subject are not a series of scientific propositions with supporting evidence, but consist instead of a few central judgments surrounded by a mass of argumentation and rhetoric designed to persuade the reader to adopt the same metaphysical and normative points of view. For example, Ayres's view that institutional values are pernicious is a value judgment, not a logical deduction from a set of scientifically determined premises.

Second, Ayres was wrong to suppose that technological operations are the same in all cultures, and that such operations therefore generate a set of instrumental values which is the same for all cultures. It is an error to suppose that the operation of a machine or the use of a computer produces the same results regardless of the institutions of the society in which it is used. The error results from focusing narrowly upon a part of a technological operation, such as the action of the valves in a combustion engine, rather than observing the wider setting in which the instrument or machine is used. The life-sustaining uses of technology do not have an independent existence, and cannot be defined without reference to the institutional framework within which they are employed. Technology and institutions interpenetrate each other, and the operation of tools and machines depends upon institutional habits of thought and action, and vice versa. Like capital, technology is embodied temporarily in ever-changing forms that are appropriate for the ends for which it is designed, because in each society the institutional and physical situations in which tools are used are unique, raising new problems which depend upon time, place, and circumstance, and which therefore require new solutions (see Frankel 1976, p. 69).

Third, Ayres contradicted his own thesis by arguing that the evil uses and consequences of technology are the result of institutional values. "Granted that the victims of industrial revolution have been exploited," he asked rhetorically, "have they been exploited by the machines, by the technology itself; or are they the victims of imbecile institutions . . . ?" (Ayres 1960b, p. 213). Similarly, Ayres assumed that nuclear fission, for example, is good in itself, and regarded evil uses of it as aberrations resulting from the external impact of institutional forces. Clearly, however, the recognition that the evil consequences of some uses of technology result from institutions should entail the recognition that the machines are ethically and morally neutral in themselves with respect to all uses, and that what are considered to be their beneficial effects are also determined by institutions. Uses of technology that are judged harmful in some or all respects are the result of decisions to employ technology in those ways. Beneficial consequences of technology result from value judgments about what is beneficial, since these result in derivative judgments regarding the uses of technology and the directions that technological change should take. The value judgments are the outcome of the social institutions that operate to select objectives and to define problems. Science and technology enable the achievement of the objectives, but do not select them, as can be inferred from the different uses to which science and technology are put in different societies. The conclusion must be that Ayres was not correct in supposing that there are universally true moral values which are objectively determined by technological operations, and that he was unable to demonstrate scientifically that culturally relative values are harmful. This rejection of his theory of value is a logical corollary of the rejection of his theory of the antithetical roles of technology and institutions in the process of economic development.

The final issue that arises is the worth of the institutional values which do in fact determine the uses of technology. It is undeniable that the institutional values accepted by a society are considered valuable by the members of that society. Culturally relative values contribute to making a living, and are an essential part of the life process in the society in which they prevail. It is also undeniable that contradictory values held by another society are equally valid to its members. This situation is a fact of life, and one can accept it or be frustrated by it. Ayres was frustrated by it, but he could not produce a successful argument against it.[5] In actuality, Ayres's work revealed on every page the indelible imprint of the institutionally determined value system to which he subscribed. By maintaining that only the values which he described as technologically defined should be retained he was manifesting ethnocentricity, for he identified as good or bad those values which his own culture and background led him to accept or reject, as evidenced, for example, by his notions that limited government intervention is good (Ayres 1938, Ayres 1949b, Walker 1978a), and that both communism (Tilman 1974, pp. 701, 705-706, n. 14; Breit and Culbertson 1976, pp. 17-19) and the policies of conservative economists are bad (Ayres 1944, pp. 201-202; Ayres 1952, pp. 118-119; Ayres 1966, pp. 76, 77, 83; Ayres 1967c, p. 5). It must have been a great solace to Ayres to believe that the conditions of economic organization and social behavior which he advocated are objectively true and good, whereas his benighted opponents were espousing ignorant superstitions, and it must have been a source of great irritation to them to be confronted with his imperturbable conviction of scientific and moral superiority.

III. CONCLUSION

Ayres did not establish his contention that institutions are always harmful to the well-being of society and impediments to economic growth. Furthermore, his procedure is tautological. Anything that hinders economic development is by definition an institution in Ayres's work. If a habit of thought or behavioral pattern that we would call an institution contributes efficiently to the process of production, Ayres would call it a technological activity. He asserted that institutional behavior does not contribute to economic development, but what kind of behavior is institutional? Ayres's circular answer is that it is the kind that impedes economic growth and technological change (Ayres 1952, pp. 103, 106-7).

Some contributions of lasting value were made by Ayres, and these should be viewed as additions to the mainstream of economic studies.

---

5. See Walker 1978b for some remarks on this issue.

By example and explicit argument, he made a convincing case in favor of an interdisciplinary approach to the study of economics and the other social sciences. His work as a cultural generalist was in the fine tradition of those who keep us aware of the limited value of abstract models which assume as their sole behavioral content that rational individuals engage in profit and utility maximization. Ayres reminded us to take account of the evolving social, institutional, and technological environment of which economic action is a part, and showed us some of the ways in which that can be done. There is no incompatibility between orthodox economics and this institutionalist insistence on the importance of the changing general environment within which economic behavior occurs.

Ayres contributed to the analysis of the process of technological development in two ways. First, he drew attention to the importance of technological change in understanding the history of cultures and economic development. Second, his theory that technological change results from the combination of pre-existing elements of technology and from cultural cross-fertilization identifies two important related reasons why technology grows in diversity and complexity.

In conclusion, an evaluation of Ayres should recognize that he was not only an economist, but also a critic of our society. He looked at Western culture as a social philosopher and from the perspective of a teacher of social ethics. As a result he inculcated in the minds of his students an inquiring attitude toward our economic institutions, and thereby made one of his most important contributions to scholarship. Many fundamental criticisms of Ayres's work can be made, but it should be observed that all such criticisms are as handfuls of dust to the segment of the intellectual world which has an emotional affinity with Ayres's outlook and personality. Just as Veblen and Marx will always have their loyal followers, so also will Ayres, to a lesser extent, always have a devoted group of admirers. With such charismatic heterodox thinkers there is some elemental spark of empathy that, like a religious bond, attracts people of a certain psychological and attitudinal persuasion to their cause. In the case of Ayres the cause was — in regard to its ultimate decency and concern for humanity — a good one, and if he was wrong-headed about aspects of economic science and of the moving forces of civilization, it must nevertheless be affirmed that he was not wrong in his ceaseless quest for the elimination of the superstitions and myths that have impeded the attainment of a better life for all.

REFERENCES

Ayres, Clarence E., *The Nature of the Relationship Between Ethics and Economics*, University of Chicago Press, Chicago, 1918a.

_____, "The Functions and Problems of Economic Theory," *Journal of Political Economy*, January 1918b, *26*, 69-90.

_____, "Fifty Years' Developments in Ideas of Human Nature and Motivation," *American Economic Review, Papers and Proceedings*, March 1936, *26*, 224-36.

_____, *The Problem of Economic Order*, Farrar and Rinehart, New York, 1938.

_____, "Capitalism in Retrospect," *Southern Economic Journal*, April 1943a, *9*, 298-301.

_____, "The Significance of Economic Planning," in *Development of Collective Enterprise; Dynamics of an Emergent Economy*. Seba Eldridge et alii, University of Kansas Press, Lawrence, Kansas, 1943b.

_____, "The Twilight of the Price System," *Antioch Review*, Summer 1943c, *3*, 162-81.

_____, *The Theory of Economic Progress*, 1st ed., University of North Carolina Press, Chapel Hill, 1944.

_____, "Addendum to *The Theory of Economic Progress*," *American Economic Review*, December 1945, *45*, 937-40.

_____, "The New Economics," *Southwest Review*, Summer 1948, *33*, 223-32.

_____, "The Value Economy," in *Value; A Cooperative Inquiry*, edited by Ray Lepley, Columbia University Press, 1949, 43-63.

_____, "The Co-ordinates of Institutionalism," *American Economic Review, Papers and Proceedings*, May 1951, *41*, 47-55.

_____, *The Industrial Economy; Its Technological Basis and Institutional Destiny*, Houghton Mifflin, Boston, 1952.

_____, "The Role of Technology in Economic Theory," *American Economic Review, Papers and Proceedings*, May 1953, *43*, 279-88.

_____, Communication to D. A. Walker regarding his critique of Ayres's views on the symbolic process, January 1956.

_____, "The Pestilence of Moral Agnosticism; Knowledge and Value in a Secular Society," *Southwest Review*, Spring 1957, *42*, 116-25.

_____, "Veblen's Theory of Instincts Reconsidered," in *Thorstein Veblen: A Critical Reappraisal*, edited by Douglas F. Dowd, Cornell University Press, Ithaca, 1958, 25-37.

_____, "The Industrial Way of Life," *Texas Quarterly*, Summer 1959, *2*, 1-19.

_____, "Institutionalism and Economic Development," *Southwestern Social Science Quarterly*, June 1960a, *41*, 45-62.

_____, "Economic History and Economic Development; Comments," in *Economic Growth; Rationale, Problems, Cases*, edited by Eastin Nelson, 1960b. Reprint, Books for Libraries Press, Freeport, New York, 1971, 211-14.

_____, *Toward a Reasonable Society; The Values of Industrial Civilization*, University of Texas Press, Austin, 1961.

_____, "The Legacy of Thorstein Veblen," in *Institutional Economics; Veblen, Commons, and Mitchell Reconsidered*, lectures by Joseph Dorfman et alii, University of California Press, Berkeley and Los Angeles, 1964, 46-62.

_____, "The Nature and Significance of Institutionalism," *Antioch Review*, Spring 1966, *26*, 70-90.

_____, "Guaranteed Income: An Institutionalist View," in *The Guaranteed Income; Next Step in Socioeconomic Evolution?*, edited by Robert Theobald, Doubleday, Garden City, New York, 1967a, 169-82.

_____, "The Theory of Institutional Adjustment," in *Institutional Adjustment: A Challenge to a Changing Economy*, edited by C. C. Thompson, University of Texas Press, Austin, 1967b, 3-17.

_____, "Idealogical Responsibility," *Journal of Economic Issues*, June 1967c, *1*, 3-11.

_____, "The Price System and Public Policy," *Journal of Economic Issues*, September 1968, *2*, 342-44.

Breit, William, "The Development of Clarence Ayres's Theoretical Institutionalism," *Social Science Quarterly*, September 1973, *54*, 244-57.

Breit, William and Culbertson, William Patton, Jr., "Clarence Edwin Ayres: An Intellectual's Portrait," in *Science and Ceremony: The Institutional Economics of C. E. Ayres*, edited by William Breit and William Patton Culbertson, Jr., University of Texas Press, Austin, 1976, 3-22.

Frankel, S. Herbert, "Clarence Ayres and the Roots of Economic Progress," in *Science and Ceremony: The Institutional Economics of C. E. Ayres*, edited by William Breit and William Patton Culbertson, Jr., University of Texas Press, Austin, 1976, 63-74.

Hamilton, Walton H., "Institution," in *Encyclopaedia of the Social Sciences*, edited by R. A. Seligman, 1932. Reprint, Macmillan, New York, 1963, *8*, 84-89.

Mill, John Stuart, *Principles of Political Economy, with Some of Their Applications to Social Philosophy*, 5th edition, 1862. 2 vols. Reprint, D. Appleton and Co., New York, 1889.

North, Douglass C., "The Place of Economic History in the Discipline of Economics," *Economic Inquiry*, December 1976, *14*, 461-65.

Tilman, Rick, "Value Theory, Planning, and Reform: Ayres as Incrementalist and Utopian," *Journal of Economic Issues*, December 1974, *8*, 689-706.

Walker, Donald A., "Thorstein Veblen's Economic System," *Economic Inquiry*, April 1977, *15*, 213-37.

_____, "The Economic Policy Proposals of Clarence Ayres," *Southern Economic Journal*, January 1978a, *44*, 616-28.

_____, Review of *Science and Ceremony: The Institutional Economics of C. E. Ayres*, edited by William Breit and William Patton Culbertson, Jr., *Southern Economic Journal*, January 1978b, *44*, 696-99.

_____, "Clarence Ayres's Critique of Orthodox Economic Theory," *Journal of Economic Issues*, March 1980, *14*.

[13]

Veblen and Commons:
A Case of Theoretical Convergence

DAVID HAMILTON
UNIVERSITY OF NEW MEXICO

THE IMPRESSION that institutional economics is a hodge podge of un-related hypotheses and descriptive monographs is of long standing among orthodox economists. Yet of late it is becoming increasingly apparent that this is not the case. There is emerging a body of identifiably institutionalist theory and work that is closely associated. The posthumous publication of *The Economics of Collective Action*[1] by John R. Commons brings further evidence of the cohesive nature of institutional theory.

For many years orthodox economists have contended that there were certain institutional economists such as Veblen, Commons, and Hamilton, but no body of institutional theory. Each was an entity unto himself and outside of some vague similarities, there were no general areas of agreement. This thesis has been challenged recently by several institutional economists. In a comprehensive volume on institutional economics and economists which covered the contributions of Veblen, Commons, Mitchell, J. M. Clark, S. N. Patten, Tugwell, and Gardiner Means, Allan Gruchy found a connecting thread in what he calls "holism" after the philosophy of Jan Smuts. As he states the case:

The post-Darwinian type of scientific thought which Smuts describes as "holistic" takes the physical world to be an evolving, dynamic whole or synthesis, which is not only greater than the sum of its parts, but which also so relates the parts that their functioning is conditioned by their interrelations.

The holistic viewpoint which has proven so fruitful in the biological and physical sciences is precisely the viewpoint of the heterodox economists whose work is the primary interest of this study. These economists all have the same holistic orientation or intellectual approach which Smuts finds to be so characteristic of modern scientific and philosophic thought.[2]

43]   In another post World War II volume, John Gambs claims that the

---

[1] New York, Macmillan, 1951. Cited hereafter as *Collective Action*.
[2] Allan Gruchy, *Modern Economic Thought: The American Contribution* (New York, Prentice-Hall, 1947), 3–4.

"hidden premise" that runs through the work of institutionalists is that of coercion. As he writes:

Monopoly, unfair competition, exploitation of weaker groups—all are recognized by standard theory. On the whole, however, such phenomena are deemed to be atypical, occasional, and relatively unimportant. Institutional theory erects the occasional into the general. Coercion is deemed to be as pervasive as the air we breathe and, normally, equally unnoticed, except when we are confronted with cruel or shocking or criminal instances of exploitation, monopoly, or unfair competition.[3]

Although some institutionalists might take issue with both authors over the emphasis on holism or coercion as the unifying thread, it can hardly be said that they fail to prove that there is some degree of unity among institutionalists along these grounds. Certainly more can be said for these efforts at finding a common ground among institutionalists than can be said about earlier attempts to find a concert of opinion.[4]

Nevertheless, further evidence of a uniform body of institutional thought is to be found by a comparison of the theory of Commons as found in his last published work with that of Veblen. In a sense Commons and Veblen have been looked upon as establishing two schools of institutional economics with not too much similarity in thought. This may have been due partially to the nature of Commons' earlier theoretical works. Because he used his theory as a basis for studying the legal aspects of economic activity, his theory is not as sharply drawn in the *Legal Foundations of Capitalism*[5] as it is in the *Economics of Collective Action*. Nor is it as clear in his *Institutional Economics*[6] which included a mass of extraneous material which seemed to hide his theory. There is a sense in which his *Institutional Economics* is an examination of the history of economic thought from his own theoretical position. With his theory obscured by these other aims, the similarity to that of Veblen was obscured. Yet upon a closer examination of the economic thought of Commons there is evident a remarkable similarity to that of Veblen.

Both Veblen and Commons put great emphasis on collective action, rather than individual action. In fact, the title of Commons' book should be evidence enough of this emphasis in his latest work. The subject of

[3] John Gambs, *Beyond Supply and Demand* (New York, Columbia University Press, 1946), 13.

[4] "Economic Theory – Institutionalism: What It Is and What It Hopes to Become," *American Economic Review*, Vol. XXI, No. 1, Supplement (March, 1931), 134–; "Round-table Conference on Institutional Economics," *American Economic Review*, Vol. XXII, No. 1, Supplement (March, 1932), 105 f.

[5] New York, Macmillan, 1924.

[6] New York, Macmillan, 1934. Cited hereafter as *Institutional Economics*.

this study is collective, rather than individual action. As he states: "This is an age of collective action. Most Americans must work collectively as participants in organized concerns in order to earn a living."[7] Commons defined an institution as "collective action in control of individual action."[8] He gives to custom an important role in shaping human behavior, stating that "individuals must adjust themselves to what others are doing [custom], regardless of logic, reason, or self-interest."[9] Although custom has a compulsory character, it varies in the degree of compulsion with which it falls upon individuals.

This position is similar to that of Veblen, who in all of his work emphasized the compulsive role of institutions. These institutions were so compulsive that "history records more frequent and more spectacular instances of the triumph of imbecile institutions over life and culture than of peoples who have by force of instinctive insight saved themselves alive out of a desperately precarious institutional situation."[10] In all of his work Veblen looked upon human behavior as cultural behavior and, like Commons, took the orthodox economists to task for laying a science of behavior on a physiological basis, hedonism.[11] Both Veblen and Commons viewed the individual as an active agent, a doer rather than a passive agent being acted upon.[12] This was in contrast with the hedonist psychology of orthodox economics. Differences of terminology aside, both Commons and Veblen looked upon human behavior as culturally conditioned behavior and as understandable only on that premise. Both dismissed without much ceremony the hedonist explanation of human behavior. In fact, Commons went so far as to call the incremental economics of Gossen, Jevons, Menger, *et alii* "Home Economics."[13]

As a consequence of the rejection of hedonism, both writers criticized individualistic economics based on hedonism as Newtonian. Commons stated:

The early nineteenth century economists patterned their work upon the materialistic sciences of physics and chemistry, instead of on a volitional science of the human will as developed by the courts. According to the materialists, the human individual acted somewhat like an atom, or like a natural law,

---

[7] Commons, *Collective Action*, 23.

[8] *Ibid.*, 6.

[9] *Ibid.*, 111.

[10] Thorstein Veblen, *The Instinct of Workmanship* (New York, B. W. Heubsch, 1922), 25.

[11] Thorstein Veblen, "Why Is Economics Not an Evolutionary Science?" in *The Place of Science in Modern Civilization* (New York, Viking, 1942), 56–81, cited hereafter as Veblen, *Place of Science*; Commons, *Collective Action*, 109, 113.

[12] Veblen, *Place of Science*, 74; Commons, *Collective Action*, 154–55.

[13] Commons, *Institutional Economics*, 85.

and only in the one direction of overcoming the resistance of nature's forces in the production of wealth.[14]

[45] Although Commons does not refer to Newton in this context, it was this aspect of classical doctrine that led Veblen to call it pre-Darwinian in contrast to an evolutionary science largely influenced by Darwinian evolution.[15] In another context Commons is more explicit in condemning classicism for its Newtonian outlook. He says, "False analogies have arisen in the history of economic thought by transferring to economics the meanings derived from the physical sciences, as we have seen in Locke's derivations from the astronomy and optics of Sir Isaac Newton, or from the more recent biological sciences of organisms, or even from the human will itself."[16] This at first might appear to conflict with Veblen's Darwinian approach, but it should be remembered that Veblen was drawing on the evolutionary aspect of Darwin and not drawing organismic analyses. In still another context, Commons claims that "individualistic economics" is static and "institutional economics" is dynamic.[17] These positions are identical with those taken by Veblen which are explicitly stated in the critical essays on classicism contained in *The Place of Science in Modern Civilization* and particularly so in "The Preconceptions of Economic Science."

Although it could hardly be sustained that either Veblen or Commons placed primary emphasis on coercion, both gave it a prominent place in their theories that the classicists did not give it. Of course it is not implied that either one used it in the sense of crude brute force. Coercion is a subtle thing, the product of culture and of status, of the relationship between superior and inferior. Commons states that coercion is used to insure conformance with what he calls the "working rules."[18] In Commons' theory the managerial transaction is a coercive relationship between superior and inferior.[19] In discussing "holism" Commons brings out the fact that coercion of the individual is a product of collective action.[20] Veblen expounds a similar idea throughout his work, but nowhere more concretely than in *The Theory of Leisure Class*.[21] Here the coercive nature of society is revealed in the usual brilliant satire.

But all of these similarities are probably well known. The significant

[14] Commons, *Collective Action*, 36.
[15] Veblen, *Place of Science*, 32–55.
[16] Commons, *Institutional Economics*, 96.
[17] Commons, *Collective Action*, 52.
[18] *Ibid.*, 40.
[19] Commons, *Institutional Economics*, 64 f.
[20] Commons, *Collective Action*, 135.
[21] New York, Macmillan, 1912.

upshot of the latest Commons volume is the similarity revealed between Commons and Veblen in their larger systems of theory.

Probably the most outstanding contribution of Veblen to economic theory is the distinction he detected in cultural behavior between "technological" and "ceremonial" behavior. All of those who evaluate Veblen point out the distinction he made between making goods and making money. Not all have understood the general significance of this distinction. It was part of a larger distinction in which Veblen held that man engaged in activities, some of which result in the furtherance of human welfare and others in the drawing of invidious distinctions. Professor C. E. Ayres, in this latest volume, contends that this distinction may "prove to be as fundamental for economics (and perhaps for the social sciences generally) as the idea of elemental substances was for chemistry."[22] Veblen made much of this distinction in all of his work. In some, it took the form of workmanship and exploit, in others the form of industrial efficiency and business enterprise, in others matter-of-fact knowledge and myth. Veblen began the *Theory of Business Enterprise* with the statement that "the material framework of modern civilization is the industrial system, and the directing force which animates this framework is business enterprise."[23] Throughout the book he showed how business enterprise and exploit work at cross purposes to the full utilization of the industrial system. Money was made and prestige acquired by "throwing sand in the wheels" of the industrial system. In the *Engineers and the Price System*[24] he compares business activity to sabotage working to thwart the industrial system. In his essay entitled "The Place of Science in Modern Civilization"[25] he contrasts matter-of-fact knowledge with the dramatized myth and legend. The matter-of-fact knowledge is the basis of the instrumental or technological behavior and the dramatic myth is that set of sentiment and belief which sustains the ceremonial behavior.

According to Veblen all culture is characterized by these two aspects. In technological behavior, activity proceeds on a matter-of-fact reasoning from means to end, subject to continued empirical verification of efficacy in the long-run life process. In the technological area valuation is in matter-of-fact terms—concerned with reasoning from means to end and the further consequences. It is identifiable with the scientific process. In contrast to this is the ceremonial aspect of culture. Here myth reigns supreme as the ultimate test of validity. All behavior must conform

[46]

---

[22] C. E. Ayres, *The Industrial Economy* (Boston, Houghton Mifflin, 1952), 25.
[23] Thorstein Veblen, *Theory of Business Enterprise* (New York, Scribner's, 1935), 1.
[24] New York, B. W. Huebsch, 1921.
[25] In Veblen, *The Place of Science.*

to myth. It is the area of coercion, of superior and inferior. In institutions the valuation process is concerned mainly in making invidious distinctions—matter of status and prerogative.

These two aspects of cultural behavior have been noted by others such as the anthropologist, Bronislaw Malinowski,[26] as well as by John Dewey.[27] And although Veblen has become well known for his effective utilization of this cultural dichotomy, not much has been said about [47] Commons' glimmerings of the same thing. Yet in his latest volume there is clear evidence that Commons had a grasp of the same ideas. Throughout the volume he demonstrates an awareness of technological and ceremonial patterns of culture.

Commons makes much of the distinction between transfer of commodities and transfer of ownership.[28] In other words he sees a distinction between the flow of goods and the flow of ownership. This is essentially the distinction which Veblen makes between business and industry, the form the dichotomy assumes in contemporary society. There is a pattern of ongoing industrial activity accompanied by the ceremonial of business transactions transferring ownership status to the usufruct of the industrial process.

The basic unit of economic investigation according to Commons is the transaction. This is in contrast to classical political economy which took the exchange as the basic unit of investigation. Commons claims that the exchange of classical political economy was one-sided. It encompassed the transfer of ownership only; it ignored the pattern of relationships involved in the exchange of commodities. He finds three types of transactions, the bargaining, the managerial, and the rationing transaction.[29] Within his system the bargaining transaction involves a legal transfer of ownership, while the physical transfer of the good is encompassed in the managerial transaction. The rationing transaction has to do with the apportionment of the wealth of production among the subordinates by the sovereignty. He states that the most frequent form this takes is a tax. As Commons puts it, "The physical and labor transfers have come to be comprehended in modern economics under the name of managerial transactions, while the legal transfers are the bargaining transactions and the rationing transactions."[30] Since the bargaining and rationing transactions involve transfers of ownership, this area of activity is comparable to what Veblen calls "business' while

[26] See his *Magic, Science and Religion* (Boston, Beacon Press, 1948), 1–71.
[27] See the opening passages of *The Quest for Certainty* (New York, Minton, Balch, 1929).
[28] Commons, *Collective Action*, 43–57.
[29] *Ibid.*, 48–56
[30] *Ibid.*, 48.

the managerial transactions concerned with the flow of goods is comparable to what Veblen calls "industry." In another way the bargaining
and rationing transactions in Commons' system are similar to the
ceremonial area in Veblen's system while the managerial transaction
in Commons is similar to the technological in Veblen.

There is one point of difference, however. The managerial transaction
has several facets. It is a relationship between two persons, a superior
and inferior. In this sense it is a coercive relationship. Veblen confined
coercion to the ceremonial area of activity, to the status hierarchy of
"graded men." But the managerial transaction has as its purpose the
production of wealth. "The universal principle of bargaining transactions
[48] is scarcity, while that of managerial transactions is efficiency."[31] Since
the managerial transaction is a pattern of organization or social relationship that has as its purpose the efficient production of wealth, it is
a technological pattern of behavior. That aspect of superior-inferior
which smacks of coercion would be ceremonial behaviour in Veblen.
But this difference, notwithstanding, there is a close similarity here also
beween Veblen and Commons.

In his distinction between assets and wealth Commons is even closer
to the fundamental distinction Veblen makes between business and industry. Commodities have a double meaning; one as assets possessing a
proprietary character, and the other, a technological meaning as wealth.
The populace at large has an interest in increasing wealth. Business
has an interest in maintaining scarcity, so as to maintain the asset value
of wealth.[32] Although Commons does not draw the sharp conclusion
that Veblen does that business thwarts the full realization of the fruits
of modern science and technology, he comes precariously close to this
position when he says:

Modern business is conducted on the basis of assets, that is, scarcity of wealth,
and not on the abundance of wealth according to Smith. With assets one
can give security for loans of money, but the security is worthless if the supply
of "wealth" is increased so greatly that assets have little or no scarcity value
when sold upon the markets for money.

This paradox of wealth and assets is confusing to common sense. But
common sense has previously injected unconsciously something that restricts
the supply and maintains scarcity value.[33]

In this statement Commons would appear to be on the same ground
as Veblen when he states that business restricts and thwarts output

[31] Commons, *Institutional Economics*, 64.
[32] *Ibid.*, 94–95.
[33] *Ibid.*

in order to maintain pecuniary values. This is contrary to classical doctrine which held to the identity between public and private interest guided "as if by an invisible hand."

To carry this distinction further, in dealing with efficiency Commons distinguishes between man-hour or engineering efficiency and dollar efficiency. As he states it:

Efficiency itself can be measured as Taylor had demonstrated. It is a ratio of output to input, which I name *man-hour* efficiency, to distinguish it from the *dollar* efficiency, which is not efficiency, but is the relative scarcity of bargaining transactions.[34]

The classicist maintained that dollar efficiency was synonymous with engineering efficiency. In fact, it was held to be the measure of engineer-[49] ing efficiency. In showing that dollar efficiency hangs on scarcity and restriction of output, Commons shows that it jeopardizes engineering efficiency.[35] In doing this he aligns himself with Veblen in such works as his *Engineers and the Price System* and puts his finger on an aspect of our culture that Veblen found to be true of all culture.

Although Commons has been called an "institutionalist of a sort"[36] and has been said to have a theory personal to himself, it is apparent that his theory was not in many respects too different from that of Veblen. The difference between the two is largely one of approach. Commons came to his theory through long years of research among labor unions, cooperatives, and government agencies. Veblen approaches the economic problem from anthropology and a long study of culture. Commons, coming without the advantage of anthropology, but arriving at a similar position to that of Veblen is further verification of the existence of the "ceremonial-technological" aspect of culture which would seem to be the chief contribution of institutionalism to modern [50] economic thought.

[34] *Ibid.*, 100.
[35] *Ibid.*, 100–101.
[36] Lewis, H. Haney, *History of Economic Thought* (New York, Macmillan, 1936), 743.

[14]

VEBLEN VS. COMMONS:
A COMPARATIVE EVALUATION

I

The only purely American school of economic thought is the Institutional School of THORSTEIN VEBLEN (1857–1929) and JOHN R. COMMONS (1862–1945), yet the two men were quite different in their views and outlook. In terms of the three fields covered by the History of Economic Thought, namely, economic analysis and theory; economic growth and development of institutions, economies, and systems of economic organization; and economic policy and welfare economies, VEBLEN basically was only interested in the second field, or economic development and growth. COMMONS, on the other hand, who regarded the history of economic thought and theory as a recapitulation of the evolution of his thinking, was interested in all three fields. Whereas VEBLEN's views on the formal economic theory of his day were rather negative, COMMONS tried to revitalize and refurbish formal economic theory and make it useful and relevant in the pragmatic sense of solving contemporary economic problems and issues. He did not try to create a new economics but rather to give 'collective action' its due place in economic theory. Thus, some economists look upon COMMONS as the more important of the two men in terms of economic theory in retrospect. This is not necessarily correct, and this is the subject of this essay.

While both COMMONS and VEBLEN were critical of the doctrinal heritage from the past, VEBLEN takes a more extreme position than COMMONS. In his famous 1919 article, 'Why Economics is not an Evolutionary Science', VEBLEN argued that economics should be treated as a branch of the natural sciences inasmuch as it studied one particular living organism, namely, man. The method of economics should be the evolutionary or genetic one. His evolutionary concept was Darwinian rather than Hegelian. Given the relationship of economics to the natural sciences, the economist should look more to biology than to physics for methodological guidance VEBLEN had little use for the concept of equilibrium, believed to be borrowed

322

VEBLEN VS. COMMONS: A COMPARATIVE EVALUATION

from physics, let alone the idea of an automatic and self-adjusting organization of the economic system.

Two implications follow for the study of economics from the evolutionary methodology. First, all economic generalizations to be valid must be empirically definite, that is, limited to a particular society and to a particular epoch in time. Second, an economist must have a sense of cultural perspective. He must recognize the importance of institutions in all economic phenomena. VEBLEN's perspective was primarily anthropological. He believed that economic conceptions should be dynamic stressing the inevitable evolutionary change of economic systems and institutions, and that scientific inquiry in economics should be directed to an examination of the causes and nature of change.

In VEBLEN's three early essays on 'Preconceptions in Economics', he suggested the reason that the English tradition in economics had been more empirical than that of the Physiocrats and earlier economists was the Industrial Revolution which was occurring in Great Britain at that time. This changed the stimulus-response environment in which people lived and made them more conscious of matter-of-fact experiences as opposed to flights of imputation of validity that characterized the animistic philosophies of the pre-eighteenth century societies.

Similarly in his *Imperial Germany and the Industrial Revolution* in 1914, VEBLEN explained why Germany was becoming the industrialized authoritarian system as opposed to the democratic bias of the industrial society of Great Britain. His explanation was that the habit of mind of conceiving things in terms of matter-of-fact, cause-and-effect relationships was much better developed in Great Britain than in Germany because of the latter's more recent dominance by feudal authority. Great Britain developed its industrial techniques over a long period of time and British lives changed in association with this industrializing process, whereas Germany acquired its major technology through borrowing it from Great Britain. Thus, the dynamic process of industrializing was not a part of the German political-social-economic way of life.

However, Great Britain had to pay a penalty for taking the lead; later developing economies could adopt merely the latest and the most efficient technology without the past-dated habits of mind as-

ERVIN K. ZINGLER

sociated with the historical development of technology. This idea has become the 'Frontier Thesis' of modern historians and anthropologists. It suggests why Japan became so imperialistic and why the United States developed so rapidly relative to Europe. It may explain why the Industrial Revolution occurred in Europe and not elsewhere. Europe was technologically continuous with the Mediterranean culture of Rome but institutionally discontinuous.

Economics was a behavioral science for COMMONS, and not a deterministic science as the physical and natural sciences. Institutional economics, which he said went back to HUME and McLEOD, involved not only conventional economics but also ethics, law, politics, and public administration. Great stress was placed on a volitional versus a mechanical or deterministic explanation of economic matters, and on an institutional and behavioral approach to all problems. The subject matter of economics should be expanded to include those vast areas wherein prices are not determined solely by supply and demand but by tradition, custom, regulatory commissions, courts, and statuatory law.

COMMONS maintained his major point of departure from VEBLEN was over 'natural selection'. He felt that the Darwinian idea of process was no more an appropriate analogy for economics than the Newtonian concept of natural laws. Basically COMMONS associated himself with the Bargaining School of Economics which stressed equality of power rather than the Managerial School of Economics which stressed rationing of power.

While COMMONS' basic concept was 'collective action', VEBLEN's was the 'institution'. Darwinian evolution was not one of COMMONS' interests, and social legislation was not one of VEBLEN's. Yet VEBLEN thought that a study of human nature and behavior was absolutely necessary and essential for the economic science. This is seen very clearly in his *Theory of the Leisure Class* (1899) and his *Theory of Business Enterprise* (1904). The comparative static assumptions of competition and the idea of normality and maximization in Neo-Classical economics (MARSHALL and J. B. CLARK) were nothing more than an extension of classical preconceptions of Natural Law to VEBLEN. They were essentially animistic and teleological in nature. For him, ceremonial versus tool behavior and activity were the two important factors in consumer wants. The first emphasized the existing social

VEBLEN VS. COMMONS: A COMPARATIVE EVALUATION

organization, mores, and institutions. This explained the drive for status, caste, and prestige. The second emphasized the technological and creative drives and motivations, productivity, inventiveness, ingenuity, and creativity.

Human wants other than survival for VEBLEN were largely social phenomena, the result of cultural and institutional conditioning. Thus, wants were either institutional with emphasis on status symbols or they were technological with emphasis on their 'tool' significance. It was only when goods were instruments to achieve some end-in-view, rather than status symbols, that value and welfare went hand in hand. Human behavior at best was only partially, never completely, rational, and often more times irrational than rational. Men were creatures of habits, propensities, and instincts; the latter being learned, conditioned responses to be distinguished from tropisms.

Thus, economics could not be rigidly compartmentalized but must always remain closely coordinated and interrelated with the other social and behavioral sciences. In terms of modern-day advertising, huckstering, and motivational research, the business world confirms the validity of the Veblenian cultural theory of consumption over the traditional rational theory of consumption.

The three main philosophical orientations of VEBLEN were: (1) The Hegelian notion of economic systems as constantly emerging and changing, (2) C. S. PIERCE's pragmatism—this involved a definition of science which insisted that scientific theories had two roots, one, empirical based on actual data and the other based on the bias or preconception of the observer, something for which VEBLEN criticized orthodox economics, and (3) SUMNER's Social Darwinianism, an appreciation of the process of continuous interaction of man and his environment, which led to MORGAN's new field, at that time, of anthropology where the concept of culture was expanding the definition of the environment.

In terms of psychology, VEBLEN believed that hedonism was defective. It required a person to be a passive player in the economic game incapable of action or learning beyond a mere response in a preordained manner to pleasure-pain stimuli. His theory of instincts came from J. LOEB and KANT (he wrote his doctoral dissertation in philosophy at Yale on KANT) which he combined with the idea of relective judgment. Basically he believed that people were products

325

ERVIN K. ZINGLER

of habits, and that they reacted much as they did in their cultural and social past. There were two checks, however, on pastbinding behavior: (1) The 'instinct of workmanship' or the desire to find a better way to perform the tasks at hand, and (2) 'idle curiosity', an inquiry into the abstract counterpart of the same. These two checks caused men to reflect on the traditional, habitual behavior which leads to an exercise in judgment—an instrumental concept where men had a significant and active role to play in shaping their lives.

The concept of change or process was the crux of VEBLEN's contribution, namely, that culture, institutions, and economic systems were a continually evolving and interacting process. The forces for change and progress were the instincts of workmanship and idle curiosity. The latter really meant the freedom for purposeful and creative activity and speculation, which often by accident led to innovations and material progress. It was almost always idle curiosity rather than deliberate research which led to new knowledge and discoveries according to VEBLEN. Deliberate research only filled in the gaps and discontinuities in existing knowledge.

The force working against progress was what VEBLEN called ceremonial habits of thought or institutional behavior. However, unlike MARX, for VEBLEN there was the idea of continuous interaction between these forces rather than a growing divergence culminating in a revolutionary change. This led VEBLEN to a more pessimistic conclusion about the possible triumph of the imbecile. Change for VEBLEN came about inversely proportional to the degree of institutional resistance to the forces of technological development. Institutions he defined as habitual, normal, and conventional modes of behavior. Skills, in turn, were functions of tools and technology.

From the technological-institutional dichotomy and his preconceptions about the primacy of evolutionary change came VEBLEN's theory of value. It can be found in no single place in his writings but the best source is his doctoral dissertation on KANT. Value to him was a standard for comparing historical, anthropological cultures and deriving a direction for the improvement of society. Values, he believed, were the product of technological processes. They contributed to the continuity of the life processes, and their locus could be found in experience guided by intelligence. Economic welfare was

VEBLEN VS. COMMONS: A COMPARATIVE EVALUATION

the result of tool activity and it depended upon the current stage of technology, science, and the industrial arts.

By analyzing cultures and utilizing scientific methodology, VE-BLEN came to view technological change as the positive source of social improvement. The instincts of workmanship and idle curiosity, the counterpart of technological behavior on the psychological level, were the source of improvement at the individual level. The forces which resisted change, the institutional arrangements on the cultural level, and their counterparts, traditional habits of thought on the individual level, became the enemies of progress. The technological process of development eroded the current institutionally structured behavior, and gave rise to change and improvement. There was continuous interaction between the two forces but in a processional, not a dialectic, manner.

As mentioned earlier, VEBLEN thought that a study of human nature and behavior was absolutely necessary for the economic science. He envisioned institutions as changing slowly but incessantly under the dual impact of human nature and material circumstances. To analyze human nature, he developed a theory of instincts. Three of them formed a substratum of human nature and were the basis of the moral absolute for VEBLEN. Primary to the system were the 'instinct of workmanship', a supposed human propensity to engage in activity tailored to the efficient achievement of an end, and the 'instinct of idle curiosity', a disinterested inquiry into knowledge for its own sake. The third instinct was that of 'parental bent', which referred to the solicitude for the future of the human race. The first two were importantly related inasmuch as workmanship, concerned with economy, efficiency, proficiency, and mastery of technical facts, helped assure the fruits of idle curiosity. These three instincts had in common the individual outwards from one's self and merging him through work, observation, and solicitude with the organic processes surrounding him.

VEBLEN's decision to make these instincts sources of the moral absolute was a product of his immersion in evolutionary methodology. One of the primary tenets of this methodology was that the environment exerted strong selectic pressures on those living organisms within it, and only those best adapted could survive. If, as VEBLEN believed, man's nature was fixed in prehistory when the

ERVIN K. ZINGLER

competitive struggle was at its height, then human nature could only afford those constituents conducive to its survival. Workmanship was a brute, biological necessity.

VEBLEN viewed human history as a process by which man at last attained surplus wealth and income which gave him a measure of security on earth for the first time. But this same surplus permitted the appearance of new self-serving motives. Emulation entered and man received pleasure through invidious distinctions at the expense of others, and emulation contaminated the instinct of workmanship. In earlier societies, the measure of a man had been his ability and productivity as a workman, but now with the accumulation of wealth and private property, wealth and leisure served as status symbols.

There is a double ambiguity in VEBLEN's theory of instincts. Human nature was considered fixed, yet it could be shaped and altered by institutions without any change in its underlying character and nature. However, if an institutional framework contaminated human nature and was unstable, human nature might reassert itself. The hope of many neo-Veblenians was the new psychology. Clearly VEBLEN was an economic determinist and he stressed the role of instincts as causal determinants.

VEBLEN used the evolutionary approach with its historical relativity and cultural perspective to analyze, among many things, consumer and business behavior. In the *Theory of the Leisure Class* he treated tastes genetically rather than in the common, orthodox framework of atomistic individuals, each trying to maximize his own utility. He traced a sociogenetic process that seeks to explain why tastes had become what they were. Similarly in the *Theory of Business Enterprise* he used the genetic approach. While he did not deny that profits were important behaviorally, he departed from traditional analysis and focused on the growing remoteness of the businessman from the mechanical, technological process and the inherent incompatibility between capitalist institutions and organizational structures with modern, progressive technology.

VEBLEN achieved an outsider's perspective on his own culture. He produced a classic, critical analysis of early twentieth century American capitalism, its institutions and ethical foundations, and the economic theory that explained and justified this economic system.

Here he developed his famous dichotomy between business which

VEBLEN VS. COMMONS: A COMPARATIVE EVALUATION

was bad and industry which was good. Business enterprise was a complex of institutions that sought to make money and acquire economic power whereas industry was a technological complex of tools and skills which sought to produce goods and services. The former sought profits which often required restricting the efforts of industry, the counterpart of neo-classical theory and the role of the entrepreneur. The dichotomy was one of vendability versus serviceability. VEBLEN saw America as a pecuniary society which was predatory, aggressive, wasteful, and noncooperative. Its aristocratic virtues were ferocity, self-seeking, coercion, fraud, and clannishness. Money, which was the center of economic life, was the corrupting and coercing influence. Coercion, aggression, and conflict over money, wealth, and economic power, not competition, were the central themes of economics.

The wasteful consumption of the property class, he believed, prevented the workers from receiving the benefits of technological advance. Yet, property was an ancient norm, at best an institutional habit of thought. The captains of industry, makers of profits not goods, were the cause of waste, exploitation, unemployment, and depressions.

Modern technology and the machine with its great productivity resulted often in production which was incompatible with the profit desires, and to combat it the capitalists resorted to sabotage to restrict supply to demand. The factory system, which at first was the great hope of civilization, now became a central problem area in that minute specialization and division of labor, and the use of interchangeable parts, destroyed the instinct of workmanship because the worker could no longer identify his handiwork in the end product. Also pecuniary, acquisitive enterprise contaminated workmanship. Somehow the instinct of workmanship became self-corrupting and negative leading to animism and destructive tendencies. VEBLEN makes the same assumption that the Classical economists made, namely, man was a 'lone wolf' or 'rugged individualist' who only had individual not group pride of workmanship. Since then the results of the factory studies of ELTON MAYO and others suggested that man was basically gregarious and worked best as part of a team, supporting the views of AUGUSTE COMTE, the father of Sociology.

Like MARX, VEBLEN felt that big business controlled the govern-

ERVIN K. ZINGLER

ment, churches, and the schools (see his *Higher Learning in America, A Memorandum of the Conduct of Universities by Business Men,* 1918), and that depressions were impossible unless the investment bankers wanted them to take place. Similarly in the international field, big business usually resulted in imperialism and wars. Unlike MARX, VEBLEN saw no forces at work in society likely to impel class consciousness on the part of the workers, but exactly the opposite. The traditional, ceremonial, past-binding forces dictated that pecuniary emulation was necessary for ceremonial adequacy in society. People were enculturated into accepting certain hierarchies of rank and stratification, and status needs (also acquired) required that they emulate those above them in the hierarchy. The mores of society reinforced this idea through ceremonial support of the existing order and their impulse was to perserve that order and the *status quo.*

While VEBLEN was very critical of what he called finance or banker capitalism, he did not wish to overthrow capitalism. The engineer, the inventor, and the machine could be our salvation; somehow they might eliminate animism, conquer the pecuniary and acquisitive forces, and remove the source of contamination of workmanship.

He developed an analysis of the laws of motion of capitalism in his *Theory of Business Enterprise* (1904), *Instinct of Workmanship and the State of the Industrial Arts* (1914), *Vested Interests and the State of the Industrial Arts* (1919), *Engineers and the Price System* (1921), and *Absentee Ownership and Business Enterprise in Recent Times* (1923). Unlike MARX, VEBLEN provided no operational theory of social change and he gave us no hints how to prevent or forestall the changes that he foresaw. Basically he was pessimistic in his outlook and conclusions, unlike COMMONS. He believed that every good and constructive idea or force had its opposite or destructive counterpart, and that in the struggle which inevitably ensued, the bad or the negative always won—note, there is a similarity here to FREUD's constructive and destructive instincts. However whatever would happen would come about in an evolutionary, not a revolutionary, manner.

In terms of his theory of economic development, inasmuch as human nature was conceived as stable, the primary factors were technology and institutions. Technology, which was spurred on by workmanship and idle curiosity, was the dynamic factor in economic progress and growth. It obeyed its own inner logic and was exogenous

VEBLEN VS. COMMONS: A COMPARATIVE EVALUATION

to the capitalist system. Institutions, which were past binding and concerned with ceremonial procedures and status, were the static factors. At best, they were permissive to change but usually they played a decidedly obstructionist role. It was the eternal and ceaseless dialectical struggle and conflict between dynamic technology and static institutionalism which caused economic and political institutions slowly to be displaced and replaced, and systems of economic organization to undergo historical change and ajustment. There was a self-generative dynamism in technology.

This difference between the roles of institutions and technology formed the basis of VEBLEN's famous dichotomy between business and industry. To analyze economic development in terms of this dichotomy, he developed a theory of occupational disciplines. His theory of economic development has often been interpreted as a kind of mechanical determinism but he strove for a psychological explanation. He stressed the pronounced influence that occupational disciplines have on habits and thoughts which later crystallize into institutions. In the case of America, businessmen began to think in terms of ownership, profit, wealth, and economic power whereas those pursuing industrial occupations thought in terms of productivity, efficiency, and technology. The latter began to lose comprehension of business values, their loyalties waned, and they became increasingly hostile to the capitalist system.

This is one of the latent effects that VEBLEN saw in the development of technology in America. A more immediate effect, however, was the subtantial lowering of costs of production and the undermining of capital values and wealth—old capital equipment quickly became obsolete. Inasmuch as the essential intangible basis of capitalist concern was capitalized value, this threw business into a state of cutthroat competition which ultimately led to depression, the latter being a business, not an industrial phenomenon. This state of affairs would lead to the formation of larger and larger business firms supported by an immense credit pyramid until finally the unity of business would become so comprehensive that competition would be crushed completely. Then, and only then, the economy would be stabilized at a level where reasonable profits could be made but at the expense of chronic and high levels of unemployment. It was at this stage that conflict would break out along occupational lines.

ERVIN K. ZINGLER

VEBLEN's theory was not, however, teleological. Whether a social-ist reconstruction of society would be achieved depended upon what the conservative classes would do. At this point, VEBLEN's theory of the state enters the picture. The state existed to protect the *status quo*. Its first duty was to safeguard private property and vested interests. The duly constituted representatives of the commonwealth had be-come a soviet of businessmen's delegates whose dutiful privilege it was to protect and to enlarge the power of the absentee owners. Democracy was not a sham in the sense that the underlying class was excluded. No government could rule without their consent. Rather they had been conditioned to accept business leadership.

VEBLEN posed the question what happens if the underclass spurred on by the discipline of the machine and modern technology decided they did not want business leadership. At this point, he argued, the conservative classes would resort to the weapons of national integrity. They would seek the militarization of society by assuming a hostile position to the outside world. Whether America moved toward a socialist reconstruction or a military state, VEBLEN felt certain that capitalism in its present state could not survive. But alas, Darwinian evolution had no predetermined goals or outcome, and no assump-tion of inevitable human progress to the point of perfection and mil-lenium. Thus, for VEBLEN retrogression rather than progress was a very real possibility. However, he kept hoping for a *utopia* in the form of an 'industrial republic'.

It is very important to point out the distinction between VEBLEN's instrumentalism and MARX's economic materialism. MARX made a fundamental metaphysical distinction between ideas and the ma-terial world, and he developed his theory as an interplay between these two different categories. The dialectic of HEGEL gave the appear-ance of motion, but between two separate beings or entities. VEBLEN's instrumentalism got around this dialect by positing that the separ-ation or distinction to be made was in the 'habits of mind' of men, not between ideas and the material world. It was the interaction between these habits of mind and institutions (past oriented) with the material world and the cumulative character of man-made tools that formed the basis of the analytical dichotomy. For MARX, the culture consisted of a line from technology to social structure to ideology whereas for VEBLEN, social structure and technology (symbolic tool

VEBLEN VS. COMMONS: A COMPARATIVE EVALUATION

using) combined to produce ideology or habits of mind which was culture. Culture evolved as tools accumulated. Tools and knowledge acquired in creating tools changed attitudes and habits of mind, which in turn were based on ceremonial authority or the past (embodied in social structure).

II

COMMONS' institutionalism can be found in his *Social Reform and the Church* (1894), *Sociological View of Sovereignty* (1898), *Legal Foundations of Capitalism* (1924), *Institutional Economics* (1934), *Myself* (1934), the post-humous *Economics of Collective Action* (1950), and perhaps to some degree in his numerous books on labor economics.

His basic point of departure from orthodox, classical economics was 'collective action', which was roughly equivalent to culture for him. This was an institutional framework established by men to settle conflicts in society. Collective action was held to be necessary in all societies to keep the interdependence of men and conflict in balance. Conflicts basically arose over private property and the scarcity of economic goods and services. The greatest want of people, COMMONS believed, was security, and because of class conflict and the system of private property, only the state or the government could give security.

Institutional economics to COMMONS meant collective rather than private action; the adaptation of past thinking to today's problems. Collective action involved more than control for by restricting the activities of a few, it freed all the others from fear and coercion.

An 'institution' was defined as collective action in control, liberation, and expansion of private action, that is, collective action with regard to changed goals, 'working rules', institutions, and 'going concerns'. Economic institutions were defined as customs growing out of 'transactions' and collective activities of going concerns, the latter being the family, union, business firm, trade association, state, or what not. The cumulative effect of collective action over time was the establishment of working rules which were codified in the legal framework of statutes and decisions of courts and administrative bodies, or in the less formal sense of prescribed behavior of going

ERVIN K. ZINGLER

concerns. Laws were regarded as the working rules of an on-going society.

Starting from the basic contention that institutions were going concerns, COMMONS concluded that the major area of economic concern should be the 'activity', and as such, 'transactions' were the proper field of economic analysis because the basic form of economic interaction and the most elemental aspect of going concerns was the transaction. The latter was defined as the rights of future ownership of things acquired and alienated through collective social working rules. It embraced three social relationships, namely, conflict, co-operation, and compromise.

Transactions were held to be the basic framework for economic decisions in society. This was the collective action that COMMONS spoke about, the building blocks of institutional economics. This differed greatly from the traditional view that the economic good or service was the elemental unit of economics. Moreover, there were three basic types of transactions, not merely one as in classical economics.

The most important was the 'bargaining' transaction which basically involved the exchange or transfer of wealth. It took place between legal equals who had alternatives open to them for the exchange of ownership. This transaction was voluntary and working rules set the limits on the use of coercion, duress, and force. 'Managerial' transactions involved the creation of economic goods and wealth. The parties to these transactions were not equals inasmuch as they were the master and the servant, the employer and employee, the boss and the worker, the superior and the inferior, with the state authority in the background. It was basically conceived as an authoritarian relationship between a legal superior and a legal inferior. This type of transaction covered the entire field of industrial relations, personnel administration, and collective bargaining.

'Rationing' transactions allocated the wealth and distributed the goods and services which had been produced. They were also based on a relationship between a legal superior and a legal inferior. Three parties, however, were involved: the superior which could be the union or the government as well as the business firm, the inferior, and the courts for enforcement of the 'rules of the economic game'. The legal superior was a collectivity—it could be, for example, the government raising tax revenue.

VEBLEN VS. COMMONS: A COMPARATIVE EVALUATION

The function of the government was conceived to be that of apportioning the benefits and responsibilities of wealth among the inferiors. All economic relationships were considered to be influenced by collective action. The latter determined the working rules under which bargaining and rationing transactions took place, and sanctioned the various types of rationing devices. Bargaining power played an important part in COMMONS' theory inasmuch as buyers and sellers were usually in a position to withhold something that the other wanted and needed. Clearly he focused on imperfectly competitive situations.

The fault that COMMONS found with traditional economic analysis was that it concerned itself with only part of the bargaining transactions at most and completely ignored the other two types of transactions. Yet all three transactions were going on continuously in all going concerns. The latter were only kept or held together by the working rules of collective action in control of private, independent action.

The key word for COMMONS was 'reasonable', reasonable value, cost, price, wage, profit, and so on, and he always viewed expectations of future economic activity (transactions) in terms of prevailing notions of equity and justice. The ultimate criterion of reasonableness with respect to bargaining and division of economic power, income and wealth was what the highest courts would accept in the final analysis. The specific manifestations of that social or collective criterion could be altered smoothly and continuously as the system evolved via a continuing reinterpretation of the law by the courts.

What COMMONS wanted to do was to bring economics up to date and to make it relevant and useful in the pragmatic or operational sense of solving current private and social problems and issues. This could be done only, he felt, by stressing the institutional and behavioral approach to all economic problems. The subject matter of economics would have to be expanded greatly, too, to include large portions of law and public administration, not to mention psychology and sociology. It should be pointed out that for a time COMMONS held a chair in sociology at the University of Syracuse.

COMMONS placed great stress on a 'volitional' versus a mechanical or deterministic theory of value. Largely values could be whatever people collectively wanted them to be. Institutional economics, in

335

ERVIN K. ZINGLER

this connection, was concerned with the evolutionary economics of growth and change in working rules, going concerns, institutions, and standards of reasonableness. Action was entirely volitional. By collective action working rules, goals, institutions, going concerns, and other things could be changed and improved upon. Again it was the transactions of going concerns which were basic inasmuch as they determined production, consumption, and distribution of wealth and income. Moreover, the legal concept of value was always future oriented.

However, COMMONS was not the theorist that VEBLEN was. Rather he was a conceptionalist. He developed ways of viewing economic phenomena, not theoretical constructs that had predictive value. His greatest simplifying concept was 'collective action'. This concept was the basis of all social interaction for him. Individuals did not meet each other on an individual basis, but rather on a collective action basis. The latter covered the complex of habits and customs which society condones and enforces upon its members, and the activities of going concerns, or organized groups pursuing specific functions. Even when an individual participated in a simple act of exchange with another person, he was operating within a framework of customs, habits, mores, and other socially and economically accepted practices. Thus, collective action influenced even the most elemental of economic activities. However, COMMONS stressed the volitional element in human activity. Although individuals were influenced by customs, habits, and laws, they did not accept them blindly, but rather in a process of interaction shaped and molded them into different forms.

Also, COMMONS did not see the necessity of providing a general theory of cultural development as did VEBLEN. Rather he used the dichotomy between 'habits of mind' and past dated institutions and the material world, and filled in the words with the historical categories of capitalist society. He did a number of histories of the emergence, rise and the contemporary scene of capitalism. His first was from the perspective of labor, another from that of the development of law and legal arrangements, and still another from that of the development of collective action as the controller of private action.

If COMMONS believed that 'collective action' was a new development in the history of man, then his work differed significantly and

VEBLEN VS. COMMONS: A COMPARATIVE EVALUATION

markedly from that of VEBLEN. However, if he meant only to trace the history of the specific brand of collective action which controlled individual activity under capitalism, then his work is not inconsistent with that of VEBLEN. The latter is probably true. COMMONS never claimed that he and VEBLEN differed in their approaches. It was just that COMMONS wanted to build a documented historical treatment (much like the German Historical School) from the general perspective of VEBLEN's dichotomy. This is what I believe he did.

VEBLEN, no doubt, would have agreed that the working rules, although essentially ceremonial in nature, were necessary for society to exist, but he probably would not have accepted the idea that they were capable of being made equitable by the internal process of institutional evolution (court decisions and law). For VEBLEN, laws were past-binding and changed not because men desired to adjust and alter them to meet changed circumstances but because the latter required men to change their laws—laws were one of the major forces resisting technological change.

As mentioned earlier, COMMONS maintained that his major point of departure from VEBLEN was over 'natural selection'. He believed that the Darwinian idea of process was no more an appropriate analogy for economics than the Newtonian concept of natural law. COMMONS saw that the pecuniary, industrial dichotomy was real but he believed that something could be done about it through a volitional, cooperative process. He was very much concerned about shaping the direction of change in his own culture, and he was much more interested in practical policy recommendations than VEBLEN. But clearly VEBLEN was the more comprehensive theorist—he was concerned with the development of a consistent and useful methodology.

One of the most significant contrasts between VEBLEN and COMMONS was their different conceptions of human behavior. COMMONS stressed the volitional aspect. Value was arrived at through the purposeful intervention of individuals operating under the influence of collective action. VEBLEN with his theory of instincts was more likely to stress the irrational aspect. Technology seemed to follow its own inner logic seemingly independent of human will and desire. In many respects VEBLEN was an armchair theorist given to propounding theories with little or no empirical basis. Indeed, in one sense he

ERVIN K. ZINGLER

became the master of the Ricardian vice of reasoning from imputed motives. In contrast Commons would make detailed, exhaustive empirical studies before theorizing, as for example, his studies of the American labor movement. But even he slipped occasionally as when he concluded that 'experience rating' which works so well in the case of workmen's compensation would work equally well in the case of unemployment compensation. However, institutional economics was the end result of his life-long work in empirical research.

Of the question as to whether oligopoly and other powers under conditions of imperfect or monopolistic competition would be used reasonably, that is, for the social good or welfare, Veblen was more inclined to give an unequivocable negative answer. Commons, on the other hand, was much more careful as to his answer. Reasonableness, he believed, could not be determined in general terms, but rather each case would have to be examined on its own merits. But this was not to say that reasonableness was anyone's opinion. After resort to private negotiation, if necessary, ultimately the Supreme Court would decide the matter. Its decision would be objective and could usually be measured in monetary terms. It was this device, *deus ex machina*, that Commons used to resolve the indeterminancy in his economic model.

Commons' and Veblen's views on value differed, too, although they both approached the subject within an institutional framework. Veblen stressed the acquisitive desire for wealth, power, and distinction as motives behind business behavior which eventually would establish one giant monopoly of interests that would entirely eliminate competition by the process mentioned earlier in this essay. Commons looked at value from an entirely different viewpoint. He approached value from the point of view of bargaining power. What was needed, he said, was to equalize the bargaining power of the participants in the exchange process. Labor unions were viewed at this time as a useful device for balancing power. What Commons wanted was something that he called 'reasonable Capitalism' or what J. M. Clark later called 'workable competition'. Like Veblen, Commons called the American Capitalism of his day, 'Banker Capitalism'.

Commons was no Marxian, just as Veblen was not. He saw many group or class conflicts, not just one as for Marx. What he wanted for America was collective bargaining on an organized equilibrium

VEBLEN VS. COMMONS: A COMPARATIVE EVALUATION

of equality. He argued that the premises of free competition had no meaning for the capitalism of his day. He was concerned with the need for the government and with the courts as arbitrators. If the middle class was ever eliminated as MARX predicted, he thought that either socialism or fascism might be better than capitalism. In this connection, he looked upon the USA, Russia, Germany, and Italy as empirical laboratories to test the theories of capitalism, communism, and fascism.

COMMONS' description of society differed, however, very much from that of MARX. The so-called class struggle, he felt, had become a bargaining process, by which the state and/or the courts became the arbitrator, not the supporter of one side against the other. His basic contention was that under changing cultural circumstances conflicts are inevitable, the government was never completely neutral, and the court system of any society was really its only major way of deciding the outcome of such conflicts. Resolving conflicts in this manner became the basis of his 'reasonable value' concept, a pragmatic solution to conflicts as they arise.

One would have to assume that COMMONS felt that ideology was not a very viable determinant of the outcome of such conflicts decided ultimately by the courts. VEBLEN and MARX would say that the courts historically have favored one party over the other. VEBLEN's 'habits of mind' were formed over long periods of time, and biased every decision made. Moreover, the social structure of any society changed as the result of technological advancement, whereas the ceremonial aspect of these 'habits of mind' reinforced the change resistent nature of the social structure. Thus, there was always a cultural lag. This suggested that to the extent that the courts decide upon instituted custom, as COMMONS contended, or upon laws and administrative procedures, then the outcome of such court decisions inherently protected the past and the *status quo*. New circumstances were never considered soley on their merits. Rather they were interpreted and defined in terms of current laws, customs, and mores, which were congealed in present-day institutions. COMMONS was aware of this, but he knew that court decisions can and do change over time, but it involved exhaustive and detailed empirical work on the part of the litigants. COMMONS showed time after time how this could be done successfully.

ERVIN K. ZINGLER

The difference between VEBLEN and COMMONS was essentially a difference in outlook. VEBLEN was not as optimistic about the volitional application of human intelligence and knowledge as was COMMONS. In this regard, VEBLEN might have called COMMONS an Utopian Institutionalist and himself a Scientific Institutionalist.

The criticism most often heard against the Institutional School is that it tried to be scientific but it was not. However, by insisting that theory must deal with process, and in terms of actual process as it occurs, VEBLEN set the stage for the further development in a science of mankind, not mathematics.

University of Houston   ERVIN K. ZINGLER

REFERENCES

ADORNO, T. W.: 'Veblen's Attack on Culture', *Studies in Philosophy and Social Science*, Vol. 9 (1941).
ANDERSON, K. L.: 'The Unity of Veblen's Theoretical System', *Quarterly Journal of Economics*, Vol. 47 (1933), Aug.
ARDZROONI, LEON: 'Veblen and Technocracy', *Living Age*, 1933, Mar.
ATKINS, W. E., *et al.: Economic Behavior, An Institutional Approach*, Boston, Houghton Mifflin, 1931.
BERNARD, L. L.: *Instinct, A Study in Social Psyohology*, New York, Henry Holt, 1924.
COMMAGER, H. S.: *The American Mind*, New Haven, Yale University Press, 1950.
COMMONS, JOHN R.: *The Distribution of Wealth*, New York, Macmillan, 1893.
COMMONS, JOHN R.: *Social Reform and the Church*, New York, Crowell, 1894.
COMMONS, JOHN R.: 'A Sociological View of Sovereignty', *American Journal of Sociology*, Vol. 5 (1899–1900).
COMMONS, JOHN R.: 'A New Way of Settling Labor Disputes', *American Monthly Review of Reviews*, Vol. 27 (1901), Mar.
COMMONS, JOHN R.: *A Documentary History of American Industrial Society*, Cleveland, A. H. Clark, 1910.
COMMONS, JOHN R.: 'Organized Labor's Attitude Toward Industrial Efficiency', *American Economic Review*, 4th Series (1911), Sept.
COMMONS, JOHN R.: *Labor and Administration*, New York, Macmillan, 1913.
COMMONS, JOHN R.: *History of Labor in The United States*, New York, Macmillan, 1918–1935 (4 vols.).
COMMONS, JOHN R.: *Trade Unionism and Labor Problems*, Boston, Ginn & Co., 1921 (2nd Series).
COMMONS, JOHN R.: *Industrial Goodwill*, New York, McGraw-Hill, 1919.
COMMONS, JOHN R.: *Principles of Labor Legislation*, New York, Harpers, 1920.
COMMONS, JOHN R.: *Races and Immigrants in America*, New York, Macmillan, 1920.
COMMONS, JOHN R.: *Industrial Government*, New York, Macmillan, 1921.

VEBLEN VS. COMMONS: A COMPARATIVE EVALUATION

COMMONS, JOHN R.: *Legal Foundations of Capitalism*, New York, Macmillan, 1924.

COMMONS, JOHN R.: 'Evolutionary Institutions as a Factor in Economic Change', *Special Lectures*, United States Department of Agriculture, 1930, Feb.-Mar.

COMMONS, JOHN R.: *Myself, The Autobiography of John R. Commons*, New York, Macmillan, 1934.

COMMONS, JOHN R.: *Institutional Economics: Its Place in Political Economy*, New York, Macmillan, 1934.

COMMONS, JOHN R.: 'Twentieth Century Economics', *Journal of Social Philosophy*, Vol. 5 (1939).

COMMONS, JOHN R.: *Economics of Collective Action*, New York, Macmillan, 1950.

COPELAND, MORRIS: 'Commons' Institutionalism in Relation to Problems of Social Evolution and Economic Planning', *Quarterly Journal of Economics*, Vol. 50 (1936), Feb.

COPELAND, MORRIS: *Fact and Theory in Economics: The Testament of an Institutionalist*, Ithaca, Cornell University Press, 1958.

COPELAND, MORRIS: 'Institutional Economics and Model Analysis', *American Economic Review*, Vol. 41 (1971), Supp., May.

DAUGERT, STANLEY: *The Philosophy of Thorstein Veblen*, New York, Columbia University Press, 1950.

DEWEY, JOHN: *Reconstruction in Philosophy*, New York, Henry Holt, 1920.

DEWEY, JOHN: *Human Nature and Conduct*, New York, Henry Holt, 1922.

DORFMAN, JOSEPH: *Thorstein Veblen and His America*, New York, Viking, 1934.

DORFMAN, JOSEPH: *Thorstein Veblen: Essays, Reviews, and Reports, Previously Uncollected Writings*, Clifton, Augustus M. Kelley, 1973.

DUFFUS, R.L.: *The Innocents at Cedro: A Memoir of Thorstein Veblen and Some Others*, New York, Macmillan, 1944.

GAMBS, JOHN: *Beyond Supply and Demand*, New York, Columbia University Press, 1946.

GROSSMAN, H.: 'Evolutionist Revolt Against Classical Economics', *Journal of Political Economy*, Vol. 41 (1943), Oct.-Dec.

GRUCHY, ALLAN G.: *Modern Economic Thought: The American Contribution*, New York, Prentice-Hall, 1947.

HAMILTON, DAVID: *Newtonian Classicism and Darwinian Institutionalism*, Albuquerque, University of New Mexico Press, 1953.

HAMILTON, WALTON: 'The Institutional Approach to Economic Theory', *American Economic Review*, Vol. 9 (1919), Mar.

HARRIS, A.: 'Types of Institutionalism', *Journal of Political Economy*, Vol. 40 (1932), Dec.

HARTER, L.G.: *John R. Commons: His Assault on Laissez-Faire*, Corvallis, Oregon State University Press, 1962.

HOBSON, JOHN A.: *Veblen*, New York, John Wiley & Sons, 1937.

HOFSTADTER, RICHARD: *Social Darwinianism in American Thought*, Philadelphia, University of Pennsylvania Press, 1944.

HOMAN, PAUL T.: 'An Appraisal of Institutional Economics', *American Economic Review*, Vol. 22 (1932), Mar.

ERVIN K. ZINGLER

Homan, Paul T.: *Contemporary Economic Thought*, New York, Harper & Bros., 1928.

Kohler, W.: *Gestalt Psychology*, New York, H. Liveright, 1929.

Layton, E.T.: 'Veblen and the Engineers', *American Quarterly*, Vol. 14 (1962), Spring.

Lerner, Max: *The Portable Veblen*, New York, Viking Press, 1950.

Mitchell, Wesley C.: 'Commons on the Legal Foundations of Capitalism', *American Economic Review*, Vol. 14 (1924), June.

Mitchell, Wesley C.: *Lecture Notes on Types of Economic Theory*, New York, Kelley, 1949.

Mitchell, Wesley C.: *The Backward Art of Spending Money*, New York, McGraw-Hill, 1937.

Mitchell, Wesley C.: *What Veblen Taught*, New York, Viking Press, 1947.

Parrington, V.L.: 'The Beginnings of Critical Realism in America, 1860–1920', *Main Currents in American Thought*, Vol. 3, New York, Harcourt, Brace & Co., 1930.

Parsons, K.H.: 'John R. Commons' Point of View', *Journal of Land and Public Utility Economics*, Vol. 18 (1942), Aug.

Parsons, Talcott: *The Structure of Social Action*, New York, McGraw-Hill, 1937.

Randall, J.H.: *The Making of the Modern Mind*, Boston, Houghton Mifflin, 1926.

Riesman, David: *Thorstein Veblen*, New York, Charles Scribner's Sons, 1953.

Russell, Bertrand: *A New Social Analysis*, New York, W.W. Norton, 1938.

Schneider, Herbert: *A History of American Philosophy*, New York, Columbia University Press, 1946.

Sharfman, I.L.: 'Commons' Legal Foundations of Capitalism', *Quarterly Journal of Economics*, Vol. 39 (1925), Feb.

Somers, G.G.: *Labor, Management, and Social Policy: Essays in the John R. Commons' Tradition*, Madison, University of Wisconsin Press, 1963.

Veblen, Thorstein: 'Kant's Critique of Judgment', *Journal of Speculative Philosophy*, 1884, July.

Veblen, Thorstein: 'The Instinct of Workmanship and the Irksomeness of Labor', *American Journal of Sociology*, 1898, July.

Veblen, Thorstein: *Theory of the Leisure Class: An Economic Study of Institutions*, New York, Macmillan, 1899.

Veblen, Thorstein: 'Some Neglected Points in the Theory of Socialism', *Annals of the American Academy of Political and Social Science*, 1891, Nov.

Veblen, Thorstein: 'The Overproduction Fallacy', *Quarterly Journal of Economics*, 1892, July.

Veblen, Thorstein: *The Theory of Business Enterprise*, New York, Charles Scribner's Sons, 1904.

Veblen, Thorstein: 'The Evolution of the Scientific Point of View', *University of California Chronicle*, 1908, May.

Veblen, Thorstein: *Instinct of Workmanship and the State of the Industrial Arts*, New York, Macmillan, 1914.

Veblen, Thorstein: *Imperial Germany and the Industrial Revolution*, New York, Macmillan, 1914.

342

VEBLEN VS. COMMONS: A COMPARATIVE EVALUATION

VEBLEN, THORSTEIN: *An Inquiry into the Nature of Peace and the Terms of Its Perpetuation*, New York, Macmillan, 1917.

VEBLEN, THORSTEIN: *Higher Learning in America: A Memorandum on the Conduct of Universities by Business Men* (formerly subtitled, *A Lesson in Total Depravity*), New York, Macmillan, 1918.

VEBLEN, THORSTEIN: 'The Intellectual Pre-Eminence of Jews in Modern Europe', *Political Science Quarterly*, 1919, Mar.

VEBLEN, THORSTEIN: *Vested Interests and the State of the Industrial Arts*, New York, B.W. Huebsch, 1919.

VEBLEN, THORSTEIN: *The Place of Science in Modern Civilization and Other Essays*, New York, Huebsch, 1919.

VEBLEN, THORSTEIN: *Engineers and the Price System*, New York, B.W. Huebsch, 1921.

VEBLEN, THORSTEIN: *Absentee Ownership and Business Enterprise in Recent Times*, New York, B.W. Huebsch, 1923.

VEBLEN, THORSTEIN: *Essays in the Changing Order*, New York, Viking Press, 1934.

WARDEN, CARL J.: *The Emergence of Human Culture*, New York, Macmillan, 1936.

WHITE, MORTON: *American Social Thought*, New York, Viking Press, 1949.

WOLFE, A.B.: 'Institutional Reasonableness and Value', *Philosophical Review*, Vol. 45 (1936), Mar.

ZINGLER, ERVIN K.: *Thorstein Veblen: An Economic Iconoclast*, San Antonio, St. Mary's University Press, 1962.

SUMMARY

The contributions of two institutional economists, COMMONS and VEBLEN, are compared and evaluated in terms of economic theory in retrospect. After summarizing their theories, it is concluded that VEBLEN made the greater contribution to pure economic theory. The concept of change or 'process' was the crux of his contribution, namely, that culture, institutions, and economic systems were a continually evolving and interacting process. The forces for change and progress were the instincts of workmanship and idle curiosity, which became the source of his moral absolute. By analyzing cultures and utilizing scientific methodology, he saw technological change as the positive source of social improvement. His theory of economic development is interpreted as one of mechanical determinism, but he strove for a psychological explanation. COMMONS was not the theorist that VEBLEN was, rather he was a conceptualist. He developed ways of viewing economic phenomena, not theoretical constructs with predictive value. His greatest simplifying concept was 'collective action'. He did not see the need of providing a general theory of cultural development as did VEBLEN. Rather he used the dichotomy between 'habits of mind' and past-dated institutions and the material world and filled in the words with the historical categories of capitalist society.

343

ERVIN K. ZINGLER

ZUSAMMENFASSUNG

Im vorliegenden Artikel wird das Werk der beiden Institutionalisten Commons und Veblen zusammengefasst, beurteilt und verglichen. Dabei wird die Schlussfolgerung gezogen, dass Veblens Beitrag für die reine ökonomische Theorie der bedeutendere ist. Kernpunkt seines Werkes bildet seine Konzeption des sozialen Wandels, der zufolge Kulturen, Wirtschaftssysteme und Institutionen sich kontinuierlich fortentwickeln und gegenseitig beeinflussen. Als ursächlich für Wandel und Fortschritt sind Arbeitsantrieb und Neugierde zu sehen. Nach der Analyse verschiedener Kulturen unter Beizug wissenschaftlicher Methoden begreift Veblen den technologischen Wandel als Quelle sozialer Verbesserung. Obwohl seine Theorie der wirtschaftlichen Entwicklung als mechanistisch-deterministisch gedeutet wird, hat sich Veblen dennoch auch um die Anwendung psychologischer Ansätze bemüht. Commons, im Gegensatz zu Veblen, ist weniger als Theoretiker denn vielmehr als Konzeptionalist einzustufen; er hat Mittel und Wege geschaffen, ökonomische Phänomene zu deuten, nicht aber theoretische Modelle, um diese vorauszusagen. Sein wichtigster, vereinfachender Beitrag ist derjenige des «kollektiven Handelns». Im Unterschied zu Veblen sieht Commons die Notwendigkeit nicht, eine generelle Theorie der kulturellen Entwicklung zu umreissen; statt dessen zeigt er die Dichotomie auf zwischen Denkgewohnheiten und überholten Institutionen, die er sprachlich in historischen Kategorien der kapitalistischen Gesellschaft skizziert.

RÉSUMÉ

L'auteur résume, compare et évalue les théories économiques de Commons et de Veblen et arrive à la conclusion que Veblen a contribué de manière bien plus importante à la théorie économique pure. Le point cardinal de sa contribution est sa conception de changement ou d'«évolution»: culture, institutions et systèmes économiques évoluent et s'influencent sans cesse. L'instinct artisanal et la curiosité en sont les motifs; Veblen en a fait sa thèse morale. L'analyse de différentes cultures et l'application de la méthodologie scientifique l'ont fait considérer l'évolution technologique comme la source positive de l'amélioration des conditions sociales. Sa théorie de développement économique est souvent interprétée comme déterminisme mécanique; Veblen par contre a tâché d'en donner une explication psychologique. Commons ne possédait pas les qualités de théoricien comme Veblen; il était plutôt conceptionaliste. Il a développé des méthodes pour considérer les phénomènes économiques et non pas des théories permettant des prédictions, son idée principale – et simplifiante – étant «l'action collective». Commons n'a pas cru à la nécessité d'une théorie générale de développement culturel, comme Veblen. Il a plutôt fait la différence entre «manières de penser», institutions viellies et le monde matériel, et il a rempli ce cadre avec les termes des catégories historiques de la société capitaliste.

[15]

Jei *JOURNAL OF ECONOMIC ISSUES*
Vol. XIV   No. 3   September 1980

The Institutional Economics of
Karl Polanyi

J. Ron Stanfield

This article is prompted by my conviction that Karl Polanyi's contribution to institutional economic theory is substantial and largely neglected by practicing institutionalists. I base my conclusion about the neglect of Polanyi upon casual empiricism. His name is seldom mentioned in the major institutionalist periodical, the *Journal of Economic Issues*, except by those authors who had a direct, personal relationship with Polanyi, such as Daniel Fusfeld, Allen Sievers, or George Dalton. Polanyi is similarly absent from the major monographs and books on institutional economics, such as Clarence Ayres's articulation of institutional theory, Allan Gruchy's survey of neoinstitutionalism, David Hamilton's overview of evolutionary economics, and others.[1] Polanyi is not even indexed in works directly concerned with the problems to which he gave his predominant interest.[2]

My argument will consider, in turn, the animating concerns of Polanyi's work, his general approach or method, and his theory and interpretation of modern capitalism. In a final section, I *suggest* the contemporary importance of his contributions.

In each phase of the discussion, it is my objective to indicate Polanyi's institutionalist pedigree. More specifically, I seek to establish his place within *mainstream* institutionalism as characterized by Gruchy.[3] I am

---

The author is Associate Professor of Economics, Colorado State University, Fort Collins. An earlier version of this article was presented at the International Atlantic Economic Conference, Salzburg, Austria, May 1979.

aware that there is considerable controversy among contemporary institutionalists concerning Gruchy's formulation, but I would note that it is
much to Gruchy's credit that he is forcing us to reconsider our work in
relation to the Veblenian tradition to which, perhaps, most of us claim
ancestry. Although I agree with Gruchy by and large, my argument here
does not stand or fall on that account. Mainstream institutionalism as set
out by Gruchy is more restrictive than the generic institutionalism to
which, of late, there has been a trend. Therefore, to establish Polanyi as
a mainstream institutionalist is to establish his position in the less restrictive sense of generic institutionalism.

Gruchy's formulaton is related to a further motivation of this article,
one not confined to Polanyi's work per se. The *intensive* definition and
typification of institutionalism provided by analysis such as Gruchy's is
important. I think that *extensive* delineation is also important. That is,
I think we should reach out and embrace intellectual traditions that are
compatible with mainstream institutionalism as well as identify those
which are not compatible. As I have argued elsewhere, I would include
Marx and Polanyi in the compatibility category.[1]

The Principal Animus of Polanyi's Work

Polanyi's work, broadly speaking, can be said to have been motivated
by two factors, one concerned with methodology and the other with a
historical problem of political economy. The methodological problem centered on the relation between economic anthropology and comparative
economic systems and the scope of economic theory in general. The historical problem involved the breakdown of the international political eco
nomic system early in this century and the subsequent development of the
welfare state.

Economic Anthropology and
Comparative Economic Systems

Polanyi's methodological animus stemmed from his recognition of the
essential theoretical affinity between economic anthropology and comparative economic systems. Theory is important to any social science, but
the nature of anthropology enhances its significance: "One of the peculiarities of economic anthropology is that neither the facts nor the folk
views of primitive economic life are in doubt. The ethnographic record
is large and detailed. What is in doubt is the most useful theoretical approach to organize the many descriptive accounts."[5] A theory of economic

anthropology is possible only if the research program on primitive and archaic social economies is viewed as being a part of comparative economic systems. The categories important to the modern social economy have their counterparts in earlier societies. "In order for anthropologists to see what is analytically important in Trobriands' economy they must first understand the structure of industrial capitalism; to understand the special usage of pig-tusk and cowrie money, they must first understand the organization and usage of dollars and francs."[6] The differentiating characteristics of a socioeconomic system emerge only through comparative analysis which makes possible the specification of a given system's peculiarities as opposed to those dimensions which it shares with other socioeconomic formations.

Although this is true of organizational comparison of economic systems of a given epoch, which therefore have much in common, it is more forcefully true in the consideration of social evolution. The capitalism of America and Europe, and even the socialisms of the Soviet bloc, have much in common with one another because they are all modern industrial economies with similar concerns and problems of efficiency, growth, urbanization, and social psychology. Comparative analysis nonetheless reveals critical historical and organizational differences, and the methodological trap of ethnocentrism and neglect of cultural relativity is considerable.

These differences and the concomitant methodological issues pale before their counterparts in the study of primitive and archaic social economies. In this instance it is even more important to avoid the neglect of the cultural context which surrounds and motivates the production and distribution of goods and services. At the same time, the very factors which promote or allow such ethnocentrism establish the importance of comparative historical analysis. All economies, that is, all the material aspects of human cultures, involve the provisioning of human purposes by the technological interaction and transformation of nature. In all but the most primitive societies, there is also division of labor with the concomitant necessity of integrative institutions to coordinate economic activities. These institutions have at least superficial similarities—marketplaces, trade, monetary objects, and accounting devices.[7]

The presence of these categorical generalities simultaneously makes it fruitful to undertake transcultural comparisons and establishes the need for methodological discipline so that fundamental and instructive differences are not swept under the rug of hasty generalizations and ethnocentrism. There is much to be learned from comparison of primitive and modern social economies *if* oversimplification and neglect of concrete cultural contexts are avoided.[8]

In addition to the need for totality and cultural context, another instruc-
:ive lesson to be learned from these categorical similarities is the need for
ı process or evolutionary focus. Socioeconomic categories have a life
process of origin, maturity, and decline. If it be true, as R. M. MacIver
credits Aristotle, that "we can learn the nature of anything only when it
has reached—and passed—its maturation," it is no less true that we can
learn about the mature category by the conditions of its origin and development.[9] The analogy to the relation of childhood environment to the
adult human being, and vice versa, seems to be entirely apt.

Polanyi's concern was a knife edge cutting both ways. He saw a principal defect in comparative economic systems that could be corrected only
by the incorporation of the insights of economic anthropology into comparative economic analysis. This latter field is primarily, and excessively
in Polanyi's view, concerned with organizational comparisons of modern
industrial economies. These comparisons are made in terms of the formal,
economizing models of a market economy. This approach is to a considerable extent inherently inaccurate: Although industrialized economies
share common traits of concern for rationality, efficiency, stability, and
growth, they also display important differences due to their cultural heritage. The neglect of the historical dimension and the cultural totality of
human behavior is a recognized limitation of the formal, organizational
approach.

When the scope of transcultural comparative analysis is historical rather
than simply spatial, the limitation of the economizing viewpoint becomes
a fatal defect. Indeed, the "attention of economists has been focused . . .
on just those aspects of our economy least likely to be found" in primitive
economies of interest to the anthropologist.[10] "The institutional structure
of the economy need not compel, as with the market system, economizing
actions. The implications of such an insight for all the social sciences which
must deal with the economy could hardly be more far-reaching. Nothing
less than a fundamentally different starting point for the analysis of the
human economy as a social process is required."[11] The pursuit of gain
through exchange is an institutionally enforced pattern of behavior that
must be analyzed as a result rather than the antecedent of the historical
process.[12]

In order to iterate these concerns, Polanyi made and very frequently
used the distinction between two connotations of the term *economic*. One,
used almost exclusively by mainstream economists, is that of economizing
or calculative behavior. Faced with the ineluctable logic of scarcity—and
scarcity itself is a postulated or stylized fact rather than an inductive, historical one—society and its constituent individuals must by one means or

another make priority decisions on the allocation and distribution of productive capacity. Coupled with the further postulate or ideal typology of rationality, economics becomes the science of choice. Indeed, society becomes but the aggregate of the decisions made by "economic man" with given preferences and capacities in the face of market situations.

Polanyi countered this conception with the substantive connotation of *economic* as material. This idea centers on the necessity that humanity, in order to obtain its living, must interact with the rest of nature. The economic system hence can be "defined as an instituted process of interaction between man and his environment, which results in a continuous supply of want-satisfying material means."[13] The economic system, or the economic function of social activity, is therefore a more or less systematic and orderly pattern of social behavior that functions to provision the material wherewithal necessary to support social and individual life.

Polanyi used this conception of the economy to counter the economistic conception or, better, the "economistic fallacy" of identifying the anthropologically generic term, economic system, with the features that characterize its market form.[14] "It is our proposition that only the substantive meaning of economic is capable of yielding the concepts that are required by the social sciences for an investigation of all the empirical economies past and present."[15]

The Political Economy of Capitalism

There is a further and more important dimension to Polanyi's concern than the methodological problems of economic anthropology and comparative economic systems. The economistic conception lies at the root of a paralytic *Gestalt* which is fixated on the market form of economic organization. This institutional fixation does more than break down what should be the *continuity* between the analyses of economic anthropology and comparative economic systems. It so delimits the vision of economic analysis that alternative institutional forms are not visible. This astigmatism similarly cripples the economist's approach to public policy and social reform, with the result that basic institutional change is unimaginable.

In other words, Polanyi was also motivated by the concerns of political economy. He began *The Great Transformation* with a discussion of the four principal institutions of nineteenth-century Europe. He classified these by their political, economic, national, and international character. The four pivotal institutions are the balance-of-power system, political and international; the gold standard, economic and international; the self-regulating market, economic and national; and the liberal state, political and national. These institutions resulted in a century of peace between the Napoleonic Wars and World War I.

In Polanyi's view, the decisive institution was the self-regulating market: "It was this innovation which gave rise to a specific civilization."[16] It was, he felt, the economic system which underwrote the "pragmatic pacifism" by creating a "peace interest." The worldwide movers of *haute finance* had a financial interest in averting world war, notwithstanding their interests in a series of colonial wars, but these were limited in extent and specific in purpose.

It follows, of course, that the breakdown of the nineteenth-century institutional pattern was based on the collapse of the self-regulating market. From the turn of the century onward, the international economic system was in process of dissolution, as was the political system based upon it. The breakdown of the gold standard in the early 1930s was the symbolic demise of one age and the harbinger of the transformation of civilization. This was Polanyi's thesis in *The Great Transformation*: "The origins of the cataclysm [of the 1920s and 1930s] lay in the utopian endeavor of economic liberalism to set up a self-regulating market system" (p. 29).

The transformation thereafter, the emergence of the welfare state, was to Polanyi a related problem of political economy. The breakdown in the nineteenth century stemmed from the belief in the self-regulating market and the conception of the state as a necessary evil. Understanding the dissolution is critical to the welfare state, because the latter is a response to the same institutional problems that toppled the nineteenth-century structure.

In other words, social reform cannot be effectively accomplished until the habits of the last century are cast aside. This is "a theme that Polanyi returned to repeatedly: that deeply ingrained beliefs about man, society, and economy, fashioned in the very special setting of early industrial capitalism inhibit understanding and further reform of the changed economy of the present day."[17]

Polanyi's vision was that the crisis of market capitalist society was rooted in the self-regulating market and the neglect of the primacy of society. The great difficulty was the semi-autonomous economy, not embedded in society. This idea shaped Polanyi's major conceptual framework. His two main interests were the origin and development of nineteenth-century market capitalism and the place of the economy in primitive and archaic socioeconomic formations.[18] The striking similarity to Karl Marx, Max Weber, and Thorstein Veblen is obvious; each sought to comprehend the phenomena of market capitalism and industrialism not only directly, by study of modern society, but also indirectly, by study of the nature of precapitalist economic formations.

Polanyi's General Approach

I have argued that Polanyi's general animus or vision was very similar to that of institutionalism. I now shall consider Polanyi's general approach to socioeconomic analysis in relation to that of institutionalism. In the next section, I shall take a closer look at the specific analysis and interpretation of modern capitalism.

The Economy as an Instituted Process

Polanyi's general approach to the economic system is perfectly consistent with the mainstream institutionalist approach. The substantivist view of the economic system is a technological perspective. In contrast to the formalist approach, the focus on materiality commits the analysis to humanity's tools-*cum*-knowledge interaction with the rest of nature. At the same time, the substantivist view emphasizes the institutional aspect of human culture: "The social process is a tissue of relationships between man as biological entity and the unique structure of symbols and techniques that results in maintaining his existence."[19] The substantive meaning of *economic* derives from man's dependence for his living upon nature and his fellows. It refers to the interchange with his natural and social environment, insofar as this results in supplying him with the means of material want satisfaction.[20]

The economy is thus an *instituted process* manifesting the essential materiality and sociality of the human being. Polanyi emphasized that "process suggests analysis in terms of motion."[21] He seems to have meant by process the technological aspect of human culture. I gather this by his references to the "process level between man and soil in hoeing a plot" and to process as the "material resources and equipment—the ecology and technology."[22] By "institutedness" Polanyi referred to the ensemble of social relationships and attitudes which give meaning and stability to the material process.

This clearly corresponds to the celebrated Veblenian dichotomy between the technological and ceremonial aspects of human culture, although some disagreement arises from Polanyi's emphasis on the stabilizing role of institutions, which Veblen tends to view as a retarding influence. Still, however different be their value judgments of the function of institutions *vis-à-vis* technology, they are nonetheless dealing with the same theoretical problem. In terms of the key focus—the problem of technological change and institutional adjustment—the two are in accord.

The similarity between the two men's ideas is brought out in Polanyi's major work on modern society, *Great Transformation*, in the title of a pivotal chapter: "Habitation versus Improvement." This is clearly kith and kin to Veblen's celebrated cultural dichotomy, but once again the tone or judgment is different: "At the heart of the Industrial Revolution of the eighteenth century there was an almost miraculous improvement in the tools of production, which was accompanied by a catastrophic dislocation of the lives of the common people."[23] Lest we overstate this contrast, it should be noted that, for Polanyi, the catastrophe was not the revolution of technology so much as the revolution of technology within a *commercial society*.[24] "The congenital weakness of nineteenth century society was not that it was industrial but that it was a market society."[25]

The Holistic and Societal Perspective

Polanyi's frequent reference to the need for a "total view of man and society" points up another general approach that he shares with mainstream institutionalism. As do the institutionalists, Polanyi stresses the need for a holistic and societal view of social science. This shows up most clearly in his characterization of the market economy as disembedded, in contrast to the general historical and anthropological evidence that the economy has no existence autonomous from culture. "The outstanding discovery of recent historical and anthropological research is that man's economy, as a rule, is submerged in his social relationships."[26]

As a rule, the process of production and consumption is not organized upon a set of distinctly economic motives, purposes, and influences. This is most importantly true of *economic* in a calculative sense, but it applies as well to *economic* in the material sense because the process of production and consumption is not an end in itself. It becomes so only in modern society, when "instead of economy being embedded in social relations, social relations [become] imbedded in the economic system."[27] The market is "imperialist" in that it tends to extend into all facets of social life;[28] production and consumption become ends in themselves, or at least self-justifying, in that they are not independent of their putative purposes, but instead exert strong influence thereon.

The errant institutional pattern of market capitalism is reflected in the concomitant social scientific paradigm, especially that of economics. Both institutional practice and economic thought neglect the essential wholeness of the human being, the web of motives and influences which underlie any action, and the web of effects which result from any action. However, "human institutions abhor unmixed motives."[29] The human being acts, thinks, and lives as a whole and must be understood as a *totality* of manifold dimensions. Irrational and arational variables are part of economic life, just as they are part of sexual, psychological, and political life.

Polanyi takes the *societal* approach to social science. That is, he does not begin with the individual, but with society. Both historically and psychologically, the individual emerges from, and is not antecedent to, society. Starting with society, one can then arrive at the level of the individual by consideration of the social process of individuation. The opposite analytical strategy, of taking the individual as the point of departure, aside from being ahistorical, is static and abstracts from the basic questions of human behavior. For example, analysis of the formation of the individual's valuations, preferences, and perspectives, in contrast to the orthodox strategy of taking the individual as given, commits the mainstream institutionalist to the scrutiny of the dynamic and concrete existence of humanity in society.

Departing from the level of society, it is then possible to arrive at important considerations and conclusions *vis-à-vis* the individual. In contrast, the image of society which emerges by way of reasoning from the level of the individual to that of society is severely limited. This approach is inherently incomplete because society is not a mere agglomeration of individuals, a mere sum of its parts. This is very clearly seen in economists' approach to value. Social value is viewed as the aggregation of individual values. While logically unassailable, perhaps, this view is severely limited as an approach to understanding human behavior in its concrete, social setting.[30]

Power and Value

Polanyi made no attempt to develop a theory of value in the sense of analyzing the determinants of market prices. He also did not offer any systematic critique of existing theories of price formation. He probably would have accepted much of orthodox theory in this regard, despite his conviction that orthodoxy embodied an economistic fallacy which severely undermined the positive contribution of its analysis. The absence of a theory of price determination by market forces is easy to explain. For Polanyi, the important issue was not the orthodox question of analyzing how prices are determined, but the Aristotelian question of deciding at what level prices should be set. Polanyi cites this difference and the scant attention in Aristotle's work to market prices versus value, price fluctuations, price formation as a function of the market, or competition as a set of forces bent on establishing a unique price in a market. "The crucial difference was that the modern economist was aiming at a description of the *formation of prices* in the market, while such a thought was far from Aristotle's mind. He was busied with the quite different and essentially practical problem of providing a formula by which the *price was to be set*."[31] In other words, Aristotle's concern was with the price issue as part of the problem of the administered economy. He had no conception of a self-regulating market mechanism and therefore no interest in the analysis of price formation by which market theory seizes order from the apparent chaos of a nonadministered economy. The function of prices in Aristotle's, and Polanyi's, conception is not to reflect impersonal market forces, but to serve as part of the information and control system by which society institutes its economic aspect.

Polanyi does provide the rudiments of a theory of value in a different sense, and this brings us to the third general area of methodological agreement between Polanyi and mainstream institutionalism: the insistence that economic science place pivotal emphasis upon the analysis of *power* and *value*. The market vision of the social economy, with its givens regarding individual preferences and capacities and its subjective and volitional theory of socioeconomic behavior, denies the prepotency of society. This leads, in turn, to the invisibility of society and obscures the crucial relationship between power and economic value.[32]

As is said often in the institutionalist literature, notably by John Kenneth Galbraith, the reality of power persists despite the denial of its existence and the refusal to come to terms with it. Also common to the institutionalist literature, notably in the works of Ayres, is the conviction that economics must be a science of value and loses all meaning when reduced to mere prediction of relative prices. Polanyi noted the obscurity surrounding power and economic value and located this obscurity in the peculiar conception of freedom in the market economy. "But power and economic value are a paradigm of social reality .... The function of power is to ensure that measure of conformity which is needed for the survival of the group. . . . Economic value ensures the usefulness of the goods produced."[33]

Power, then, is the institutedness of the productive process. The vestiture of the discretionary authority to make and execute decisions is a power process, as is the legitimation of this discretion. Value is an expression of the power process: Economic values are sociological entities. Taking the individual as a datum obscures this pivotal fact because it ignores the socialization process which precedes and molds economic values. There is, of course, a technical component of values—production functions, physical transformation functions, and the like. But this cause-and-effect, manipulative knowledge derives its significance from its institutedness—social relations, customs, and power. Knowledge plus institutional context yields value judgments.

Polanyi's orientation to value is similar to the instrumental value focus of mainstream institutionalism. This much is clear from the quotation just above. At that place Polanyi referred to the function of power as sustaining the survival of the group. This focus is similar to institutionalism in another way, namely, the essential *normativity* of economic theory. "That which ensures justice . . . is good since it is required for the continuance of the group. Normativity, then, is inseparable from actuality."[34]

In sum, Polanyi's view of the economy focuses on social reproduction. The basic function of the economic process is to reproduce society, with or without expansion. Power and value, hand in hand, manifest the reality of society and the necessity of reproducing it. The economy does not merely involve production of goods and services; although it does that, its primary significance lies in the reproduction of society. That process involves, in addition to the simple production of material, the reproduction of the species acculturated to the manner of social existence. Classes and social strata, instrumental competency, and aesthetic appreciation must be reproduced. For example, the ways and means of modern social existence require the normally competent individual to be able to balance a checkbook, operate a motor car, and appreciate the nuances of cinema, football, and the like.

Social reproduction is not merely intergenerational; it is an ongoing process. The perspectives, values, and skills of individuals are continuously evolving. The individual is formed and reformed throughout his or her lifetime.

Viewed in this light, in terms of social reproduction, power and economic value take on new meaning. They are the key categories of *social control*. This is of considerable importance because such a perspective permits social control to enter the discussion at level one; there is no question of social control being absent in this focus. The only relevant questions concern the form and content of the control and whether or not they are functional and legitimate. *Social reform* is equally comfortable in this conceptualization since it is a conscious reconstruction of the form and content of social control in order to remedy some deficiency of function or legitimacy.

This approach is in sharp contrast to the orthodox economic analysis which departs from the isolated individual. In that view, the questions of social control and, by extension, social reform, enter the analysis in terms of *whether* rather than how. This neglect of the primacy of society inevitably embodies a distortion of social control and reform and, all too often, a suspicion toward them. Social control and social reform are thereby reduced to political intervention into the affairs of individuals. This distortion of the social existence of human life exerts an important and pernicious influence on the conventional approach to social policy. As Adolph Lowe has observed, "it is the essence of the [controls of the conventional approach to economic policy] that they take the behavior of the micro-units for granted. . . . In contrast, Control as here understood refers to a public policy that concerns itself with the shaping of the behavioral patterns themselves."[35] In contrast, by taking society as their methodological point of departure, Polanyi and the other social economists bring social control and reform into the analysis "naturally," that is, in a fashion which is consistent with the realities of human life.

One final note on Polanyi's discussion of power is in order. He denied that social change could be understood solely in terms of class struggle. He insisted, instead, that interest groups representing various socioeconomic sectors and geographical sections were involved.[36] It is important to note that this was not pluralist apologia: There is no reasonable way that Polanyi can be portrayed as such. Rather, Polanyi's denial of the primacy of class interests in social change plays an important role in his theory by enabling him to separate the social problems of market society and industrialism. I shall return to this point later.

Polanyi's Theory of Modern Capitalism

Polanyi's theory of modern capitalism is also essentially similar to that of mainstream institutionalism. This can be easily seen by considering the relation between industrial and market society and between industrialism and social reform.

The Industrial Revolution and Market Capitalism

Polanyi, similar to institutionalists, insists that two very different cultural processes, industrialism and market capitalism, emerged together two centuries ago. As I noted above, he stressed that the social catastrophe concomitant to the origin of modern society is not due to industrialism per se, but to industrialism as instituted via market capitalism. Industrialism as a way of life must be distinguished from its effects in tandem with the attempt to establish a self-regulating market economy. It is precisely the obscurantism of the market myth that stands in the way of human adaptation to and mastery of industrialism as a way of life.

One major source of enervation in the market myth is the distorted and obsolete conception of *freedom*. The liberal conception has yet to transcend its origins. Born into a cultural milieu in which the state represented the most serious obstacle to liberty, the liberal view of freedom has always been freedom from government. Liberal economic theory has been preoccupied with free (from government) enterprise and private property and neglectful of the vital changes in the social situation.[37] This distorted view of freedom parallels the distorted view of social control and social reform already discussed. The conventional economic perspective places freedom, and social control, in an unrealistically narrow context of political intervention into "private life." "With the liberal the idea of freedom thus degenerates into a mere advocacy of free enterprise—which is today reduced to a fiction by the hard reality of giant trusts and princely monopolies. This means the fullness of freedom for those whose income, leisure and security need no enhancing."[38]

Similar to Ayres, other institutionalists, and Marx, Polanyi envisioned a more positive and just freedom made possible by the wealth created by industrialism as a way of life.

> The passing of the market-economy can become the beginning of an era of unprecedented freedom. . . . Freedom can be made wider and more general than ever before; regulation and control can achieve freedom not only for the few, but for all. Freedom not as an appurtenance of privilege . . . but as a prescriptive right extending far beyond the narrow confines of the political sphere into the intimate organization of society itself. Thus will old freedoms . . . be added to the new fund of freedom generated by the leisure and security that industrial society offers to all. Such a society can afford to be just and free.[39]

This vision of an intensive and extensive increase of freedom made possible by industrialism is a centerpiece of Marxian and institutionalist social theory.[40]

The similarity extends farther in that each of these intellectual traditions stresses that the expansion of human freedom remains largely latent, distorted, and one-sided so long as the market capitalist social order remains in place. "Yet we find the path blocked by a moral obstacle. Planning and control are being attacked as a denial of freedom. Free enterprise and private ownership are declared to be essentials of freedom. . . . The freedom that regulation creates is denounced as unfreedom."[41]

The shared vision of the principals in question includes the institutional adaptation necessary to realize the latent potential for human liberation. Economic planning and social control are necessary to contain and utilize, effectively and equitably, the manifold potentialities of industrialism as a way of life. The institutional adjustment that is required involves the need to extend the reach of collective action and organization so as to restrict predation and conflict, or at least channel them into more manageable and less disruptive spheres than the contexts they assume in market capitalism. Ultimately, collective action can be expected to breed cooperation and competition on a new scale and in a renascent ethical milieu.

I shall return to the consideration of industrialism and social reform below. For the moment, I want to consider Polanyi's essential similarity to Marx and institutionalism *and* his advance beyond them in one important respect. The similarity is clear enough. Industrialism manifoldly increases the human capacity for mastery of nature, with all the pernicious and beneficial implications that this new technological scale entails. To cast the balance toward the desirable implications, institutional adjustment must occur. Here, Polanyi touches familiar ground. For Marx, the forces of production, developed to historically incredible heights by the capitalist socioeconomic formation, must eventually burst asunder the constricting fetters of capitalist social relations and superstructure. For Veblen, who eschewed teleology and historical necessity, at least in part of the Marxist sense,[42] and who was rather more cynical than Marx, it was a contest of imbecilic institutions and the protean power of the industrial age.

I think, however, that Polanyi, writing several decades later and drawing upon Marx, although apparently not from Veblen,[43] made an important new departure. He did not rest with posing industrialism and all its might to the pernicious legacy of the market myth. He combined the position with an identification of a basic institutional tendency created by the attempt to conform social practice to the self-regulating market model. This tendency he identified as the *protective response*. The exposure of human beings, nature, and economic organization to the vagaries of the competitive market created spontaneous collective action to protect society from the debilitating consequences of its market idolatry.

Human society would have been annihilated but for protective countermoves which blunted the action of this self-destructive mechanism.

> Social history in the nineteenth century was thus the result of a double movement. . . . While on the one hand markets spread all over the face of the globe . . ., on the other hand a network of measures and policies [arose] to check the action of the market relative to labor, land, and money. . . . Society protected itself against the perils inherent in a self-regulating market system.[44]

The strength of Polanyi's formulation lies in the forceful demonstration that this protective response was not even solely political, in the sense of belonging to the realm of government, much less motivated by a general advance toward leftist ideology.[45] Polanyi denied that the protective response had any unifying theme except the *primacy of society* and the necessity of taking steps to preserve society in the face of the disruptive onslaught of the uncontrolled market. Dalton recognizes the importance of this point. "One of Polanyi's most perceptive and telling arguments concerning the social divisiveness of uncontrolled market economy emphasizes the spontaneity with which social control of labor, land, money, and some product markets was imposed in England and the continent. . . . Not only were similar controls in different countries instituted . . ., but the sponsors and supporters of the market controls varied radically in politics and ideology."[46] This protective response, in addition to its visibility in the progression of state intervention in industrial relations, natural resources and environment, banking, and so on, can also be seen to be the operative factor in the development of the modern corporation, trusts, and unionization.[47] The historical lesson in all of this is the untenability of the self-regulating market economy.

The protective response is an instructive way to view another set of phenomena of interest to institutionalists and Marxists: the diminished flexibility of the market pattern toward the turn of the last century. This was, of course, due in large part to the concentration of wealth concomitant with the accumulation of capital. However, the development of institutions and associations for control of and protection from the market threat was also involved. Moreover, concentration and accumulation, on the one hand, and control and protection, on the other, display circular causation. As the scale of the decision-making entity increases, so also do its reach and impact. This increases the need for economic entities, other than the one embodying the decisive discretion, to protect themselves. At the same time, the increase in scale and the decline in the number of entities involved facilitate association and control.

The result of the protectionist movement, as recorded often by Marxists and institutionalists, was monopoly capitalism. At the same time, imperialism was the expression of protectionism in the world economy.[48] The result, all in all, was a decisive retreat, in practice, from the fabled and still celebrated autonomy and automaticity of the market economy. "Protectionism helped to transform competitive markets into monopolistic ones. Less and less could markets be described as autonomous and automatic mechanisms. . . . More and more were individuals replaced by associations, men and capital united to non-competing groups. Economic adjustment became slow and difficult. . . . Eventually, unadjusted price and cost structures prolonged depressions."[49] This carries Polanyi's theme to the Great Depression. In the brief final section, I suggest its importance to the development of capitalism after World War II. Before doing so, however, I want to consider industrialism as a way of life and its embodiment of social reform in order to round out the case of Polanyi's institutionalism.

Industrialism and Social Reform

One of the basic propositions of mainstream institutionalism is that there is a logic of industrialism and a derivative logic of social reform.[50] In the emerging epistemological concept of "research programmes," after the fashion of the late Imre Lakatos,[51] I believe this proposition belongs to the hard core of institutionalism and not to that outer circle of hypotheses that can be surrendered without jeopardizing the fundamental character of the institutionalist research program. This is, of course, somewhat controversial. By simply stating my conviction here, I do not mean to preempt that controversy; it is simply not appropriate to enjoin it in this article.[52]

Polanyi clearly appreciated the logic of industrialism and the logic of social reform: "How to organize human life in a machine society is a question that confronts us anew. Behind the fading fabric of competitive capitalism there looms the portent of an industrial civilization."[53] Polanyi goes on to note the dehumanizing implications of the machine age in a way with which Veblen would not, perhaps, have agreed. But Veblen would have agreed with Polanyi's further development of the logic of industrialism theme. Agreement would likewise occur on Polanyi's insistence that to deal effectively with this industrial logic it is first necessary to throw off the market myth. The problem

is not merely the search for a solution to the problems of capitalism. It is a search for an answer to industry itself. Here lies the concrete problem of our civilization. . . . We find ourselves stultified by the legacy of a market-economy which bequeathed us oversimplified views of the function and role of the economic system in society. If the crisis is to be overcome, we must recapture a more realistic vision of the human world and shape our common purpose in the light of that recognition.

Industrialism is a precariously grafted scion upon man's age-long existence. The outcome of the experiment is still hanging in the balance.[54]

This is very reminiscent of Veblen's famous statement about the precarious institutional situation of Christendom.[55] Polanyi points out "the need for a new response to the total challenge of the machine," the irreversibility of industrialization, and the key problem of "adapting life [in an industrial setting] to the requirements of human existence."[56]

Polanyi's reading of the logic of industrialism is also in agreement with mainstream institutionalism with respect to social reform. The problem of "freedom in a complex society" can be resolved only by "planned intervention," or "conscious and responsible action." This, in turn, requires the discipline of "a total view of man and society very different from that which we inherited from market economy."[57] Elsewhere, Polanyi notes that socialism is an inherent tendency of industrialism bent on transcending "the self-regulating market by consciously subordinating it to a democratic society."[58] Polanyi, too, reads from the logic of industrialism the logic of social reform and the necessity for socioeconomic planning.

Polanyi bases his argument in this and other regards upon the primacy of society. He regards the recognition of this primacy as one of the "three constitutive facts in the consciousness of Western man: knowledge of death, knowledge of freedom, knowledge of society."[59] Living in modern industrial society, man cannot fail to recognize the reality of society. It molds individual character and provides conditions and situations within the context of which the individual can exercise his freedom of interest, personal development, and life-style. Acceptance of the reality of society, and the "power and compulsion that are a part of that reality,"[60] renders invalid any conception that would remove them from social life. The ideal of conventional economic theory is powerless; free individual agents and the reality of society invalidate that ideal and necessitate new conceptions of power, freedom, and responsibility.[61]

Polanyi's discussion with regard to society and freedom is very similar to J. M. Clark's views on "the changing basis of economic responsibility": "We have gone through a revolution of late [1916] in many realms of thought and policy. We have swung far away from narrow individualism toward a sense of solidarity and social-mindedness."[62] Clark went on to elaborate his point with examples from religion, philosophy, ethics, the role of the state, and economic practice. He then noted that this revolution "is all part of a movement we cannot escape. . . . It is the product of new situations and new knowledge, and we must make use of the knowledge to make the best of the new situation."[63] Clark insisted that new knowledge of cause and effect could of necessity alter an ethical situation, for such a situation involves a value judgment based on knowledge of fact and of valuations.

An important part of Clark's new knowledge was the primacy of society. The development of knowledge in behavioral psychology, nutrition, and child development indicated *social responsibility*; the nineteenth-century wisdom pointed to divinity, genetics, or individual corruption. Human misery that is divinely ordained or genetically determined is one thing; human misery that is due to human evil or institutional ignorance is quite another matter. The former elicits religious observation or animistic idolatry; the latter inspires indignation and demands for social reform. Even the view that misery is engendered by individual frailty, being secular but not social, leads only to stern lectures about bootstraps or appeals to humanitarian charity.

The point is no less than the *demystification* of social forces. Cause-and-effect knowledge of the social determinants of the human condition carries with it an alteration of the social situation. Social responsibility becomes recognized, and collective action toward social reform follows in the wake of the awesome recognition of human self-determination. "One of the greatest things that the progress of science and industry has done for us is to give us responsible causes of a social and environmental sort."[64] This matter-of-fact, cause-and-effect bent of mind with regard to the social determination of the character of human existence, pragmatism in the best sense, is the underlying animus to the institutionalist commitment to social reform, just as it earlier prompted Marx's revolutionary vision. To this frame of mind, to this commitment, and to this vision, Polanyi was wholly dedicated.

Polanyi's Vision and the Welfare State

In conclusion, I wish only to mention the instructiveness of Polanyi's socioeconomic theory with regard to the emergence of the modern welfare state. His central concern is the place of the economy in society. His anthropological study revealed that the general rule of human culture is the embeddedness of the economy in the web of social and political life. The *experiment* of market capitalism violated this rule, that is, within this social order the economy is disembedded and conceived to run as an autonomous, self-regulating sphere of human activity.

But this experiment proved to be an utter and catastrophic failure. Human society of necessity responded to protect itself from the ravaging entailed in this failure. This protective response has culminated, roughly a century later, in the modern welfare state. As Dalton observed, "in Polanyi's terms, the welfare state is a movement toward 're-embedding' economy in society."[65] But the task is far from complete,[66] and there is no better instruction available to guide us in its completion than that of Karl Polanyi's institutional economics—holistic in scope, evolutionary in method, and fervently committed to economics as a moral science.

"I plead for the restoration of that unity of motives which should inform man in his everyday activity as a producer, for the reabsorption of the economic system in society, for the creative adaptation of our ways of life to an industrial environment. . . . Today, we are faced with the vital task of restoring the fullness of life to the person."[67]

Notes

1. C. E. Ayres, *The Theory of Economic Progress* (New York: Schocken, 1962) and *Toward a Reasonable Society* (Austin: University of Texas Press, 1961); Allan G. Gruchy, *Contemporary Economic Thought* (New York: Kelley, 1972); David Hamilton, *Evolutionary Economics* (Albuquerque: University of New Mexico Press, 1970); Joseph Dorfman et al., *Institutional Economics* (Berkeley: University of California Press, 1964); Carey C. Thompson, ed., *Institutional Adjustment* (Austin: University of Texas Press, 1967); William Breit and W. P. Culbertson, Jr., eds., *Science and Ceremony* (Austin: University of Texas Press, 1976); and Rolf Steppacher et al., eds., *Economics in Institutional Perspective* (Lexington: Lexington Books, 1977).
2. Clark Kerr et al., *Industrialism and Industrial Man* (New York: Oxford University Press, 1960); and K. W. Kapp, *The Social Costs of Private Enterprise* (New York: Schocken, 1971).
3. Allan G. Gruchy, "Institutional Economics: Its Development and Prospects," in Steppacher, ed., *Economics*, pp. 13–14 and 23–26.
4. On Marx and institutionalism, see J. Ron Stanfield, "Limited Capitalism, Institutionalism, and Marxism," *Journal of Economic Issues* 11 (March 1977): 61–71, and "Radical Economics, Institutionalism, and Marxism," *Social Science Journal* 15 (January 1978): 47–54.
5. George Dalton, ed., *Primitive, Archaic, and Modern Economies: Essays of Karl Polanyi* (Garden City: Doubleday-Anchor, 1968), p. xxxviii. It is convenient to note here the debt we owe to Dalton for his efforts to sustain and develop the insights of his mentor. My personal debt to Dalton's work for the current article is considerable, although, of course, all errors are my own.
6. Ibid., p. x.

7. See ibid., pp. xli–xlii.
8. It is interesting to note the similarity of the methodological viewpoint to that of Marx in *Grundrisse* (New York: Vintage, 1973), p. 105: "Bourgeois society is the most developed . . . historic organization of production. The categories which express its relations . . . [provide insights to precapitalist economic formations]. Human anatomy contains a key to the anatomy of the ape. The intimations of higher development among the subordinate animal species, however, can be understood only after the higher development is already known. The bourgeois economy thus supplies the key to the ancient, etc. But not at all in the manner of those economists who smudge over [obliterate] all historical differences and see bourgeois relations in all forms of society."
9. Karl Polanyi, *The Great Transformation* (Boston: Beacon Press, 1957): p. ix.
10. Dalton, ed., *Essays*; Dalton is here quoting Herskovitz.
11. Ibid., p. 118.
12. Compare this to Marx, *Grundrisse*, p. 83: "Smith and Ricardo . . . [follow] the eighteenth-century prophets, in whose imaginations this eighteenth-century individual [of the society of free competition]—the product on one side of the dissolution of feudal forms of society, on the other side of the new forces of production developed since the sixteenth century—appears as an ideal whose existence they project into the past. Not as a historic result but as history's point of departure. As the Natural Individual appropriate to their notion of human nature, not arising historically, but posited by nature."
13. Dalton, ed., *Essays*, p. 145.
14. Ibid., p. 142 n.
15. Ibid., p. 140.
16. Polanyi, *Great Transformation*, p. 3.
17. Dalton, ed., *Essays*, p. xxxvi.
18. Ibid., pp. xi–xii.
19. Ibid., p. 116.
20. Ibid., p. 139.
21. Ibid., p. 146.
22. Ibid., pp. 147 and 307.
23. Polanyi, *Great Transformation*, p. 33.
24. Ibid., pp. 40–41.
25. Ibid., p. 250, italics omitted.
26. Ibid., p. 46.
27. Ibid., p. 57.
28. Applications of the economistic paradigm reflect this tendency. See the revealing statement on the scope of economic science in Lord Robbins, *An Essay on the Nature and Significance of Economic Science*, 2d ed. (New York: St. Martin's, 1969), p. 17. For a remarkable recent example, see Richard B. McKenzie and Gordon Tullock, *The New World of Economics: Explorations into the Human Experience* (Homewood: Richard D. Irwin, 1975).
29. Dalton, ed., *Essays*, p. 71.
30. On social value, see J. M. Clark, *Preface to Social Economics* (New York:

Kelley, 1967), pp. 44–65: and Kapp, *Social Costs*, pp. 255–62.

31. Dalton, ed., *Essays*, p. 108.
32. Polanyi, *Great Transformation*, p. 258.
33. Ibid.
34. Dalton, ed., *Essays*, p. 96.
35. *On Economic Knowledge* (New York: Harper, 1965), p. 131.
36. Polanyi, *Great Transformation*, pp. 151–56.
37. See Ayres, *Theory of Economic Progress*, pp. 189–90 and 300–303.
38. Polanyi, *Great Transformation*, p. 257.
39. Ibid., p. 256.
40. For example, compare Polanyi to Marx, *The German Ideology* (New York: International Publishers, 1970), pp. 115–16: "In reality . . . people [have] won freedom . . . to the extent permitted . . . by the existing productive forces. All conquests of freedom hitherto, however, have been based on restricted productive forces. The production which these productive forces could provide was insufficient for the whole of society and made development possible only if some persons satisfied their needs at the expense of others, and therefore some . . . attained the monopoly of development, while others . . . were for the time being (i.e. until the birth of new revolutionary productive forces) excluded from any development."
41. Polanyi, *Great Transformation*, p. 256.
42. I think the matter of Marx's teleology has been overemphasized by institutionalists, following Veblen. Clearly, Marx foresaw socialism as the teleological result of the evolution of socioeconomic formations. But this was no Hegelian absolute state of final development. Social evolution will continue beyond socialism in Marx's view, but this further development will be of a fundamentally new character due to the development of the productive forces to a profoundly new level. The social practice of abundance must be far different from that of scarcity, as institutionalists frequently point out.
43. If anything, Polanyi's failure to cite Veblen, Ayres, Clark, and so forth, is an even more serious sin of omission than the lack of attention given Polanyi by his institutionalist contemporaries. Polanyi is, as a rule, generous in his acknowledgment of sources. Thus, his failure to cite the root stocks of institutionalism, except for one inconsequential mention of Wesley Mitchell, must be taken at face value.
44. Polanyi, *Great Transformation*, p. 76.
45. Ibid., pp. 140–56.
46. Dalton, ed., *Essays*, p. xxiv.
47. It is interesting to compare this with Galbraith's analysis of the corporate quest to stabilize its market environment and preserve its autonomy. See *The New Industrial State* (Boston: Houghton-Mifflin, 1967).
48. Polanyi, *Great Transformation*, p. 217.
49. Ibid., p. 218.
50. See Gruchy, "Institutional Economics."
51. See Imre Lakatos, "Falsification and the Methodology of Research Programmes," in *Criticism and the Growth of Knowledge*, edited by Imre Lakatos and Alan Musgrave (New York: Cambridge University Press,

614 J. Ron Stanfield

1970), pp. 91–195; and Spiro Latsis, ed., *Method and Appraisal in Economics* (New York: Cambridge University Press, 1977).

52. I have entered the controversy elsewhere. See *Economic Thought and Social Change* (Carbondale: Southern Illinois University Press, 1979), chapter 6.

53. Dalton, ed., *Essays*, p. 59.

54. Ibid., pp. 59–60.

55. Thorstein Veblen, *The Instinct of Workmanship and the State of the Industrial Arts* (New York: Kelly, 1964), p. 25.

56. Dalton, ed., *Essays*, p. 60.

57. Ibid., pp. 76–77.

58. Polanyi, *Great Transformation*, p. 234.

59. Ibid., p. 258A.

60. Ibid.

61. As noted above, the persistence of the reality of power in the face of the tendency of mainstream economics to assume it away is one of Galbraith's themes. See, for example, "Power and the Useful Economist," *American Economic Review* 63 (March 1973): 1–11.

62. Clark, *Preface to Social Economics*, p. 67.

63. Ibid., p. 70.

64. Ibid., p. 74.

65. Dalton, ed., *Essays*, p. xxvi.

66. See William A. Robson, *Welfare State and Welfare Society* (London: George Allen and Unwin, 1976), for an instructive discussion.

67. Dalton, ed., *Essays*, pp. 72–73.

[16]

Jei JOURNAL OF ECONOMIC ISSUES
Vol. XVII No. 3 September 1983

J. R. Commons's Institutional Economics

Malcolm Rutherford

J. R. Commons is widely recognized as having possessed one of the more obscure styles of presentation to be found in the history of economics, an obscurity that may be connected with two of the salient features of the secondary literature concerning his work. The first feature is the comparative lack of adequate analyses of Commons's overall theoretical system. Although a great deal of work has been done on particular aspects of Commons's thought, much less has been produced on those general ideas concerning institutions and institutional change that provide the context within which Commons's more particularist effort can be placed.[1] Indeed, even among Commons's own pupils there are those who would deny that Commons ever managed to generate any overall theoretical framework.[2]

The second, although related, feature is the extremely wide variety of opinion that has been expressed on the nature and value of Commons's theoretical contribution. For example, D. Hamilton interprets Commons as belonging in the mainstream of institutionalism, his work adding to the central institutionalist analysis of the dichotomy between institutions and technology (a dichotomy most explicitly stated by T. Veblen and C. E. Ayres);[3] D. Seckler places Commons in a "wing" of the institutionalist movement quite distinct from that inhabited by Veblen and Ayres, and

The author is Assistant Professor of Economics, University of Victoria, British Columbia, Canada. Helpful comments and suggestions were provided by numerous colleagues at the University of Victoria and by Warren Samuels, William Dugger, Allan Gruchy, A. W. Coats, and anonymous referees. Any remaining errors are the author's responsibility.

also argues that Commons's work is naive, unsophisticated, and inherently uninteresting;[4] M. Blaug contends that Commons's theoretical writings are "suggestive" (although also obscure); and K. Boulding would seem to agree, calling Commons's work "a tangled jungle of profound insights."[5] Most recently a number of writers have argued that Commons's ideas could be useful in the creation of a synthesis of institutionalist and orthodox analysis in the area of law and economics,[6] but J. M. Buchanan has dismissed the work of institutionalists (including Commons) as descriptive and lacking in analysis.[7]

This article represents an attempt to interpret and evaluate Commons's work in the light of some recent thinking on institutions and institutional change. The argument here supports those who would place Commons ouside of the Veblen/Ayres tradition within institutionalism, but, more important, Commons is found to have provided a more general, coherent, and potentially valuable theoretical contribution than has often been supposed. This contribution, however, will be seen as lying more in the area of institutional theory than in the field of law and economics as such.

Fundamental Concepts

Commons, as other institutionalists, was concerned that orthodox economics failed to take full and proper account of institutional factors, but, unlike a number of other institutionalists, Commons did not entirely reject orthodox theory and he thought of his analysis of institutions more as a supplement to orthodox theorizing.[8] This attitude shows up clearly in Commons's approach to the question of institutions, which shares elements with both the orthodox and institutionalist programs. The traditional approach to institutions displayed in classical and neo-classical economics is to treat institutions as having the role of given *constraints*. On the other hand, institutionalists have tended to be more concerned with questions of institutional change and many have emphasized the *instrumental* role of institutions. It has been argued that much of the difficulty of dealing with institutions in economic theory comes from this apparent contradiction in roles,[9] and it is therefore of interest that Commons attempts to deal with both of these aspects of institutions. In Commons's analysis institutions are constraints on individual and group action and yet can be altered and used as instruments by individuals and groups.

Commons conceived of institutions as embodying collective action. Collective action controls individual action through physical, moral, or economic sanctions. Collective action thus constrains individual action, but Commons goes beyond this idea and argues that institutions are not *simply* constraints. Collective action may also involve the liberation or expansion of individual action. Liberation for some individuals may be achieved by constraining the acts of others. In particular, institutions may liberate individuals from coercion, duress, or discrimination at the hands of others. In addition, institutionalized authority or power over others can result in the expansion of the "will of the individual," enabling the individual to achieve goals that require the organization and control of others.[10]

In Commons's terminology an organized form of collective action is a "going concern," and within this category he places the state, political parties, courts, unions, firms, churches, and the like. The rules, regulations, common practices, customs, and laws that regulate the actions of individuals and concerns are the "working rules of collective action." The concept of working rules is extremely broad and applies equally to those rules that operate only within particular concerns, the broad social framework of custom and law, and to constitutions. Working rules determine what individuals or concerns can, cannot, must or must not, and may do.[11]

The key to Commons's approach to institutions is that it is problem-centered. Institutions are problem solving instruments that operate through the control of individual action. Commons's analytical starting point is surprisingly orthodox and consists of the problem situation created by the fact of economic scarcity. Scarcity is, of course, the basis of the economist's concern with the efficient use of resources, but Commons argues that scarcity also generates a problem in human relationships. Scarcity creates conflicts of interest, conflicts that in the absence of institutionalized constraints will be resolved by private violence to the detriment of productive efficiency.[12] Without an institutionalized system of rules to create a degree of order and certainty or "security of expectations," there could be "little or no present value, present enterprise, present transactions, or present employment."[13] In Commons's words, institutional rules "are necessary and their survival in history is contingent on their fitness to hold together in a continuing concern the overweening and unlimited selfishness of individuals pressed on by scarcity of resources."[14] The institutional system serves to "ration" economic benefits and burdens, and, if successful, generates a "workable mutuality," if not a harmony, out of conflict.[15]

Commons, of course, was particularly interested in the evolution of institutions, and it is in this aspect of his work that he departs most clearly from the orthodox approach. Commons explicitly rejects the use of any contractarian logic or any "eternal reason binding upon men henceforth without change" as a basis for a positive theory of institutions.[16] For

Commons, institutions evolve under pressure from the requirement of workability. Workability involves a degree of efficiency and a distribution of benefits and burdens that allows the system to survive, but inefficiencies and injustices may remain. Workability is an entirely pragmatic requirement: there must be a set of rights and rules, some authority for enforcing rights, and some degree of adherence to common customs or norms. Commons was quite aware of the role of power struggle, sometimes leading to war and revolution, in institutional history, but social order, for Commons, required both a balance of opposing interest groups and the existence of a system of common belief.

Working rules, and changes to the working rules, come from two main sources. Firstly, there are the rules that arise from the power of monarchs or other absolute rulers by conquest or subordination, or from the acts of legislative bodies. Secondly, there are rules that arise from customs and common practices and the decisions of common law courts in resolving disputes. In Commons's view the "great bulk" of working rules come from the latter source.[17] These working rules evolve and change over time, and Commons thought of institutional history as a process of the selection of one set of practices or rules over the other, alternative, sets— a process of pragmatic decision making involving "the concerted but conflicting action of human wills in an historical evolution of determining what is workable within the changing economic, political, and ethical sequence."[18]

Given these fundamental ideas and concepts, Commons's principal tasks were: (1) to analyze in more detail the way in which the structure of rules constrains economic behavior; and (2) to deal with the mechanisms involved in the selection of rules over time—the behavior of private collectives, courts, and governments.

I. *Working Rules and Transactions*

The detailed analysis of how working rules constrain and effect economic behavior and economic outcomes is contained in Commons's treatment of transactions. Commons concentrates on the distributional aspect, on how working rules determine the terms upon which economic transactions take place.

While orthodox economics tends to look at the voluntary exchange of commodities between individuals of equal legal standing, Commons looks at the transfer of rights of ownership and control between individuals and groups standing in various legal relationships to each other. As is well known he distinguishes three major types of transaction: the rationing transaction, the managerial transaction, and the bargaining transaction, a classification based on both legal and functional criteria.[19] Rationing and managerial transactions are transactions between a legal superior and a legal inferior. The rationing transaction involves the "rationing of wealth or purchasing power by a superior authority," for example legislators agreeing on taxes or protective tariffs or judicial decisions transferring wealth from one party to another.[20] Managerial transactions involve the organization and control of production and consist of the relationship of command and obedience between "manager and managed, master and servant, owner and slave."[21]

Bargaining transactions involve the transfer of rights of ownership between legal equals, but legal equality is compatible with the exercise of economic power.[22] Economic power is determined by the alternative opportunities and bargaining power (ability to withhold) available to the parties involved. The available alternatives define what Commons calls the "limits of coercion," and where the terms of the bargain will settle within these limits is determined by the bargaining power of the parties to the transaction.[23]

Transactions thus involve the use of legal or economic power, but these powers may have limits placed on their use. Working rules can constrain the use of power by requiring that some alternatives be avoided, or by limiting the use of power to reasonable levels. For example, the working rules may require such things as equal opportunity and fair competition, prevent the unreasonable use of bargaining power or the issuing of unreasonable commands, and ensure due process of law.[24] Also, changes in law or other working rules may shift certain transactions from the rationing to the bargaining type, or may restrict the range of rationing or managerial authority and provide more room for bargaining. The abolition of slavery involved the substitution of bargaining for rationing authority while the establishment of a socialist state would work in the opposite direction.[25] The type of transaction used and the terms upon which they take place depend, therefore, on a process of negotiation carried out within a context of working rules that determine legal and economic power and the limits on the use of such power.[26]

Commons's treatment of working rules obviously provides for the analysis of economic transactions within a *given* set of institutional constraints, but the concept of transacting also provides Commons with a basis for his critique of orthodox economics and a link to the analysis of institutions as dynamic instruments. Commons deals with this point by providing another classificatory scheme for transactions, this time dividing them into "routine" and "strategic" transactions. Commons relates this division to his idea of "limiting" and "complementary" factors. A strategic transaction is one that gives control over a limiting factor. Once the limiting factor is controlled the complementary factors can be dealt with through routine transactions. The limiting factor may change over time, but as long as the limiting factor is controlled, the complementary factors will generate the result sought. Commons explains that his "formula" of strategic and routine transactions "has become a highly important instrument of investigation, by means of which the older analogies of equilibrium give way to the actual process of human ability in controlling, through transactions, the physical and social environment."[27]

As pointed out by L. Harter, strategic transactions can be seen as those that "become the basis for establishing customs, resolving conflicts of interests, and establishing working rules."[28] The strategic transaction represents the dynamic element, the transaction that alters the set of incentives or constraints that will bear on routine transactions. Thus, the process of transacting involves more than can be captured by notions of market exchange and equilibrium within given institutional constraints. Transacting involves negotiation, persuasion, power, and the attempt to affect and alter working rules when they are the limiting factor. Individuals and concerns do not necessarily accept the legal or institutional status-quo. Individuals and concerns are *active* and attempt, through strategic transactions, to control their environment in order to ensure or increase their expectations of beneficial routine transactions, whether managerial, bargaining, or rationing in nature.

Institutions and Institutional Change

The above treatment of institutions implies that institutions have a function in constraining individual action, and yet individuals and concerns may attempt to pursue their interests even into areas that affect the existing structure of rules. In Commons's work institutional change does indeed arise out of the actions of individuals and concerns, but here again the operation of individual action is constrained, most obviously by ethical and customary norms and by the political and judicial institutions that govern the process of changing other rules or institutions. Political and judicial institutions are, however, also subject to change, and although Commons usually deals with a system of representative democracy and a developed judicial system in the Anglo-American mold, it is clear that he thought of political and judicial institutions as evolving under pressure from the requirement of workability. Political and judicial institutions must themselves be workable and result in workable solutions to problems and conflicts over other institutional rules. In other words, political and judicial institutions are also a response to a problem situation: that of maintaining workability over time as new problems and conflicts arise.

As noted above, Commons thinks of the structure of institutions and rules and the changes made to them as the outcome of a process involving human will and choice, in particular the "conscious determinations of legislatures" and the role of the courts in approving rules or practices as good and workable.[29] Laws, both statute law and common law, are backed by the power of the state. The state is a concern that has taken over the power to use physical sanctions, and that operates according to its own working rules built up out of custom, precedent, judicial opinion, statute law, and constitutional articles.[30]

What is important, however, is the control of the sovereign power of the state, and in representative democracies political parties have become the concerns "through which the sanctions of physical force are directed towards economic gain or loss."[31] In order to serve the interests they represent or choose to support, political parties aim at "selecting and getting control of the hierarchy of legislative, executive, and judicial personalities whose concerted action determines the legal rights, duties, liberties, and exposures involved in all economic transactions."[32] Parties are subject to lobbying and pressure from other organized groups seeking legislation in their advantage, and Commons argues that the legislature in a representative democracy operates through a process of "log-rolling."

Log-rolling, for Commons, is a pervasive phenomenon and is to be regarded as simply the way in which members of a legislature reach voluntary agreements on the legislative acts that will affect the distribution of economic burdens and benefits. Commons objects to the usual outright "crimination" of log-rolling, but although log-rolling is "as nearly a reasonable reconciliation of all conflicting interests as representative democracy has been able to reach," it still has difficulties.[33] The process is slow and inefficient and, particularly if many differing interests are involved, a legislature may become deadlocked. Also, the decisions made benefit only a few at the expense of others. While there are constraints on the actions of legislatures in the form of the customs, opinions, and beliefs of the populace, and, in the case of nations such as the United States, the ability of the courts to rule legislation unconstitutional, there is a real possibility that minority or less well-represented groups will be ignored, or poorly organized groups maneuvered out of opposition to measures not in their interests. Political leaders are experts in mass psychology and play on the "passions, stupidities, and inequalities of masses of people."[34]

Private collectives, then, engage in what is now called "rent seeking" by attempting to influence legislation to their advantage. Political processes are a method of reconciling politically important interests and of "maneuvering the populations into a unity of national government and a distribution of economic privileges."[35] Statute law is a "kind of organizing and experimenting with the efficiencies, scarcities, customs, and expectations of the people, sometimes expediting them, sometime inhibiting them."[36]

Commons pictures common law in a not entirely dissimilar fashion, although he does not believe judicial decisions are a matter of pressure groups. Common law arises out of the working rules of collective organizations or from custom or habit. An organization may be formed or adopt new practices or rules in order to promote or protect or advance its interests. This may amount to an attempt to establish, *de facto*, certain rights, liberties, or immunities. If a dispute arises the collective may succeed in having its practices and rules established in law through the decisions of the courts. Commons argues that the evolution of common law is very largely a matter of the courts deciding disputes concerning the rules or practices of concerns, but it is obvious that a similar process operates with rules or practices that arise not from any particular concern but from broader social customs.[37] Again, as disputes arise the courts will decide whether the practice or rule in question is to be given legal sanction.

When a dispute arises and is brought to court, the court must decide whether the rule or practice at issue is desirable. The court makes this decision on the basis of what it thinks to be "reasonable," and in deciding what is or is not reasonable the court must consider not only the existing statute law, but also "the inducements to Efficiency, the circumstances of Scarcity at the time and place, the expectations of the Future, the good and bad practices of the two parties, as well as the good and bad Common Practices of similar persons under similar conditions."[38]

While the court considers efficiency and scarcity aspects, an ethical or ideological element is also present. Court decisions are, therefore, not simply a matter of reducing transactions costs. The criterion of reasonableness is relativistic and based on the "habitual assumptions" of the court. The habitual assumptions of judges are subject to change with changing circumstances and on the basis of experience, but Commons was concerned that the rapid growth of private collective organizations had made the habitual, individualistic assumptions of judges obsolete. Also, the complexity of many issues required detailed investigation and the courts did not have the "agencies for making such extensive investigations as would be required."[39]

Neither political nor judicial processes are perfect means of developing or maintaining workable institutions, but both are concerned with the working rules of individuals and concerns "in their mutual adjustments to scarcity of resources and in their competitions and conflicts imposed upon them by that scarcity."[40] The "phenomena of political economy" are "the present outcome of rights of property and powers of government which have been fashioned and refashioned in the past by courts, legislatures, and executives through control of human behavior by means of working rules, directed toward purposes deemed useful or just by the law-givers and law interpreters."[41] Through these political and judicial processes the structure of working rules will respond to emerging problems and conflicts, to the formation of new collectives and interest groups, and to changing concepts of what may constitute a reasonable and workable solution.

Institutional Reform

Commons was far from being a radical critic of the social and institutional order of his time, but he certainly felt that there was room for improvement. His efforts at reform proceeded on two levels. First, he was concerned with the development of new practices and rules that would help overcome the particular economic and labor problems that concerned him. His work on business cycles, unemployment insurance, workmen's compensation, and collective bargaining are all well known. Second, he proposed what can be seen as more fundamental constitutional reforms designed to make the political and judicial processes work more effectively in resolving conflicts and solving problems. On both levels Commons's approach was pragmatic. He rejected attempts to return to "any of the individualistic devices of our founding fathers."[42] He wished to preserve and increase liberties while recognizing the existence of collective organizations and unequal political, legal, and economic power. What was important to Commons was to ensure that the power of one individual or collective was not used to control the behavior of others in an unreasonable fashion, and in practice that could be done only by creating new forms of collective action and working rules designed to equalize power, provide representation of interests, and liberate those currently operating under coercion, duress, or unfair competition. Commons's philosophical pragmatism is clearly displayed in the following quotation:

In modern economics the fears are mainly the fear of collective action, whether by governments, by corporations, or by labor unions. All collective action is looked upon with fear as leading straight to some form of dictatorship. But actually, in the cases as they arise, all kinds of collective action can be investigated to see whether, at the time and place, they are conducive to more real and equal freedom from individuals than the type of collective action which they displace.[43]

On the constitutional level Commons put forward two main proposals. First, and unlike some institutionalists, he rejected any further extension of direct government economic planning, and in fact argued that the power of political parties should be reduced.[44] This could be done, according to Commons, by encouraging the formation of voluntary collectives to represent all interest groups. It was the collective bargaining of these groups that Commons found the only refuge from totalitarianism. He took this line of argument to the point where he claimed that such collectives could form an economic or "occupational parliament of the American people, more truly representative than the Congress elected by territorial divisions," and that the "preservation of the American economic system against a totalitarian world, and against its own internal disruption, consists mainly in the collective bargaining between organized capital and organized labor, as against government by the traditional political parties."[45]

Commons's second proposal concerned the development of a "fourth branch" of government that would investigate and administer working rules. These administrative agencies would have the authority to experimentally institute rules of behavior. The legislature's function would be to set only the general working rules and terms of reference of the agencies, and the courts would hear any disputes arising out of the actions of the agencies. Within these limits the agencies would be free to undertake investigations and make rules designed to prevent possible disputes. They would try to develop rules that would provide for mutual advantage and gain the cooperation of the parties concerned. They would differ from courts in that courts decide disputes only after the event.[46]

In these ways Commons hoped to reduce the role of rationing by legislatures and courts and to *substitute* a process of collective bargaining, cooperation, and experimental rule making conducted in the light of the best available information. Such a process represents "pragmatic social philosophy" that "brings together again, this time by methods of scientific investigation, the separated fields of economics, ethics, and jurisprudence."[47]

Commons and Institutional Theory

To those familiar with the Veblen/Ayres and neo-classical approaches to institutional theory, it should be obvious that Commons does not fit clearly into either camp. Indeed, except for their shared interest in institutional change it is sometimes difficult to see why Commons has usually been classified along with writers such as Thorstein Veblen and Clarence Ayres.

A different point of view has been expressed by D. Hamilton, who claims that Commons utilized the key Veblenian concept of a dichotomy between business institutions and industry or technical efficiency, but although it is true that Commons sometimes uses similar terminology there is a profound difference between the meanings that each attaches to it.[48] Veblen's analysis of business institutions holds pecuniary gain to be the dominant criterion of social choice, with the only real solution to the domination of business over industrial efficiency being the replacement of business institutions by a system based on technological criteria. In contrast, Commons's analysis works in terms of reasonableness and workability. While Commons does discuss the problem of monopoly restriction leading to inefficiency and utilizes Veblen's conception of monopoly power as intangible property, in Commons's view these are problems that can be overcome without such radical institutional reconstruction.[49] Indeed, Commons explicitly attacks Veblen's sharp dichotomization of business and industry:

> The historical explanation of Veblen's cynical antithesis of business and industry is in the failure to trace out the evolution of business customs under the decisions of the courts, as he had traced the technological customs. Such an investigation reveals the evolution of his 'intangible property,' which has consisted in making the distinction, not allowed by Veblen, between goodwill and privilege, goodwill being the reasonable exercise of the power to withold, and privilege being the unreasonable exercise of that power.[50]

In Commons's work there is no dichotomy between business and industry as fundamental as Veblen would have us believe. Institutions can act as *constraints* and business power can be restrained to reasonable levels through the working rules resulting from court decisions. The business principles of profit seeking are not the sole criterion. This difference in attitude can also be seen in the treatment of unions. Veblen came to regard unions as just another vested pecuniary interest with adverse effects on technological efficiency. Commons saw unions as an attempt to gain a reasonable equalization of bargaining power.[51]

The differences between Commons and Veblen outlined above are reflective of much deeper points at issue. Commons is much more of a pragmatic reformer than Veblen, but he also differs from Veblen in his treatment of knowledge and its relationship with institutions and in his methodological individualism. To take the last point first, Commons's analysis is, for the most part, of individual decision makers and their reactions to the situation and problems they face. This is not to say that Commons utilizes individualism in the psychological form in which it is found in orthodox economics (where the goals and aims of action are taken as psychologically determined givens), or that he adopts individualism as a political or ideological position, but merely that in his work institutions and institutional change emerge from a process of decision making and problem solving that involves individual decision makers responding to the logic of their situation (including the institutional situation).[52] On the other hand, Veblen, in rejecting the psychologistic individualism of orthodoxy, abandons a consistently individualistic approach to the explanation of institutions and institutional change.[53] Veblen's contention is that as institutions *condition* individual thought and action, institutional change, at least of a radical sort, has to be explained by reference to some other conditioning "force" that counteracts the influence of existing institutions.

Veblen conceives of technological change as the major cause of substantial changes in the basis of the institutional system. Veblen's argument is that technology introduced under the exigencies of a prevailing system can result in the formation of new habits of life and thought that may come to displace the prevailing system. Commons's work is not inconsistent with technological change playing a role, but his work does not lead to the position that technology is the only, or even the major, source of change. Commons's primary concern was with the resolution of problems and conflicts, whatever their source, and his analysis is of choice, of selection, of judicial and political processes through which disputes are resolved or certain solutions to problems given sanction. The fault with Veblen's approach, however, is not his stress on technology or his view that institutions can condition goals and aims, but that he fails to provide an adequate or convincing analysis of the decision making process, of exactly why individuals abandon some conventions and adopt others, and of how a new consensus is formed and comes to find legal and political expression.

This brings up the question of the relationship between ideology, knowledge, and institutions. In Veblen's work a major source of social problems is to be found in the fact that institutions resist change even when they are obsolete and interfere with the attainment of more effective social arrangements. The fact that institutions have, in some sense, failed does not, however, necessarily lead to a shift in ideas. For Veblen, institutional systems embody and are built around an ideology that governs the course of action that will be taken in the face of new problems and opportunities. More substantial changes in institutions require a *prior* shift in ideology or preconceptions, which comes about only as a result of new habits of livelihood (technology) that instill new ways of thinking. It should be noted that only in the case of modern machine industry with its associated scientific approach does Veblen believe that the induced habits of thought involve clear matter-of-fact insight into the nature of problems and their solutions.

Ideas such as these clearly lie behind M. A. Copeland's objection to Commons's analysis. Copeland's argument is that in Commons's theory ethical tastes and ideology, which define what is thought to be workable and reasonable, depend in part on the existing common practices and that, therefore, these ethical precepts cannot be seen as the basis for the selection of practices. In Copeland's words,

> it would seem that we must consider separately those ethical tastes that constitute the 'artificially' selective conditions which practices survive or fail to survive, and that these selective tastes cannot be considered as evolving on a par with the practice selected. Otherwise we shall have the practices acting as selective conditions for the survival of the tastes quite as much as the tastes acting as selective conditions for the survival of the practices.[54]

However, Commons's work can, if one is generous, be interpreted in a way that avoids circularity. Commons saw institutional change as a response to new problems, difficulties, and conflicts. Solutions to problems are sought within a context provided by the existing state of knowledge, ethical beliefs, the "best" existing practices, and political possibilities, but the process is *dynamic*. The "best" practices will change as individuals and collectives seek their own solutions to problems. In addition, Commons's conception of decision making is experimental, a process of trial and error in search of workable solutions, and involves a dynamic interplay between knowledge and belief on the one hand, and the success or failure of proposed solutions on the other. This is not to say that Commons does not realize that ideologies may change only slowly or that he does not provide a role for scientific investigation. His comments on the habitual assumptions of judges and his own reform proposals indicate that he felt that changes in ideological preconceptions sometimes came tardily and that scientific investigation could aid the process of finding workable solutions, but a recognition of these points does not require a dichtomization between institutions and technology, with technology being seen as the only source of changes in social knowledge or ideology.

The relationship between Commons and Ayres is more complex, as while both adopt an instrumentalism based on John Dewey, Ayres presents his ideas in a framework closer to Veblen's than to Commons's. Ayres links technological advance with the growth of "true" knowledge in contrast to the "false" or "ceremonial" criteria of adequacy (ideology) embodied in institutions. Ayres views institutions as attempts to solve problems, but in the absence of correct knowledge, and he accepts the Veblenian argument that established norms and ideologies will strongly resist the promptings of the advance of knowledge and technique.[55]

Admittedly, some of the differences between Ayres and Commons are purely definitional in nature, in that Ayres tends to include in "technology" all instrumentally effective knowledge and organizational devices, but genuine differences do remain. Ayres's treatment maintains a heavy emphasis on the role of technology (even as more narrowly defined), and includes an element of technological determinism in that the growth of instrumental ability is seen as connected with not only the growth of knowledge but also the adoption of particular ("true") values. Ayres's work also tends to operate at the level of broad social "forces" and gives relatively little attention to the analysis of the situation of the individual decision maker and the political and judicial processes of change. In addition, Ayres adopts an extremely optimistic view of science, both with respect to its ability to discover "clear and certain knowledge" and to create a consensus around its findings.[56]

The above interpretation of Commons's work implies the rejection of D. Seckler's view of Commons's analysis as naive and uninteresting. Seckler's opinion is based on the idea that Commons's arguments imply that all institutions are deliberately designed and that his analysis leaves no room for errors or unintended consequences of any kind.[57] Although Commons's methodological individualism means he must analyze decisions according to the problem situation and the purposes of the decision maker, the whole tenor of Commons's pragmatic conception of experimental decision making is at odds with the notion of perfect foresight or perpetually successful decision making. In fact, unintended consequences can have a significant role in Commons's work—first, as the source of new problems that then give rise to legislative or judicial decisions, and, second, as the source of institutions that develop through custom. It might be argued that Commons does not devote enough attention to the development of customs and common practices, but his point is that even in the case of customs, judicial or legislative decisions will be required as a result of the problems and conflicts that arise in connection with customs.

On the other hand, Seckler is correct in placing Commons in a separate wing of the institutionalist movement. The differences between Commons and other institutionalists are not minor. They touch on fundamental methodological and theoretical matters and explain the fact that Commons's work has never been well integrated into the institutionalist tradition—a tradition that, with some exceptions, has been dominated by the joint influence of Veblen and Ayres.[58]

Commons's work also has areas of similarity and dissimilarity with the neo-classical approach to institutions. Recently, neo-classical theorists have attempted to endogenize institutions, and when one compares this literature with Commons's work a number of points emerge. Firstly, it is clear that Commons's treatment has a number of serious omissions as it lacks proper or full discussions of free ridership, transactions costs, public good and externality problems, and contains no theory of bureaucratic behavior. Admittedly, Commons does make comments that clearly indicate his awareness of transactions costs, and his discussion of unions and collective bargaining demonstrates his knowledge of the problem of free ridership, but these are ideas that remain underdeveloped.[59] A fuller treatment of these issues would, however, have little effect on Commons's system—except perhaps for his reform proposals, and particularly his ideas concerning the occupational parliament.[60] A fuller treatment of free ridership problems might pose a difficulty for Commons's positive analysis, but as Douglas North has argued, "casual empiricism provides ample evidence that large groups have sometimes acted to alter the structure of the state."[61]

Secondly, and despite the omissions mentioned above, Commons's work contains clear anticipation of the neo-classical literature in a number of important respects. Commons's awareness of the need for collective action to secure some system of workable rules in place of private violence and anarchy is the basis of much of the work by J. M. Buchanan and others.[62] Commons must be credited with anticipating the Coasian emphasis on the transaction as the basic unit of analysis, and much of the modern concern with the rent-seeking activity of collective organizations and the distributional aspects of the structure of rules.[63] As do many writers in the public choice field, Commons views democratic decision making as a process of "log-rolling"; Commons's refusal to "criminate" log-rolling and his argument that it is simply a method of reaching decisions on the basis of a consensus could easily come from Buchanan or G. Tullock.[64] In addition, few would argue that efficiency is the major determining factor in government legislative action. For instance, R. Posner argues that legislative action tends to be based on distributive considerations.[65] Commons was among the first economists to develop a detailed analysis of the role of the courts and the development of common law, issues that have been taken over more recently by writers such as Posner. It is true that Commons's treatment of court decisions differs from Posner's in vital respects (a point dealt with below), but Commons and Posner could agree that court decisions have the role of establishing "rules of conduct designed to shape future conduct."[66]

Thirdly, Commons's considerable opposition to further direct government control or planning, and his desire to substitute bargaining for rationing or managerial transactions, are worthy of note. Of course, Commons did not accept that there could ever be a purely individualistic system and did not simply equate market exchange with liberty. He would doubtless have objected to the contractarian analysis of the Buchanan type as artificial and ahistorical, and to Buchanan's constitutional proposals as overly restrictive, failing to take account of economic power, and insufficiently pragmatic.[67] Nevertheless, Commons's support of an expanded role for both private collective action and administrative agencies came from a conviction that only through such means could individual liberties and institutional flexibility be secured and preserved.

In contrast to the foregoing, Commons's fundamental concepts of reasonableness and workability provide a context for analysis significantly different from the neo-classical. Commons does not regard voluntary exchange as a sufficient basis for the creation of a workable mutuality and he approaches questions of efficiency only within a broader context that emphasizes power relationships, distribution, and the need for a "reasonable" framework of rules. Commons is obviously aware of efficiency considerations, but his work is centered on the concepts of workability and reasonableness, and takes account of efficiency only within such a framework. One aspect of this can be found in Commons's treatment of court decisions, which contrasts sharply with the view of writers such as Posner, who would see court decisions as tending to efficient solutions. There are, however, a large number of authors who adopt a position closer to Commons's, but to introduce ideological criteria such as reasonableness creates obvious difficulties for a consistently neo-classical theory of institutions.[68]

The fundamental difficulty with a *purely* neo-classical approach to institutions is that it cannot provide a satisfactory treatment of institutional change. Douglass North has expressed the problem as follows:

> The simple fact is that a dynamic theory of institutional change limited to the strictly neoclassical constraint of individualistic, rational purposive activity would never allow us to explain most secular change ranging from the stubborn struggle of the Jews in antiquity to the passage of the Social Security Act in 1935. Secular economic change has occurred not only because of the changing relative prices stressed in neoclassical models but also because of evolving ideological perspectives that have led individuals and groups to have contrasting views of the fairness of their situation and to act upon those views.[69]

What this criticism amounts to is a questioning of the psychologism and standard assumption of correct knowledge inherent in much orthodox theory. Institutional change is more than simply the dynamic consequences of constrained maximization. The goals and aims of action are, in large part, determined by the problem situation faced by individuals and groups and the state of their knowledge and belief. Despite the fact that North has often defended neo-classical theory, the fact of the matter is that his own sense of the limitations of that theory has led him to adopt an approach to institutions and institutional change that is notably similar to Commons's.

North argues that a theory of institutions must contain (1) "a theory of property rights that describes the individual and group incentives in the system," (2) "a theory of the state, since it is the state that specifies and enforces property rights," and (3) "a theory of ideology that explains how different perceptions of reality affect the reaction of individuals to the changing 'objective' situation."[70]

In his discussion of the first two parts, North makes much use of the neo-classical work on transactions costs and the neo-classical theory of the state, but even in these sections he frequently warns of the limitations of the neo-classical approach for the analysis of stability and change in institutional systems. He regards the efforts to reduce transactions costs as taking place within constraints that are both distributional (maximizing the income of the ruler and his group) and ideological (maintaining the legitimacy of the ruler and his decisions), and these constraints mean that relatively inefficient forms of organization may persist.[71] Also, North admits that when the distribution of political power is diffuse (many pressure groups) it becomes difficult "to predict or explain the ensuing forms of property rights which will develop."[72] More importantly, he argues that "in the absence of ideological convictions to constrain individual maximizing, the viability of economic organization is threatened," a point so close to Commons's concern with workability that the similarity need hardly be stressed.[73]

On the third part, the theory of ideology, North refers to the "immense amount of resources invested throughout history in attempting to convince individuals about the justice or injustice of their position."[74] Reference to such investment is quite compatible with Commons's ideas on persuasion and mass psychology, but not with neo-classical notions of correct information and rational choice. In addition, North can be found arguing that "the clearest instance of the dominant role of ideology is the case of the independent judiciary. Judges with lifetime tenure are relatively immune from interest group pressure. It is true that their initial appointment may reflect such pressure . . .; but their subsequent decisions over a wide range of policies reflect their own convictions of the 'public good.' "[75]

North's treatment of ideology also deals with shifts in ideology as a result of unsuccessful decision making, in the sense that the accumulation of anomalies between the ideology and experience will lead to an eventual shift to some alternative ideological perspective. Indeed, North's whole approach relates very directly to Commons's emphasis on institutions as a response to social problems and conflicts, workability and reasonableness as criteria of choice that contain an ethical and ideological element, and on decision making as a kind of experimentation.

Conclusion

Commons attempted to provide an integral and logically coherent treatment of (1) the nature and function of property rights and other rules and their effect on economic transactions, (2) the behavior of private collectives and judicial and political processes of decision making, (3) institutional change, and (4) proposals for institutional reform. His work can be seen as standing between the neo-classical and Veblen/Ayres approaches. Commons rejected the psychologism of orthodoxy, and anti-individualism of the Veblen/Ayres tradition, and the treatments of knowledge in both. Because of his individualism Commons shares more with orthodox theory than do most institutionalists, but his rejection of psychologism and his instrumentalism bring him closer to other institutionalists.

Commons's work does have faults. The style of presentation diminishes its accessibility, points of importance are left undeveloped, and there are many omissions. His work could be strengthened by a more extended consideration of transactions costs, public goods, externalities, free ridership, and bureaucratic behavior. These faults most severely affect his normative proposals and the applicability of his work to the range of problems usually considered under the heading of law and economics, but despite these problems Commons did make a significant analytical contribution. In particular, his view of institutions as a response to scarcity and conflicts of interest, his choice of the transaction as the basic unit of analysis, his treatment of political processes as log-rolling, and the importance he attached to legal and economic power and to common law and judicial decision making are all worthy of note, but the aspects of Commons's work that are of greatest interest and have continuing relevance even for today's theorist are to be found in his awareness of the need to deal with institutions both as constraints on the actions of individuals and groups and as instruments, alterable through the actions of individuals and groups, and in his treatment of the relationships between knowledge, belief, and institutions. While Commons may not always have been clearly aware of the precise nature of the theoretical and methodological problems he was grappling with (which may explain much of the obscurity of his work), there can be little doubt of the insightfulness of his treatment and his substantial anticipation of modern thinking on institutions and institutional change—an anticipation that is particularly remarkable given that many of the fundamentals of Commons's system can be found (at least in embryonic form) in his articles on "A Sociological View of Sovereignty," first published in the *American Journal of Sociology* in 1889 and 1900. Commons's contribution is to be found not only in his very considerable influence in the world of affairs, as some have claimed, but also in his attempt to develop what can properly be called a *theory* of institutions.[76]

Notes

1. The major exceptions are L. G. Harter, *John R. Commons: His Assault on Laissez-Faire* (Corvallis: Oregon State University Press, 1962) and K. Parsons, "John R. Commons's Point of View," reprinted in J. R. Commons, *The Economics of Collective Action* (New York: Macmillan, 1951). Also useful, although of narrower focus, are R. A. Gonce, "The New Property Rights Approach and Commons's *Legal Foundations of Capitalism*," *Journal of Economic Issues* 10 (December 1976): 765–97; R. A. Gonce, "John R. Commons's Legal Economic Theory," *Journal of Economic Issues* 5 (September 1971): 80–95; and W. M. Dugger, "Property Rights, Law, and John R. Commons," *Review of Social Economy* 38 (April 1980): 41–53.
2. In a personal interview with Ewan Clague, Clague expressed the view that Commons never managed to develop a theoretical "roof." Most of

Commons's pupils did not pursue the more general aspects of Commons's work but concentrated on particular areas and problems such as labor, public utilities, social security, and unemployment compensation. See Harter, *Commons: His Assault*, p. 209.

3. D. Hamilton, "Veblen and Commons: A Case of Theoretical Convergence," *Southwestern Social Science Quarterly* 45 (September 1953): 43–50.

4. D. Seckler, *Thorstein Veblen and the Institutionalists* (Boulder: Colorado Associated University Press, 1975), pp. 5, 130.

5. M. Blaug, *Economic Theory in Retrospect*, 3d ed. (London: Cambridge University Press, 1978), p. 721; K. Boulding, "A New Look at Institutionalism," *American Economic Review* 47 (May 1957): 1–12.

6. See in particular the articles by H. H. Liebhafsky, V. Goldberg, R. A. Gonce, and V. Ostrom in the *Journal of Economic Issues* 10 (December 1976). See also A. Randall, "Property, Institutions, and Economic Behavior," *Journal of Economic Issues* 12 (March 1978): 1–21.

7. J. M. Buchanan, "An Economist's Approach to 'Scientific Politics,' " in *What Should Economists Do?* ed. J. M. Buchanan (Indianapolis: Liberty Press, 1979), p. 147.

8. J. R. Commons, *Institutional Economics* (Madison: University of Wisconsin Press, 1961), p. 5.

9. L. A. Boland, "Knowledge and the Role of Institutions in Economic Theory," *Journal of Economic Issues* 13 (December 1979): 957–72.

10. J. R. Commons, "Institutional Economics," *American Economic Review* 21 (December 1931): 648–57.

11. Not all working rules are laws, but this can be translated into legal terminology as the structure of rights (which impose duties on others), exposures (no rights), duties, and liberties (no duties). Commons distinguishes a right from a liberty on the basis that rights involve the ability to gain the backing of collective power to assist "in compelling others to obey" what has been commanded. A liberty is a rule of permission only, and the power of collective action will be limited to ensuring the non interference of others. Similarly, a duty is a rule of compulsion while an exposure is a rule of non-assistance. See J. R. Commons, *The Legal Foundations of Capitalism* (Madison: University of Wisconsin Press, 1968): 134–53; J. R. Commons, "The Place of Economics in Social Philosophy," *Journal of Social Philosophy* 1 (October 1935): 7–22; J. R. Commons, "The Problem of Correlating Law, Economics and Ethics," *Wisconsin Law Review* 8 (December 1932): 3–26.

12. Commons, *Institutional Economics*, p. 6; Commons, *The Legal Foundations of Capitalism*, pp. 3–4. See also Commons, "Institutional Economics," p. 656; J. R. Commons, "Law and Economics," *Yale Law Journal* 34 (February 1925): 371–82; Commons, *The Economics of Collective Action*, pp. 97–103; Commons, "The Place of Economics in Social Philosophy," p. 21.

13. Commons, *The Economics of Collective Action*, p. 104.

14. Commons, *The Legal Foundations of Capitalism*, p. 138.

15. Commons, "Institutional Economics," p. 656.

16. Commons, *Institutional Economics*, p. 50. This passage is taken from Commons's critique of Locke.

17. Commons, *The Legal Foundations of Capitalism*, pp. 134–38.

18. Commons, *Institutional Economics*, p. 719. See also J. R. Commons, "A Sociological View of Sovereignty," *American Journal of Sociology* 5 (July-November 1899) : 1–15, 155–71, 347–66; 6 (January-May 1900) : 544–52, 683–95, 814–25; and 6 (July 1900) : 67–89.

19. Commons, *Institutional Economics*, pp. 59–60.

20. Ibid., pp. 67–68.

21. Ibid., pp. 64–67.

22. Commons, "Institutional Economics," p. 652; Commons, "The Problem of Correlating Law, Economics and Ethics," p. 5; and Commons, *Institutional Economics*, pp. 59–64.

23. Commons, *Institutional Economics*, pp. 307–17, 331–39.

25. Commons, *The Legal Foundations of Capitalism*, pp. 217–18; Commons, *Institutional Economics*, pp. 68, 761–63.

26. Commons, "Institutional Economics," p. 655.

27. Commons, *Institutional Economics*, p. 627.

28. Harter, *Commons: His Assault*, pp. 230–31. See also the same author's "John R. Commons: Conservative or Liberal," *Western Economic Journal* 1 (Spring 1963) : 226–32.

29. Commons, *The Legal Foundations of Capitalism*, pp. 134–37.

30. Commons, *Institutional Economics*, p. 684; Commons, *The Legal Foundations of Capitalism*, pp. 149–50.

31. Commons, *Institutional Economics*, p. 752.

32. Ibid., p. 751.

33. Ibid., pp. 755–56.

34. Ibid., pp. 684–85, 752–53, 756, 762, 881–90; Commons, "Law and Economics," p. 376; Commons, *The Economics of Collective Action*, pp. 212–23, 270, 271.

35. J. R. Commons, "Twentieth Century Economics," *Journal of Social Philosophy* 5 (October 1939) : 29–41; see especially p. 35.

36. Commons, "Law and Economics," p. 382.

37. Ibid., pp. 372–76; Commons, *The Legal Foundations of Capitalism*, pp. 138–40.

38. Commons, "Law and Economics," p. 380.

39. Commons, "The Problem of Correlating Law, Economics and Ethics," pp. 24–25.

40. Commons, "Law and Economics," p. 374.

41. Commons, *The Legal Foundations of Capitalism*, p. 378.

42. Commons, *The Legal Foundations of Capitalism*, p. 126; Commons, *The Economics of Collective Action*, p. 291.

43. Commons, *The Economics of Collective Action*, p. 237.

44. Commons, *Institutional Economics*, p. 891.

45. Commons, *The Economics of Collective Action*, pp. 33, 262. An abiding theme in Commons's work was the representation of interests. Early in his career he considered proportional representation but his later work concentrated on the occupational parliament. One must conclude that

Commons came to think that traditional political representation contained flaws that could not be overcome by expedients such as proportional representation. See J. R. Commons, *Proportional Representation*
(New York: T. Y. Crowell, 1896).
46. Commons, "Twentieth Century Economics," pp. 38–41. See also *The
    Economics of Collective Action*, pp. 277–83. The "fourth branch" was
    not an uncommon idea among progressives. R. G. Tugwell also utilized
    the concept, although for Tugwell, the branch would have the function
    of advising on economic planning, particularly the allocation of capital.
47. Commons, "Twentieth Century Economics," p. 33. For a more extended
    treatment of Commons's approach to reform see W. M. Dugger, "The
    Reform Method of John R. Commons," *Journal of Economic Issues* 13
    (June 1979): 369–81. See also W. F. Kennedy, "John R. Commons,
    Conservative Reformer," *Western Economics Journal* 1 (Fall 1962):
    29–42; and Harter, "Commons: Conservative or Liberal," pp. 226–32.
48. D. Hamilton, "Veblen and Commons," pp. 46–50.
49. Commons, *Institutional Economics*, pp. 656–73.
50. Ibid., p. 673.
51. Ibid., pp. 672–73. Compare T. Veblen, *Absentee Ownership* (New York:
    Huebsch, 1954), pp. 403–16. Of course, Veblen's and Commons's ideas
    on unions are not necessarily entirely incompatible, but Commons ob-
    viously thought that union power, like business power, could be restrained
    to reasonable levels.
52. This, of course, does not rule out group or collective action. Indeed, much
    of Commons's work is directed at charting the growth of group action
    and the reasons for it. The only possible difficulty is that Commons does
    not given sufficient attention to the free rider problem, or discuss in much
    detail the reasons for group action failing to occur. In his earlier work
    Commons did talk of institutions arising from basic psychological pro-
    pensities, but if this work is read carefully it can be seen that he rejects
    orthodox psychologism and is really talking about the logic of the situa-
    tion (particularly that of scarcity) leading to certain types of behavior, in
    particular conflict and the need to combine for group action. See Com-
    mons, "The Sociological View of Sovereignty." For an insightful discus-
    sion of the various types of individualism see L. A. Boland, *The Founda-
    tons of Economic Method* (London: George Allen & Unwin, 1982),
    pp. 27–43.
53. Useful surveys of Veblen's views can be found in D. Seckler, *Veblen and
    the Institutionalists*, and in D. A. Walker, "Thorstein Veblen's Economic
    System," *Economic Inquiry* 15 (April 1977): 213–37. My own interpre-
    tation of Veblen is contained in M. Rutherford, "Thorstein Veblen and
    the Processes of Institutional Change," *History of Political Economy* 16
    (Fall 1984), forthcoming. See also T. Veblen, *The Theory of Business
    Enterprise* (New York: New American Library, 1958), pp. 144–81. For
    Commons's critique see his *Institutional Economics*, pp. 649–56. It
    should be noted that the portion of Veblen's work that deals with action
    within a given overall framework of institutional principles is not incom-
    patible with methodological individualism. Also various types of less

radical institutional change can take place in Veblen's system within such an overall framework. Institutions are thus not to be seen as entirely static or resisting any and all changes.

54. M. A. Copeland, "Commons's Institutionalism in Relation to Problems of Social Evolution and Economic Planning," *Quarterly Journal of Economics* 50 (February 1936): 333–46; see especially p. 343.

55. See C. E. Ayres, *The Theory of Economic Progress* (New York: Schocken, 1962); and M. Rutherford, "Clarence Ayres and the Instrumental Theory of Value," *Journal of Economic Issues* 15 (September 1981): 657–73.

56. Rutherford, "Clarence Ayres and the Instrumental Theory of Value," pp. 665–69.

57. D. Seckler, *Veblen and the Constitutionalists*, pp. 126–31.

58. For an indication of the dominance of the Veblen/Ayres tradition see D. Hamilton, "Why is Institutional Economics not Institutional?" *American Journal of Economics and Sociology* 21 (July 1962): 309–17; C. E. Ayres, "Institutional Economics: The Co-ordinates of Institutionalism," *American Economic Review* 41 (May 1951): 47–55; P. A. Klein, "American Institutionalism: Premature Death, Permanent Resurrection," *Journal of Economic Issues* 12 (June 1978): 251–76; W. Gordon, *Institutional Economics* (Austin: University of Texas Press, 1980), pp. 9–33. A penetrating critique of such definitions of institutionalism by a writer influenced by Commons can be found in W. J. Samuels, "Technology *vis-à-vis* Institutions in the JEI," *Journal of Economic Issues* 11 (December 1977), pp. 871–95. Commons did have an influence on E. E. Witte, Selig Perlman, K. Parsons, and some others, but little development of Commons's theoretical system occurred until recently. For an example of the more recent work in the Commons tradition see A. A. Schmid, *Property, Power, and Public Choice* (New York: Praeger, 1978).

59. Commons, *The Economics of Collective Action*, pp. 57, 268–69.

60. M. Olson, *The Logic of Collective Action* (Cambridge, Mass.: Harvard University Press, 1973), pp. 114–31.

61. D. North, *Structure and Change in Economic History* (New York: Norton, 1981), p. 31.

62. See, for instance, J. M. Buchanan, *The Limits of Liberty* (Chicago: University of Chicago Press, 1975), pp. 6–24.

63. O. E. Williamson, "The Modern Corporation: Origins, Evolution, Attributes," *Journal of Economic Literature* 19 (December 1981): 1537–68.

64. J. M. Buchanan and G. Tullock, *The Calculus of Consent* (Ann Arbor: University of Michigan Press, 1962), pp. 134–35.

65. R. Posner, *Economic Analysis of Law* (Boston: Little Brown, 1972), pp. 327–28.

66. Posner, *Economic Analysis*, pp. 98–100, 320–22.

67. For a critical commentary on the contractarian literature, see Scott Gordon, "The New Contractarians," *Journal of Political Economy* 84 (June 1976): 573–90.

68. For example: W. Z. Hirsch, *Law and Economics: An Introductory Analysis* (New York: Academic Press, 1979), p. 7.

69. North, *Structure and Change*, p. 58.
70. Ibid., pp. 7–8.
71. Ibid., pp. 28–32, 43–44.
72. Ibid., p. 43.
73. Ibid., p. 44.
74. Ibid., p. 51.
75. Ibid., pp. 56–57.
76. Seckler, *Veblen and the Institutionalists*, p. 130. In contrast, Harter argues that Commons's real legacy is to be found in his treatment of economic evolution. See L. G. Harter, "The Legacy of John R. Commons," *Journal of Economic Issues* 1 (June 1967): 63–73.

Name Index